NUMBERED DAYS

NUMBERED DAYS

Diaries and the Holocaust

Alexandra Garbarini

Yale University Press
New Haven & London

Published with assistance from the Mary Cady Tew Memorial Fund.

Set in Postscript Electra by Tseng Information Systems, Inc.
Printed in the United States of America by
Sheridan Books, Ann Arbor, Michigan.

Library of Congress Cataloging-in-Publication Data
Garbarini, Alexandra, 1973–
Numbered days : diaries and the Holocaust / Alexandra Garbarini.
p. cm.
Includes bibliographical references and index.
ISBN-13: 978-0-300-11252-8 (alk. paper)
ISBN-10: 0-300-11252-1
1. Holocaust, Jewish (1939–1945)—Historiography. 2. Holocaust, Jewish (1939–1945)—Personal narratives—History and criticism. 3. World War, 1939–1945—Personal narratives—History and criticism. 4. Holocaust, Jewish (1939–1945), in literature. 5. Jews—Diaries—History and criticism. 6. Diaries—History and criticism. I. Title.
D804.348.G37 2006
940.53′18072—dc22   2006003339

A catalogue record for this book is available from the British Library.

10 9 8 7 6 5 4 3 2 1

To my parents,
with love and gratitude

Contents

PREFACE

In April 1942, Fela Szeps, a young Jewish woman who but for the onset of war would have been finishing her studies in psychology at the University of Warsaw, began writing a diary clandestinely in a German forced labor camp. Two months earlier she had been sent from her hometown of Dąbrowa Górnicza to Grünberg, a small women's camp in Silesia that eventually became a subcamp of Gross Rosen. The women imprisoned in Grünberg worked in textile production for the German army. Fela was deported there with her younger sister, Sabina. They were separated from their parents and brother, all of whom remained in the Dąbrowa Górnicza ghetto for several more months before her parents were deported and killed in Auschwitz and her brother was deported to a succession of concentration and forced labor camps.

Throughout the more than two years she spent in the Grünberg camp, Fela faithfully, though intermittently, recorded entries in her diary. How she procured paper for her diary is unclear, but she did—lined paper and graph paper, torn from composition tablets around eight inches high by six inches wide. She wrote in pencil in legible but messy Polish script, and she maximized the space on each page, leaving little to no margin on the left- or right-hand sides, although bafflingly she sometimes ended an entry in the middle of a sheet and neglected to utilize the remaining space on the page.

Fela wrote about life in the camp, her hopes and dreams, her concern about the fate of her parents, and the pain she felt remembering the lives they had lived before the Germans destroyed them. In addition to keeping the diary, Fela and her sister, along with other women, organized illegal educational and cultural activities in the camp. On their day off from work, generally Sundays, Fela lectured to the other women from memory on history, sociology, and Jewish culture. She also wrote and distributed an illegal newsletter, "Żywe Gazetki," which included recitations, songs, and film scenes.

Copies of that newsletter and Fela's diary survived the war; Fela did not. She and her sister were forced on a death march with the other female prisoners from Grünberg in the final months of the war. Postwar testimonies suggest that two transports were marched out of Grünberg in January 1945. One contingent headed northeast to Bergen-Belsen; the other, including Fela and her sister, headed south to Helmbrechts camp in Bavaria. They were forced to walk and occasionally to ride in cattle cars the three hundred miles to Helmbrechts in the dead of winter. As Sabina Szeps described in a written testimony she gave in 1964 to Yad Vashem archives in Jerusalem, Fela was sick, probably with pneumonia, even before the death march began. But before leaving Grünberg, the two of them sewed the diary between the layers of an empty haversack. They carried the diary the entire time they marched, from Grünberg south to Helmbrechts and from Helmbrechts east to Volary in the Protectorate (present-day Czech Republic). Fela was so sick her sister had to drag her much of the time. They were liberated from the Germans on 6 May 1945, but Fela died less than a week later in a hospital in Volary.[1]

Sabina survived. She was reunited with her brother in a displaced persons camp in Salzburg, and together, in 1946, they emigrated to Palestine, carrying Fela's diary with them. Sabina, now known as Szewa, held on to the diary until 1963, at which time she donated it to Yad Vashem. Over time the paper has yellowed with age and the edges of the diary's pages have become brittle and chipped; the archivists at Yad Vashem have painstakingly attempted to stabilize the pages by adhering a high-quality rag paper to the edges.

The story of Fela's diary—how it came to be and how it came to be read by others—is but one of hundreds such stories. This book is an analysis of why Fela and other people sustained such seemingly herculean writing efforts and of what their diaries reveal about their perceptions of Nazi exterminatory policies in the midst of their implementation.

Like most people with an interest in the history of the Holocaust, I encountered early in my studies a number of diaries written by Jewish men and women and was transfixed. Indeed, an unscientific sampling of my students has revealed that the majority of them were inspired to learn more about modern Jewish and German history through their exposure to Anne Frank's diary. In this respect the current generation of college students would appear to be no different from preceding generations: diaries have long been central texts in the popular awareness of the Holocaust. Anne Frank's diary alone has been translated into dozens of languages and reportedly has sold more than thirty-one million copies since it was first published in 1947.[2]

It was not Anne Frank's diary but the diaries of three men in the Warsaw ghetto—Chaim Aron Kaplan, Emanuel Ringelblum, and Abraham Lewin—and that of the Dutch woman Etty Hillesum that set me on the path of this study. These and the German publication of Victor Klemperer's Nazi-era diaries in 1995 prompted me to write to archives in several countries inquiring into the possible existence of other diaries as yet unpublished and gathering dust on their shelves. I learned that hundreds of diaries written by Jews during the Second World War, like that of Fela Szeps, are extant in archives in Israel, Europe, and the United States. In most cases, again as in Fela's, the fate of the diaries diverged from the fate of the diarists. In some instances, little to no information other than the diaries themselves is available about the diarists' identities—sometimes not even their names, much less their family situations or fate during the war. Discovered in the ruins of the ghettos or passed along from one person to the next, they arrived at archives without a history, save the one they described. Most of these diaries, for a variety of reasons, have never been published, and most likely will remain unpublished.

I have focused largely on unpublished diaries in an effort to make audible new voices from the past, thereby enlarging the breadth of source material upon which existing historical and literary studies of Holocaust diaries have been based. What is more, unlike widely read published diaries, most of which were written in ghettos during the first half of the war or while the diarists were in hiding in western Europe, many of the diaries I analyze in this book were written by Jews in hiding in eastern Europe in the second half of the war as well as by little-known diarists from Germany and France. Diarists in eastern Europe, for instance, who had witnessed mass shootings and deportations to extermination camps and temporarily evaded them, developed a different perspective on Jewish wartime experiences and thus wrote with a different intention and tone than diarists writing earlier in the war. These texts and others illuminate the self-awareness and responses to news of the genocide of Jews living in a broader range of circumstances in western, Central, and eastern Europe during other periods of the war.

In relying on these largely unpublished diaries, I trace the attempts of Jews over the course of the war to make sense of and adapt to a world of shrinking prospects. In particular, I explore the function and meaning of diary writing within individual Jews' struggles to make meaning of events that seemed incomprehensible. Alternating between close analyses of individual diaries and larger thematic perspectives, I examine the different impulses—familial, ethical, theological, and historical—that compelled individuals to record their experiences. I also detail how people's reasons for writing their diaries changed over time, in response to mounting knowledge about the ensuing extermination. Particularly in the latter years of the war, Jewish diarists frequently alluded to the unrepresentable nature of their experiences, while at the same time they were the first people to attempt to represent the extermination of European Jewry. They possessed a keen sense of the historicity of their experiences and wrote in their dual capacity as victims and witnesses. Some were concerned with recording the history of their families, in particular, rather than with contributing to Jewish history or European history or human history, in general. But even in instances in which diarists wrote for more limited audiences, they conveyed an awareness of the difficulty they faced in making their experiences of life in extremis comprehensible to their readers.

Language skills are always a limiting factor in conducting research in this field. I have read approximately one hundred diaries written in German, Polish, and French in combination with the available published translations of diaries written in other languages. These three languages have permitted me to read the original diaries of Jewish men and women in Poland, Germany, Austria, Czechoslovakia, France, Belgium, and the Netherlands. Although there are many diaries that are beyond the scope of my reading abilities—particularly those written in Yiddish that have not been translated and which constitute the second largest language group of diaries—I am confident that these one hundred diaries offer a fascinating cross section of Jewish experiences during the war. Those written in Polish constitute the largest single language group of diaries, numbering slightly more than those in Yiddish.

In the polyglot world of Polish Jewry in the first half of the twentieth century, Polish Jews who wrote in Polish instead of Yiddish typically appear to have been educated in Polish schools in cities and towns during the interwar years. Thus, they consisted largely of young adults or the parents of young children, although there were certainly exceptions. In many instances, there is evidence from the diaries themselves or from materials accompanying the diaries, such as letters or postcards, that these individuals also knew Yiddish. Their choice to write in Polish may have reflected their greater facility in that language, although it may also be a clue to their intended audience. Individuals writing diaries in Poland late in the war were aware of the fact that few Yiddish-speakers would be alive at war's end and therefore may have believed their diaries would reach a broader audience if written in Polish. Lacking explicit discussion on the part of a diarist of his or her language choice, we can only surmise. Diaries written in Yiddish may illuminate other segments of the Polish Jewish population during these years—those who were older or were politically engaged with the Bund or were Hasidic. Without question, Yiddish-language diaries offer access to Jewish experiences in other regions of eastern Europe. Thus, undoubtedly, our understanding of Jewish experiences under German occupation and of the place of diary writing would be enhanced by such additional research.

What follows, then, does not purport to be a comprehensive study of Holocaust diaries. Indeed, there may be an infinite number of studies that can be done of Holocaust diaries depending on a person's language abilities, scholarly background, and interests. Nevertheless, I have attempted to group and frame the material in a way that will (I hope) offer fresh insights. As the historiographical and theoretical discussion in the first chapter indicates, my framework does not necessarily contradict existing ones; sometimes it deepens and supports existing scholarship. By focusing on the concepts Jewish diarists used and the strategies they employed in their efforts to understand the calamity befalling them, I aim to make it possible to see diarists as active subjects in this history—not as passive victims or heroic resisters, but as ordinary men and women who were subjected to extraordinary events and who tried in different ways to cope with them.

We have to assume that most diaries written by Jews during the war were not salvaged, as Fela Szeps's was. The hundreds of diaries in archives recall the thousands of texts that are missing—and the millions of people who never wrote a diary. And all of the texts we have, however vibrant the voices that resound within them, should not permit us to forget how physically ravaged most of their authors were. I myself was reminded of this—of how difficult it can be to keep an image of their physical devastation in mind while reading these texts—when I came across a photo of Fela Szeps taken by a U.S. Army Signal Corps photographer the day before she died. In it she lies naked and emaciated on a hospital bed. It is a devastating photograph, reminiscent of so many other photographs of skeletal Holocaust victims that have been reproduced countless times over the past sixty years, and yet still more powerful for being of a woman I felt I had come to know. As tempting as it was to include a photograph of a diary writer when so few photographs of diarists remain, it seemed disrespectful somehow to publish it. At the time the photograph was taken, Fela Szeps was no longer capable of writing in her diary, no longer able to frame her story. She surely wanted us to read her diary, but she may not have wanted us to see that image.

Diaries do not convey all dimensions of Jews' experiences during the war—not even all the experiences of the diarists themselves—but they do shed light on their efforts to make meaning of and understand their experiences. Diarists were themselves conscious of the incomplete nature of their chronicles, yet this in no way undermined the importance to them of people reading their accounts. Their pages clamor with the desire to be read.

A Note on Translations

Whenever possible, I have worked with the handwritten original diaries. In some instances, the original copy of the diary has been lost or remains in private hands, in which case I made use of a typescript or, in rare instances, of the translation of a diary when it is the sole copy of that diary deposited in an archive. I specify which version of a diary I consulted in the notes accompanying each chapter.

Unless otherwise noted, all translations are my own. For diaries that have not been published or that are difficult to find despite having been published, I have chosen to cite entries in their original language in the notes in order to facilitate more direct access to the cadences and expressions of the diarists for readers who can read the original. With the same purpose in mind, I have aimed for accuracy in my translations, staying close to the original punctuation and sentence structure. Any additions or changes to a text appear in brackets. This applies as well to instances in which I have omitted any part of an entry. In those instances, I have inserted square brackets with ellipses in order to differentiate my use of ellipses from the diarists' use of them.

Finally, a special note is in order about the quotations I include from Chaim Aron Kaplan's Hebrew-language diary. Because the published English edition of Kaplan's diary is substantially abridged yet lacks any indication of where passages or entire entries have been eliminated, I found it necessary to supplement that translation with translations of omitted passages from the published Hebrew edition. Furthermore, in some instances I have included a different translation of passages that were included in the published English edition. When I quote a passage that mixes translations, i.e., that is part from the published English translation and part from the new translation, I include the newly translated lines in italics. When individual words or sentences pertinent to the quotation at hand were omitted in the published English translation, I reinserted them in italicized form. However, in order not to interrupt the visual flow of the text, when I cite an entire passage that has been newly translated, I have opted not to italicize that passage and instead to indicate in the corresponding note that it is a new translation.

Numbered Days

Historical and Theoretical Considerations

Notebook Nr. 1

Entreaty

The person into whose hands this diary should happen to fall is strongly urged not to discard it, or to destroy it.

In case it is not possible to deliver it to the intended address—one is kindly asked to give it over to competent hands so that a future historian might ladle out the true evidence, illuminating at least partially those terrible days of ours full of murder, conflagration, blood, and tears unprecedented in the history of the world, the suffering of a defenseless nation. From the chaos, in the shrouded mist, will emerge the outlines of the true and unprecedented crime, whose atrocity and unprecedented abomination will penetrate even the most hardened hearts and will wrap the perpetrators in eternal shame.[1]

From April through October 1943, Kalman Rotgeber wrote about the previous three and a half years of German occupation from the vantage of a hiding place on the "Aryan" side of Warsaw. He filled twenty-three notebooks, all the while remaining conscious of the possibility that they might never reach his intended audience.[2] For Rotgeber as well as for other European Jews who were persecuted and killed between 1939 and 1945 providing the future with a written testimony of what was in the process of being destroyed was one response to living in the shadow of annihilation. Through their diaries, they attempted to make sense both of the unimaginable genocide as it unfolded around them and of the meaning of their own lives in this radically altered world.

Hundreds and perhaps thousands of European Jewish men and women from different national backgrounds and linguistic-cultural traditions and in various wartime contexts kept diaries during the period of the Holocaust.[3] These texts are a window onto Jewish victims' responses, in the midst of the killings, to the perpetration of genocide. They also constitute one component of their responses. While the Nazis endeavored to destroy all traces of their murder of European Jewry, the victims of that genocide produced written testaments for their relatives abroad and for the world at large in order to ensure that the memory of their extermination would not become the Nazis' last victim. While Jews were being expelled from their homes, systematically starved, shot in mass graves, or ultimately, for the majority of the victims, gassed, some attempted to preserve evidence of the murderous methods employed by the perpetrators and thereby to prevent their killers from controlling the knowledge of their deaths.[4] In so doing, they demonstrated their keen awareness that annihilation is incomplete when memory is preserved.

The diaries that have survived because of the painstaking care taken by the diary writer and by chance comprise an extraordinary body of source material. Jewish men and women registered in their diaries the evolving process that eventually culminated for some in the realization that their fate was collective annihilation. Looked at together, diaries represented a broad social, intellectual, and cultural phenomenon that unwittingly linked Jews from all over Europe in a similar activity during the years of the war. As both "personal expressions" and "cultural products," diaries not only gave voice to their authors' personalities but also articulated the expectations and values of the cultures to which they belonged.[5]

In their turn to diary writing during the Second World War, Jews were not alone, although their reasons for writing differed in certain fundamental respects from those of non-Jews. In an essay that appeared in the newspaper *Deutsche Allgemeine Zeitung* in November 1942, the German journalist and diarist Ursula von Kardorff commented, "For several years, it appears that, in general, the practice of keeping a diary is again on the rise despite the total demand that today's existence makes on the individual's time."[6] The French scholar Michèle Leleu was likely inspired to take up an investigation of diaries in 1943 because of the popularity of diary writing during the war. In her book, published in 1952, Leleu claimed that "more than any other, the Second World War favored the blossoming of diaries of revolt. French and Germans sought in them a relief from the oppression of their consciences."[7] Leleu and others have accounted for the profusion of diary writing under German occupation—by Jews and non-Jews— by arguing that totalitarianism led people to keep diaries because politics was off-limits as a subject of conversation and because people sought to escape by the only means available to them: turning inward. Whereas studies of primarily non-Jewish diaries from the Second World War have by and large equated the motivations of Jewish and non-Jewish diarists—even though it seems clear that Jewish diarists did not need to document their distance and independence from the Nazi regime—studies of exclusively Jewish Holocaust diaries have described the phenomenon as having emerged from a deeply rooted Jewish literary tradition of bearing witness to tragedy as a means of transcending it. Yet the fact that so many Europeans took up diary writing during this period attests to how widespread an endeavor it had become, reaching beyond its Jewish roots. Thus, Jewish diary writing during the Holocaust reflected Jews' particular wartime circumstances and also connected to broader European cultural practices of the nineteenth and twentieth centuries.[8]

Jews employed many strategies in response to the Nazi threat to Jewish existence and the crisis of meaning it precipitated. The key problem this book details is, how did Jews make sense of the horror while it was being perpetrated? Rather than portraying "the Jewish response" to the Holocaust, I consider the range of responses of different people. First and foremost, then, this book contributes to our knowledge of the heterogeneity of the victims, of their experiences, of their wartime perceptions and coping strategies. By exploring the differences among Jews, I have tried to heed one scholar's warning and resist "reducing all Jews to a single, undifferentiated category with one common destiny."[9] Jewish experiences of the Holocaust cannot be boiled down to a single narrative or conceptual framework. Instead, I suggest new ways of categorizing Jewish wartime experiences based on diarists' strategies of interpretation. Jews' positions as the theologically inclined, the historically minded, the news-reading, the family-oriented were born of their meaning-making struggles, which emerged out of the intersection of their prewar identities and wartime situations. Looking at the variety of ways in which diarists attempted to make sense of the catastrophe gives us an alternative means of categorizing Jewish experiences from this period, one which highlights both the shared experience of being a Jew under German occupation —as meaning-makers rather than passive victims—and the diversity of modern European Jewry in the mid–twentieth century. Even diary writing did not mean one thing or function in a single way for Jews.

I also show that several of the issues central to postwar scholarly discussions about this period were pertinent to the women and men who wrote diaries. For instance, some diarists grappled with whether the Nazi extermination of the Jews challenged the limits of representation. For them, direct knowledge of the Holocaust did not lead to understanding and the ability to construct narratives about their experiences. On the contrary, when they became aware of the genocide, they faced the core problem of how to make sense of and represent to others the destruction of their people. In this respect, questions that have been considered as belonging to recent theoretical and historiographical debates were already present in the diary sources of the period.

Remaining attuned to the perspectives of diarists suggests a new periodization of the war years based not on the actions of the perpetrators but on the responses of the victims. For Jews who remained alive and knew about the fate of their fellow Jews—for the most part, Polish Jews who were geographically at the center of the German killing operation and had thus far evaded being killed—the period 1942 to 1943 was one of rupture. Most diaries written before that time reflect a limited understanding of the threat the writers faced. The annihilation of Jewish communities in large cities, towns, and villages produced the realization that there could be no postwar return to what had been. This provoked new questioning about God, humanity, the future, and the continuity of their identities and a sense of total alienation from the outside world.

Attention to time, to the periods of the Holocaust, is inextricable from a concern with the emotional lives of Jews. Understanding emotions may be acutely important for a history of this period. Indeed, the first major call for the historical study of emotions was by the French *Annaliste* historian Lucien Febvre in 1941. Febvre's interest in the general question of emotions in history stemmed from his particular concern with the emotions that dominated Europe in the 1930s and during the war. He believed that historians needed to take seriously emotional life and its historicity in order to understand fascism's appeal and, thereby, to prevent its recurrence.[10] Many Jewish diarists shared Febvre's conviction that what appeared to them to be fundamentally irrational—in this instance, the drive to murder millions of children and adult civilians—would have to be rationally analyzed by historians after the war because such an impulse carried to such an extreme could hardly be left unexplained. At the same time, some diarists indicated it was also essential to study the emotional lives of Jews during this period. These diarists conveyed the idea that without becoming familiar with the complexity of Jews' emotional responses, people in the outside world would never come to understand what it was like to be a Jew during this period and thus would remain ignorant of the full range of human experience. For this reason, I take up the question of emotions and consider categories such as hope, despair, anger, and defiance as communal responses and as aspects of Jews' relationships during different periods of the war. Emotions played an essential role in Jews' interpretive strategies: in their reading of the news, of history, and of the meaning of their diaries.

The historiographical discussion in this chapter and the textual analyses in the following four chapters address fundamental issues of experience and agency, representation, and diarists' changing strategies of confrontation with the unimaginable. To be sure, one of my goals has been to impart a sense of dignity to those who suffered, yet I have tried to avoid suggesting that Jews were ennobled by their suffering. To do so would invest their misery with an ultimate meaningfulness, as if they had derived some positive benefit from it.[11] This applies to my reading of the act of diary writing as well. Jewish diarists have been glorified; in the words of one scholar, "Like soldiers who die for their country, these Jews obeyed the imperative to document over the imperative to live."[12] Rather, it seems to me the "imperative to document" was inseparable from the "imperative to live." Lacking allies and having no hope of being rescued, Jews clung to one of the last threads of life available to them: writing themselves into the future. The last words of Chaim Kaplan's Warsaw ghetto diary, "If my life ends—what will become of my diary?" are frequently interpreted as evidence that Kaplan valued his diary more than his life, yet they can also be read as indicating that he regarded his diary to be intertwined with his existence. The condition of his death meant that his diary would end and, even more, that he would cease to control its fate. As much meaning as these diarists invested in their writing, they did not "martyr" themselves for the sake of their documentary endeavors.[13] And, as we shall see, in many cases they bore witness to their experiences with the deepest reluctance.

CATEGORIES OF VICTIMS AND THEIR DIARIES

An examination of Jews' values and perceptions must wrestle with an issue familiar to historians of the Holocaust in particular and to social and cultural historians in general: how to depict mass experience without effacing individual differences. Indeed, some diarists expressed concern about this eventuality, namely, that the complexity of Jewish identities and wartime lives would remain unknown to "the outside world." The Dutch diarist Etty Hillesum pessimistically conjectured in a letter she wrote in 1943 that "the outside world probably thinks of us as a gray, uniform, suffering mass of Jews, and knows nothing of the gulfs and abysses and subtle differences that exist between us. They could never hope to understand." Despite wondering, "Could one ever hope to convey to the outside world what has happened here today?" Hillesum continued to grapple with the depth and scope of Jewish suffering, feeling herself duty-bound to "bear witness where witness needs to be borne."[14]

Thanks to Hillesum's diary and those of other Jews, we can glimpse the ways in which Jewish men and women portrayed their lives, their worlds, their persecution, and, most specifically, their realization that they were individually and collectively facing death. In examining the self-perception and conduct of Jews during the Holocaust, I have been influenced by other social and cultural historians who have been drawn increasingly to study individual experience. Historians have always mined personal documents for information about important historical figures, but only in the past two decades, under the influence of feminism and poststructuralism and the methodological innovations of microhistory, have they sought out first-person accounts produced by ordinary people. An openness to what Joan W. Scott referred to as "the literary" has given rise to new questions about human experience, new areas of historical research, most notably on the historicity of the self, and new possibilities for thinking about narrative construction.[15] In analyzing the relationship between writing and experience in Jewish Holocaust diaries, therefore, I ask questions similar to those of other cultural historians about the function and meaning of cultural production under varying historical circumstances.[16] My book thus joins the growing tide of historical works that make use of diaries and memoirs in writing about the perspectives of the Holocaust's victims.[17]

At stake in an investigation of Jewish men's and women's diaries is the possibility of discovering traces of the human struggles of this epoch. People's efforts to render their suffering meaningful are discernible in their diaries. So, too, are their repeated doubts about these efforts because of their ongoing suffering. Thus, the potential exists to explore these men's and women's construction of narratives—what was historically imaginable to them—and the ways in which such narratives molded their possibilities for agency—both the actions they took and the strategies they developed to make sense of the destruction of their worlds.[18] Though Jews from all backgrounds met with the same end, nonetheless, they "'saw'—i.e., understood *and* witnessed—[their] predicament[s] differently, depending on [their] own historical past, religious paradigms, and ideological explanations."[19] Moreover, variations among individuals' wartime situations played a crucial role in their interpretations of Nazi persecution. How these differences manifested themselves is evident in each chapter of this book, ranging from Jewish diarists' approaches and responses to reading the news to the unremitting hope for the future retained by diarists whose children had reached the safety of distant shores.

[My analysis of Jewish diaries builds on the efforts of scholars who have consistently challenged the monolithic representation of Holocaust victims in histories that focus on the motives and actions of the perpetrators‚ One early strategy some historians pursued to counter the objectification and homogenization of Jewish victims in Holocaust histories was to document resistance in response to accusations of Jewish compliance. Raul Hilberg, in *The Destruction of the European Jews* (1961), the first significant history of the Holocaust to be published in English, condemned European Jews for their "almost complete lack of resistance"

and, even worse, accused the German-appointed Jewish Council leaders of assist-
ing in the destruction of their communities. Hannah Arendt amplified Hilberg's
reproach against alleged Jewish passivity and Jewish complicity in her famous
analysis of the Eichmann trial, originally published in the *New Yorker* in 1963.[20]
Their works generated a strong negative response among a newly emerging generation of Israeli historians of the Shoah in the 1960s and 1970s. To counter the
critiques of Hilberg and Arendt, historians such as Yisrael Gutman and Yehuda
Bauer challenged their monolithic portrayal of the majority of Jews—derived
from German bureaucratic documents, which would naturally paint Jews in a
highly unfavorable light—and investigated instances of Jewish armed and unarmed resistance.[21] They and others made clear what is perhaps today a commonplace assumption: that Jews reacted to German policies in a variety of ways,
albeit within a narrowly circumscribed field of action.

Before the late 1960s, historians of the Holocaust were divided into two schools
of thought on the question of how to evaluate cultural activities like writing literature, poetry, diaries, and songs, staging theatrical performances and lectures,
printing underground newspapers, and educating children. One side equated
such activities with escapism, while the other side saw them as an assertion of Jewish viability and spiritual resistance.[22] For the former, the central issue was how
cultural activities *functioned* politically (that is, did they further Jewish armed
struggle?); for the latter, the central issue was what they *meant* symbolically.
Those who adhered to the former position defined political activity narrowly, as
physical resistance to genocide. However, as social and cultural historians have
pushed for a broader reading of the political implications of culture, there has
been a marked shift away from evaluating the cultural activities of Jews as non-
resistance. Gutman has shown how, in Warsaw, for example, youth groups that
supported underground cultural production in the first two years of the war
began, in 1942, to call for armed resistance upon learning of the deportations
of Jews from the Lublin area and the massacres of Jews in territories captured
from the Soviet Union. Similar-minded historians now see the relationship between unarmed and armed resistance as more complementary than contradictory. They have found that the political function and symbolic meaning of cultural activities frequently overlapped.[23]

Historians no longer merely opposed the figure of the heroic fighter to that of
the cowering victim. Instead, scholars of this bent maintained that the prior conception of the overwhelming majority of Jews as having faced their murderers
by going "like sheep to the slaughter" was grossly inaccurate. They were eager
to show that the Jewish masses were not passive but resisted their oppressors by
whatever means were available to them. Along with partisans, therefore, "ghetto

scribes" have gained posthumous recognition as figures of resistance who attempted to subvert the Nazis with writing instruments as their weapons.[24] The broadening of the category of resistance has since become the prevailing interpretation of Jewish cultural production during the Shoah. This historiographical development has followed on the heels of changes from within and outside the field of Holocaust history.

Historians' general assessment of Jewish wartime cultural life has been, in part, a reaction to important new findings by scholars of German anti-Jewish policy. These findings show that the decision to murder the Jews during the war, rather than drive them out of Europe or murder them after the war's end, was not made until sometime in 1941. They also reveal that local German officials pursued different policies toward Jews in various districts of Poland, Ukraine, Belorussia, and the Baltic States. Understanding the complexity of German policy has allowed for a new appreciation of the equally variable Jewish efforts to survive the war by making themselves invaluable to the German war economy. Seen in this light, morale-building activities made sense for people who understood their predicament to be not trying to survive against all odds but trying to persevere against very bad odds. At the same time, the differences in German treatment of Jews also explain to a great extent why, in many locales, Jews apparently did not engage in cultural pursuits: conditions were just too horrendous to support them.[25]

This reappraisal of the implications of Jewish cultural life during the war should also be set against the larger backdrop of developments in the fields of cultural history and literary theory. In her introductory essay to the volume *The New Cultural History* (1989), Lynn Hunt described how historians were increasingly incorporating literary and art historical approaches into their readings of texts and images. According to Hunt, she and others had taken up the issue of representation in order "to examine the ways in which linguistic practice, rather than simply reflecting social reality, could actively be an instrument of (or constitute) power."[26] Several recent discussions of diaries and other literature produced during the Holocaust have attempted to do just that: to show how, for the individual who wrote, the act of writing did not merely reflect their experiences but also granted a sense of agency.[27]

It is necessary to distinguish between the function diaries served and the meaning they held for their authors. Diaries may have constituted a form of individual and collective resistance, but that does not mean the process of writing a diary necessarily conferred on an author a sense of relief or that it was an effective means of preserving selfhood. The power of diary writing should not be overstated. Perhaps under normal life circumstances, diaries can "create the illusion of control, lessen the sensation of risk, or make their [diarists'] restricted situation seem more satisfying," but for many Jewish diarists of the Holocaust, especially those who wrote in the wake of the mass deportations, diary writing neither positively affected their emotional state, nor had the power to maintain their sense of equilibrium.[28] While diary writing may have constituted a considerable *effort* "to preserve a shred of one's self before it is rubbed out," that does not mean it was armor strong enough to withstand the Nazi assault.[29] Thus, while diaries are not evidence of successful resistance to genocide, they are texts of struggle that document Jews' efforts to maintain a sense of an individual self, even as that possibility was being erased.

The general appraisal of typically individual, unarmed acts as having constituted a form of cultural-political resistance unintentionally homogenizes a remarkably diverse body of writings and the manifold messages communicated by their authors(While I accept the basic premise that diary writing could serve as a form of resistance, I am not centrally concerned with this issue, thanks in no small measure to the work of other scholars who have already called attention to the element of resistance.) Instead, I focus on issues that may be obscured by an emphasis on resistance. Thus, in addition to writing diaries to resist German oppression, Jewish diarists wrote for many other reasons, in part depending on their religious, cultural, national, political, and familial backgrounds, and in part depending on the period of the war and their experiences of Nazi persecution. Some diarists, especially those in Poland during the second half of the war who had witnessed the worst atrocities, wrote to communicate their anger and desire for revenge, and some diarists who knew their children would survive the war wrote to reaffirm the possibility of humanity to act for the good and the just. Some, above all those in western Europe, conveyed their sense of the total moral bankruptcy of both the Axis *and* Allied powers, while others believed the world would right its wrongs after the defeat of Nazi Germany. Some who had family living outside German-occupied Europe addressed their diaries to a specific audience, while others who were politically active or had lost everyone dear to them wrote for the world at large. Some diarists, particularly those who wrote during the first half of the war, hoped their diaries would help repair the Jewish world after the war, while others, particularly who wrote during the second half of the war, feared that no repair was possible.

The range of responses to Nazi persecution reflected two centuries of profound change in European Jewish life. During this period, Jews integrated to varying degrees into the societies in which they lived, creating new divisions among themselves as well as complex modern individual identities. Diary writing was one of the European cultural practices in which Jews participated during the nineteenth and twentieth centuries, and they continued to practice it during the Shoah as they tried to reconstruct meaning and register the destruction of their lives and worlds. In this respect, diary writing, like other dimensions of Jewish wartime existence, should not be viewed solely as a reaction to German atrocities. As Dan Michman has argued, it is essential to see how Jews' responses to their persecution and extermination were also "the results of modern Jewish history" which "came into play on different levels and in different settings" during the war.[30] For example, why the ardent Hebraist and Zionist Chaim Kaplan, writing a diary in the Warsaw ghetto, put his trust in history to make sense of the catastrophe, whereas the Alsatian diarist Lucien Dreyfus, writing from exile in Nice, reaffirmed his faith in the Hebrew God and looked disdainfully on history writing, makes sense only in light of their prewar relationships to history, religion, national identity, and humanist values in conjunction with their different wartime circumstances. In order to decipher the complexity of Jewish responses to the Holocaust, it is necessary to study them within the broader context of nineteenth- and twentieth-century European history.

This broader contextualization of Jewish wartime diary writing differs from most scholars' previous depictions. They have tended to describe the phenomenon of Jewish diary writing during the Shoah in one of two ways. They have either connected it to a specifically Jewish literary tradition or they have contended that diaries, along with other literature produced by Jews during and after the war, came to constitute their own literary genre. The former portray diary writing as having emerged from a deeply rooted Jewish tradition of bearing witness to catastrophe in order to transcend it and restore the relationship between God and the people of Israel. Jewish diary writing during the Second World War constituted one noteworthy instance in a thousand-year-old literary effort to write "against the apocalypse," as David Roskies argued in his magisterial study of Yiddish and Hebrew literature.[31] Whereas this interpretation is based on a notion of continuity, albeit a complex, dialectical one, the understanding of Holocaust literature as its own genre of writing comes out of a sense of exceptionality. As a reaction to an unprecedented social universe, Holocaust literature is seen as bearing the imprint of that particularity and as ultimately dissimilar from other literature in its content and meaning. Given the politicized fights over genres in Western literary criticism, which have determined what gets included and excluded from the canon, the argument for the recognition of Holocaust literature as its own genre can also be construed as a political statement advocating the necessity of devoting time and attention to this literature.[32]

Ostensibly, Jewish cultural production during the war was a reaction to German oppression. Yet the concept of Holocaust literature implies that the German occupation created *sui generis* works of literature which lacked other influences and literary models. As a rubric, it tends to discourage the forging of connections, especially between Jewish wartime diary writing and traditions that predated the war. Instead, as Ruth R. Wisse has argued, "the nature of literature during and after the war depends in large part on the language and context within which it was written . . . and . . . where problems of language reflect conflicts of identity, they predate the war and were not caused by Hitler alone."[33] Furthermore, the category Holocaust literature fails to distinguish between those texts written from the perspective of hindsight, with an awareness of the larger narrative we understand as the Holocaust, and those that were not. It erroneously implies that all such texts—memoirs, diaries, poetry, novels, and so on—are unified by a set of internal characteristics, thereby flattening divergences in the narrative strategies, perspectives, and motivations of their authors.[34] When one analyzes diaries separate from, rather than in conjunction with, survivors' testimonies, the specificity of Jews' contemporaneous perceptions and reasons for writing a diary becomes apparent.

Most literary studies of Jewish writing during the Shoah have devoted some attention to broader influences; however, with few exceptions, their focus has remained on internal Jewish developments.[35] Rather than a specifically Jewish phenomenon, Jews' wartime diary writing was the result of diverse and complex impulses and goals. Jewish diarists from the war modeled their writing on diverse literary sources, and in some cases the models shifted over time. Etty Hillesum began her diary with Augustine clearly in mind. Initially, her diary was a form of personal confession in which she recorded her spiritual awakening. As she became convinced of the importance of "bearing witness" to the plight of Jews under German occupation—and perhaps also as she shared her writing in the Dutch transit camp Westerbork with her friend Philip Mechanicus, a journalist who also kept a diary—Hillesum's writing became more journalistic and less self-revelatory in tone and subject matter. By contrast, Yitzhak Rudashevski, a youth in the Vilna ghetto, conceived of himself as a ghetto historian and observer in the tradition of scholars at YIVO, the institute founded in Vilna in the 1920s which was dedicated to research on Jewish history, folklore, and the Yiddish language. And a number of older Jewish diarists of the Holocaust, including Victor Klemperer, Willy Cohn, and Lucien Dreyfus, began their diaries decades prior to the war. Their turn to diary writing exemplified several trends that commenced in western Europe in the mid–nineteenth century, such as the use of diary writing as a pedagogical and moral exercise for school-age children and the use of the diary as a medium of "self-realization."[36] Thus, Jewish men and women who wrote diaries connected their writing to Jewish and non-Jewish writing practices that included lamentation literature, autobiography and confession, the literature of dissent, modern historiography, journalism, jurisprudence, the private diary (*journal intime*), and family correspondence. During the war, diaries became sites and vehicles for Jews to reconceptualize different versions of the religious, to employ a range of cultural practices, and to cling to familial and increasingly Jewish national frameworks.

Although thousands of Jews may have written diaries during the Holocaust, millions did not. Indeed, Bauer has signaled the need to be wary of "overdrawing" the portrait of an "active, unarmed Jewish response" for fear that "a reader might get the impression that while there was suffering, the majority of the Jews were busy educating, learning, putting on plays or making music or painting, giving or listening to lectures, publishing illegal newspapers," or, one might add, scribbling away in their diaries.[37] Among those who were unable to write diaries were the overwhelming majority of concentration camp inmates, who simply lacked the opportunity, the means, and the physical strength to do so. While this book enlarges our perspective of the victims, it is imperative to recall that it remains limited to the small number who wrote diaries.

THE HOLOCAUST, REPRESENTATION, AND HOPE

Among the issues with which diarists grappled, one question became notably acute as the killing of Jews increased. Diarists wondered if it was possible to represent their experiences in language, and what the implications were of the representations they were in the process of creating. The quotation from Rotgeber that begins this chapter shows one diarist engaging this issue of historical reality at the very outset of his diary. Rotgeber's repeated insistence on the "true" and "unprecedented" nature of the "crime" committed against a "defenseless nation" suggests that he feared people in the future would not believe his stories of atrocity. This questioning by Rotgeber and others as to whether the ensuing genocide would be ultimately unassimilable to those who had not personally experienced it is related to the now-familiar discussions among scholars about the potential inadequacies of traditional historical narratives to represent the Holocaust. Diarists' representational struggles force us to reconceptualize what has until now been thought of as a historiographical and philosophical issue that emerged in the wake of poststructuralism. In addition, these theoretical discussions, in conjunction with reading Jewish men's and women's diaries, suggest alternative approaches to thinking about narrative construction, approaches which I have attempted to incorporate into the structure of this book.

Scholars' theoretical discussions have centered on two interrelated issues. First, is it possible to render the Holocaust by the conventional means historians use to narrate and analyze the past? Second, does reality exist independently of the act of its construction by the observer? As Berel Lang observed, underlying the question of historical representation were two assumptions: the existence of a standard representational form employed by historians and the notion that the Holocaust constituted a kind of conceptual limit case.[38] If traditional forms of historical narrative, whether chronological, analytical, or topical, attempt to organize the past in a coherent form with a beginning, middle, and end, then some historians questioned the suitability of such representational forms for histories of the Holocaust. They contended that the sense of resolution, or closure, created at the conclusion of a historical narrative contradicted the excess of suffering of the victims, their experiences of chaos and disorder, and ultimately the silence of their deaths.[39] By concluding a history of the Holocaust with either the chronological end point of Allied victory and the liberation of the camps or the rhetorical tying together of loose ends by answering the questions laid out at the beginning of one's study, the historian suggested a movement from catastrophe and the unknown to redemption (of meaning, of victims who became survivors) and the establishment of stable truth.

An investigation of Jewish diaries would seem to avoid being susceptible to "simplistic and self-assured historical narrations and closures" because it places the experiences of the victims—their suffering and dislocation—at its center.[40] Yet as the generally "uplifting" readings of Anne Frank's diary indicate, even a study written from the perspective of the victims can extract "hope from desolation, good from evil, and celebration from tragedy."[41] In order to resist constructing a redemptive narrative that implies a return to normalcy with the end of the war or an unflagging confidence in the goodness of humanity, neither of which reflects the view of most Jewish diarists, I have organized this book thematically, staying close to the issues and emotions conveyed by diarists. So rather than proceeding time-wise in linear fashion, the book spirals, each chapter retracing the war's chronology from a different thematic vantage point. In this way, it suggests two movements simultaneously: change over time and repetition.[42] Each chapter proceeds chronologically yet tries to forestall the overall narrative thrust toward a denouement, thereby not only highlighting continuities and discontinuities among Jews' experiences over the course of the war, but also pointing to the inescapability of death for most Jews under German occupation.

The combination of repetition and change also relates to the experience of reading one diary after another. The themes, subjects, and even words of one diary often closely resemble those of other diaries, but always with a shift in perspective and a change in detail. I have tried to replicate the sense of repetition and newness derived from reading diaries by taking different approaches, from

one chapter to another, in analyzing them. Two chapters are organized by extended discussions of individual diaries and the other two by the interspersal of
references to over fifty diaries. While each chapter could benefit from the other
kind of analysis, my hope is that the richness from one chapter, with more in-
depth analyses of individual sources, could be taken as background for another
chapter that moves from text to text, and vice versa. Moreover, by handling the
material in different ways, I mean to suggest a degree of open-endedness in interpretation as another means of avoiding closure.[43]

As for temporal boundaries, this book focuses on the years of the war rather
than on the Third Reich in its entirety. Although a few of the diarists considered
here wrote entries before the war and in some cases survived and continued to
record entries even after the war, I have centered my analysis on those parts of
their diaries that treat the period of the war itself. Nevertheless, since few Jewish diarists lived to see the end of the war, Germany's defeat does not figure as
the end point of this historical study. Indeed, the chronological ending of each
chapter has been determined not by an event as much as by a shift in the conceptual awareness of some of the Jewish men and women who are the protagonists
of this historical narrative. From the point of view of those victims who wrote in
Poland in the midst of the mass deportations to the death camps, the end of the
war might save their individual lives, but it would not bring about the resumption of a European Jewish collective life. It is this consciousness from the second
half of the war of a fundamental rupture in Jewish history that frames the outer
limit of this study.

Not only did some diarists convey the sense that what they were experiencing
constituted a fundamentally new historical reality, but they also made explicit in
their wartime diary writing their struggles with the problem of how to represent
the ensuing destruction. Representation was a core epistemological and ethical
problem for victims of the Holocaust, just as it has been for postwar scholars. The
contemporaneous problem of representation concerned how to understand and
communicate their present—not a historical—reality. Lacking the perspective
of hindsight and the bird's-eye view that retrospective vision affords, many diarists believed their experiences to be unprecedented and conveyed the fear that
they were potentially unrepresentable to the outside world. On the one hand,
they sought to ensure that the outside world would learn about the horrors to
which Jews had been subjected. On the other hand, they feared that language
would efface or misconstrue the particularity of their experiences. These Jewish
diarists thus called attention to the lack of transparency in their own representational endeavors at the same time that they insisted on the ethical, historical,
and juridical value of their writing.

The difficulty diarists encountered in trying to represent their experiences resonates with the second historiographical issue over the limits of representation "probed" by the Holocaust. This discussion among Holocaust scholars about the epistemological and ontological status of the past has been part of a larger "linguistic turn" among historians.[44] First, poststructuralist theories call the reality of the past into question, hence challenging history's ability to know it. They challenge historians to abandon the privileging of a recoverable, *real* reality. Second, the very principle of coherent individuals is challenged by poststructuralism, and that, in turn, appears to invalidate history's attempts to know human experience. In other words, some historians have challenged the notion that a past reality exists, independent of the act of its construction by the observer, and, at least in theory, is knowable on its own terms. Historians have been left to wrestle with "the paradox that, on the one hand, there is no straightforward way to match our propositions about events with events themselves, yet, on the other hand, the historian is justified in claiming she can tell the truth."[45]

These wider debates about historical truth have had a dramatic significance for Holocaust historians. Scholars reflecting on the Holocaust have asked whether it is possible that "after Auschwitz poetry can be written, but history, as the 'realistic' interpretation of the past, cannot."[46] The questioning of the referentiality of historical representation provoked a heated response among those scholars who recognized the potential relativization of "truth" if taken to its logical extreme. The ethical stakes became especially clear in considering the possibility that Holocaust denial could be regarded not as an untruth, but as an interpretation no less (and no more) valid than any others. Thus, "the status of alternate Holocaust-narratives . . . demonstrate[s] graphically what is at stake in the issue of historical representation more generally."[47]

Again, it is striking that in their contemporaneous writing many Jewish diarists wrestled with issues similar to those historians would confront later. Diarists often invested tremendous faith in history and envisioned their diaries as evidence for future historical writing about their plight. At the same time, they expressed doubt that historians who had not shared their experiences would be able to understand and accurately depict them. Diarists thus anticipated the paradoxical ordeal of the (post)modern historian: they seemed to recognize and fear "the productive quality of discourse" yet, on the basis of their own attempts to represent their experiences, asserted that material reality is separate from the realm of discourse.[48] What had happened to them did not conform to existing norms of the plausible or conceivable. It was a moment of excess in which experience either would change discourse or would remain unrepresentable. With this contention, they put forth a view that contradicts Joan W. Scott's later argument that experience is constituted in and through language, not prior to or separate from a "discursive system."[49]

Rather than resolve this paradox by arguing either that experience cannot precede interpretation or that experience can be directly apprehended in representation, Edith Wyschogrod's concept of the "heterological historian" offers another possibility. Wyschogrod's theorizing about history has been driven by a concern for those who have been erased from history and for whom, she feels, the historian is responsible. Yet this ethical responsibility is not easily discharged. The heterological historian takes as her starting point the irony that "obligated by her vow to restore the past in its actuality, she nevertheless recognizes the impossibility of doing so." In addition to this philosophical conundrum, Wyschogrod's historian contends with the psychological dilemma of having to combine "disinterestedness" with "a sense of inescapable urgency": "The heterological historian is driven, on the one hand, by an impassioned necrophilia which would bring to life the dead others for whom she speaks. On the other hand, as 'objective,' she consciously or otherwise assumes responsibility for a dispassionate relation to events."[50] Thus, the heterological historian struggles, uncomfortably yet hopefully, with the ethical, philosophical, and psychological contradictions of the historical endeavor.

The heterological historian is the closest approximation to the figure of the future historian called for by many Jewish diarists. Wyschogrod conceptualizes the writing of history as emanating from hope, which is "the interface of possibility and improbability, as that which is not only improbable but also possible, [and] can become programmatic and, as such, is hope that enters into history."[51] My own study has proceeded from a hopeful imperative, animated by the diary material whose fragmentary nature both serves as a perpetual reminder of the impossibility of apprehending the victims in their fullness and offers one of the few possibilities of encountering them "proximately."[52]

RETHINKING GENERIC PARADIGMS

Every author of a work on diaries feels compelled to define what constitutes a diary. Yet, as one literary scholar wrote, "almost everyone knows what a diary is until it becomes necessary to define one."[53] Definitions generally start with the premise that a diary is structured around a series of dated entries. Yet even this proposition runs into problems, since the appearance of dated entries does not guarantee that the writer recorded the events of a day on the same day as their occurrence. It is common practice for diary writers—including the emblematic Samuel Pepys—to write up entries for a number of days in one sitting. Moreover, considering the chaos of Jews' lives under German occupation, the criteria of dailiness, or even of regularly dated entries, does not seem to be the best way to distinguish diaries from other forms of writing.

I have considered as diaries those texts that "preserve the gradual acquisition of knowledge and shifting of values that occur in life."[54] In other words, I have delineated diaries on the basis of temporal perspective, or the author's changing point of view, rather than the texts' uniformity of structure. Thus, the writings that I am calling diaries do not all resemble classic diaries, although some of them do.[55] Among the sources for this book are private diaries, in which the writers were also the main subjects of the diaries and reflexively explored their thoughts. But some of the sources do not fit a traditional definition of what constitutes a diary, either because they were products of a group effort to record Jewish experiences, because the texts more closely resemble reports in which the writers tried to remain objective and inconspicuous, or because the texts were written as a series of letters to absent loved ones. What they share is context: they were written by men and women who were subjected to German occupation, who were identified as Jews by German racial laws, and who wrote during the war years. The texts under consideration here are "discontinuous series of more or less self-contained responses to the writer's present situation and recent experience."[56]

These diaries are hybrid texts that melded and adapted preexisting literary forms in order to respond to the circumstances of different phases of persecution. One might think of them as improvisational texts which, like theatrical improvisation, drew from multiple, studied elements.[57] In considering diaries as such, I take my cue from literary scholars who increasingly tend to dispense with generic paradigms in favor of considering all texts "as modes of signification, as linguistic representations derived from many discourses available at a particular historical moment."[58] Rather than attempt to define the ideal-typical diary or autobiography, scholars have become increasingly interested in boundary crossings and overlaps between genres.

My book extends scholars' efforts to break down generic boundaries, in particular, the separation of diaries from correspondence. Scholars have differentiated the two on the basis of audience. Diaries are typically represented as being private and lacking a specific audience beyond the diarist, whereas letters are portrayed as being written with a recipient in mind. However, the general situation of war and, within that, the extreme isolation of Jews under German occupation made it impossible for many Jews to correspond with relatives in Allied countries for long stretches of time. For this reason, many Jews wrote series of unsent letters that functioned for their writers in ways indistinguishable from diaries. The act of writing, which emerged from a desire to contact distant loved ones, also helped individuals to try to connect with their prewar identities rooted in family and community. In this way, letter-diaries carried a similar symbolic meaning as diaries whose entries were not structured in letter format. They represented to their writers the existence of a community rendered present through the process of writing.[59] The differentiation typically made between diary and correspondence thus did not hold for some Jews during the Holocaust.

This book challenges generic paradigms in another way as well, namely, by arguing that historical diaries or war diaries should be considered forms of self-writing. War diaries have generally been construed as having little in common with private diaries because they tend to point to the external world rather than to "the internal world of a single ego."[60] Since they are focused on a definite historical episode and were usually written with an audience in mind beyond the author him- or herself, literary scholars have placed such diaries in their own category or subgenre. It is true that most of the diaries I have examined were not "self-sustaining piece[s] of autobiography" but were written only because of the diarists' separation from loved ones and the consciousness that they were witnessing historically important events.[61] Though not classical *journaux intimes*, however, they do reveal aspects of their authors' thoughts and feelings.

Many private diarists also wrote for an eventual audience. Once diaries were published and became popular literature in the late nineteenth century, the dichotomy between public and private diaries became untenable. Ordinary diarists, those who were not professional writers, wrote with literary self-consciousness and were attuned to style and a potential readership. In contrast to the conception of diarists writing in a vacuum, most diarists had models of diary writing in their heads gained by reading other people's diaries, either those that were published or the diaries of family members that were shared within the family. Private diarists thus came to possess a sense of the value of diary writing and of the form of writing and connected their own work to that of others. Even diarists who never imagined a broader audience of strangers "hovering at the edge of the page" often shared their diaries, willingly or not, with other readers, like their husbands.[62] In the *journal intime*, the development of the self was interconnected with public performance.

Jewish men and women who addressed their diaries to absent family members and to the world at large were part of this longer tradition of diary writing as public performance. When parents attempted to use their diaries to impart moral lessons to their children, they were drawing upon an established function of diary writing as a moral and pedagogical tool. So, too, when Jews struggled, by means of their diaries, to make sense of the world around them, they were taking part in a European cultural practice that was premised on the notion that individuals' lives had meaning and purpose.[63] Thus, diary writing often emanated from the hope that, by narrating their experiences to others, it would be possible for people in the future to determine the underlying causes of the Germans' perpetration of such horrific crimes and to prevent their recurrence. Whether the explanation for the extermination of the Jews was located on a human or theological plane, Jews' victimization would be connected to a larger narrative. Diarists wanted to ensure that the Jewish cataclysm shook the world to its core and had an effect on the future.

The chapters that follow illuminate the strategies of interpretation that diarists employed in their attempts to comprehend their personal fates and that of European Jewry as a whole. Chapter 2 explores the divergent responses of two diarists, Chaim Kaplan in the Warsaw ghetto and Lucien Dreyfus in the south of France, to the onset of the extermination of European Jews. Both of these men attempted to make sense of Jewish wartime experiences by means of their preexisting belief systems. Neither was able to retain his prior conceptions of God and humanity. Kaplan questioned the Hebrew God and relied upon rationalism and historical justice to ensure that Jews' suffering would not be forgotten and would have meaning in the future. Dreyfus became disillusioned with liberal enlightened society and reaffirmed his faith in God to fill the existential void. This in-depth look at the diaries of these two men reveals how the persecution of European Jews and the onset of genocide pushed Jews in opposite directions, driving some toward deeper religiosity and pushing others away. Examining such extreme positions, I establish the wide spectrum of Jewish responses, exposing the range of individuals' attempts to render their experiences meaningful. Many diarists did not respond in the same ways as Kaplan and Dreyfus, but practically all of them wrestled with the same theological and moral questions.

The third chapter explores another epistemological approach to comprehending what one diarist described as "things that we would not believe if we were told about them."[64] That approach consisted of building rational knowledge about the crisis on the basis of reading the news. Jewish diarists avidly tracked the news. In entry after entry, they recorded the latest news reports about the fighting on the fronts and rumors about the fate of Jewish individuals and communities. News was a product that, by means of its exchange and consumption, sustained Jewish existence under German domination. Examining Jews' strategies of interpreting news expands our sense of the sources to which Jews turned in their confrontations with genocide. In addition, this chapter takes us further into the diversity of individuals' responses by widening the lens from two to more than thirty-five diarists. It also underscores the rupture in hope and understanding that followed the commencement of the mass deportations to the death camps, a rupture evident in Kaplan's diary. Diarists conveyed an emotional shift from dislocation and the hope that lay in confusion to the anger and despair of comprehension.

Chapters 4 and 5 focus more explicitly on the function diaries served and the meaning they had for Jews during the war. I examine the implications of diary writing: what it signified to different people to write a diary and how the process of writing about their experiences affected them. In the fourth chapter I argue that, for families that were separated during the war, diaries were an essential medium for communicating thoughts and experiences to absent loved ones. Parents separated from their children tried to "parent at a distance" through their letter-diaries and to bridge the gap in knowledge and understanding created by the Hitlerian universe between them and their families in the outside world. The intermeshing of diaries and letters for some Jews during the war also illustrates how it can be fruitful to consider the hybrid nature of these genres. Furthermore, what emerges from these letter-diaries is a conception of the future different from that most news-readers articulated, thus building on the previous chapter's discussion of how people's notion of the future changed over the course of the war. Some diarists who knew their children were safe continued to believe that future generations of Jews would follow a meaningful life course even if their own lives were to be prematurely ended. Thus, through the close reading of a smaller number of texts, we see how people's responses were affected by their personal circumstances as well as by their understanding of the scope of the Germans' murderous actions.

The fifth and final chapter examines how the function of diary writing was transformed as diarists came to believe they faced a predicament that lacked historical precedent. Whereas earlier in the war, diary writing was a means of mental escape for many Jews, it ceased to function in this capacity for some Jews writing after the mass deportations, from 1942 onward. Instead, it made manifest the seeming unrepresentability of Jews' predicament and their sense of alienation from the outside world. As the outside world became more distant, some diarists expressed the belief that they had experienced a rupture not only in the realm of epistemology, but also in the continuity of the self. Writing could not help them connect to the past and the future. Indeed, some diarists believed that they had been fundamentally altered by their wartime experiences and that there could be no return to what had been, in terms of national identity, belief in progress, or faith in divine justice or humanist ethics. These diarists struggled with the impossible task of expressing what they had experienced and witnessed, yet simultaneously felt duty-bound to attempt to represent and make known to the outside world the extermination of the Jews.

Jews tried to transcend the boundaries that were forcibly inscribed ever more tightly around them. As they were forced to live in smaller and more crowded spaces, Jewish diarists tried to carve out a private realm in their diaries. They attempted to write themselves into a future they were being written out of and to reach an audience of human peers from whom they had been physically and categorically separated. And they wrote in the desperate hope that they might bridge the chasm between their wartime experiences and their self-understandings developed before the war. This book explores the strategies Jews employed in their search for meaning, the preliminary answers they arrived at, and the periods during which meaninglessness intruded despite their best efforts to suppress it.

HISTORIANS AND MARTYRS

On 1 September 1939, as Germany invaded Poland, Chaim Aron Kaplan recorded in his diary, "We are witnessing the dawn of a new era in the history of the
world."[1] For a man just shy of sixty years old (he was born in 1880 in Horodyszcze,
Belorussia) who had witnessed some of the most tremendous upheavals in modern European history, including pogroms, revolution, and world war, this was a
bold declaration. It reflected in part his discernment, in part hyperbole, and in
part premonition. Kaplan had received a Talmudic education at the celebrated
yeshiva in Mir and had attended the Government Pedagogical Institute in Vilna
before moving to Warsaw at the turn of the century. For forty years before the
outbreak of the Second World War, he was the principal of a Hebrew elemen-
tary school which he had founded and which was named for him. A passionate Hebraist and Zionist, Kaplan faithfully penned his diary in Hebrew in order
to preserve memory of the "horror and destruction" then befalling Warsaw: "I
will write a scroll of agony," he wrote, *"for the future period in my life."*[2] He had
kept a diary since at least 1933, but with the start of the war his writing acquired
new meaning and importance. Indeed, just four days later, he promised, "I have
made a rule for myself in these historic times not to let a single day go by without making an entry in my diary."[3]

Kaplan's diary stands as one of the most remarkable chronicles of Jewish experiences during the Holocaust. He recorded the suffering of Warsaw Jewry in
six notebooks replete with irony, literary flourishes, Talmudic and scriptural references, and a modern historical sensibility. In impeccable handwriting in black
and purple ink, Kaplan filled a notebook of two to four hundred pages roughly
every six months—twice as fast during the war as previously—until shortly before he and his wife were deported. His diary survived thanks to the efforts of
two men: a friend of Kaplan's in the ghetto named Rubinsztejn whom Kaplan

entrusted with his diary in August 1942, asking him to keep it safe until the end of the war; and a Polish friend of Rubinsztejn's named Władysław Wojciek, who took the diary from Rubinsztejn when it appeared the ghetto's end was fast approaching and buried it in several locations on his father's farm outside Warsaw.[4] Today, Kaplan's notebooks are scattered in archives in Israel and Poland. And, as Kaplan had hoped, versions of the diary have been available in print since 1965.

While Kaplan wrote about the ever more desperate circumstances of Warsaw both before and after the establishment of the ghetto, Lucien Dreyfus kept a diary from the "margin of events" in the south of France.[5] Dreyfus, too, was just shy of sixty at the outbreak of the war and, as a native of Alsace, was no stranger to the historical upheavals of the late nineteenth and early twentieth centuries. Despite having resided in German-annexed Alsace for the first half of his life, he remained a strong French patriot who identified equally with being Jewish. Dreyfus had struggled with his faith before the war: he had deserted his rabbinical studies in Berlin four decades before and had subsequently become a teacher of modern languages and history at a *lycée* in Strasbourg, where he had taught for over thirty years. Nevertheless, in the editorials he wrote for the leading Jewish newspaper of Alsace and Lorraine, *La Tribune Juive de Strasbourg*, he consistently urged his coreligionists to lead Jewish lives while remaining faithful to France. Although he had kept a diary since at least 1925, during the war it took on a new function, that of a locus for working out the relationship between the two identities he embraced: the French "warrior" patriot and the Jewish "believer."[6]

Although Dreyfus's diary has never been published, it is a significant chronicle of the response of a prominent Jewish intellectual from the provinces to the persecution of European Jews. His wartime diary is the culmination of decades of sustained reflection on the condition of French-Jewish identity. At four hundred pages plus, the diary is much shorter than Kaplan's, though it is written in an equally meticulous hand and in a similar type of composition book, the kind commonly used at that time by students all over Europe. Seven notebooks written in French span the period from 22 January 1925 to 24 September 1943. When Dreyfus and his wife were evacuated from Strasbourg in July 1939, moving first to Poitiers and then to Nice, he must have carried at least part of his diary with him. It is unknown who safeguarded the diary after he and his wife were deported. Donated anonymously to the archives of the United States Holocaust Memorial Museum in the 1990s, it was dropped in the mail one notebook at a time without a sender's name or address and sent by regular, uncertified first-class mail. Gaps in the chronology and notebook numbering suggest that some notebooks are now missing. It is possible, therefore, that more diary notebooks are in private hands or were destroyed or even lost in the mail. It is also entirely possible that Dreyfus had kept a diary for years before 1925 and that those and other note-books were lost when Dreyfus's family left Strasbourg.

The national and geopolitical contexts in which Kaplan's and Dreyfus's lives unfolded before and during the war were obviously distinct. As we shall see, Kaplan's east European background made his wartime path fairly predictable, whereas Dreyfus's French background made his path all the more surprising. In other respects, however, Dreyfus's biography bore some striking similarities to Kaplan's. Each belonged to the generation of writers born in the 1880s whom the literary scholar David Roskies identified as having written "some of the central responses to the Holocaust," because of the perspectives on upheaval and catastrophe gained over their lifetimes.[7] Both were educators and writers who supported a Jewish cultural and national identity long before the Nazis began to wage their "cold pogrom" against German Jews in the 1930s. Kaplan wrote mostly children's books on Jewish history and tradition and the Hebrew language, contributed articles and essays to Hebrew periodicals on Jewish education, and participated in Warsaw's Society of Writers and Hebrew Journalists. Dreyfus was a dedicated journalist who contributed articles to several French Jewish periodicals and was the behind-the-scenes editor in chief of *La Tribune Juive*.[8] Thus, they were both deeply engaged in the political, social, and religious questions of their time. What is more, they were also both strongly opinionated men whose diaries reflected their intellectual involvement in general and their meticulous dedication to diary writing in particular.

Despite these shared traits, these two men interpreted the meaning of the German destruction of Jewish life in dramatically different fashions. Kaplan's and Dreyfus's perceptions were complex products of their backgrounds and wartime experiences. Both attempted to make sense of the Nazi persecution of the Jews and the complicity or indifference of most non-Jews and the Allied nations by means of their preexisting belief systems. Neither was able to assimilate Jewish wartime experiences into his prior conceptions of God and humanity. For each man, only one faith held strong.

Kaplan's story—the flickering and final extinguishment of religious faith in the face of catastrophe—would seem to be the more familiar. When news reached Kaplan of the mass killings of Jews east of Warsaw, he felt God had deserted his chosen people. God's disappearance from the human realm of activity proved God's injustice or even God's nonexistence. Kaplan could not attribute the ensuing extermination to divine justice, and he came to believe that if there could be any possible justice for the Jews it was in historical research. By means of rational analysis, historians might be able to explain the motivations of the Nazis and to ensure that the outside world learned of Jews' suffering. The mass destruction of

Jewish life resulted in Kaplan's losing faith in a just divine order, although it did not end his faith that humans would remember and learn from what was being done to the Jews.

Dreyfus's thinking moved in the opposite direction from Kaplan's. Rather than finding his religious faith wavering, Dreyfus was pulled toward deeper religiosity. France's capitulation to Germany and the failure of the Western powers to help the Jews shattered Dreyfus's belief in the values of Western civilization. He became convinced that religion, not liberalism or science, supported the freedom and equality of human beings. In addition to regarding religion as a moral doctrine, he turned to it as a source of solace and understanding. In his wartime exile in Nice he recognized that "religious principles inconvenience in periods of euphoria but reassure in periods of crisis."[9] He believed that there existed a theological explanation for Jewish suffering, and his faith provided him with a way to respond to his entrapment: to die as a martyr. Thus, in contrast to Kaplan, the Germans' murderous campaign against the Jews severed Dreyfus's faith in humanist values, but it did not lead him to question God's righteousness.

The two men's fundamental questioning of faith and liberal enlightened society resonate deeply with post-Holocaust theological, philosophical, and historical discussions. Kaplan's belief in history as both an arbiter of justice and custodian of Jewish memory is a powerful suggestion of what history writing could accomplish in the view of a man who was steeped in Jewish tradition and history.[10] Moreover, Kaplan's ultimate rejection of the biblical and rabbinic image of a historically active God is similar to many survivors' positions as well as to certain postwar Jewish theology.[11]

Dreyfus's deepened belief is barely represented in the historical literature on Jewish responses to the Shoah—especially given his identity as a bourgeois, acculturated west European Jew—even though there were other victims who became more believing Jews during the Holocaust.[12] Furthermore, Dreyfus's theological interpretation of the meaning of Jewish wartime suffering was common among Orthodox Jews during and after the Shoah.[13] We will never know if Dreyfus's religious belief faltered when he arrived at Auschwitz, but regardless of this possibility, the change that Dreyfus underwent before being deported—of increasing faith—was shared by others.

At the same time that the reinforcement of Dreyfus's religious faith is less familiar to historians than Kaplan's religious disenchantment, Dreyfus's questioning of Western civilization and humanist values has become central to post-Holocaust scholarly discussions.[14] Many Holocaust victims and survivors shared his sense of the betrayal of liberal enlightened society.[15] And in the early twenty-first century with the rising popularity of far-right political parties in France and elsewhere in Europe, Dreyfus's concern with ensuring the viability of liberal democratic states seems pertinent once again. What is more, his disillusionment with France and the other Western Allied powers, as well as his refusal to exonerate France from culpability in the persecution of the Jews, anticipated the leading postwar interpretations of Vichy France and the Allies. This aspect of Dreyfus's analysis was trenchant, even if some of the answers he arrived at seem incongruous, in particular that he maintained his trust in God rather than becoming deeply cynical or nihilistic.

This chapter traces the efforts of these two men to cope with and even to find meaning in the Nazi persecution of European Jews. I explore how they interpreted the individual and collective destruction of Jewish life in relation to science and reason, history, and faith in God as well as the role played by their respective backgrounds in determining their strategies of interpretation. The story of these two diarists' responses does more than elucidate two of many possible reactions. It analyzes two divergent perspectives, thereby establishing a spectrum of responses: between those who moved toward deeper religiosity and those who questioned divine providence, and between those who despaired of and those who continued to place their faith in liberal enlightened society. Many Jews may not have responded in the same ways as Kaplan and Dreyfus, but they were pulled in these opposing directions. Indeed, the theological and moral questions with which Kaplan and Dreyfus struggled were central questions for practically all Jews during the war as well as for Holocaust survivors and postwar scholars. Investigating Kaplan's and Dreyfus's attempts to render their experiences meaningful by reference to Jewish theology and the values of Western civilization — and their sense that Jews' experiences revealed the limits of those belief systems — plunges us deep into the subject of how Jews comprehended the unimaginable genocide of their people.

The chapter is divided into two sections. First, I contrast Kaplan's abiding faith in humanity to Dreyfus's despair. In the second section, I analyze their opposing theological interpretations. Ultimately, Kaplan's and Dreyfus's understandings of the meaning of Nazi persecution affected the meaning they invested in their diaries.

BETWEEN CIVILIZATION AND BARBARISM

Did the actions of the Germans and other Europeans against the Jews mean that Western civilization carried the seeds of barbarism within itself? Or were such barbaric actions the outgrowth of ideas aberrant to Western civilization? Kaplan's and Dreyfus's different answers to these questions were bound up with their personal identities. The actions of the Germans and other Europeans against the Jews provoked a crisis of identity for Dreyfus, but they did not for Kaplan. Kaplan had always embraced a particularist conception of his Jewish identity. He defined his Jewish identity in religious, political, and ethnic terms, supporting the creation of a Jewish state in Palestine and opposing Jewish acculturation into Polish society. Kaplan had harsh words for those Jews who were not Zionists, especially for "Polonized" Jews and outright converts. In this respect, Kaplan was typical of Litvaks, Jews who came from Lithuania-Belorussia to Congress Poland in the late nineteenth and early twentieth centuries and who imported Jewish nationalist political doctrines, including Jewish socialism and Zionism.[16] Yet even though his views were shared by others of his generation and despite his many professional, associational, and personal connections, he remained a self-imposed outsider in Warsaw Jewish circles. In an entry about his "cherished friend Reb Jakub Zajac," Kaplan expounded his view of Polish Jews and his relation to them:

> Sometimes it bothered me that he [his friend Zajac] was a superior person among the millions of lesser people, for as a type he contradicted my opinion about Polish Jewry. That is, the existence of Jakub Zajac clashed with my opinions about the Jews of Poland, which are not too positive. Forty years ago I settled among the Jews of Poland and I am known among them. I deal with them and I am well acquainted with their way of life and their cultural level as human beings and as Jews. To my great sorrow, I have not always spoken well of them. My opinions are based upon concrete examples, and from year to year the instances proving the validity of my opinions multiplied. Then here came Jakub and demolished all I had built up. If Polish Jewry can bring forth such a person, it is a sign that within it there exists something of the very finest.[17]

At the same time Kaplan seemed to regard himself more as a Jew in Poland than a Jew of Poland, he was far from dismissive of Jews in the Diaspora and regularly remarked upon their accomplishments, claiming that "Jewish creativity never ceased throughout all the days of our exile."[18] Yet despite his admiration for Diaspora Jews, the events of the Second World War confirmed for Kaplan that he had been right all along, that Zionism was the only viable political option for Jews. When Palestine too faced the threat of German occupation, he feared that "if she [Palestine] is conquered," it would constitute "total destruction for the hope of a people."[19] He placed his hope for the Jewish future in the creation of a Jewish state, and German and Polish anti-Semitism only deepened his conviction.

Like Kaplan, Dreyfus supported Zionism from before the war; however, his

Zionist sympathies stemmed from different origins. Dreyfus regarded Zionism as essential for French Jews' less fortunate brothers—Polish and other east European Jews—and strongly criticized those French Jews who withheld support for Zionism for fear of the negative repercussions it might have on their situation in France. In this respect, he was typical of Alsatian Jews, the majority of whose rabbis and notables were Zionists for reasons similar to those of Dreyfus and because they saw Zionism as a means of preserving Judaism against the pressures of modern urban life.[20]

Dreyfus's backing of a Jewish nationalist politics had not precluded his adopting French culture. His support of Zionism was part and parcel of his larger conviction that Jews could "have Jewish souls, [while] speaking the French language."[21] Whereas Kaplan did not think of his identity in bifurcated terms as both a Pole and a Jew, Dreyfus believed that the French and Jewish aspects of his identity complemented one another, a conviction that was consonant with the ideology of "Franco-Judaism." Vicki Caron has defined *Franco-Judaism* as the belief that "Jewish messianic hopes and prophetic ethical ideals culminated in the Enlightenment and the French Revolution. Emancipation thus marked the end of Jewish exile and [. . .] messianism would be realized in the Diaspora. France became the 'Promised Land,' the 'New Jerusalem.'"[22] Dreyfus evinced an affinity with this ideology in his prewar journalism and diary writing. He regarded France as a "free nation by instinct and a liberator by hereditary vocation. [. . .] France's destiny has required it to fulfill the calling of its secular vocation, which invites it continually to fight and to conquer in defense of civilization and liberty."[23] In an editorial he wrote on the occasion of Bastille Day, 1939, Dreyfus professed the depth of his faith in France: "France has stayed young. She has remained the nation of liberty, the land of thinkers and soldiers of Europe, still standing, invincible heroes at their posts of peril and honor, seemingly incapable of resting as long as there exists the barbarism of human injustice on the ravaged globe and under the stormy sky. All of the persecuted, our co-religionists and others, those of Berlin and those of Rome, all place their supreme hope in this generous and courageous country [. . .]. Everyone prays with us that France endures."[24] At the same time he avowed his allegiance to France, he insisted that "even emancipated, there exists a Jewish life. The generations that underwent emancipation knew to take part in the culture of their time and to enrich Jewish ideals. Are we going to let that effort perish? Those who do betray Judaism [. . .]."[25] Dreyfus was like most Jews from Alsace-Lorraine; according to Caron, they "viewed their participation in liberal politics, not as an effacement of their Jewish identity, but as a means of reconciling their Jewish interests with their desire for acculturation."[26]

Dreyfus's moral and cultural confidence in France and its universalist nationalism progressively crumbled over the course of the war.[27] Wartime events called into question his identity as equally French and Jewish. Although Dreyfus was constantly modifying his ideas, it is possible to tease out two stages in his thinking. The first stage followed France's defeat by Germany and the issuance of the first anti-Jewish legislation by the Vichy regime on 3 October 1940, which resulted in Dreyfus's dismissal from his teaching post in Nice.[28] France's defeat and Vichy anti-Jewish policies provoked Dreyfus to question the fundamental morality of Western civilization. During this stage of his thinking, he analyzed the relationship between science, religion, and politics in order to uncover the causes of France's demise.

The question of what had caused France's defeat was absolutely essential to Dreyfus. If he could understand that, then he could determine the conditions necessary for France's resurgence. Most of all, he was concerned about whether France would once again embrace Republican values and defend the rights of all its citizens. He was trying to evaluate the viability of his French Jewish identity. Indeed, because this question was so central to who Dreyfus was and how he coped with wartime persecution, it is necessary to spend some time considering his analysis of French politics in order to understand the changes within Dreyfus himself.

Not surprisingly, as a proponent of Franco-Judaism, Dreyfus did not see religion and nationalism as being in conflict, and in fact he criticized the removal of religion from nationalism as the cause of the Republic's failure. He viewed religion as a moral and social integument rather than as a doctrine of transcendence. He argued that the strict separation of religion from politics in the Third Republic had had a negative impact on France's morality as well as on its intellectuals' perspicacity. In particular, intellectuals' abandonment of religion and embrace of science had weakened France. His critique of French intellectuals was tantamount to his blaming them for France's defeat.

In a 1940 diary entry which Dreyfus undoubtedly would have worked over for an editorial in *La Tribune Juive* if the newspaper's publication had not been suspended, he expounded on the relationship between religion and the state. Dreyfus believed that religion taught people to be subservient to God, and this religious posture translated into submissiveness to the state. In keeping with the perspective of the mainstream of French Jewry, he saw no apparent conflict between traditional religious observance and the Republic. Indeed, he contended that the existence of the Republic depended on the moral foundation provided by religion, for Judaism and Christianity were based on the notion of the equality and unity of all humans created in the image of God. The embrace of democratic political principles would follow from the democratic basis of both religions.[29]

Central to Dreyfus's analysis of what had gone wrong with the Third Republic was his notion of warrior leaders and believing masses. He maintained that
"the warrior, the statesman, represents the most elevated type of human being;
he is superior to the thinker who is not familiar with action."[30] The dominance of
thinkers in the Third Republic had resulted in the loss of religion in public life.
Without religion, he argued, the state had been unable to inspire the masses as
well as to maintain discipline and obedience. To Dreyfus, religion was not a tool
of oppression but a springboard for action. It supplied the necessary condition for
the work of warrior-statesmen, who would ensure the survival and future thriving
of France. Religion was "an essential weapon in the fight for existence" because
it offered "not only a consolation to those who are distressed, tormented by daily
troubles and miseries, [but also] it offers a harbor and reward for faithfulness,
patience, submission, and all other warlike virtues. Since time immemorial, the
philosophers who count, the statesmen who laid the foundations of a new order
were opposed to impiety and respected religions."[31] Dreyfus esteemed "warlike
virtues" that conveyed a unity of purpose, an acceptance of higher authority, and
the primacy of the collectivity over the individual. Yet the qualities he sought to
cultivate in the masses betrayed his deep mistrust of the crowd. Wartime legislation and public expressions of hostility against Jews had only heightened his fear
of the crowd and intensified his conviction that, in the absence of religion in public life, legal measures were an insufficient guarantee of civil rights and equality.[32]

Dreyfus's suspicion of the masses did not lead him to reject democratic prem-
ises of governance and justice, however. Instead, he worried about how to win
over the support of the masses to the Republican faith in light of the clear failure of Third Republic politicians and intellectuals to do so.[33] The latter—"the
intellectual representatives of the last two generations"—had incorrectly judged
science and religion, or liberalism and religion, to be diametrically opposed and
hence had rejected "the ideal of the warrior and the believer" as being "reaction-
ary" and antirepublican in spirit. Yet what they had failed to recognize, according
to Dreyfus, was how their own attitude toward science was infused with religious
feeling. Intellectuals may have abandoned religion, but that did not mean they
had ceased to be driven by religious sensibilities: "The truth is that science, idol
of cultured Europeans for more than half a century, arose on the piled-up ruins
left by the demolitionists of beliefs and accepted political principles."[34] Their rejection of God had made a god of man and reason.[35] Dreyfus pointed out the
further irony that not only had science become a new god to secular intellectuals, but also intellectuals had become proselytizers to the masses. He called
attention to the futility of their efforts since "you cannot persuade people who
don't share your opinions [. . .] Most people accept the ideas that please them,

that easily adapt to their temperament; very few men settle on ideas on the basis of well-founded arguments."[36] To his intellectual contemporaries, science might have represented hope and progress. To Dreyfus, however, its transparently false stance of neutrality made it a weak substitute for religion in its ability to rally people in support of the "French spirit of universalism."[37] France and the Western world would prevail over Nazi Germany only if they "proclaim[ed] the ideal of the warrior and the believer."[38]

During the first stage of his thinking Dreyfus attempted to salvage the ideals of Franco-Judaism. Restoring religion to the state would, he hoped, restore to France her faithful followers. A further shift in his thinking is discernible in the spring of 1941, on the eve of the promulgation of Vichy's second Statut des Juifs, which imposed tighter restrictions on Jews' economic activity, but it became much more explicit in response to the first news of mass killings of Polish Jews in July 1942.[39] During this second stage he became even more alienated from his French bourgeois identity. He became convinced that "the success of the patron of Berchtesgaden [Hitler] can only be explained by the complicity of the entire European bourgeoisie who shared his antipathies or exploited them."[40] He conjectured that, ultimately, the bourgeoisie's hateful instincts and need "to be superior to their fellow man" had fueled disdain for the stranger and made war a necessity.[41] He condemned as amoral all of European bourgeois society.

Dreyfus became increasingly certain that, without religion, humans were bound to act amorally. Commenting in his diary on the infamous Riom trial of 1942, in which the political and military leaders of the Third Republic were put on trial for having caused France's defeat in 1940, he insisted, "After a country has abandoned religion, it will not cultivate the virtues that produce and preserve great powers."[42] Whereas previously Dreyfus had called attention to some of the similarities between science and religion, during this second stage he began to emphasize science's essential difference from religion in the realm of morality. Unlike religion, which he considered an unwavering morality, science was morally malleable. He claimed that "those who have faith" were not drawn in by the vagaries of "logic, which adapts to every changing circumstance." Instead, they "hold onto faith, which gives a direction, a time frame, and an end to life, which dictates all convictions and all hopes." In contrast to the faithful, "those who assess things with logical reasoning are not far-sighted, succumb to specious arguments, and give themselves over all the more easily to convictions that they did not believe they held, [but] which were born all the same in their subconscious thanks to propaganda or hopes which came from outside."[43] The establishment of the collaborationist Vichy regime convinced him that the origins of authoritarian societies could be attributed to people's lacking "the modesty of preferring divine law" over "horrible regulation and decrees."[44] With the decline of religion, there was no check on human malice.

The news he first heard in early July 1942 about the massacre in Poland of seven hundred thousand Jews only served to reconfirm Dreyfus's pessimism about human nature and his conviction that the entire Western world shared responsibility for "the catastrophe of this war."[45] "Everyone is guilty," he wrote, even the Americans, who "did not send boats to set up some five to six hundred thousand Polish, German, and French Jews in the center of the United States, which would have alleviated the general situation without burdening the expansion of agriculture and industry in a country of more than 120 million souls."[46] Understanding the full scope of the ensuing Nazi extermination of the Jews was not essential to his regarding Western civilization as morally bankrupt. Throughout the West, people had abandoned religion and thus had "totally neglected the culture of the spirit and the soul."[47] Their actions during the war proved that religion was as necessary to human society in modern times as before. Dreyfus also argued that science and reason were worse than value-neutral: they constituted pernicious ideologies in and of themselves: "The decline of the religious idea facilitated the explosion of anti-Jewish hatred and the catastrophe of this war. [. . .] That which does not agree with science and human reason can all the same be indispensable to life in society. It is necessary to prove that science and reason have in themselves destructive tendencies, and this reflection forces a person to the necessity of recognizing a [higher] authority."[48] Dreyfus assigned responsibility for the war and the murder of hundreds of thousands of Polish Jews to proponents of science and reason as well as to the obvious perpetrators, the Germans. This conclusion led him to despair of the possibility that human beings would create a just society.[49] During this second stage, he let go of any last hopes he had harbored that France would reemerge as the beacon of civilization and liberty through the work of warrior-statesmen. Bitterly disillusioned, he abandoned his French identity and moved much closer to Kaplan's particularist Jewish identity. He turned to religious faith in a desperate effort to rescue hope in justice and morality.

Kaplan did not undergo a similar disillusionment with Western civilization. Perhaps he was less idealistic than Dreyfus from the start. Certainly, his lack of patriotism for Poland was starkly different from Dreyfus's feelings for France. Dreyfus expected better from the French, whereas Kaplan held a low estimation of the Poles.[50] Moreover, his wartime situation played a large role in his retaining faith in the Allied powers. From Kaplan's writing, it seems his world was divided into three physical spaces, each inhabited by distinct population groups.

The Jews in the Warsaw ghetto were set off sharply from the Germans and Poles in "Aryan" Warsaw, and beyond the borders of German occupied territory was the outside world. Whatever the Allies' failings, they represented Jews' sole hope for liberation and survival, for "in this conflict between two worlds, we are in the middle. If democracy falls, we fall forever. If Nazism wins, we are better off committing suicide."[51] Furthermore, the cruel treatment meted out to Warsaw's Jewish population on a daily basis by the Germans and Poles rendered the moral failings of the Allied powers negligible in comparison. By contrast, Dreyfus was technically living outside German occupation, in the southern zone of France under the Vichy regime. While he was subject to many fewer deprivations than Kaplan, he did experience anti-Semitic discrimination and persecution, and when he did, it was primarily at the behest of French authorities. Perhaps as a result, he did not exempt the outside world the way Kaplan did.[52]

Whereas Dreyfus's faith in humanism collapsed, Kaplan embraced it fully, turning to history for meaning. Indeed, Kaplan's faith in liberal enlightened society was the fundamental underpinning of his belief that modern history would render Jewish suffering meaningful. His continued faith in a just world beyond Nazism also allowed him to carve out a role for himself in response to Nazi persecution. He determined that he would be a collector of facts and information about Jewish wartime experiences for the future. Convinced as he was that "Hitlerian Nazism will ultimately be defeated, for in the end the civilized nations will rise up to defend the liberty which the German barbarians seek to steal from mankind," he sought to ensure that the Allied nations would know about the German crimes against the Jews.[53] Thus, he considered his diary a contribution to future justice, and as a diarist, he was actively participating in that struggle to defend liberty against German barbarism.

Kaplan's drive to preserve evidence of the German treatment of Polish Jews was also driven by his deep historical consciousness. His sense of the importance of history emerged in part from his knowledge that in the past Jews had written history in response to tragedy. However, his historical consciousness was equally a product of the centrality of modern Jewish historiography in the nineteenth and twentieth centuries "as a cultural and spiritual phenomenon within Jewry itself."[54] Indeed, essential to his Zionist vision was the role history played—a rationalist, positivist history—in defining Jewish national culture. Furthermore, his use of Hebrew in his diary was as much an outgrowth of his Zionist vision for a new Jewish future as it was a reference to Jewish literary tradition.[55] His imbrication of the traditional and modern reflected his east European Jewish milieu and his notion of modern Jewish culture as both a continuation of and a departure from the Jewish past.

From his first wartime entry, in which he stated that "we are now witnessing the dawn of a new era in the history of the world," Kaplan suggested that his impulse to write was not merely in keeping with the tradition in Jewish culture to bear witness to history as the realm of God's activity.[56] He sensed from the beginning of the war that the events then transpiring were unlike those that had come before. Within this "new era," he viewed himself as a witness to this break with the past and to the daily occurrences of "these historic times." He promised to write everyday in order to preserve some sort of record because, among other reasons, he was filled with foreboding about the implications of this new era for Jews. Already on 1 September 1939, he speculated, "Wherever Hitler's foot treads there is no hope for the Jewish people. Hitler, may his name be blotted out, threatened in one of his speeches that if war comes the Jews of Europe will be exterminated."[57]

Throughout the first two years of the war, Kaplan conveyed a tension between looking at the present from a modern historical viewpoint—in which he sought to identify and analyze the specificity of Jewish persecution by German hands— and from a literary-archetypal viewpoint—in which he regarded the present in cyclical terms as a return to the past or revival of the past.[58] In his early entries, on the one hand, he conveyed his sense that Jews were on the brink of untold persecution and that the nature of such persecution was potentially unprecedented. On the other hand, his formulation for cursing Hitler ("Hitler, may his name be blotted out") recalled the curse against Amalek, the biblical enemy of the Jews. This traditional imprecation placed Hitler, the new Amalek, in line with past enemies of the Jewish people. In so doing, Kaplan suggested that the suffering of the present resembled that of the past and that, as at other times in history, the Jewish people would persevere.

Whereas Dreyfus had come to distrust science and reason, Kaplan placed tremendous faith in them, attributing to them not only analytical properties but also ethical ones. He trusted that future historians would be able to understand and explain the motives of the perpetrators through psychology and social science analysis, and he recorded what he judged to be symptomatic of Nazi psychology in order to assist them. He adduced that "when an individual is afflicted with a psychological illness it is a private matter for the doctor who is treating him. But when an entire community has been afflicted with a psychological illness it is a sign of the times, and is of interest to historians of the future as well."[59] He also offered his analysis of the Nazis, believing that the only way to properly assess the nature of the threat to the Jews was to evaluate "the character of the conquerors."[60]

Kaplan's diary became a site for analyzing the historical significance of German actions as well as for recording the actions themselves. In his analysis, he sometimes placed recent events in the framework of former catastrophes in order to assert that the scale of Jewish suffering was without parallel. Indeed, he questioned early on the idea that the present persecution was the same as that of old, recognizing in the Nazis' anti-Jewish hatred a qualitatively different ideological underpinning. He differentiated, for example, between the Bolsheviks' persecution of the Jews and the Nazis': "There is plunder on the one hand and plunder on the other, but the Russians plunder one as a citizen and as a man, while the Nazis plunder one as a *worthless* Jew."[61] He also recognized what appeared to be a contradiction between the Nazis' consistent ideology and unsystematic actions: "It is a mistake to think that the conqueror excels in logic and orderliness. We see quite the opposite of this. Everything that is done by those who carry out his exalted will bears the imprint of confusion and illogic. The Nazis are consistent and systematic only with regard to the central concepts behind their actions—that is, the concept of authoritarianism and harshness; and in relation to the Jews—the concept of complete extermination and destruction."[62] The seeming discrepancy between the Nazis' ideology and their actions opened up room for debate among Jews about whether and how to take action as well as pendulous swings between hope and despair. Kaplan tried to predict the extent of the calamity that would befall Polish Jews by resorting to his powers of observation and logic and his knowledge of history.[63]

Using such methods to gain insight into Polish Jews' wartime predicament, Kaplan remained convinced throughout the first two years of the war that Polish Jewry as a collective would survive. The collective's survival made Kaplan's writing particularly valuable for him, since he felt accountable to the Jewish nation and to its history. Thus, during this period, he imagined that the author and primary audience of future history writing would be other Polish Jews. On 26 October 1939, he wrote, "*Individuals shall perish, but the Jewish collective [קיבוץ] shall live, shall live.* Therefore, every entry is more precious than gold [. . .]."[64] Throughout the fall and winter of 1939–40, Kaplan regularly prophesied that Polish Jewry was "on the brink of total extinction," but his notion of "total extinction" was not identical to the meaning those words would come to have in the wake of the Final Solution. What Kaplan imagined at that time was nonetheless unprecedented in Jewish history:

If a sudden salvation does not arrive by way of nature or even not by way of nature, because in such moments of distress one even begins to believe in miracles, then we should be witness to a tragic phenomenon dissimilar to anything in the chronicles of Israel [. . .]—total extinction and extermination of a Jewish collective that played such an important role in our historical life. Polish

Jewry shall exit the stage of Israel. Its dying has begun. A third shall die in hunger; a third shall be exiled to the Soviets; a third shall live a life of poverty and misery, the life of a pariah, which shall reach down to the last echelon of the social ladder, who shall live off of the despised livelihoods, shall not be capable of any cultural creation, and in its economic and cultural plight, shall be so low until it reaches the level of the Jewish collective in Yemen or in Iran.[65]

Upon reading the forced labor decree of mid-January 1940 subjecting all Jewish men in Poland aged twelve to sixty and all Jewish women in Poland aged fourteen to sixty to mandatory physical labor, he feared all the more that Polish Jews had never before encountered such a threat to their existence: "If we are not saved by some outside help, our end is complete annihilation, for nothing like this has been inscribed before in our historical scroll of agony." Two months later the situation had deteriorated further, yet he still imagined that one day "the Jewish community [קהלה] of Warsaw" would narrate the story of "its own martyrology."[66] Of the role he would play in the community's memorial effort, he wrote, "I sense within me the magnitude of this hour, and my responsibility toward it, and I have an inner awareness that I am fulfilling a national obligation, a historic obligation that I am not free to relinquish. [. . .] My record will serve as source material for the future historian."[67] He hoped his diary would be an essential contribution both to the community's future memorial effort and to future historians' analyses of their experiences.

A modern historical consciousness had taken root in eastern Europe to such an extent that Kaplan, who was not a historian, looked to history writing as a form of collective memory and arbiter of justice. Indeed, during Kaplan's lifetime — and during a period of competition among nascent views of Jewish nationalism — a modern historical consciousness had first developed among Jews living in the regions of Poland under Russian and Austro-Hungarian rule.[68] In that setting of revolutionary ferment and rival national minorities, the notions of Jewish history that dominated in Poland differed from those in western and Central Europe. Rather than defining Jewish history in literary religious terms, as it had been by nineteenth-century German Jewish scholars, Russian and Polish Jewish historians like Simon Dubnow and Ignacy (Yitzhak) Schiper gave pride of place to the society and economy of the Jewish nation.[69] Evidently, both models of history writing influenced Kaplan.

Dubnow and several Yiddish writers helped set in motion a grassroots effort in historical documentation, calling upon the Jewish masses to record their folklore and experiences. This effort culminated during the interwar period in the establishment in 1925 of the Yidisher Visnshaftlekher Institut (YIVO, or Jewish

Scientific Institute). As the first institute of its kind, YIVO became the beneficiary of the efforts of local collectors, or *zamlers*, who sent their contributions to
YIVO's archive in Vilna. Beginning in 1927, these voluntary contributions were
augmented by collections of questionnaires and the sponsoring of essay contests
targeting specific population groups and historical experiences. Among the top-
ics YIVO historians pursued were Jews' First World War experiences and the
autobiographies of Jewish youths aged sixteen to twenty-two.[70] Schiper described
how YIVO historians sought to expand the range of subjects covered by Jewish
historians: "We know the Sabbath Jew with his festive spirit, but it is now high
time to become acquainted with the history of the workday Jew, and his workday
ideas and to turn the spotlight on Jewish labor. They [the early historians] gave
us a splendid picture of the spiritual leaders of Diaspora Jewry. We are, however,
left completely in the dark about the history of the untold hundreds of thousands
whose claim to recognition rests not on the riches of the spirits but on their toil
and labor."[71]

During the Second World War, YIVO's ambition to portray the "history of
the workday Jew" lived on most obviously in the work of Emanuel Ringelblum,
who was one of the key organizers of and contributors to YIVO's historical work
in the 1920s and 1930s. Ringelblum also kept a diary in the Warsaw ghetto and
spearheaded the creation of the Warsaw ghetto's underground archive, *Oyneg
Shabbes*, which utilized methods of documentation and collection similar to
those of YIVO. Although scholars have more often pointed to the contrasts between the diaries of Ringelblum and Kaplan, it is their similarities in content and
intention that are most striking in this context. Kaplan's diary was described by
one scholar as "a diary to bare one's soul," whereas Ringelblum's is quite rightly
depicted as a historical diary.[72] Yet as different as the two writers' tones may
be, they both wrote with an eye to modern historical methods. Kaplan likewise
stressed the objectivity and comprehensiveness of his writing. He did not perceive
an inconsistency between his tone of lamentation and his goal to record facts.
He declared that "a future historian will find material here that may be relied
upon, not just stories out of the imagination."[73] His concern with the accuracy
and accountability of his writing was an aspect of his larger goal of ensuring there
would be sufficient material for the future historian. He was like his contemporaries, to whom, as Roskies described, "there was no felt contradiction between
a subjective point of view, an intimate narrative voice, and strict adherence to
observable reality."[74] As Kaplan himself contended, "It is beyond my capabilities
to record every event in organized form. Perhaps other people will do this when
the appropriate time comes. But even events recorded in reportorial style are of
historical value."[75] The meaning and importance Kaplan attributed to his diary

writing reflected a modern historical consciousness inasmuch as he was attuned to the need for individual Jews to record, document, and collect reliable information for the purposes of future historical writing about the Jewish nation.

While lamenting the dearth of talented poets who would be able to immortalize the suffering of Polish Jewry under the Germans, Kaplan attributed more space in his diary to the potential of history to ensure the transmission of memory.[76] The historian, along with the poet, became a "primary custodian" of Jewish memory.[77] Kaplan ultimately placed his hope in historians to confer meaning on the deaths of untold numbers of Polish Jews by explaining the Nazis' motivations and the complexity of Jewish responses to living in the shadow of death. His trust in history attested to his abiding faith in science and reason as essential frameworks of understanding. Through his diary, Kaplan sought to contribute to civilization's triumph over barbarism.

Dreyfus also contemplated the value and implications of history writing. Not surprisingly, in contrast to Kaplan, he did not place his confidence in history to render Jewish suffering meaningful, nor does it seem he envisioned his diary as a contribution to the historical enterprise. Quite the contrary: since he had lost faith in Western civilization, he was highly critical of its commitment to history writing. Even before the outbreak of the war, he had been skeptical of historians' belief in their ability to be rational and objective, and the experience of wartime dislocation only reinforced his distrust of historians.[78] His critique of history was part of his broader critique of science and Third Republic intellectuals.

For Kaplan, history was a nationalist endeavor associated with the continuity of the Jewish nation—and so tied to tradition and modern Jewish culture and politics. Dreyfus also regarded history as a nationalist endeavor, but he associated it with French nationalism during the Third Republic rather than with Jewish national politics and thus tied it to reason and science and the failure of Enlightenment civilization. In the French national context, after France's defeat to Prussia in 1870 and the establishment of the Third Republic, the academic study of history shifted in conjunction with the overhaul of the French educational system under the new regime. In the spirit of the anticlericalism and rationalism undergirding the Republic, French historians turned toward positivism and claimed to be truth-seeking, free from bias and the taint of philosophy or theory. Yet these positivist historians, like Ernest Lavisse and Fustel de Coulanges, whose work Dreyfus mentioned in his diaries, had a well-defined political agenda that their historical work was intended to promote. They played a role in state educational reforms that were designed to unify French national sentiment in support of the new Republic. Lavisse and Coulanges tied history to science instead of to art, but to a science of collecting and classifying documents, which supposedly relegated the historian to the role of a receptive assembler of facts who should seek "their objectively existing relatedness."[79]

Dreyfus was highly critical of this view of history. Throughout the war, he wrote disparagingly about historians' supposition that history belonged to the sciences and not to the arts: "History and historians, like museum curators, take pleasure in changing the placement of objects, in modifying the way one observes and the vantage point from which one observes, and especially in replacing labels. That's what their science is to them, and they imagine that others believe as they do, that intelligent people regard their amusing and useless occupation as a scientific activity. History has nothing to do with science."[80] By casting aspersions upon the scientific basis of history writing, Dreyfus registered his disbelief in the potential of historians to reconstruct what he referred to as the truth of an epoch. Of all fields, he believed that "history least approaches the truth," and he contrasted the perspective of historians with that of contemporaries to an era: "For a long time I have considered contemporaries to be the only good judges of men and things: they do not need to await the discoveries of historians who go through archives."[81] He contested the notion that retrospective vision was twenty-twenty and suggested that contemporaries—like himself—were better qualified to analyze their own epoch.

By contrast, Kaplan believed that historians were better able than contemporaries to understand the significance of an epoch, although he also wavered on this point. On the one hand, he expressed the view that historical events were "like paintings, they require perspective."[82] On the other hand, he contradicted himself one week later, writing that a person who had not lived under Nazi dominion would "not be able to express the truth of Nazism's cruelty and barbarism."[83] One year later, though, he seemed to have reverted to his original position—the opposite of Dreyfus's. After having described the work of a philanthropic organization in the ghetto, he called attention to the limitations of his account: "No doubt the Self-Aid will find its own historian who will tell future generations of its scope and magnitude, and of the greatness of its influence and its educational value, using facts and figures. I do not intend to compete with him. I wrote this out of my own impressions as someone who is close to it, on the inside, and thus sees only certain aspects of it rather than the entire picture. *I just tried to give a general assessment and that's enough for me.*"[84] Kaplan put his faith in historians to sort out his impressionistic notes.

Although Dreyfus lacked faith in the analyses put forth by historians, he did believe there was much to be learned from the past. In a 1935 entry, he recorded, "One can have one's doubts about historians without questioning history. With its torch it sheds light on the path followed by humanity. Without it, we would not avoid any precipice, nor would we know how to find the river's ford."[85] The past illuminated the present, not only by shedding light on how society evolved from then to now, but also by imparting lessons about how to proceed in the future. Ironically, Dreyfus's regard for history as an important source of knowledge about human experience was part of the legacy of modern Jewish historical writing. Indeed, during the war he applied a historical perspective, derived from reading works of history, to the Nazi persecution of the Jews. Writing about Ismar Elbogen's work on German Jewish history, he commented, "The Nazis have not invented anything." He cited the damage to Jewish property and the loss of Jewish lives during the "Hep-Hep" riots of the early nineteenth century as well as the anti-Semitic language of a nineteenth-century Romantic author as evidence of the similarities between the actions taken against Jews in the past and the present.[86]

Dreyfus penned this entry about historical parallels in late June 1942, at which time the difference between his situation and Kaplan's could hardly have been more profound. While Dreyfus recorded reflections about how the Nazis were merely repeating earlier forms of Jewish persecution, Kaplan's experiences in the Warsaw ghetto had led him to the exact opposite judgment—that the Nazis' actions were unprecedented. At this time, Dreyfus exalted the martyrdom of Jews in the Middle Ages, seeing in their self-sacrifice a model for Jewish behavior in the face of persecution: "The sacrifice of oneself is the sublime act of a Jew exposed to the blows of assassins."[87] For Kaplan and other Warsaw ghetto Jews, it was the sanctification of God's name through self-preservation—not through self-sacrifice—that became an appropriate mode of response to the Nazis' exterminatory policies.[88] Thus, their different wartime locations and exposure to Nazi actions played a significant role in shaping their perspectives on the historical significance of contemporary Jewish suffering. At the same time, their wartime circumstances cannot entirely explain their diverse attitudes toward history.

Both Kaplan and Dreyfus turned to the past to make sense of the perpetrators' and victims' actions. Although they both looked to history, it was a different undertaking for each of them. For Kaplan, history was part of the project of Jewish nation building. It was also a means to investigate the interaction of Jews and non-Jews and to adjudicate on the innocence of the victims and the guilt of the perpetrators. Hence, history for Kaplan was both a scientific and moral pursuit. For Dreyfus, the historical project Kaplan esteemed was part of the wider culture that had betrayed him. Its association with the French Third Republic tainted modern historical scholarship. As a result, the concept of history Dreyfus valued was the traditional variant that sought to incorporate the new within the old. As a study of patterns and repetitions, history—not modern historical scholarship—could reveal the meaning of the present. Although both Kaplan and Dreyfus concerned themselves with history, the different versions of history to which they looked for meaning reflected their differing faith in enlightened liberal society.

While Dreyfus continued to identify patterns of action and response, Kaplan could find fewer and fewer historical lessons relevant to Jews' present suffering. Their divergent interpretations of the relationship of the present to the past, as well as their different perspectives on Western civilization, played a major role in their changing religious beliefs.

GOD AND HISTORY

In Judaism, history is invested with meaning, for it is in history that God's relationship to the Jewish people is revealed. How, then, should Jewish wartime suffering be interpreted: as an act of God and proof of God's inscrutable ways? or as proof of God's absence from history? These questions of God's presence or absence in history—of how to approach theologically Jews' unimaginable wartime predicament—became fundamental to Kaplan and Dreyfus.

Kaplan's mounting sense that the present could not be understood by reference to literary archetypes strained his belief in divine justice. If God was good and just, then why would he permit such offenses to be committed against his people and allow the perpetrators to go unpunished? "It seems as though even our Father in Heaven—the mainstay of our fathers—has deserted us," he intoned. "Are we indeed to sing with the poet [Bialik]: 'Heavenly spheres, beg mercy for me. Behold, the path to God no longer exists! God of Israel, where art thou?'"[89] Kaplan indicated that though he was not prepared to harmonize with Bialik's chorus, he was also not prepared to refute Bialik's suggestion that God had broken his covenant with Israel. A few months later he cried out, "Lord God! When will you tell the angel of destruction: let go! Shall you destroy the remnants of Israel in Poland?"[90]

To Kaplan, the inscrutability of God's ways was an unacceptable explanation for the fact that the Germans' crimes continued and remained unpunished. He railed at an imaginary interlocutor: "The abominations committed before our eyes cry out from the earth: 'Avenge me!' But there is no jealous avenger. *Our Torah calls the nation's God: 'Envier and Avenger.' If our Torah is not untrue,* why has a 'day of vengeance and retribution' not yet come for the murderers? Do not answer me with idle talk—I won't listen to you. Give me a logical reply!"[91] Justifying or explaining why God permitted evil to exist in the world could not satisfy Kaplan at this moment. Indeed, when it was announced that the edict to establish a ghetto in Warsaw would be put into effect, he related an incident that suggested he was far from alone in questioning God's righteousness:

> There is a rumor that in one of the congregations the prayer leader came and dressed himself in a kittel and prepared to lead his poor and impoverished people in the *Neilah* service [at the end of Yom Kippur], when a boy from his congregation broke in with the news about the ghetto. At once that Jew dispensed with *Neilah*, took off his kittel, and went back to his seat. There was no point in praying when the "Gates of Mercy" were locked. *I am not sure that this actually happened. However, if the public invented such a rumor in its imagination—it is a sign that this is how things could have been, because the masses have started to think heretic thoughts. . . . One has to mention that heretics and Epicureans have increased among the Jews. Finished [is] the belief in the "Leader of the City," "whose all ways are justice, a god of faith with no evil who is righteous and honest."* [. . .]
> —Has Israel no God? Why has He refrained from giving us aid in our time of trouble? [. . .] The wrath of the conquerors and of our God is poured upon us at once.[92]

Kaplan again conveyed an unwillingness to accept that an omnipotent God would stand idly by or that such evil was a just response to Jewish sins. Uncomprehending of God's ways, overwhelmed by the Nazis' capacity for hatred and sadism, he questioned whether the God of Israel, who traditionally intervened and revealed his will in history, existed. One day later, he ruminated, "I gazed at the Dantean scenes in the streets of Warsaw, and could not stop thinking: Are we really guiltier than any nation? Have we sinned more than any people?"[93]

While faith in God's righteousness became untenable for Kaplan personally during the war, during the first two years of the war he seemed to admire the abiding faith of most Jews around him. He tied their faith to their will to survive, analyzing how messianic faith fueled hope in this-worldly redemption and worked as social glue to keep the community fighting for survival. As hardships piled up, he paid homage to the defiant hope of the Jewish people: "A nation which for thousands of years has said daily, 'And even if he tarries, I will await the coming of the Messiah every day,' will not weaken in its hope, which has been a balm of life and has strengthened it in its miserable survival."[94] Jews' hopes for redemption may have been pinned on this-worldly political powers; however, such "fantasies" bore traces of an otherworldly messianism. Kaplan's language in an entry a few weeks later made this connection more explicit still: "Even though we are now undergoing terrible tribulations and the sun has grown dark for us at noon, we have not lost our hope that the era of light will surely come."[95]

During these initial years of German occupation, faith for Kaplan was more than just a question of pure belief. He associated religious faith and observance with practical defiance, as a coping mechanism and form of spiritual resistance. He looked to faith as, in the words of one religious scholar, a "practice-oriented approach to evil," and he became attuned to "how faith is a plausible response to coping with evil by showing the pragmatic resources of belief in God."[96] Kaplan described the secret assembly of prayer groups, or *minyanim*, during the high holy days of 1940, despite the ban on public worship, as evidence of the fact that the Jewish community of Warsaw "still exists," however "debased and impoverished" it had become.[97] Later that year, he recorded how even though *"from day to day, we become more impoverished, more poor, and more wrinkled, more 'proletarian-ized,'"* nevertheless *"there were never more Hanukkah celebrations in Jewish Warsaw as in a drought year like this."* The parties, organized *"in hiding, in a room within a room,"* incited "a feeling of national kinship. [. . .] After sixteen months of Nazi occupation *that is unprecedented in terms of sadistic cruelty*, we came to life again, *and we say 'a thorn in the eyes of Satan'! In spite of you, we shall continue to live and we shall see your defeat!!"*[98] During the high holy days of 1941, Kaplan noted that Warsaw's Jews continued to flock to *minyanim* even though wartime experiences had made "agnostics" of many Jews. "Everyone sought the Hebrew gathering, the companionship, the religious atmosphere," in the three synagogues the Judenrat had been allowed to use for religious services for the first time in three years.[99] While the covenant between God and Israel could hardly justify or render meaningful the Jews' suffering at the hands of the Germans, it continued to draw the community together, thereby providing moments of spiritual uplift. The power of this communal solidarity furnished him with hope of a different kind: that the Jewish people would outlast the Nazis because of their strength as a community and their ability to withstand torment.[100] Faith became a way of acting in the face of evil, a defiant stance against the deprivations of ghetto life.

Kaplan's perspective on religious faith was similar to his interpretation of diary writing. In both instances, his view underwent a transformation as a result of his wartime experiences. According to Abraham Katsh, Kaplan's diary entries from before the war focused mainly on the personal sphere: his daily experiences, his troubles at work, and other routine issues that arose in his life. In the summer of 1939, with war on the horizon, the character and style of his diary entries changed radically. From that time forward, described Katsh, "Kaplan leaves behind the private sphere from a deep sense of danger and the measure of catastrophe that is going to hit Polish Jewry. He breaks the limits of the individual and reacts from the point of view of the nation and collective."[101] Kaplan himself acknowledged this shift in the focus of his diary. In an entry describing how he, like other Jewish teachers, was trying to eke out a living, he explained, "Contrary to my custom since the outbreak of the war, I have written this personal entry in my diary today."[102] Kaplan almost never alluded to his wife and family situation in his wartime diary. He never mentioned his wife's name, nor did he discuss his health problems, which surely worsened in the ghetto for he was a diabetic and must have struggled to obtain medication.[103] Thus, during the war, the practice of writing a diary became, for Kaplan, a quasi-religious deed; it came to have a function and meaning not unlike attending synagogue in the ghetto. Engaging in diary writing was an expression of Kaplan's defiance. It was also an outgrowth of his commitment to the Jewish community and served simultaneously to reinforce those communal ties in the present and in the future. And, finally, as was the case with participating in religious rituals and messianic dreaming, diary writing was another "balm of life" in the midst of unmitigated suffering. The most personal revelation in Kaplan's wartime diary consists of his passionate outpouring about the emotional solace he found in diary writing: "This journal is my life, my friend and ally. I would be lost without it. I pour my innermost thoughts and feelings into it, and this brings relief. When my nerves are taut and my blood is boiling, when I am full of bitterness at my helplessness, I drag myself to my diary and at once I am enveloped by a wave of creative inspiration, although I doubt whether the recording that occupies me deserves to be called 'creative.' Let it be edited at some future time—as it may be. The important thing is that in keeping this diary I find spiritual rest. That is enough for me."[104]

Despite such occasional outbursts, Kaplan remained a cynic. He considered the hopes of his fellow ghetto Jews to be illusory even though he frequently drew inspiration from their optimism. Indeed, he let slip his ambivalence toward the community's emotional yearning when he commented that "the masses comfort themselves with groundless rumors, offsprings of *their* own imaginings. Man believes what he wants to believe. In the thick darkness surrounding us, *we* have ample opportunity for imaginings. This time, they are not Messianic dreams but political fantasies" (italics added).[105] Kaplan both set himself apart from the Jewish masses and their unjustified "imaginings" and simultaneously grouped himself among the hopeful. Such was his ambivalence. Later, he openly acknowledged that coping with ghetto life required some form of messianic dreaming, even for him. After one year of war but prior to the establishment of the ghetto in Warsaw, Kaplan included himself among those for whom "a certain stubborn optimism has made its nest among the Jews, and we are all certain that the murderers' days are numbered, that the end of the despot and tyrant will be death. The God of Israel will not betray his people; he will not abandon them."[106] Faith in an immanent God continued to move Kaplan during the first two years of the war despite his overwhelming conviction that God had deserted them. In the face of Jewish suffering, his own need for hope kept him clinging at times to the image of a historically active God.

Dreyfus, much more than Kaplan, turned to God for solace and understanding. As we have seen, Dreyfus did not regard the present as unprecedented when viewed from the perspective of eternal time; however, from the standpoint of recent history, he saw the current persecution of European Jewry as shocking for what it revealed about the amorality at the core of modern secular society. Religious faith grew to fill the void created by his disillusionment with France and Western civilization. Out of his need for there to be greater meaning behind the calamity befalling European Jews, he grasped at the notion of an immanent God who meted out divine justice, the very notion Kaplan could not abide. Dreyfus was conscious of the psychological comfort this notion furnished him, confessing that it helped him "to escape from the necessity of seeing all around me an inextricable heap of contradictions and human maliciousness, which directs the course of events."[107] His loss of faith in humanity caused him to turn to God ever more since he could not accept that injustice reigned in human society without any greater justice prevailing.

Dreyfus yearned for a theological explanation to account for Jewish suffering. He linked the present suffering of European Jews to the dilemma of how to reconcile belief in a just and all-powerful God with the existence of evil in the world. He explained: "These ideas correspond to my temperament, and if in these notebooks I occupy myself with nothing other than the highest principle of man, the fact is that the rest of what preoccupies my loved ones, even the war, is nothing vis-à-vis the problem posed by the Bible. There is a God who punishes and rewards. [. . .] I will not seek to convince those opposing, but I intend to keep intact the spiritual traditions that date back to Sinai."[108] To account for Jewish suffering, he returned to a traditional Jewish view of history. Beginning with the Bible, Jews injected history with meaningfulness, as Yosef Hayim Yerushalmi explained, since "it was human history that revealed his [God's] will and purpose." God was radically other, his ways inscrutable, and yet human history offered clues about how God judged his creation's exercise of free will. Dreyfus thus revisited what Yerushalmi deemed "the paradoxical struggle between the divine will of an omnipotent Creator and the free will of his creature, man, in the course of history; a tense dialectic of obedience and rebellion."[109] Dreyfus had resort to theodicy, attempting to make known God's reasons for "punishing" the Jews.

Dreyfus speculated, as did many Orthodox Jews during and after the war, that

Jewish assimilation had provoked God's wrath.[110] He could not help but think that Jews' wartime suffering was "a celestial punishment [*châtiment*] brought about by Jewish defection [*la defection juive*]."[111] This punishment would, he hoped, serve a larger purpose: "He who believes that, according to the word of the prophet, Heaven also creates evil, sees in the action of the Führer only something that had become necessary to Jews. It reminds them of their origin, their history, their calling, forgotten in the abandonment of all traditions in the aid of—in the last analysis—an unrealizable assimilation."[112] Dreyfus hoped Jews would learn from their wartime experiences and "return to Judaism." Crediting Theodor Herzl with having foreseen the inevitability of this process of oppression and return, he implied that Jewish wartime suffering could advance the cause of Jewish nationalism.[113] In fact, he noted with astonishment when the war did not appear to be having this effect, "The lesson of the war is not changing their *mentalité*."[114] French Jews were not embracing Judaism, and their rejection of the path he had chosen exacerbated his feelings of alienation and loneliness. Unlike Kaplan, who seemed to derive strength and courage from the Jewish community around him, Dreyfus felt "the general atmosphere [to be] hostile to everything that I am. One is terribly isolated with others and one's own."[115]

The extent of Dreyfus's pain and isolation was evident not only in his ruminations on assimilation and divine justice but also in the change his diary writing underwent during the war. Interestingly, the character of Dreyfus's diary writing changed in the opposite way from Kaplan's. Before the war, Dreyfus's diary mainly served an intellectual function as a reading journal in which he transcribed passages from books and reflected on the broad political and philosophical questions of his day. From 1925 to 1940, he wrote sporadically, maybe two or three entries each month, and he never discussed his family or social milieu. The self he projected in his diary was that of the free-floating thinker who lacked personal traits. During the war, however, Dreyfus's diary became predominantly a journal of the quotidian in which his diary-writing self was embedded in family and community. He wrote much more frequently, and the content of the entries changed dramatically. Most entries were devoted to the mundane matters of everyday life, like visits he made and received, private tutoring sessions he gave, walks he took by the sea, and mediocre sermons he heard at the temple he attended. Interestingly, his religious observance did not seem to undergo a transformation during the war; what was new was his *mention* of his synagogue attendance. In this respect, his goals and ambitions for his diary seemed to multiply during the war. Especially after his daughter, son-in-law, and granddaughter emigrated from France in mid-May 1942 (eventually making their way to the United States), he wrote for several reasons. On the eve of the

one-year anniversary of their emigration, he wrote in order to conjure their figures before him. Since he could neither talk to them nor send a letter, he had to
resort to writing in his diary about how he wished he could tell his children they
had been right to leave.[116] A few weeks later, he transcribed a letter he had received about the sale of their jewelry by the Commissariat-General for Jewish Affairs (CGQJ) so that "the children know the text of the letter."[117] Dreyfus clearly
imagined his children reading his diary in the future, and through it he communicated information he could not relay to them by any other means. In contrast,
on the basis of his prewar entries, one would barely have known he had a daughter. His family played no role in his writing from the 1920s and 1930s. During
the war, he also described his social engagements and discussions with friends
and acquaintances and recounted conversations he overheard among strangers.
Like the almost complete absence of references to his family, accounts of conversations were also missing from his prewar entries. Consequently, at the same
time that diary writing became part of his wartime theological quest, it became
more of a log of daily activities. Dreyfus's grand theological reflection was inextricably linked to his observation of himself and the people around him.

Dreyfus's self-disclosure in his wartime diaries revealed how fundamentally
altered his life was in Nice from the life he had lived in Strasbourg and how
difficult that new life was for him, even though he also recognized that he was
better off than Jews throughout most of the rest of Europe. He divulged his misery
while reflecting on the views of other writers about writing: "I myself am the material for my book. This line of Montaigne is well taken but does not go nearly
far enough. He could have calmly said that the book, the very sentence that we
write or think contributes to making us known to ourselves and to others. We
always speak of ourselves, said Anatole [France], when we don't have the strength
to be silent."[118] Dreyfus expressed the view that writing was an exercise in and
through which an individual gains self-knowledge. Yet the Anatole France quote
suggested a distinction between writing in general and writing about oneself. To
write about oneself implied that a person could no longer prevent him- or herself
from speaking out because things were too unbearable. His need to write about
his daily life attested to how much pain he was in and how disconnected he was
from his earlier life.

As his world fell apart, messianic hope consoled Dreyfus. In a fascinating and
shocking entry, he expressed how thankful he was to live through such terrible
times: "This period is terrible and terribly interesting. [. . .] I thank heaven for
having made me live in this epoch and for having favored me with the gift of
understanding this epoch."[119] He believed that "it is necessary to be [a] contemporary in order to savor an event," and it was in his capacity as a contemporary,

but especially as a religious Jew, that he thought himself able to understand his epoch's "particularity and its meaning." In addition to other meanings, here he made explicit his messianic hopes: "Israel remains the witness to the prehistory that prepares the messianic times and that is still a long way from being over." [120] In a slightly later entry, he clarified that he did not "wish for evil [*le mal*]" out of his desire for redemption, but he was able to accept evil. He felt grateful that God had shown him the "exploits and miracles" of Creation and wondered, "is redemption [*la guéoula*] far off?" That proponents of "atheism, agnosticism, rationalism, and *jemenfichisme* [not giving a damn]" were unable to probe the depths of meaning of wartime events further proved to Dreyfus the worthlessness of those philosophies. [121] They addressed only the human realm, which Dreyfus dismissed as mere "literature," whereas reality consisted of "the end of days when the Messiah will appear." [122] Wartime events were significant to Dreyfus because they more fully revealed the spectrum of divine activity. Furthermore, that they were so terrible augured the relative nearness of divine redemption. Dreyfus's faith helped to mitigate his suffering.

As long as Kaplan believed that the Nazis intended to starve the Jews to death, he found Jewish messianic hope to be praiseworthy, if also at times naïve. He deemed its symbolism and practical benefit to be potent because it might help sustain a large number of Jews until the Germans' defeat. This appraisal began to change with the building of the Warsaw ghetto. The creation of the ghetto spurred him to consider how metaphors were losing their analogical status. "If it were said that the sun has darkened for us at noon it would not be merely a metaphor," he wrote. [123] So, too, "the concept that 'all Jews are responsible for one another' has stopped being merely a slogan or a metaphor. *The saying that 'I learned from all my teachers' was realized in us—this includes even from my whole-hearted enemy.*" [124] Metaphors became reality when the gap he had once noted between the Nazis' ideology and their actions began to close, making words meaningful in new ways. As Kaplan became attuned to the literal meaning of words, he endowed the Jewish capacity to hope with less value.

Kaplan became increasingly critical of the Jewish masses' inclination to hope as conditions in the ghetto became more horrific in the months prior to the deportation of Warsaw Jews. At that time he deduced, as many Jews did not, that "the Führer has decided to rid Europe of our whole people by simply having them shot to death. [. . .] The day before yesterday we read the speech the Führer delivered celebrating January 30, 1933, when he boasted that his prophecy was beginning to come true. Had he not stated that if war erupted in Europe, the Jewish race would be annihilated? This process has begun and will continue until the end is achieved. For us the speech serves as proof that what we thought were rumors are in effect reports of actual occurrences."[125] Kaplan realized the Germans were acting and would continue to act in a manner entirely consistent with Hitler's pronouncements. Perhaps it was the distance he had maintained from the Jewish masses' hope for redemption that enabled him to comprehend, in the spring of 1942, the extent of the threat confronting Polish Jewry. A little over two months later, eyewitness reports confirming rumors about the extermination of the Jews of Lublin — "the fact is that reality surpassed imagination by far" — removed any lingering disbelief Kaplan may have had as to what the Germans had in store for them in Warsaw.[126]

According to Kaplan's previous view, the hope that had sprung from religious attitudes and practices could help them outlast their tormentors. Now, in light of his conclusion that the Nazis were intent on exterminating the Jewish population, he considered hope to be delusionary:

> Never were we so hopeful of the final Nazi downfall as during these days, days in which our tribulations grow worse from hour to hour. [. . .] But we were always a nation *of prisoners of hope*—and so we shall remain. Jewish faith is marvelous; it can create states of mind that have nothing to do with reality. Like the believing Jewish grandfather who in anticipation of the Messiah always wore his Sabbath clothes, so we too *wait for good news*, "and, though he tarry, I will wait daily for his coming." [. . .] Hirsch [Kaplan's fictitious self], my wise friend, is an exception. He is the only one who sits like a mourner among bridegrooms. "Idiots!" he shouts, and his face becomes red with anger. "Your hope is vain; your trust a broken reed. All of you are already condemned to die, only the date of execution has yet to be set. We are doomed to pass from the world without seeing the Nazi downfall because the physical annihilation of European Jewry is one of Nazism's cardinal principles. You have eyes and yet you do not see the fulfillment of this horrible goal has already been started. What hope do we have that it will not be carried out? Over half a million Jews who used to live in Poland have already been murdered; some by hunger, some by disease, some by the Nazi sword. [. . .] Optimistic fools! [. . .]" And thus he goes on and on. Would that Hirsch's predictions prove to be untrue.[127]

Kaplan was still amazed by Warsaw Jews' capacity to hope, yet now he regarded it as the faith of doddering fools rather than a display of defiance by age-old survivors. At the same time, he distanced himself from total pessimism by letting the character Hirsch be the one to voice his doubts. Nevertheless, he indicated that he agreed with Hirsch, however reluctantly.

News of the murder of Lublin's Jews immediately returned Kaplan to the theme of history and his responsibility to it. By recording what he had learned from eyewitnesses, he was planting "the seed of history," convinced that, "for future generations, every word will be valuable."[128] His continued faith in modern history was coupled with his ultimate rejection of the traditional view of history: "We have a Jewish tradition that an evil law is foredoomed to defeat. This historical experience has caused us much trouble since the day we fell into the mouth of the Nazi whose dearest wish is to swallow us. It came to us from habit, this minimizing of all edicts with the common maxim, 'It won't succeed.' In this lay our undoing, and we made a bitter mistake."[129] Kaplan refused to place the extermination of European Jewry on a historical continuum and attributed the Jewish tendency to assimilate the new within the framework of the old as having led them to respond inappropriately to the Nazi threat to their existence. Messianic faith had fueled Jews' misplaced hope that they would live to see the defeat of Nazi Germany.[130]

Because he no longer believed they would outlast the Nazis, Kaplan assumed that the future historian for whom he collected documentary material would not belong to his generation, but to succeeding ones. And it was to succeeding generations that the task of comprehending the perpetrators' motivations would fall—a task Kaplan had once taken up himself. The combination of Jews' wartime suffering, the certain knowledge that death awaited them, and the onset of the great deportation from the Warsaw ghetto on 22 July 1942 made it impossible for Kaplan to engage in any further rational analysis of the Nazis. The extermination was so horrific he could imagine only that "such a plan could have been invented only by Satan."[131] While Kaplan now located the Nazis' evil on a theological plane, he absolutely denied the existence of a historically active God. After learning of the extermination of other Jewish communities in Poland in the spring of 1942, Kaplan had still felt the pull of messianic hope and redemption. But in the midst of the deportation of Warsaw Jewry just a few months later, he could no longer imagine that a just God existed: "In these two days the *space* [חלל] of the ghetto has been filled with cries and wails. If they found no way to the God of Israel it is a sign that He doesn't exist."[132] Over the course of the great deportation, his doubt was confirmed: "From hour to hour, even minute to minute, Jewish Warsaw is being demolished and destroyed, reduced and decreased. Since the day the exile was decreed, ruin and destruction, exile and wandering, bereavement and widowhood have befallen us in all their fury. *It is so that there is no God to Israel!*"[133]

If God would not exact vengeance and see that justice prevailed, then history and history alone had the power to ensure that Jews' suffering and deaths had not been in vain. Kaplan invested history with the redemptive capacity to render

Jewish suffering meaningful, not as a record of divine justice, but as a guarantee of earthly justice. Historians would thwart Hitler's genocide by ensuring that the murder of Polish Jewry did not remain a secret. If the civilized nations learned the full truth about Nazi barbarism, then partial justice would be served. Kaplan's loss of faith in divine justice left him with the hope of historical justice, yet even this was not guaranteed. Kaplan's final words attested to his fear that his exhaustive efforts to preserve evidence for the future historian would come to naught. "If my life ends," he wrote, "what will become of my diary?"[134]

Dreyfus's religious belief remained intact until his diary writing was interrupted on 20 September 1943. From his perch on the Mediterranean coast, Dreyfus still looked forward to the perpetuity of the Jewish people, and individual suffering did not change his ability to be consoled by faith.[135] The solace Dreyfus found in faith, however, was not the same as for the Jewish masses in Warsaw that Kaplan depicted. Religious faith allowed Dreyfus to believe there was a reason for Jews' suffering, but it did not lead him to hope for a this-worldly redemption or, in other words, to hope he would survive the war. He seemed to know he was going to die in the impending catastrophe. But the prospect of his life as well as the lives of massive numbers of other Jews ending prematurely did not sever his belief that divine justice would prevail.

Dreyfus's interpretation of the Nazi threat to European Jewry played a role in his continuing reliance on theology to explain Jewish suffering. His understanding of the menace was similar to Kaplan's from the start of the war until he heard about the murder of Lublin's Jews. Dreyfus foresaw the removal of Jews from Europe, presumably by means of forced emigration, which he considered to be the logical outgrowth of a virulent European anti-Semitism: "The end of this movement will be the elimination of Jews from this continent."[136] At the same time, Kaplan's and Dreyfus's different wartime circumstances are hardly the complete explanation of why Dreyfus saw God as active in history whereas Kaplan could not. After all, there were many religious Jews throughout Poland whose faith endured the Shoah unchanged. However, even if the difference in their circumstances was not the whole story, it was an essential factor.

When Dreyfus heard reports in the second half of 1942 about mass murders of Jews in eastern Europe, his faith was not shaken. Curiously, the murder in Poland of hundreds of thousands of Jews did not strike him as unprecedented or as requiring a causal explanation beyond what he took to be the hideous nature of human beings. By contrast, he regarded the betrayal by the French regime in Vichy, by dispossessing Jews of their rights as French citizens, as having broken a covenant between the French and the Jews. That betrayal begged a larger explanation; it constituted, in his eyes, divine reprisal for the sinfulness of French Jews, although it also attested to the moral bankruptcy of secular democracy. Yet the killings in Poland he understood to be in line with pogroms from the past: "They speak of 700,000 Jews killed in Poland and the surrounding area. This figure is not necessarily an exaggeration. In proportion to the number of Jews dispersed world-wide, it is not as many as during the epoch of Chmielnicki persecutions."[137] He did not regard this murder as qualitatively different from, or even as surpassing in scale, other instances in history in which Jewish lives were lost en masse. And comments recorded elsewhere in his diary about the depth of Jewish feeling among east European Jews and the honor of Jewish martyrdom during the Crusades suggest that Dreyfus regarded the murder of Polish Jews as conferring honor—not shame—on the victims. What is more, his reaction to news of the killing of Polish Jews was also consistent with his prewar view of Polish Jews as "unfortunate Polish co-religionists."[138] In modern history, Polish Jews had always been in a different—and worse—situation than French Jews.

Dreyfus did not view the Polish wartime situation as related to the French one. He did not seem to link the massacres of Polish Jews with the deportations— first of foreign Jews, then also of French Jews—from the occupied and unoccupied zones of France.[139] Of the first wave of deportations of Jews from France, he recorded: "The atmosphere in Nice is heavy, both from a hotter than normal heat spell and from the rumors that fill our heads of the arrest and sending away of foreigners to camps and to Germany, where they are being sent to work. It is impossible to know the details, but there are facts that justify people's apprehensions and contribute to the denigration of our country. [. . .] They say that the same atmosphere hangs over Marseille. From Paris come alarming rumors that the Germans demanded 20,000 Jewish, able-bodied workers, and that they are separating families in a barbaric manner. All of this is unverifiable, but the Jewish population's nervousness is tremendous."[140] (In chapter 3 I will pick up on this issue of Jewish diarists attempting to make sense of rumors and news reports.) Dreyfus seemed to connect the fate of foreign Jews being arrested in Nice and Marseille to rumors from Paris that the Germans were going to send Jews to Germany for forced labor.[141] Similarly, when rumors circulated about the impending arrest and deportation of French Jews soon after the Axis powers occupied southern France in November 1943, he interpreted them to mean that French Jews would also be sent to Germany.[142] Dreyfus had a premonition that he would not survive the war, but it did not seem to be linked to a fear for the fate of European Jewry as a whole. He assumed that Jews were being sent from France to Germany to perform forced labor and that he, as a man beyond the prime of his youth, would not be able to withstand the harsh treatment.[143]

The comparatively decent conditions of Jews living in Nice reinforced Dreyfus's sense that the fate of Jews in eastern Europe was separate from the fate of
Jews in Nice. He was conscious of the disparity between Jewish life in Nice and
elsewhere in Europe—even elsewhere in France—and he repeatedly returned
to the theme of how abnormally "peaceful" their lives were "on the margin of
events."[144] Nice was located in one of the eight French *départements* occupied by
Italy instead of Germany, and Jews streamed into Nice from other areas of western Europe in the belief that the Italians would protect them from the Germans.
Conditions actually improved for Jews in Nice during the spring and summer of
1943. The new Vichy prefect who took charge of Nice in May 1943 curbed the
brutal treatment of Jews that had been initiated in August 1942. In several entries,
Dreyfus commented that the food situation got better in April 1943 and that his
children would be shocked to see how well he and his wife were living.[145] At a re-
move from events in Poland and having limited information, Dreyfus could not
grasp the enormity of the ensuing extermination of European Jews.[146]

Dreyfus may not have comprehended that the Germans were in the midst
of exterminating Jews from all of Europe, yet he resigned himself to the likelihood that he would be killed. Dreyfus turned sixty in 1942, and from the time
of the emigration of his daughter, son-in-law, and granddaughter from Marseille
to the United States, via Algeria and Morocco, in May 1942, his anxiety about
the future had lessened. Knowing they were out of harm's way filled him with a
newfound attitude of resignation toward his own fate and toward that of Jews in
Europe generally. For example, in response to the first news of the killing of Jews
in Poland, he accompanied his condemnation of the Western world with the
self-conscious comment that "these are the reflections of a man who fears nothing, who has seen a lot, and who exercises judgment all the more dispassionately
since his children are saved."[147] Similarly, when the arrests of non-French Jews
began that same summer, he recorded, "Everyone is living in a state of anxiety except me. When you have ceased to regard your existence as up against the world,
you no longer fear anything. My children are saved."[148] His sense of the future—
that his children's lives were assured and that, through them, he was leaving behind a lasting legacy—not only rendered the perpetuation of his own life less
important, but also reinforced his belief in divine justice: "But my calm amidst
the anguish [. . .] can only be explained by the certainty that I will be survived
by my loved ones, established in America. At my age, you have shown what you
are, what you have, and what you are capable of. If I have to give up seeing them
again, the satisfaction of having often and for a long time been surrounded by
them will console me. If the Germans cut my life short, they will have the satisfaction of having had a little martyr. God will bless them and they will continue

to stay among the best of Israel."[149] Secure in the knowledge of his children's survival and unable to procure visas for himself and his wife, he placed his hope in God for help. His religious faith provided him with a meaningful response to his entrapment: the righteousness of the martyr.

Dreyfus chose to regard his death as that of a martyr. What he understood martyrdom to mean recalled his earlier discussion of the warrior and believer. It combined defiance and submission in a manner consistent with the "warlike virtues" he had once held up as necessary for France's spiritual renewal. Martyrs possessed "souls of fire, capable of energizing the crusade against the German barbarian with their breath and their faith."[150] Martyrdom was a practice that emerged from belief; deep religiosity compelled the martyr to fight for morality. He believed that "the sacrifice of oneself is the sublime act of the Jew who is exposed to the blows of assassins."[151] It was a statement of Jewish identity and a form of protest. Dreyfus conceived of his imminent death as a religious and moral act, which was in keeping with his investing human history with theological significance. Martyrdom also connected him to his forebears—the Jews of Alsace and Lorraine who had chosen death over conversion during the Crusades.[152]

Long before Dreyfus faced his own death, he had contemplated the martyr's legacy and was drawn to the ideal. His reflections on martyrdom and heroism did not change substantially during the war. If anything, his admiration of martyrdom from before the war, combined with his wartime messianic yearning, led him to conceive of his own death as another instance of martyrdom. Dreyfus believed that when the martyr is killed, "a sacred legend will eternally surround him in the memory of posterity."[153] Although he did not explicitly equate martyrdom with heroism, the martyr seems to have possessed heroic qualities in Dreyfus's eyes. He regarded heroism as a posture of courage and hope: "The hero is a person who has been the victim of some tremendous tragedy and has withstood his disgrace with courage. [. . .] When one hopes for something very great, one derives from the beauty of one's ambition the courage to withstand obstacles."[154] His admiration of Jewish martyrdom in the past seemed to influence his choice to regard his own death as that of a martyr.

When the Germans and the French Milice began arresting French Jews in September 1943, Dreyfus again cast himself in the mold of a martyr.[155] As he faced deportation, he recorded,

Thursday 16. [September 1943] Alarming rumors are spreading. In Nice, people are being arrested in large numbers, in the streets, in hotels, in the villas of the Promenade des Anglais. It's the Germans assisted by the Milice who proceed without pity. We don't know what to do. There is only one thing to do: trust that God will help.

Still and all, I have lived past age sixty, and my children will console themselves heroically that they had a martyr as a father.[156]

One week prior to being deported, the only hope Dreyfus could find was in God. Attributing guilt to the Germans and, to a lesser although not inconsiderable degree, to the French, he conveyed his sense of helplessness in the face of human malevolence, and he reaffirmed his faith in the eternity of divine justice. Possessing no other choice of action than to determine his attitude toward death, he responded with dignified resignation and faith. Now, however, he foresaw the transmission of heroism from the martyrs to the survivors. Resembling other parents, he imagined that, for his children, mourning his and his wife's deaths would entail a heroic effort.

Each man's concern for the fate of his diary was justified, for neither Dreyfus nor Kaplan survived the war. Although we do not know how Dreyfus's diary got from France in 1943 to Washington, D.C., over forty years later, we do know that in late September 1943, Dreyfus and his wife, Marthe, were deported to Drancy, a concentration camp on the outskirts of Paris of which Dreyfus had heard mention. Two months later, on 20 November at 11:50 in the morning, they began the hellish, five-day journey by train from the Paris-Bobigny station to Auschwitz-Birkenau, a place that by all indications Dreyfus did not know existed. Of the 1,200 Jews who were deported along with the Dreyfuses on transport number sixty-two—634 men, 556 women, and 10 "unspecified"—1,181 arrived in Auschwitz. Because of their ages, Lucien and Marthe Dreyfus were undoubtedly among the 914 people from their transport who were gassed immediately upon arrival.[157]

Despite knowing quite a lot about the fate of Kaplan's diary during and after the war, we know very little about the deaths of Chaim Aron Kaplan and his wife. They were probably deported during the second phase of deportations from the Warsaw ghetto to Treblinka, between 31 July and 14 August 1942, when German forces and their helpers took over primary control of the roundup of Jews from the Jewish police. At the end of the forty-six days of the great deportation, 253,743 Jews were deported from the Warsaw ghetto to their deaths. Of the more than 300,000 Jews who had lived in the Warsaw ghetto, it is estimated that "when all the selections, transfers, and evacuations were over, no more that 1,000–2,000 of the Warsaw Jews had survived."[158]

As both men had foreseen, their diaries would survive in their stead, testifying to the changes wrought by their wartime experiences on their lives and views of the world.

However, their thinking moved in opposite directions. Kaplan could not abide that God would permit such atrocious acts to be perpetrated against the Jews, and for this reason he rejected the belief that God was active in history. Dreyfus came to the opposite conclusion. France's betrayal of the ethical promise of Franco-Judaism created a void for Dreyfus that he filled with religious faith. He became convinced that religion was essential to the foundation of a just society. Moreover, religious faith became indispensable to him as an explanatory framework for the suffering being inflicted on European Jews in general and on French Jews in particular. Dreyfus invested history with theological meaning, whereas Kaplan could no longer believe in an immanent God.

Both men sought to understand the causes of Jewish suffering. They hoped some sort of meaning could be attributed to it or extracted from it. In their respective searches for meaning, they ultimately grappled with different questions. For Dreyfus, the central question was why this calamity was befalling the Jews. The question Kaplan sought to answer was how to historically contextualize and explain the underlying causes of the Nazi extermination. For each man, the function diary writing had and the meaning they attributed to it were inextricably related to their strategies of interpretation.

Though unusual among Polish Jewish ghetto diaries for being written in Hebrew and not Yiddish or Polish, Kaplan's diary exemplified the trilingual cultural "polysystem" of interwar and wartime Polish Jewish life much more than it has been credited with doing.[159] In preserving evidence of the suffering of the multitudes, Kaplan, like Ringelblum and Herman Kruk, wrote with an eye to modern history. He looked to future historians to explain the causes and meaning of Jewish suffering under German occupation. Implicit in Kaplan's hopes for modern history was his sense that history held the power of ultimate justice: it could function either as a medium of redress or as a final stage in the extermination of a people. He assumed Germany would eventually lose the war. Its defeat as a ruling power would not constitute its just deserts, however, if the Jews did not outlast the Nazis or if, at the very least, the Jews were unable to prevent their killers from controlling the knowledge of their deaths. Kaplan, like many other Jewish victims, produced a written testament out of his steadfast confidence in the morality of Western civilization. He wanted to ensure that the civilized world would know about the Germans' barbarity and that the memory of the victims would be passed down to future generations.

Dreyfus's religious awakening was not representative of French Jews. Indeed, his feeling of alienation from other French Jews was likely a product of the different path he took during the war.[160] Yet from the perspective of Jewish tradition, his turn to God for answers was a familiar response to catastrophe. Indeed, his theological interpretation was common among Orthodox Jews. Dreyfus's attempt to render meaningful the catastrophe befalling the Jews recalled the process at work in the biblical book of Lamentations. As described by the Hebrew literature scholar Alan Mintz, the "alleviation of the pain comes only when, by asserting a willed recollection of past truths, the sufferer makes the connection between suffering and sin. This realization releases him from his isolated victimization and allows him to join in a communal appeal to God. God remains silent in Lamentations, but the sufferer's emergence from soliloquy to prayer enables him at least to recover God as an addressable other."[161] During the war, Dreyfus's faith in God deepened, and he developed a notion of divine justice out of his loss of faith in humankind. Since he could no longer participate in the French society and culture that had betrayed him, he turned to the divine realm for answers. In so doing, he made use of an age-old Jewish strategy of interpretation: he incorporated the Jews' new suffering by placing it within the framework of past suffering, which rendered history as theologically meaningful.

Kaplan and Dreyfus can be regarded as emblematic of Jews' confrontations with the unimaginable genocide occurring in their midst. The events of the war threw them up against their systems of making meaning out of the world. Both men had two systems available to them—their Jewish one and their European enlightenment one. Each man felt one system give out, and the other—perhaps as a result—seemed more viable and valuable. In a sense, both men had their faith broken; they both asked where God or Civilization had gone. But they also had their faith deepened, Kaplan in civilization (in the form of modern history) and Dreyfus in God.

Jews made use of strategies of interpretation other than the theological and the historical-humanistic in their attempts to understand the destruction of Jewish life as it was unfolding. Indeed, these two diarists' meaning-making struggles open up to the dozens of diarists who employed similar strategies. Thus, we shall see not only how Jews were drawn to grand theological and historical narratives about God and humanity, but also how, as members of modern mass society, they were readers of popular media. Diarists turned to ephemeral sources—newspapers, radio broadcasts, and rumors—as a way to gain insight into their wartime predicament. Their interpretations of international and local news reveal other epistemological approaches Jews took in their confrontation with the murder of their people.

3

NEWS READERS

"A few ounces of news" could become "a ton of hope." So wrote Jurek Becker, a Holocaust survivor, in his novel *Jakob the Liar*. Published in East Germany in 1969, *Jakob the Liar* vividly portrayed how news helped sustain Jews living under German occupation. In the narrative, Jakob, an inhabitant of an unspecified ghetto, convinced his fellow Jews he was in possession of a radio. Forbidden from having radios and desperate for news of the outside world, the characters in Becker's novel hounded Jakob each day for the latest report on the Red Army's progress. Jakob's make-believe radio broadcasts buoyed the spirits of his fellow ghetto inhabitants, and Becker's novel explored the impact of these "lies" and the moral ambiguity of such lies in the context of the ghetto. Becker showed, on the one hand, how Jews' desperation drove them naively to give credence to their fantasies by believing the fictitious news reports to be true. On the other hand, he admiringly depicted how Jews turned fiction into reality, transforming mere words into communal viability, albeit short-lived.[1]

Few historians have taken up the issues raised in *Jakob the Liar* about Jews' wartime consumption of news. Scholars have written histories of the German official press during the Third Reich and of the production and distribution of underground newspapers by non-Jews and Jews during the Second World War.[2] Studies of the Jewish press and of other Jewish wartime writings have sought to determine what Jews knew, and when, about the Nazi intention to exterminate them.[3] What scholars have not analyzed is the social and emotional centrality of Jews' efforts to gain knowledge about their predicament—displayed in their news reading—and how the significance of those efforts changed over the course of the war. Rather than scrutinizing the information about the Final Solution available to Jews from various sources during the war—a line of investigation which seems to lead ineluctably to the question of whether Jews should have known more than they did and to a retrospective assignation of blame that they did not do more to save themselves—I want to explore Jews' hermeneutics of news. Investigating how Jews read the news elucidates a great deal about their wartime social interactions, coping strategies, and hopes for the future. Fundamentally, it reveals their efforts to make sense of what they read, heard, and experienced.

News reading was meaningful to Jews in different ways during the war. It can be understood as an example of what Yehuda Bauer in his recent discussion of Jewish resistance during the Holocaust called *Amidah*. Bauer roughly translates the Hebrew concept *Amidah* as "'standing up against'" and uses it to mean forms of armed and unarmed resistance that reflected a "refus[al] to budge in the face of brutal force."[4] *Amidah* included individual or group actions that defied German orders and could be seen as demonstrations of Jews' human dignity in the midst of dehumanizing circumstances. As instances of activities that bolstered morale and physical strength he cites cultural, religious, political, and educational efforts, along with the smuggling of food and the medical care provided by Jewish doctors and nurses. The goal of such activities, undertaken by many— though certainly not all—Jewish communities, was the maintenance of Jewish collective and individual existence until the time of Germany's presumed defeat. Bauer's expanded conception of Jewish resistance reflects recent scholarship that has, as noted, proven the Germans did not decide to murder the Jews until sometime in 1941. To quote Bauer, "If the Germans did not know, the Jews cannot be expected to have known either. Their problem, as they saw it, was how to survive an occupation that would end one day."[5] Thus, to paraphrase Bauer, the question of why Jews succeeded or failed to comprehend the Germans' intentions during the first three years of the war should be set aside. Instead, we might ask, To what did Jews attach importance in their efforts to stand up to the German threat, as they perceived it?

The reading of news was one of several such mechanisms of perseverance employed by Jews throughout the war. Jewish diarists all over Europe filled pages upon pages with news reports. Rumors abounded about the fate of individuals and communities as well as about the progress of the Allied war effort and projections of the war's duration. As Kaplan's angry litany of news demonstrates— "Vilna, Kovno, Lublin, Slonim, and Novogrudok have proved that the Nazi may be relied upon to keep his word"—is representative of how diarists honed their expertise in reading beneath the surface of propaganda-laden newspapers and in gleaning knowledge from the muddle of unconfirmed reports and secondhand stories.[6] As consumers of news, Jews were not docile readers. They did not passively absorb the information that reached them from newspapers, radio, letters, and hearsay but rather approached reading as an active pursuit. In addition to theorizing about how to analyze news sources and, when possible, making practical decisions therefrom, individuals responded to news in other, palpable ways. Most significantly, they interpreted news in order to construct hopeful narratives about their wartime situation. While the uses Jews made of news could be understood as their merely having "made do" under the circumstances, that assessment obscures the particular activities involved in much of their news reading during the Holocaust. The exchange and consumption of news, like other cultural activities mentioned by Bauer, acquired a different valence in the context of German occupation.

This economy of news had a tremendous impact on Jews' experience of the war and made an important contribution to sustaining Jewish existence, despite the fact that individuals' news reading had no impact on the outcome of the war.[7] Here I want to examine the types of news Jews followed, the sources from which they gathered information, the techniques they applied to its comprehension, and the implications of this economy of news in various parts of German-occupied Europe. Furthermore, I chart continuities and changes in the function of news reading over the course of the war. *Jakob the Liar* suggested—and Jewish diaries confirm—that Jews regarded news as more meaningful than mere information. Thus, what emerges are some of the ways in which the exchange and consumption of news sustained Jewish existence under German domination.

Kaplan's and Dreyfus's dramatically different accounts of the meaning of the Nazi persecution and extermination of European Jewry are emblematic of diarists' diversity. By contrast, the disparate entries of the thirty-odd diarists considered here illuminate how, in spite of the dissimilarities among diarists, including their wide-ranging backgrounds and wartime experiences, many shared interpretive strategies during the war. Indeed, diary evidence demonstrates that Jews throughout Europe—diarists and nondiarists—fairly consistently engaged in the tactic of tracking news. News reading as a project crossed borders and elided the many differences among Jews. Kaplan and Dreyfus, so unlike in their interpretations of the meaning of Jewish wartime suffering, shared the habit of frequently analyzing news in their diaries. The search for news and the effort to make sense of it were common experiences.

In examining the interpretation of news, I also return to the question of diarists' struggles to build rational knowledge about the surrounding crisis. The examples of Kaplan and Dreyfus revealed that Jews looked to traditional literary and historical sources to comprehend their suffering. When people read the news they were turning to other sources to make sense of their predicaments, contemporary sources such as newspapers, radio broadcasts, and rumors. These sources, in a much less abstract way, provided vital information with which people could try to make sense of their lives.

What makes the subject of Jews' wartime news reading particularly interesting is that news reading had captivated Europeans long before the outbreak of the Second World War. In chapter 1 I touched on how Jewish wartime diary writing was part of a broader phenomenon of diary writing in Europe that dated back to the nineteenth century and earlier, while at the same time it acquired new functions and meanings as a response to Jews' particular situation during the Holocaust. In similar fashion, Jews' wartime hermeneutics of the news grew out of the European history of readership and the popularization of the press from the second half of the nineteenth century.[8]

Many factors contributed to the increased consumption of newspapers in the nineteenth century, not least of which was the fact that newspapers had become the central political forum for progressive ideas and government critique as European states became increasingly democratic. In addition, a new reading public came into being with the migration of masses of people to industrializing metropolises. New city dwellers turned to newspapers, which now cost less thanks to advertising, for information on how to find their way in the cities. Besides enormously popular serialized novels, newspapers offered glimpses of other people's hardships and pastimes as well as advice about how to adapt to city life. New residents could find employment, housing, and theater listings; advice on how to be a good pedestrian or streetcar rider; and recommendations for where to go for quality meats and dairy products in the indoor markets. Newspapers were entertainment for city residents, but they were something more: guides that helped orient people to rapidly expanding cities. In a kaleidoscopic cityscape of rapidly shifting events, what was stable was news reading itself.[9] These functions of news reading—entertainment, orientation guide, and anchor—persisted into the Second World War.

A common thread connected news reading throughout Europe in the nineteenth century, and that was the development of a mass press as a central feature of urban cosmopolitan culture. Within city life, the press played a social function in addition to providing entertainment and local guides. As Benedict Anderson argued, the sight of people reading copies of the same newspaper on the streets and in cafés helped create a sense of "community in anonymity."[10] Newspapers constituted social relations of an anonymous kind among strangers. This function, too, would persist for Jewish news readers during the Second World War under totally different circumstances.

Jews from all over Europe participated heavily in this flourishing mass journalism as both producers and consumers of news. They too were swept up in the "reading revolution" of the late nineteenth and early twentieth centuries. Large numbers of Jews were among those who migrated from rural areas to urban centers in the mid to late nineteenth century, particularly in western and Central Europe, where they won political freedom and equality. Jews, like non-Jews, used newspapers to assist in their adaptation to new surroundings. Moreover, for those Jews who had gained newfound freedoms, the press furthered their identification with the nation in which they lived, and for those Jews who did not have the option to assimilate into the supposed majority national society and culture, the Jewish press reinforced their identification with a Jewish cultural milieu and politics.[11]

For Jewish and non-Jewish news readers, the hankering after news acquired new meaning after the Nazi regime took power in Germany. Before this development, local news had taken precedence over national and international news. Now, world events supplanted city life as the focus of people's attention.[12] Even before Germany invaded Poland in September 1939, international political changes outpaced the commotion of the metropolis. In 1938, the uncertainty of world affairs kept one German Jewish diarist who was living in Holland up until two o'clock in the morning listening to the news on the radio. As England and France repeatedly acquiesced to Germany's annexations of its neighbors, she felt like "three times a day the entire situation of the world turns inside out."[13] International news was more sensational than local news had ever been. Indeed, beginning in the 1930s and certainly after the start of the war, world affairs had ceased to be a matter of distant curiosity; they had become personal. Especially for Jews in Europe, the events unfolding in the news bore an unprecedented urgency.

Just when world affairs became newly meaningful, the press became the instrument of repressive regimes. The Nazi regime crushed the freedom of the press in Germany in the fall of 1933 with the passage of the Editor's Law and the creation of the Reich Press Chamber within the Reich Chamber of Culture. These measures brought the German press under state and party control, requiring that journalists, editors, and publishers "regulate their work in accordance with National Socialism as a philosophy of life and as a conception of government."[14] In practice, this meant that those people whose political sympathies or racial "pedigree" did not conform to National Socialism—all "individuals who were liberal, leftist, or Jewish"—were excluded from the profession.[15] Many periodicals were immediately forced out of existence, most conspicuously the Socialist and Communist press, and those that remained were subject to forced takeovers, consolidation, and censorship. Nazi Germany extended these publishing controls to the territories it annexed in 1938 and 1939. With the invasion of Poland, these measures were made stricter and encompassed the countries under wartime German occupation.[16]

As the war unfolded and the concentration and deportation of Jews began, fewer and fewer Jews under German occupation were in a position to be able to follow the news directly. Jews' radios were confiscated, and even government-controlled newspapers were often difficult to obtain. By July 1942, Jews in Germany were prohibited from buying newspapers.[17] Yet more than ever, Jews throughout Europe hungered for news, believing it to have direct relevance to their lives. In fact, Jews' hermeneutics of news was the most literal version of their effort to make sense of what was happening around them and to them. Ultimately, news reading constituted a crucial piece of Jews' efforts to render their present and postwar future meaningful as they connected their fate to that of Europe as a whole.

STRATEGIES OF READING UNRELIABLE SOURCES

Jetzt stürmen die Ereignisse con brio
Wir brauchen nächstens eine zweite
    Klio.
Die Eine kommt ja nicht mehr zum
    Verschnaufen
Und muss sich einen neuen Griffl
    kaufen.
Der Duce sitzt! Italien Republik
Baroglio Präsident! Und in der
    Schweiz—
Der Einen Unglück ist der Andern
    Glück—
Macht man Quartier für Könige
    bereits.
Indem ich schreibe kommt schon neue
    Mär.
Brioglio in Italien ist erschossen,
Die Eisenbahner streiken, und ein
    Heer
Von Deutschen ist in Welschland
    eingeschlossen.
Und Mussolini kommt vors
    Kriegsgericht!

Now current events rage *con brio*
We will need before long a second
    Clio.
The first no longer comes to take a
    break
And must buy a new pencil of slate.
The Duce holds out! Italian Republic
Baroglio President! And in
    Switzerland—
Where one man's misfortune is
    another's luck—
The accommodation for kings is
    already in hand.
Even whilst I write there are new
    tidings.
Brioglio in Italy was shot,
The railwaymen strike, and an army
Of Germans in French Switzerland
    has been locked up.
And Mussolini is being brought before
    the military tribunal!

Das Sternenbanner weht schon über Rom!	The Stars and Stripes wave over Rome!
Ob sich wohl Adolf jetzt den Kopf zerbricht?	I wonder will Adolf rack his brains now?
Der Draht bringt jede Stunde neuen Strom.	The wire every hour imparts a new tome.
Ist alles wahr? ist's etwa nur Gedicht?	Is it all true? is it only a poem? —Rudolf Geissmar, 28 July [1943], [poem] 241, Theresienstadt Diary

Rudolf Geissmar, a former jurist in Germany who was in his seventies during the war, kept a diary in verse in Theresienstadt. This entry documents one instance of how news continued to stream into the ghettos, concentration camps, and forced labor camps of German-occupied Europe. It reads like a newsreel of the major stories of the day. The "hot off the presses" emissions outpaced Geissmar's ability to set them to rhyme. Yet as the last line of this entry attests, it was hard to discern truth from poetry among the rumors.[18] Where did these news stories come from?

A variety of sources fed Geissmar's and other Jews' "newswires" in ghettos, camps, and hiding places. They included letters and postcards, authorized and underground newspapers, German and foreign radio broadcasts, German officials, other Jewish and non-Jewish prisoners who had just arrived in a ghetto or camp, and rumors. None of these sources was reliable, and none transparent. News reading ceased to be a straightforward process thanks to German guile and deceit. Still, Jews took up the challenge directly, often convinced it was possible to grasp reality if one approached the task methodically and creatively.

Two main subject areas, the fate of the Jews and fighting on the front, fell under the rubric of news in people's diaries. Although the sources for each type of news varied, in both cases we see the same process at work: Jews attempting to figure out their situation under German occupation. The most important news to most diarists—that of other Jews—was also usually the least accessible.

THE MYSTERY OF JEWS' FATE AND THE CLUES OF CORRESPONDENCE

For news of family and friends, there were no mass circulation newspapers and no radio broadcasts; the post and rumors were the only available sources. Nevertheless, neither could be described as dependable or consistent. Postal regulations frequently changed over the course of the war and varied from location to location. As a rule, communication with people in Allied countries was nonexistent apart from Red Cross postcards. Jews in the territory of the Reich and else-where in German-occupied Europe often were able to send letters, postcards, and packages to individuals in other German-occupied countries and in neutral countries like Switzerland, Sweden, Spain, and Portugal, though this possibility also faded in and out and depended on location. And even when correspondence was allowed, many letters did not reach their destination.[19]

The changeable nature of postal service during the war is exemplified by the circumstances in Łódź and in Theresienstadt. The official archivists of the Łódź ghetto, who worked for the ghetto's Jewish administration, recorded that in the first year of the sealed ghetto's existence, when the ghetto's population consisted of approximately 160,000 people, "the post office delivered 135,062 parcels mailed from the Reich (and territories incorporated into it), and 14,229 from abroad. The telegraph service processed 10,239 wires, and the number of letters and postcards handled reached 1,074,351."[20] The stream of mail slowed consider-ably after the Germans invaded the Soviet Union, at which time parcels sent from the Soviet Union, formerly the largest source of parcels, were no longer delivered. Shortly thereafter, mail sent to the United States, western Europe, and Sweden was "returned to the senders and stamped: *Zurück. Kein Postverkehr* [Send back. There is no postal service]."[21] German authorities suspended the outward flow of mail from the ghetto altogether in January 1942 as a cautionary measure in advance of the mass deportation of Jews from Łódź to the extermination camp in Chełmno nad Nerem, the first death camp used to kill Jews.[22] This ban con-tinued for two and half years, during which time the only mail that people in the ghetto could send were preprinted postcards, and even those were limited in number and could be sent only to other Jews. The diarist Oskar Rosenfeld, who kept a personal diary in addition to his work chronicling the history of the Łódź ghetto for the ghetto's official archives, objected to these "preprinted cards" for the reason that "*address and name written by the postal official so that the ad-dressee doesn't even get to see the original handwriting*" (original emphasis).[23] By the time the ban on sending mail was lifted, the much-reduced population of the ghetto feared they no longer had anyone to whom they could write. As re-corded by the ghetto's official chroniclers,

> But to whom should the others [that is, those without "Aryan" relatives] write? To family members who at one time fled from Łódź? Who knows whether they are still alive and where they might be? To the fathers, mothers, or children resettled from the ghetto? Who knows whether they have survived and, if so, where they are. Similarly, the people resettled here from the Old Reich and from Vienna have little hope of contacting their relatives since they have no

idea of their whereabouts. Indeed, if all the Jews in the Reich, the Protectorate of Bohemia and Moravia, and the Generalgouvernement learn that the mail ban has been lifted, and thereupon write to the ghetto, then perhaps communication could be restored. Many people—alas, too many—fear such communication because the news can only be bad.[24]

Even when letters could be sent, they were subject to strict limitations, and letter writers could impart little information in their correspondence. Correspondence sent from Theresienstadt to the Protectorate (Bohemia and Moravia) in 1942, for example, could consist solely of the postcards distributed by the Jewish administration of the ghetto and could contain a message of no more than thirty words, written in German in block letters or on a typewriter (to which only workers for the Jewish administration had access). The content of the message could not contain any political references or "untrue or misleading information about life in the Ghetto." The Jewish administration in Theresienstadt conducted the first round of censorship on all correspondence leaving the ghetto and thus was vulnerable to punishment along with the sender if the German censors found any "objectionable text."[25] What this meant in practical terms, as Philip Mechanicus described in his diary written in a transit camp in Holland, was that letters received from Theresienstadt and Lublin were "varied and often detailed, but strictly personal. There is nothing about their environment or their work activities."[26] Mention in a Stanislawów ghetto diary of the correspondence between the diarist's aunt in the ghetto and her aunt's son in Italy indicates just how little letter writers in Poland could communicate of their circumstances: "Yesterday, with tears flowing, aunt brought over a letter from her son in Italy. He reproached her for not letting him know sooner about his father's illness. In his naiveté he declares that he would have come to save his father (from the jaws of the lion). He requests that she put flowers on his grave. (What ignorance of our circumstances). [. . .] It is after all utterly ridiculous but there is a need to say how like honey it [the letter] is for us, even in this form."[27] It is possible to imagine how painful it was for this son to learn of his father's death in this manner, and how frustratingly powerless he felt in the face of this news. At the same time, his mother was perhaps angry and hurt by her son's reproaches, knowing he remained utterly ignorant of conditions in the ghetto. The diarist picked up on the absurdity of their situation: that her cousin's letter could fill them with such joy despite the frustratingly limited nature of their correspondence as a result of censorship.

Although Jews were not supposed to write explicitly about what was happening to them, they could encode messages. One method they employed was to use the names of long-deceased family members to refer to people who had recently died and to hint at their shared fate. Another encryption device was to transliterate Hebrew or Yiddish words (since Jews were forbidden from writing in Hebrew or Yiddish) and to use them as people's names.[28] For example, as Walter Laqueur analyzed, a letter sent to Switzerland with news about the mass deportation of Jews from the Warsaw ghetto said, "Mea Alafim (hundred thousand) had been invited by Mr. Hunter to his countryhouse 'Kever,' meaning grave."[29]

Although most letter writers closely guarded their language, there were instances of letters sent by Jews that contained explicit references to their suffering, even of the deportations and killings. Naturally, letters sent through illegal channels contained more explicit information. Jews in Theresienstadt, for example, had various means of smuggling letters out of the ghetto, most frequently through the Czech inhabitants of the town, and these letters were, predictably, of a different character. However, the punishment for sending correspondence illegally was severe. In the case of Theresienstadt, individuals who were caught were automatically included on a transport to Auschwitz.[30] Even some letters sent legally, though, could impart a great deal of information. This is evident in the postcard sent from a man named Herman in May 1942 from the town of Delatyn in eastern Galicia to his uncle in Basel, Switzerland. The main text of the card reads,

> Delatyn 17 May 1942
> Dear Uncle
> I received your card from 5 February. Out of our entire family only I and my younger brother Artur are left. We have had to move from our home [and] find ourselves in Delatyn without any means of living. If it would be possible for you to help us a little we would be very much grateful. Please don't forget about us. I send heartfelt greetings from my wife and child, and also from Artur, to you, dear Uncle and Aunt.
> Herman[31]

In another instance, the diarist Fela Szeps in the Grünberg forced labor camp mentioned receiving letters from her brother and parents until they too were deported in the summer of 1942. These letters informed her of the deportation of Jews from the ghetto in her hometown, although they did not know where the Jews were being sent.[32] (It turns out that the deportation they reported was the first of two deportations of Jews from Dąbrowa Górnicza to Auschwitz in 1942.)[33] Fela and her sister also received postcards from friends, several of which they managed to smuggle out of Grünberg and preserve along with their diary during the death march in 1945. In one postcard, the sender, who appears to have been the father of a friend of Fela's who had been killed, told Fela that her brother had been sent to a camp with a hundred other "young people" but that no one knew anything more specific. Remarkably, in a second postcard to Fela postmarked less than a month later, the same man wrote again, saying he was glad to learn from Fela's last card that she had heard from her brother and learned where he was, in a camp in Klettendorf.[34] These two postcards reveal the frequency and frank nature of correspondence in some instances, most likely in this case because the correspondents resided in the same administrative district under German occupation. Indeed, the existence of other people's correspondence, also sent from the Szepses' hometown to Grünberg and to another camp in the vicinity, suggests that the Szepses' correspondence activity was typical for Jews in that region.[35]

The most revealing correspondence, however, is five letters and postcards which described in clear language the killing operations being conducted at Chełmno. They were discovered among the documents preserved in the Warsaw ghetto's underground archives, *Oyneg Shabbes*. The letters were written by Jews who lived near Chełmno and were sent to friends and family in Warsaw in the hope that the information would be passed along to Warsaw's Jewish leaders. The preservation of these five pieces of mail suggests there were likely many others sent within Poland describing the deportations and killings being committed.[36] Indeed, it was precisely for fear of such news spreading that German authorities had imposed the ban on outgoing mail from the Łódź ghetto at the time of the first deportations to Chełmno. To be sure, though, letters of this sort rarely made it into the hands of their intended recipients.

In many cases, the content of Jews' correspondence had to conform to a specified model. Indeed, Jewish prisoners in concentration camps and extermination camps were sometimes forced to write to their friends and family in order to reassure them that conditions in the camps were tolerable and that they were healthy. For example, in a postcard written on 8 August 1943 from "Arbeitslager Birkenau," a woman named Helene Faltin wrote to friends in Prague, "Dear Friends, We are no longer in Theresienstadt but all four [of us] arrived here today. We are all healthy and send you all our heartfelt greetings. Yours, Helene." This postcard bears obvious traces of German intervention. Not only was it postmarked 22 September 1943, a month and a half after it was written, but it also bore the imprint of another person's hand. Below the return address in Helene's handwriting, someone added "bei Neu Berun." "Arbeitslager Birkenau bei Neu Berun" was the denotation given to the Theresienstadt family camp established in Auschwitz-Birkenau on 8 September 1943, in which some 17,500 inmates from Theresienstadt were kept alive for several months, separate from other inmates in Auschwitz-Birkenau, until they, too, were gassed.[37] Thus, this postcard was sent by the German authorities to give the impression that Helene and her three friends or family members were alive, healthy, and living in the Theresienstadt family camp. This was undoubtedly not so.

Letters written in extermination camps often deliberately lacked dates so that German officials could send them in batches during the subsequent months—after the vast majority of the letter writers had been killed—in order to deceive Jews who had not yet been deported that the deportees remained alive.[38] For Jews in western and Central Europe, who had not yet seen firsthand the ghettos and camps of eastern Europe, even a glimpse of handwriting on a preprinted postcard or on a package receipt was interpreted as confirmation that deported family members were still alive. On 10 May 1942, Frieda Reinach recorded in the diary she and her husband kept jointly in Berlin, "We cannot write to Max [her older brother] and Jule, we can only send them money and also some food, weeks afterwards we receive a receipt from them through the ghetto in Litzmanstadt [Łódź]. As long as we see their handwriting, we know they are alive."[39] This entry confirms the Łódź diarist Oskar Rosenfeld's sense of how important it was to the addressee to glimpse the sender's handwriting. Moreover, German and Austrian Jews may also have interpreted preprinted postcards as a sign of life because similar postcards acknowledging receipt of packages had been used in the First World War during a postal ban.[40] Not surprisingly, Chaim Kaplan was more circumspect in his interpretation of the significance of a person's handwriting. Almost two weeks into the mass deportation of Jews from Warsaw, Kaplan recorded, "We have no information about the fate of those who have been expelled. When one falls into the hands of the Germans he falls into the abyss. [. . .] One person says that a certain family has received news of one of its members who was deported, that he arrived in the place intended for him alive and well—but he doesn't name the place nor give his address, and he doesn't ask them to write to him."[41] Although Kaplan did not know the specifics about what happened to the deportees, he knew enough about the fate of Jews from other Polish towns to doubt that the letter writer was "alive and well."

More often, Jews did not receive any correspondence from people who had been deported. Diarists in Germany, France, and Holland waited anxiously for news from their loved ones as a sign that they were still alive. A diarist writing in Berlin half a year after Jews began to be deported from Germany to Poland wrote, "There is still no clear indication as of now with regard to the destination of several transports, since no news was received from any of the people in those transports. This applies to the November transports so that family members living here are without any news."[42] A fifteen-year-old girl recorded in entry after entry in August and September of 1942 that there was no word from her parents, who had been deported to an unknown place from the transit camp Drancy in early August.[43] A German Jewish man who had emigrated with his elderly parents to Holland before the war noted in December 1942 that a half year had passed since his relatives in Germany had been deported: "Are they still alive? We have heard nothing more from any of them."[44] One year later, a German Jewish woman in Berlin, who had evaded deportation by obtaining false papers, passed a memory-laden New Year's eve reflecting on her fate and that of her loved ones during the prior year. One year had passed since she had assumed her false identity and she wondered, "Where are all the people who were close and distant to me and went away from here.—Will they be heard from again?"[45] These diary writers were desperate for news of their family and friends. They also wanted to gain information about what had happened to Jews who were sent away and thereby to learn what might await them as well.[46]

The lack of information about loved ones fed people's hopes as well as their suspicions. Even in Poland, where since the beginning of the war Jews were beaten and killed daily in the clear light of day, the lack of concrete knowledge about the fate of relatives who had been carried off by the Germans gave families a sliver of hope that their missing relatives might still be alive. For example, Dina Rathauserowa, a diarist in hiding in western Ukraine, did not know what had happened to her husband, yet she continued to hope that he, like her and her son, was still alive and in hiding or maybe had escaped to Lwów, the region's capital, or been sent to a work camp. She did not reach the conclusion that her husband was dead, even though she had witnessed the Germans drive "our Jews to death" in the *Aktion* in her town.[47]

Rathauserowa was not alone in harboring such hopes. Another diarist, Margarete (Grete) Holländer, was in hiding in the same region of Poland as Rathauserowa.[48] She reflected with the advantage of two years' hindsight on their disbelief in August 1941, when many of the Jewish men from their town were rounded up, taken to the forest, and shot. At that time, families believed their relatives had been taken to a forced labor camp. Such hopes were supported by "ever new tales" that "they had been seen in this or that town. Messengers came who transmitted greetings and took away cash remittances and letters. Of course, these messages were without exception forged or fabricated. [. . .] Because of them, people believed in soap bubbles for a longer time and did not give up hope."[49] While Holländer blamed extortionists' lies for people's refusal to recognize the truth of what had happened—and surely those lies were fodder for their hope—Rathauserowa's writing suggests that people could also clutch at the absence of news to reinforce their hopes, since silence left their loved ones' deaths unconfirmed.

The combination of truth and lies in the available sources of news about other Jews' fate opened a space for hopeful conjecture. Where there was incomprehension or ignorance, there was hope. The limited information also compelled Jews to turn to the press for additional clues about the war and what it might mean for their future. Regarding newspapers as personally relevant was hardly new to the war, nor was it unique to European Jews during the early war years. The intensity of Jews' suffering, however, did invest their news reading efforts with special urgency.

READING BETWEEN THE LINES

Though war news was seemingly less personal, Jews believed it to be absolutely pertinent to their lives and devoted considerable energy to the development of techniques for apprehending it. If Jews were forced to rely on cryptic letters, glimpses of handwriting, and allegations of chance sightings in their attempts to ascertain the fate of those who had been deported, they gathered news of the war mostly through newspapers and hearsay. They were privy to unconfirmed rumors, "which spread like wildfire" through towns, ghettos, camps, and bunkers.[50] Those diarists who referred to reading actual newspapers as opposed to hearing news were almost always outside the ghettos and camps. Within the ghettos and camps, there were so few copies of newspapers—if there were any at all—that the relay and acquisition of news was conducted for the most part through word of mouth. A contributor to the *Oyneg Shabbes* archive shed some light on the news relay process in the Warsaw ghetto in an entry of his diary. Nehemiah Titelman read in a paper being sold on the street outside the ghetto that there was some tension within the inner circle of the Nazi Party. He felt "compelled to share the joy, and since there are few papers brought in or read in the ghetto, I feel it my duty to tell whomever I meet on my way, while running to tell same to friends and acquaintances."[51] While Titelman could assure his friends that he himself had read the news in a newspaper, his friends would not be able to make the same guarantee when they relayed this piece of news to others, as they surely did. For this reason, it was often difficult to distinguish between rumors and real news, as attested to by the last line of Geissmar's diary entry in verse: "The wire every hour imparts a new tome. / Is it all true? is it only a poem?" Indeed, the combination of Jews' isolation, the Germans' efforts to deceive the Jews (and the world as a whole), and the Germans' control of the press often made it impossible for Jews to know what was true. During the last month of the Łódź ghetto's existence, one diarist recorded, "The truth is mixed with lies, we do not know what to believe and what not to believe."[52]

Jews in concentration camps and forced labor camps were so cut off from the outside world that, out of desperation, they derived news from any conceivable source. They became, in a sense, ragpickers of news. In the Grünberg forced labor camp in Silesia, Szeps's first words in a diary entry of 5 July 1943 were, "News, I want news, news from which hearts quicken, eyes burn, fists clench weakly and yet still with strength [. . .] That news, by force of spirit [and] hypersensitive imagination, is detected in insinuated words, is read on the faces of new arrivals, is decoded in printed and written words."[53] Szeps depicted her desperation for news in terms associated before the war with hysteria.[54] She described how she and other women in the camp seized on every word or expression to invigorate their will to live. Newcomers to a ghetto or camp provided information about the outside world, about the progress of the war, and especially about the fate of Jewish communities. For example, French prisoners at Grünberg, who had more access than others to the outside world, imparted news of the war to the Szepses and other Jewish prisoners.[55] Several diarists in Theresienstadt mentioned the news and rumors that circulated when new transports arrived.[56] In addition, Jews tried to infer news about the war's progress from the sounds in their vicinity. Air sirens at night filled Szeps with hope that liberation, whether through death or Soviet victory, was not far off.[57] And, in a fashion similar to Jews who tried to interpret the significance of having received no letters from those who had been deported, a woman in hiding in Poland tried to deduce what it meant when she heard no planes or trains for an entire day.[58]

The extreme isolation experienced by Jews in some ghettos and camps and their desperation for news of the outside world are apparent in the example of two men who worked in the crematorium in Bergen-Belsen. Arnold Keller and Hans Horwitz compared their isolation as crematorium workers in Bergen-Belsen to their previous situation in the Dutch transit camp, Westerbork. Keller wrote in his diary from Bergen-Belsen, "One is completely cut off from the outside world, hears and sees nothing about the war, as the whole day long the SS-men, who appear to believe still in a German victory, are so self-confident in their manner. I think that they are also being left in the dark about what is going on outside and how things stand on the Front. In Westerbork we heard some about outside the camp through newspapers, radio, and reports, and the state of affairs gave us all reason to be optimistic about the duration of the war. But here??? I think that things will come to an end for us quite suddenly and unexpectedly."[59] Keller and Horwitz were totally cut off from the rest of the camp—and, by extension, from the world outside the camp—and would sit by the window of their hut whenever possible to eavesdrop on the conversations of people in their vicinity.[60]

Diarists who did have access to newspapers often expressed confidence that, despite German control of the press, they could read between the lines and make out the pertinent news. They were convinced it was possible to grasp reality if they approached the task artfully and scientifically. In the case of official newspapers, they generally assumed that nothing appearing in the press was arbitrary, and they set to analyzing the meaning behind the printed news. The strategies they developed reflected not only their specific wartime experiences and emotional registers but also the knowledge they had gained before the war.

Diarists who had access to multiple sources of news would often compare and contrast them in order to extract news. The practice of reading multiple newspapers and comparing versions of a story was common before the war as well, with one major difference: at that time there was a free press. Then, people read several newspapers in order to gain exposure to a wide array of political perspectives. During the war, Jewish diarists compared versions of stories in order to try to detect the markings of the propagandist's pen.[61] When the only newspapers available were the German official press, this comparative method yielded few additional insights. The German Jewish diarist Victor Klemperer noted the sense of repetition one experienced when reading different German papers. Klemperer was a professor of Romance languages before the Nazis came to power and a lifelong diarist who remained in Dresden throughout most of the war, recording his keen observations of everyday life in Germany under the Third Reich. On reading various German official papers, he commented,

> In place of the *Frankfurter Zeitung*, which ceased publication, Lewinsky is subscribing to the *Deutsche Allgemeine Zeitung* [DAZ] and brought a couple of copies with him. It contains exactly the same commentaries on the situation as the *Dresdener Zeitung*, in a little more detail, accommodating its style to the regular readership [of] aristocracy, senior civil servants, ecclesiastics — but literally identical in all arguments and catchwords and slogans. Quite obviously, every day a central office issues the official blurb, which all newspaper authors have to print or paraphrase. Just as Goebbels once said with delight of marching Hitler Youth: the same face everywhere.[62]

State control of the press was so blatant and heavy-handed that Klemperer was able to deduce how it was carried out. Another diarist, the renowned Polish Jewish writer Yitzhak Katzenelson, made a similar observation about the unity of the German press: "After some hours of utter depression, I read the 'Pariser Zeitung' of today's date. It is some years since I read this paper. There is really only one newspaper in the whole of that part of Europe occupied by the German beast. It resembles that devouring ogre of the thousand eyes, the Hydra of a thousand heads; in reality only one evil eye and one monstrous head."[63]

Diarists did find discrepancies between German and non-German sources of news, even between German newspapers and those printed in countries under German occupation in the local language. Two diarists in Holland, both German émigrés, specified reading other news sources in addition to German ones. While imprisoned in Holland in the fall and winter of 1940, Jacob Müller had a subscription to a Dutch newspaper for four months until prisoners were prohibited from obtaining non-German newspapers. Not only were the Dutch papers more revealing, he believed, but the German prison officials, who were unable to read the Dutch, would also ask Müller for news, convinced as they were that the Dutch papers imparted more information.[64] Grete Steiner mentioned listening to English radio broadcasts until as late as December 1941 in Zeist, Holland. Steiner commented that, contrary to what one would assume, it was easier to figure out what was happening in the war from the German newspapers than from English radio. While this preference might have reflected her language proficiency, perhaps her comment stemmed more from her evaluation of the ineffectiveness and transparency of German censorship: "The German reports in the local newspapers are tragi-comic. Even if a person was not informed through English reports, he could gather everything of importance."[65] All German newspapers on a given day were alike, but that did not mean they revealed no meaningful information.

A diarist in eastern Poland echoed Steiner's preference for German news reports. Klara Kramer (née Schwarz), a teenage diarist who, along with seventeen other people, was being hidden by a Gentile couple of German background (*Volksdeutsche*) in Żółkiew, stated her preference for "the German communiqué" over "English radio." The Germans "give more details, they admit they are retreating. They say for strategic reasons, but they are retreating." Kramer assumed that what was hidden in the German press was the intention or goal of the army's actions but not the actions themselves. Moreover, the German war coverage focused on the eastern front, which was more pertinent to Kramer's situation than English radio's coverage primarily of the "northern front."[66]

Kramer and Steiner listened to or read the German news reports with a measure of confidence. Steiner believed she could gauge the significance of what appeared in the newspapers by remaining cognizant of how German control of the press worked. Like Klemperer, she understood that "[the newspapers] can only print what the Germans give them, and sometimes that is very meaningful." When the newspapers reported nothing about the war in Russia, for example, she interpreted that as a sign that the German army had made no progress in Russia. "So one hopes that one is a day nearer to liberation," she concluded.[67] Steiner grounded her sanguine news analysis in what she believed to be her intimate knowledge of the psychology of the German people, undoubtedly derived from the fact that she was German herself. She was convinced that the majority of Germans did not want to sacrifice their lives for a war they had no hope of winning, and thus that German newspapers would not print anything that would constrain the German people's sense of hope.[68] Building on this foundation, her technique of reading the papers fell somewhere between science and art. Before the start of the war, in late September 1938, Steiner applied the language of scientific research to describe the process of news reading—she spoke of "dissecting" [*zerlegen*] a speech of Hitler's. In the fall of 1941, reading around the censors was "a peculiar art."[69] It required method and creativity, both.

Klemperer also expressed confidence in his ability to extract the truth from German-controlled news even when he lacked the assistance of non-German news reports. Reading the newspapers was, to Klemperer, like learning a language. After gaining fluency in the language of the Third Reich, which he referred to as LTI, or *Lingua Tertii Imperia*, it became possible to engage in literary analysis of news reports.[70] He recorded proudly,

> I have learned to read reports, which in the last war I naively accepted. Yesterday a summary of the Crimean campaign just ended. The big talk of the amount of booty and of enemy losses and of the insignificance of our losses has as little effect now as the words "battle of extermination." But it concludes: This is a great German victory, which the lies of enemy propaganda present as a German defeat. From this one can say with certainty—and one does not need to commit a broadcasting crime [i.e., listen to foreign radio broadcasts] to know—that the opponents are writing: Germany has lost an irreplaceable amount of time and men before Sevastopol. Now it is certain that the enemy figures of German losses will be greatly exaggerated (I assume that England and Russia exaggerate by 100 percent, Goebbels and co. by 200 percent); but they are nevertheless basically right.[71]

Klemperer drew upon his background as a scholar of literature and languages to analyze the news. He believed his familiarity with Nazi hyperbole and stock phrases helped him to understand the meaning of reports. Indeed, he was so certain his analysis of German reports was correct that he extrapolated other versions of the news the Allies could have written. His mastery of LTI made it possible for him to track the progress of the war despite the Nazis' efforts to twist the truth. It also affirmed his intellectual abilities and professional competence, which had been undermined by his dismissal from his teaching position in 1935 and his inability to secure a position abroad.

Other diarists also proffered modes of reading the newspapers. M. Landsberg had access to a Polish underground paper and to German newspapers while in hiding with another man named Rudy in Krzemieniec [Kremenets] in Volhynia in western Ukraine. Little information exists about Landsberg's identity, including his first name. Perhaps he was related to the Zionist leader in Krzemieniec, Benjamin Landsberg, who committed suicide during the liquidation of the Krzemieniec ghetto. What can be extracted from his diary is that Landsberg was in his early thirties and appears to have participated in the ghetto revolt initiated by Krzemieniec's Jews in July 1942, during which they set fire to parts of the ghetto and attempted mass escapes to the forest. The Germans brutally suppressed the revolt during a two-week *Aktion* in August, and it was during this period that Landsberg and Rudy went into hiding. Most of the fifteen thousand Jews living in Krzemieniec were shot in trenches near the town's railway station, and some fifteen hundred were sent to perform slave labor. After the war, fewer than two dozen individuals survived. Landsberg was among the few Jews who lived to see Soviet troops roll into Krzemieniec, having survived in hiding until March 1944 thanks to the help of a Polish woman active in the underground whom he referred to as H. or Halina in his diary. It is unclear what happened to him after March 1944, when his diary ends.[72]

In his diary, Landsberg explicated in detail how he and Rudy systematically approached news reading. Rudy read the Wehrmacht reports aloud, and Landsberg would track the war's progress on a map they had in their hiding place. Then they would read the articles from the German newspaper and translate them—first literally into Polish and then figuratively—in order to determine what he described as the "flashes of objectivity."[73] Landsberg provided an example of the process they followed by quoting a story in German from the 21 November 1942 *Völkischer Beobachter* about the U-boat sinking of British ships and then including their precise Polish translation of it. From this they concluded that the reported number of ships sunk was absurd, and they proceeded to repeat their system for the next article. Later in the entry, he summarized their findings: "After reading through the news, we begin to 'translate' it into 'our' language. Thus we know: that in the Caucasus the Soviet army is attacking, that in Stalingrad it also goes 'like a nosebleed' for the Germans, that on the [river] Don the first move is with the Russians, [. . .] that . . . in general things are going well. We have 'our' own key, which we employ to read the German newspapers."[74] For Landsberg, news reading took the form of code breaking. His method of reading German newspapers suggested his likely familiarity with a state-controlled press gained as a subject of Soviet occupation from 1939 to 1941. He and Rudy believed it was possible first to decipher the overall thrust of the news and then to apply that "key" to the comprehension of different stories.[75] Driven by their desire to get even with the Germans, they seemed to derive a sense of superiority from their news reading system. News reading helped them to maintain their dignity while they hid for months on end in a dark, dank cellar crawl space.

One week later, Landsberg elaborated further about their news reading techniques. "Yes, yes!" he exclaimed. "We are all the more confirmed in our belief that one must know how to read the newspapers."[76] Though they did not trust the precise numbers reported in the papers, he and Rudy tracked, for example, the proportion of German to English planes shot down in order to procure a sense of the Allies' progress. They believed the German press, while always exaggerating the numbers, was in fact revealing a partial truth. Furthermore, they interpreted the printing of trashy articles in a fashion similar to the way in which Steiner looked upon the absence of any mention of fighting on the eastern front: as a good sign because it meant the Germans had space to fill on the page. Chaim Kaplan advanced the same interpretation: "Sometimes we learn more from what is not reported than from what is."[77] Silence, according to their "key," also constituted a piece of indirect news.

Not all diarists believed themselves able to extract kernels of truth from the newspapers, however. There were also diarists who found the newspapers to be incomprehensible. Cypora Zonszajn wrote about the significance of news and rumors in the diary she kept for a brief period in the wake of the deportation in August 1942 of more than ten thousand Jews from the Siedlce ghetto in eastern Poland to Treblinka. In the subsequent months, Zonszajn recorded what she had witnessed during those fateful days, including whatever details she knew about her parents, so that her eleven-month-old daughter "will one day know how they died." She and her daughter were among the two thousand Jews from Siedlce and the surrounding area who had not yet been killed as of November 1942. Her daughter survived the war in the home of Polish friends. Zonszajn allegedly committed suicide shortly after writing the entry that appears below. Knowing of the killing operations at Treblinka, she attempted to make sense of the news that reached her:

> Our lives depend on one thing, news! Who is saying what? What is happening in the stations? Are the wagons rolling, filled with people? Who is new here? What are they telling? On the 6 of November there is a news item in the official paper. It stated that there would be new districts created by combining towns including Warsaw and Lublin. In view of this all the Jews need to be moved there. Siedlce is also named in that group. We don't believe a word of this that they are going to allow us to live. We believe that the verdict will be accomplished in a while. We calm down for a day or two, but even that is not to be allowed. On Sunday we begin to hear that in Lukow, which is one of the

mentioned districts, all the Jews have been gathered together, even the ones in the barracks [. . .] and taken to the outpost. The murmurs, which were not affirmed before, are now true. So what were all the new items, what was the purpose of the newspaper article? We don't know anything, we don't understand anything except that we innocents have been condemned to a terrible and tragic death and we are waiting until the sentence is carried out.[78]

Zonszajn's attitude toward the news betrayed an impossible contradiction. On the one hand, she continued to feel that the news learned both from other people and from newspapers could determine their fate. On the other hand, she understood that the news had little bearing on their futures. They would certainly be killed, as most of the Jewish residents of Siedlce had already been, and she did not delude herself into imagining they could evade their death sentence. Thus, Zonszajn tracked the news despite knowing it was false and finding the entire web of murder and deception to be incomprehensible. They knew nothing and everything at the same time.

Another diarist found the newspapers to be entirely opaque, though for different reasons. Hiding in the same region as Landsberg, Grete Holländer also recorded in her diary her responses to the news. Unlike Landsberg, however, Holländer was not a native of that Polish-Ukrainian borderland. She, her husband, and young daughter had fled there from her hometown of Teschen [Cieszyn] to stay with her husband's family at the outbreak of the war. Holländer began her diary several years later, after she had lost her husband and given her daughter to Ukrainian peasants in an effort to save her, as I will discuss in chapter 4 in greater detail. Holländer had escaped the liquidation of the Czortków ghetto and had fled from another camp thereafter, and she ultimately survived the war in hiding in a tiny village named Świdowa, in the vicinity of Czortków. The Polish farmer who sheltered her and two other Jews sometimes brought them a Polish underground newspaper and German papers to read.

Holländer found the Polish paper to be "very interesting, unfortunately still nothing of significance has happened." She scoured the German papers to unearth any meaningful information, but, in marked contrast to most other diarists, she did not feel rewarded for her efforts. Confounded, she commented, "The newspapers are riddles with 7 seals of which a person can absolutely not make heads or tails. A flood of reports that contradict each other and only the gods know what is really going on."[79] Holländer was unable to find the key to unlock the mystery of the newspapers. By means of the biblical image of the "7 seals," she conveyed the sense that newspapers blocked the path to revelation—to the truth of the war. Though newspapers offered little concrete information, she trusted them more than rumors, even rumors based on alleged radio broadcasts: "Jozek [the Pole who hid her] just returned and delivered barely believable news: Italy is to have finally surrendered. He heard it from a *Volksdeutsche* who owns a radio. [. . .] Unfortunately we have been terribly disappointed so often already that I do not believe anything until it appears in the newspaper."[80] She doubted the local German populace knew any more than she did about what was going on in the war. And, as the front drew nearer, she found the newspaper reports and rumors about the war only became more contradictory, indeed, "the longer things go on, the more confused we become."[81]

Holländer was unable to crack the code of news reports on the basis of knowledge gained either before or during the war. What makes Holländer's confusion revealing is that she had intimate knowledge of German news production. Before going into hiding, she worked in the Czortków office of the *Gazeta Żydowska*, the German-controlled weekly newspaper published for the Jews of the General Government in Poland, a German administrative entity that, after the invasion of the Soviet Union, consisted of the five districts of Cracow, Warsaw, Lublin, Radom, and Galicia. Thus, it was not for lack of familiarity with the workings of German press production that newspaper stories appeared opaque to Holländer. Her sense of being at a loss when reading newspapers suggests that censorship and propaganda were not the only issues. She felt herself to be the object of forces she could not control, and this feeling seemed to be exacerbated by the chaos of news reports. Moreover, with the back and forth of fighting on the eastern front, Holländer's confusion reflected how difficult it could be to figure out what was happening in the war. This is borne out by Klemperer's admissions of confusion during the same period. After the Allied invasion of Italy, he continued to analyze the news, but the complexity of the war seems to have surpassed his analytic ability: "Absolute opacity of the situation. Emphasis on the seat of government being transferred to the Quirinal, that 'in a solemn ceremony'—why solemn?—the king is assuming supreme command of the army. Badoglio's words: 'The war goes on.' But nothing about victory, about common cause with Germany. Only: 'We remain true to our word.' To which one? Who is fighting whom in Italy now? There, too, after all, there is army and SS (Camicie nere). What about the people? The royal house? Where are the Duce and his party? Why did he go? Nothing is clear. And so no conclusion can be drawn as to the new German situation."[82]

Even though some diarists continued to believe themselves able to extract basic information from news reports, during the last two years of the war they were perhaps the exceptions and Holländer the rule. Nevertheless, whether individual Jews perceived newspapers as being ultimately impenetrable or as yielding "flashes of objectivity," they continued to try to develop reading strategies. So, too, Holländer and Klemperer persisted in tracking the contradictory news reports instead of throwing up their hands in frustration and despair.

Emanuel Ringelblum regarded Jews' engagement with literature of all kinds as evidence that "though we have been sentenced to death and know it, we have not lost our human features; our minds are as active as they were before the war."[83] News reading was part of *Amidah*, that is, as mentioned earlier, Jews' efforts to maintain their individual humanity amidst circumstances that were created to negate it. Moreover, news provided Jews with much-needed succor, even though its opacity was often impossible to clear and its truthfulness could not be confirmed. In response to a rumor that the war would not last another year, one woman responded, "Whether it was true or not, that is of no consequence, but the very words comfort, are worth millions."[84] More than for any other reason, Jews tracked news—they became amateur journalists and strategists—in order to find something to give them hope.

WARTIME IMPLICATIONS OF NEWS READING

Jews' reading of war news was inextricable from their desire to keep hope alive. Little about their situation was encouraging, so they looked to news of the war for signs of German weakness, news which could support the forecast of an ultimate Allied victory and their liberation. In trying to make sense of their present circumstances and link them to a redemptive narrative, they not only relied on God or the courts of history, but also set their hopes on the military might of the Allied powers to ensure that Jewish suffering would be avenged.

Some aspects of Jews' wartime attempts to interpret information grew out of earlier practices and applications of reading news, while others were reactions to the particular predicaments Jews faced during the war. As it had been before the war, news reading was an obsession and a form of entertainment, an orientation guide and a medium of social relations. The context had changed, however, the stimulation of modern life in the metropolis being replaced by the horrifying conditions of war and mass murder. In that new context, the implications of news reading differed from what they had been. Now Jews extracted news from various sources in order to map time, not the city, and their timelines became factors in the few decisions some Jews were in a position to make. News reading became the main source of hope for the future. However, after Jews realized that war news would have no bearing on their future, which was different from that of other Europeans, the implications of news reading changed yet again—from hope to despair and greater indifference. How news informed Jews' choices and, most of all, how it shaded their existences during the years of the Holocaust are central issues.

NEWS READING, HOPE, AND FALSE HOPE

During the first half of the war—and despite the steady stream of German victories—news of fighting on the fronts was the foundation of Jewish communal hope. Furthermore, throughout the war and in different contexts, war news functioned as entertainment and as the coin of social relations. Because of its communal and individual importance, news formed the basis of interpretive efforts, arguments, and strategy discussions. For Landsberg and Rudy, who avidly tracked the news from their hiding place in Krzemieniec, reading the news almost took on more significance for them than food. Though famished in the morning when the woman hiding them delivered their food, they would first devour the newspaper if there was one that day: "but who could eat it [the food] when there are newspapers!" Each day, after they had both undressed, tended to their personal hygiene, tidied their bunker, and gotten dressed again, they spent the rest of their time reading and discussing the same three subjects: "'Will they find us?' 'Will we make it?' 'When will the war end and how?'"[85] These two men whiled away the endless hours in hiding by discussing news. Undoubtedly one important factor that underlay their obsession with news was knowing they would be fed every day. Nevertheless, the discussion of news played a major role in helping to sustain them. It broke the monotony of wretched days and became incorporated into their daily routine.[86]

So, too, in Gurs, a concentration camp under Vichy authority in southwestern France, a German Jewish diary writer described the main street, along which Jews gathered and passed on news and rumors, as the "life nerve" [*Lebensnerv*] of the camp. He elaborated, "The street is at the same time the news center where rumors and information are exchanged and commented on, it is stock exchange and marketplace where a person can acquire any valuables, e.g., a piece of bread or even a quarter pound of fat [. . .], it is full of adventures and secrets [. . .] it is relaxation, diversion and life outlet of the camp, everything in one place."[87] The illicit exchanges of food and news—nutritional and moral sustenance—shared sites of relay and comprised the central social interaction in Gurs. Yet the social function played by news in Gurs was different from that of newspapers in the metropolis. Rather than creating "imagined" communities of strangers, the consumption of news required and fostered face-to-face interactions among the camp inmates. News gave them something to talk about.

This sense of news as the currency of social relations was echoed in a diary entry recorded by Kaplan shortly before the creation of the Warsaw ghetto. As he made clear, however, news was not just any currency: it was the currency which, whether real or counterfeit, purchased hope and sustenance. Kaplan described how out-of-work, starving young Jews congregated in small groups in the Warsaw streets in order to hear and pass along the latest news. As in Gurs, it seems that the clandestine exchanges of news and foodstuffs were commingled in the streets of Warsaw in September 1940. For this reason, food and news became geographically and conceptually linked. While food was nutritional sustenance, news was moral sustenance, and they were both for the most part contraband. Kaplan recorded,

> Everyone is hungry for news. [. . .] Small groups of half-starved people, burdened with worries, with pained spirits and dulled eyes, strain their ears for any sound, and the rumors they catch pass in whispers from one to the other, making their way around as open secrets. *And everything, either truthful or fabricated, develops wings within seconds and like an arrow from a bow, it penetrates every corner from one edge of town to the other. And that "news," when it comes back to its father-generator and the one who gave birth to it, has already been transformed beyond recognition. The masses do not have a periodical. And the periodicals of the occupier are considered to be lying. And therefore everyone feeds off rumors. And here we should mention a psychological insight that affirms the proverb: "the will is the father of the idea."* You will never hear a rumor of good news for the murderers. Always they suffer defeats, always the sword is at their throats. The lying radio that the street corner idlers listen to on the sly builds lies upon lies, which are like a balm to their aching hearts. There are many ready customers for these lies [. . .] Any time you meet an acquaintance you hear the stereotyped request: "Open your mouth and tell me what you know. Has anything happened?"[88]

In Kaplan's entry, we again see the conceptual linkage between food and news, between physical hunger and being, in Kaplan's words, "hungry for news." In part because of its scarcity and illicit nature, news had become a precious commodity, and Kaplan employed a metaphor of the marketplace in describing those desperate for news as "ready customers." But news was not some luxury item. Kaplan also suggested that the circulation of news was a broader phenomenon that extended from the most destitute to his own acquaintances, who also hankered after news. War news was an item desperately needed for maintaining the Jewish community's emotional and spiritual strength.

Yet there is another important dimension to Kaplan's description in this entry. In referring to the news as "lies," Kaplan practically accused Jews of not exercising their critical faculties, of being taken in by a bunch of lies out of their desperation for a reason to hope. Elsewhere in his diary, as we have seen, Kaplan portrayed Jewish hopefulness in a more sympathetic light. Here, however, he attributed Jews' optimistic responses to news both to naiveté and to a Jewish predilection to face tragedy with hope.

Other diarists also traced the origins of optimism, disparagingly, to a Jewish predisposition to hope. They expressed a viewpoint much like Kaplan's about Jews' tendency to interpret the news optimistically and thus to derive hope from it. "The well-known optimism and life will of our co-religionists again asserted themselves even in this abnormal situation," remarked Richard Ehrlich, amazed that this quality could persist under the conditions in Theresienstadt.[89] Ehrlich seemed to associate optimism less with a basic disposition toward favorable outcomes than with a markedly Jewish metaphysical faith that good would predominate over evil.

An optimistic response to news or believing in the veracity of a news report, however, were not necessarily the result of naiveté or of Jewish tradition. Certainly the diarists who consciously employed reading strategies were hardly naïve in their consumption of the German press. Nor was optimism necessarily a product of reading the news through the lens of traditional Jewish narratives. Holländer, for example, who often found the newspapers to be opaque, explained her inclination toward optimism by reference to her passion for adventure stories. In an early diary entry, she imagined herself to be a protagonist from one of her favorite novels: "I have always had a great predilection for adventure stories. Life has done me the favor and bestowed upon me the most improbable adventure. But I am an incorrigible optimist. Maybe I will succeed in smuggling myself through."[90] Placing her present experiences in the context of an adventure story and identifying with the heroines of her favorite literary genre—and not Jewish tradition—fueled her optimism that she might make it through the war alive. It was as if the news reports updated her on her own adventure's plot development.

The tendency to derive hope from the news was the prevailing tendency among Jews during the first half of the war. People's extraordinary need for hope led them, as Ringelblum wrote, to "buil[d] complete castles in the air—about an armistice, peace being declared" on the basis of mere rumors.[91] In the words of Arthur Flaum, a diarist imprisoned in Prague, "Optimism makes this life bearable for us."[92] Ringelblum recorded in September 1940 that good news was so important to Jews' morale that they were willing to pay more for newspapers with pictures of the destruction in Germany caused by Allied bombing attacks.[93]

As the war dragged on, Jews did not simply rely on reading strategies that revealed the facts, squeezed through the lines of the German censors; they also developed analytic strategies wherein every piece of news could somehow be turned into good news. Kaplan described how people were able to build feasts of hope from the smallest morsels:

> The English radio, whose listeners endanger their lives, strengthens our hope. [. . .] Every word gives us courage; every small detail that points to any military weakness is carried through the length and breadth of the ghetto as though on eagles' wings, with even the children talking about it. When the news doesn't tell us what we want to hear, we twist and turn it until it seems full of hints, clues, and secrets that support our views. [. . .] Everyone asks everyone else about the news, certain that this time the report will be favorable. And the news from Reuters always contains a certain intonation or expression to satisfy and comfort a spirit thirsting for a speedy and quick redemption.[94]

Optimistic readings of the news sustained Jews who, by 1942, could not "bear it any longer, that's why we try our utmost to see the war's end as imminent."[95] By 1942 and 1943, the search for hope began to outweigh the search for information. "To sit with a death verdict with a little hope, one can hope," explained Kramer, "but to sit and lose hope, one can lose one's mind."[96] Indeed, by the spring of 1942, Kaplan had created a fictional friend, Hirsch, to give voice to his pessimistic analyses in his diary. Whatever else Hirsch accomplished, his presence allowed Kaplan to create distance between himself and his encroaching sense of hopelessness.

Other diarists also recognized the value of illusions. As Fela Szeps wrote in a letter to her brother from the Grünberg camp, "Like you I ask myself if I am not too naïve, if I do not live excessively in a world of illusions? But no other world exists for me. People living under such conditions [. . .] walk through reality blindfolded, dreams are for us the fullness of life."[97] Szeps's assessment of the value of illusions, likely written in early 1942, recalls Kaplan's analysis of the naïve hope that emanated from messianic belief. Tremendously self-aware, Szeps acknowledged that her dreams were an escape from reality and thus delusionary. Yet she stressed that they were a necessary coping strategy.

Because of Jews' extraordinary need for hope, those who expressed pessimistic interpretations of the news could be distrusted or even shunned. Often they were labeled in Yiddish as *Mismakhers,* or people who were up to no good. Writing about the debates that ensued between optimists and pessimists in Theresienstadt, Ehrlich made it clear that optimists—no matter how hopelessly naïve their views—were more popular than pessimists and held the majority among the people he knew in Theresienstadt: "Understandably the war situation and the future of the Jews was also much debated, in which more often than not an optimism that bordered on naiveté came to the fore. Woe is he who dared to have a different opinion; he would become notorious as a pessimist and *Mismakher* and was welcome nowhere."[98] While Ehrlich intimated his own critical view of most Jews' optimism, he did not reveal in this diary entry if he had become one of the unwelcome people. Whether or not he was viewed as a *Mismakher*, the prevailing view of such people was that they hindered people's coping efforts by reciting a narrative nobody wanted to hear.

Flaum, while imprisoned in Prague, did not challenge the validity of a pessimistic reading of Jews' prospects, but he did question the value of publicly expressing such pessimism: "The only one who remains skeptical of all rumors is Dr. Bohrer. A Polish journalist who wrote for various big Polish papers in Prague [. . .] he gathers a large number of people around him every evening and gives lectures mostly on the theme: the civilian as internee. His expositions mostly have a pessimistic undertone. [. . .] Although I am personally opposed to spreading such pessimistic views, among people who are a cut above the others, I like the Doctor very much."[99] While Flaum clearly held Dr. Bohrer in high esteem, he seemed to feel that the journalist was not living up to his responsibility to his fellow Jews to help them endure their period of internment. Pessimism created one more misery to fight against. This viewpoint was in keeping with the basic consensus among all segments of the Jewish population from the start of the war until the winter of 1941 to 1942, namely, that their goal should be the maintenance of Jewish existence in defiance of German efforts to deplete and kill large numbers of Jews.[100] Flaum implied that, to the extent that optimism helped sustain Jewish life, it should be commended. Thus, a strategy of optimistic if self-deceptive news reading was part of a larger strategy of Jewish perseverance. Interpreting the news was commonly regarded by people at the time as central to Jewish communal endurance.

Diarists' references to optimists and pessimists often created the impression that they were entrenched positions; indeed, Holländer went so far as to ascribe a metaphor of war, "the Bunkerfront," to the strife between her, "an incorrigible optimist," and one of her bunker mates, "the habitual prophet of misfortune [*Gewohnheitsunglücksprophet*] Ozias."[101] Yet the two attitudes were more akin to roles people played and became associated with in public discussion. Klemperer, for example, confessed that "in the Jews' House I always play the role of the optimist. But I am not quite sure of my position at all."[102] Since the tidings of the war changed constantly, it was impossible to maintain one stance consistently. Thus, optimism did not take on the quality of a fixed outlook but was one moment in time, one swing of a pendulum, between hope and despair. Flaum wrote in the fall of 1939, "I so vacillate between hope and depression that I do not know how I am feeling." He described the progression from upbeat rumor to optimistic prediction to disappointment and despair in cyclical terms. When a new rumor unleashed a new wave of hope, he commented, "The same game begins again."[103] Nevertheless, his awareness of the cycle did not preclude his succumbing to hope. Klemperer also illustrated how variable his and other Jews' moods were: "My mood and that in the Jews' House changes daily, almost hourly. England has occupied Iran: Up. Will Turkey go with Germany? Down. [. . .] "At Zscheischler's bakery five women said 'Good Afternoon,' two said 'Heil Hitler.'" Up. At Ölsner's they all said 'Heil Hitler.' Down."[104] In May 1941, Ringelblum recorded that even the most committed optimists were losing hope in the face of news of Allied defeats in North Africa and Greece.[105] In the meantime, another Warsaw ghetto inhabitant recorded in the same month that the "sworn pessimists" had found reason to hope. In response to the sensational story, reported in German newspapers, that Hitler's deputy, Rudolf Hess, had flown to England on a self-appointed mission to make peace: "The sworn pessimists, who never doubted a German victory[,] are now the loudest of all, asserting that this is exactly what they predicted, that thus must Hitler end. Those that had only yesterday urged to start preparing for the winter self-relief program turned into believers in the opening of peace talks not later than tomorrow."[106] At least until 1942 or 1943, individuals moved back and forth regularly between hopeful and despairing interpretations of the news.[107]

As vulnerable to pessimism as hopeful interpretations of the news were, they nonetheless dominated public discourse. Optimism sustained Jews' morale—the only thing most people *could* control in an otherwise impossible situation. In addition, there were times when news interpretations and the hope they nourished became the basis for individuals' potentially life-altering decisions.

DECISION MAKING BASED ON HOPE

Until the mass deportations of Jews to death camps began in 1942 and became somewhat known in the following months, deriving hope from the news about the prospects of Jewish communities in Europe was possible, if also changeable. The hope people extracted was based on their estimates of the war's duration. On the most general level, Jews interpreted news about fighting on the eastern front and in North Africa and Italy to calculate a timetable to German defeat and their own liberation. Depending on their forecasts, some individuals who were in positions to do so made decisions about whether to relocate or when to go into hiding. They factored news into their strategies for taking potential life-saving courses of action and practicing subversive tactics. The optimism or pessimism they derived from the news still yielded them highly tangible results.[108]

The identical news story could inspire differing predictions of German defeat and differing plans for hiding or taking subversive action. Within two days of one another in December 1941, Grete Steiner, the artistic-scientific German Jewish news reader in Zeist, Holland, and a young woman in Poland named Elsa Binder, who was known as Eliszewa, recorded the same piece of news in their diaries. "A stunning turn of events," wrote Steiner on December twenty-second in response to the news that Hitler had taken over as sole commander in chief of the German armed forces. It was "an obvious sign of decline," she thought, in light of Goebbels's request of the preceding night that German civilians donate any and all winter clothing for German soldiers fighting in Russia. Steiner no longer believed "that Germany will keep it together even 3 months more."[109] Two weeks before this announcement, Steiner had expressed her firm conviction that the war would not last much longer, despite the fact that other people around her thought the war would continue for two more years. Hitler's taking over the reins of the military confirmed what she already believed, that "Germany is actually already beaten."[110]

Over the next two months, despite the ups and downs of the Allied war effort and her first mention in the diary of deportations of Jews from another town in Holland "to a camp [*Kamp*]," Steiner remained hopeful the war would end soon. She rejected her daughter's suggestion in mid-February to move to Amsterdam: "One cannot see into the future, too many precautions can just put us in danger. We wait here calmly, whatever happens. [. . .] In spite of all the Jap[anese] successes and the failures of the Eng[lish] and Amer[icans], we are very much expecting a speedy end."[111] Many factors undoubtedly contributed to Steiner's decision to stay in Zeist, among them the network of people she had created there, independent of her children, and her sense that Jews in Zeist were subject to fewer restrictions than those in Amsterdam, where a curfew was already in effect. Moreover, if she had wanted to find a hiding place, it was generally easier to secure shelter outside of Amsterdam in small towns, although it is also extremely unlikely she would have done so as early as February 1942, when deportations of Jews in Holland to Poland were not yet under way. Nevertheless, her belief in "a speedy end" to the war, supported by her interpretations of news reports, likely contributed to her assessment that the safest option was to stay put and wait out the remainder of the war.[112] One month later, on March twenty-eighth, Steiner's diary ended. I do not know what happened to her thereafter. Most likely, she was deported to Poland via the Dutch transit camp Westerbork and killed in Auschwitz or Sobibór.[113]

Writing about the same news from the Stanislawów ghetto, Eliszewa recorded the seemingly wild speculations of Jews in response to the story from, "yesterday's newspaper [. . .] that 'the Fuehrer' took over the army high command." She stood apart from the ghetto rumor mill in her recounting and used the grammatical third person to refer to other people's responses: "Jews draw the most far-reaching and most auspicious conclusions from it. And so: Hitler, seeing his imminent defeat, and the hasty retreat of his till now invincible army, wanting [. . .] also to consolidate the entire command under one man, took this commission upon himself." For many people in the Stanisławów ghetto, this story was the first instance of renewed hope since 12 October, when ten thousand Stanisławów Jews had been taken to a cemetery and shot.[114] In contrast to other Jews in Stanisławów, however, and to Steiner in Holland, Eliszewa clearly did not believe this was proof of Germany's "imminent defeat." "The Reds [Red Army] advance slowly but steadily," she wrote, indicating her sense that Germany would eventually lose the war, just not that winter.[115]

Although Eliszewa did not succumb to the general optimism about the war's proximate end, she did share another assumption common at the time. Like other Jews in Stanisławów, she believed the Germans would spare the lives of those Jews with work assignments. Despite the rumors that the Red Army had "not found a single Jew" when they took back Kharkow, she believed that, "for Jews today [the question of work] is a matter of 'to be or not to be.'" This was confirmed by the combination of German orders that every man from age twelve to sixty-five and every women from age eighteen to thirty-five was required to perform forced labor and of rumors that a camp was being built for young women.[116] Three weeks later, when her name appeared on the list drawn up by the Judenrat, the Jewish Council under German control, of people who would receive work, she thought it was "pleasant news," even though she did not feel it ensured her survival. She prayed that her strength would hold out.[117] Eliszewa continued to record entries in her diary until 18 June 1942. From March until June, weeks passed between entries, whereas previously, in December and January, she had written every few days. Her last entry trails off midsentence, and her fate is unknown. The Germans resumed mass roundups and shootings of Jews in Stanisławów during the summer of 1942 and sent transports to Bełżec during September and October. Her diary was found by a Polish secondary school teacher in a ditch along the road that led to the cemetery where Stanisławów's Jews were executed.[118]

Certainly in Eliszewa's situation, and arguably in Steiner's as well, there was nothing they could do in response to the news to save their own lives. Desperate efforts to procure a position in a workshop or factory were rewarded with hard labor and a briefly delayed death.[119] Though little substantive information was available outside of Poland about the fate of Jews in Poland, Jews in western and Central Europe heard enough to imagine that conditions in Poland were far worse than those in Germany, Holland, and France.[120] Nevertheless, that did not make it financially or logistically feasible for the overwhelming majority of Jews to avoid deportation by going underground. And while hiding was a means of rescue for some, it was far from a guarantee of survival.[121] Most Jews, therefore, were not in a position to make life-altering decisions, and the few who were usually managed only to postpone their fate for a period of weeks or months. One exception, not to be altogether discounted, was Holländer, who recorded from her hiding place that good news from the front temporarily drowned out her and her two bunker mates' thoughts of suicide.[122] Since the three of them survived the war, war news could be regarded as one factor in their survival.

Despite the limitations on Jews' power to act, individual decision making on the basis of interpretations of news constitutes another dimension of the implications of news reading for Jews during the war. As Jews struggled to make sense of what was happening to them, they used news to stoke the fire of hope that their present suffering would soon end. When hope was smothered, the implications of news reading fundamentally changed.

THE END OF HOPE

Reading the news to calculate a timetable to liberation preoccupied Jews and non-Jews alike. Yet for Jews the significance of the war's duration changed dramatically with the mass killings of Jews, begun in the wake of Germany's invasion of the Soviet Union on 22 June 1941. The expansion of the war had brought millions more Jews under German control in eastern Europe and, soon thereafter, the tightening of the vise on Jews in western and Central Europe. Although Jews' knowledge of the means and the scope of Germany's annihilation of European Jewry varied, many understood that their future as a collectivity was in jeopardy. Before 1942, most Jews had assumed that Germany would ultimately be defeated and that the end of the war would usher in a return to normal life. In 1942, many Jews began to realize that the outcome of the war might no longer decide their fate. As a result, during the second half of the war, optimism as a viable communal emotional and interpretive posture fell away.

Those Jews who were still alive in Poland in 1943 generally assumed they would eventually be killed. Szeps now wrote, "We placidly surrender ourselves to the report that no one will remain alive, that very likely towards the end they will make a mass grave for us, as the girls say, they will wall us in behind the doors and let the gas in, the beds will be our graves, the cabinets our monuments, the future will find our name according to the numbering."[123] Szeps exhibited a jumbled knowledge of the methods employed by the Germans to murder the Jews. Nevertheless, by this point it was clear to her that working in a forced labor camp would not safeguard her life. Unlike rumors about war fighting, which were difficult to confirm and changed daily, the information available on the fate of the Jews through eyewitness reports corroborated the most horrific rumors and fears. Indeed, several diarists in Poland looked back on the events of 1942 to set down at what moment it had become clear to them that the Germans intended to murder all Jews. One diarist after another had reached the conclusion that no segment of the Jewish population would be spared when the Germans began to deport Jews during that year regardless of their designation as workers.[124]

The perpetration of genocide radically altered the implications of war news. Klemperer recorded in October 1942 that even though new rumors of peace negotiations between Italy and the United States brought renewed hope that Germany would soon be defeated, such news could no longer provide succor to Jews: "But the earlier distinction between optimistic and pessimistic Jews can no longer be maintained. Everyone, but everyone, says the same thing, usually formulated in exactly the same way: 'They are lost in the foreseeable future, utterly lost, but if things don't happen quickly—and it does not look as if they will—they will finish us off first.' Truly murder is horribly at our heels as never before."[125] Klemperer registered an emotional shift in Jews' response to the news as the pace of deportations of west and Central European Jews to Poland accelerated. Whereas previously optimistic and pessimistic interpretations of the news had both garnered supporters, now pessimism was the only legitimate position. Disagreements over varying interpretations of the news were replaced by a unanimous despair that the war's outcome would have no bearing on the fate of the Jews.

Landsberg, who had described in detail his and his bunker mate's news reading techniques the previous month, communicated a fear that matched Klemperer's in his mention of the war news of late December 1942. Landsberg had learned from the person who sheltered him "that things are going well on the front. In Brody a massacre is taking place. They say H.'s order is that by New Year's not a single Jew should exist on German occupied territory."[126] While the timetable for killing the Jews was exaggerated, the overall sense conveyed by Landsberg revealed a cognizance of a changed reality. The war news may have been favorable, but as far as news of the fate of the Jews was concerned, it was devastating.

This consciousness that the war's end would not bring about the resumption of Jewish communal life reverberated throughout Jews' diaries from the last three years of the war. Diarists in Poland, in particular, who wrote in the wake of mass shootings and deportations to extermination camps and still feared for their lives, conveyed both their desperate yearning for liberation and the sense that liberation could not offset the irreparable destruction of families and entire communities that had already occurred. One diarist who, together with his wife, crouched in a field for almost three weeks trying to escape deportation to Bełżec and secure a hiding place for their one-year-old son, recorded, "We are looking forward to some political changes, which alas are failing to materialize. The 'Second Front' is but a fairy tale taken out of 'A Thousand and One Nights.' When will it come — when not even a single Jew will remain alive here?"[127] Four months later, Kramer, who had compared German reports to English radio broadcasts from her hiding place in Żółkiew, wrote, "It is already twelve months that we are sitting here. I don't see any help from anywhere. They fight on the eastern front, on the western front. They confer in Moscow, but it's all moving with the pace of a tortoise. There are not many Jews left, only in the concentration camps. They are being killed every day. Every day that passes decides the life (or rather the death) of many Jews. Hitler keeps his word. He killed all of the Jews and now he starts on the converts."[128] Szeps echoed the disjuncture between the outcome of the war and the fate of the Jews: "Though admittedly the political news is very good, their defeat comes crashing down on our heads. The *Judenvernichtung* [extermination of the Jews] is nearing completion."[129] While the Allies might win the war, Holländer, the self-described optimist, raged, "For [the Jews], the war is already lost."[130] Analyzing war news no longer helped these diarists to make sense of their predicament; news of fighting on the fronts had lost its collective meaning.

For some Jews, the meaninglessness of war news insofar as their own fate was concerned made them increasingly indifferent toward it. Klemperer reported that, among Jews in Dresden, a disinterest in the news had become more widespread by November 1942: "We do not see any newspapers for days on end and know even less about the true situation than the Aryans. Since they started preparing their departure for the barracks, our fellow-sufferers have lost all taste for political events."[131] "There are changes in the political situation, but we have other things on our mind than politics," wrote a mother in hiding in Amsterdam in a diary addressed to her children. "We are accustomed to the nearness of death, and we are hungry and there is nothing to eat."[132] A woman in the Riga ghetto wrote in a letter to her sister, who was hiding outside the ghetto, "We don't have news [about] what is going on in the world. We are so scared about our everyday living, that we really have no time to ask what is going on on the front line."[133] For these diarists, world news had ceased to be relevant to their daily struggles.

Most diarists writing in the last years of the war did continue to track political

news. For them, it still had individual meaning, even if it had become meaningless on a collective level. In hiding in a Pole's apartment in Warsaw, Calel
Perechodnik recorded his and his bunker mates' response to the newspaper in
midsummer 1943:

> In the evening when our lady arrives, we grab the newspaper, read the com
> muniqué, and, depending on the text, the next day is either good or bad. [. . .]
> We had to believe our eyes: Marshal Badoglio had taken over the government
> of Italy. We could not sleep the entire night for the excitement; it was both
> joyful and painful at one time. Joyful because we had lived to have the satis
> faction that the war would soon be over, that our suffering would end—but
> at the same time our hearts wept at the thought that our wives had not lived
> to this happy moment. The same thought came to our minds: We longed for
> the end of the war, prayed for its early termination, and at the same time we
> trembled at the thought that the war would end. Where would we go then?
> With whom would we celebrate? [134]

News of the war continued to influence some Jews' moods, even though its significance had changed. War news, which had earlier meant the end of the war
and, with it, the end of Jewish suffering, still promised the longed-for lifting of
Jews' death sentence. Now, however, the possibility no longer existed of sharing that joy with loved ones. A woman in Bergen-Belsen, upon hearing the announcement of a prisoner exchange, wrote in her diary to her husband, who had
died four months earlier in Bergen-Belsen at age fifty-four, "My love, how we
had hoped for this moment, and now I shall have to conquer all of life through
everything by myself." [135]

Individual Jews still clung to the hope that they would survive, yet they struggled with the issue of why they continued to want to survive if there was no longer
any chance of being reunited with family and community. When Szeps tried
to fantasize about life after liberation she found herself unable to do so: "I will
leave, I will set out from G. [Grünberg], for home—to where? to home? to which
home, where do I have a home? To whom will I go? [. . .] I do not have the courage to commit suicide, some kind of subconscious awareness in me wants to live,
to live! Yet on the other hand, I cannot imagine that life, that future without my
nearest and dearest." [136] Holländer also wondered why she and her bunker mates
wanted to live: "For seven months we have been sitting in the bunker. What are
we expecting and what are we hoping for anyway?" [137] And Gabriel Mermall, who
hid in the Carpathian Mountains with his six-year-old son, asked similar questions in an entry from 20 September 1944 of his diary-memoir: "If we got out of
this alive, where would we go? Who would be alive—wife, brother, sister, friend?

Would there still be a house to go to, my beautiful house? There would probably be no one and nothing left."[138]

Whereas previously the projected end of the war had signaled the resumption of a collective future, at this time it augured merely an individual future devoid of content. For Katzenelson, the future was unbearable: "What kind of survival is this when the whole of your nation has perished!"[139] Almost two years after his wife and two of his three sons were deported to Treblinka, Katzenelson and his only remaining son were killed in Auschwitz. Szeps likewise expressed her fear about the meaninglessness of the extermination of the Jews and liberation: "But maybe it is not at all the beginning of something new, only the end of what was?"[140]

News reading filled many functions for Jews during the Holocaust. Throughout the war, the reading of ephemera distracted and entertained when other forms of literature were scarce. The discussion of news was central to social interactions in many different wartime circumstances. The unreliability of news sources allowed for a culture of interpretation and argument to be built around it. Most of all, Jews read the news in their quest for hope, and during the first half of the war, they were rewarded for their efforts. Many Jews developed strategies of "hopeful reading," which allowed them to find hope even in the slimmest bits of news and silence. Indeed, the hope they extracted from the news had political connotations for it helped Jews to persevere in the face of escalating persecution.

During the second half of the war, news reading no longer furnished Jews with the answers they sought about the future. Up to roughly 1942, its implications had been collective: the hope for the future was a collective hope that the war's end would bring with it the resumption of European Jewish life. For this reason, Jews read war news and news of the fate of fellow Jews with equal interest since it was all perceived as being personally relevant. Around mid-1942, however, when news trickled out that the Germans were in the process of killing the entire Jewish population of vast swathes of eastern Europe, the implications of war news changed as the collective hope for liberation became an individual hope. Many diarists who apprehended the scope of the genocide continued to be desperate for news of German military defeats and still calculated how much longer they would have to stay alive in order to see liberation. Yet they now understood the war's timeline to be separate from the fate of the Jews as a collectivity, and the hope for the future was for individual survival. Other diarists, bereft of their families and communities, became increasingly indifferent toward the news as they tried to imagine a future alone. Having gained knowledge of genocide, they could no longer read the news to construct a narrative that connected their fate to that of other Europeans. Thus, a rupture in hope for the future existed here as much as in Kaplan's and Dreyfus's diaries.

This account of news-reading strategies and goals should be seen as more than just a catalogue of a set of Jewish activities during the war. It is a particular and significant example of the struggle of interpretation and meaning making that Jews waged during the war. If Kaplan and Dreyfus wondered into which framework of history or theology they could place unfolding events, many more Jews struggled with interpretation at a much more human level. Rather than wondering about God and history, they pondered the implications of frontline movements for their own liberation. They tried to make sense of the propaganda and reportage in order to plot or imagine their own futures. And, at perhaps a deeper level, they tried to construct narratives around what they learned that pointed toward a happy ending. From their code breaking, they built narratives of hope. Thus, their struggle of news analysis was always also a struggle about sustaining their hope, sustaining their belief in their future.

Clearly, Jewish diarists dedicated a large portion of their diaries to the discussion of news. Of course, diarists were not only consumers of news; they were also engaged in the process of relaying news to others in the form of their diaries. Indeed, many Jews were motivated to write diaries in order to inform their loved ones and the world at large about their wartime experiences out of their concern that otherwise the Germans would be the only source of information about their experiences.

4

FAMILY CORRESPONDENTS

For some diarists, diary writing was predominantly a family affair. For families that were separated during the war, diaries became an essential medium for communicating thoughts and experiences, albeit in an imaginary form, to absent loved ones, a function we have already caught a glimpse of in Lucien Dreyfus's wartime diary writing.[1] Since no means of open communication were available to Jews living under German occupation, diaries became a form of correspondence, and correspondence became a form of diary writing, with diaries quite literally addressed to missing individuals. These letter-diaries were marked by the physical and epistemological distance separating the diarist and intended family-readers, while at the same time they attempted to bring the correspondents closer together.[2] Fathers and mothers, sisters and brothers tried desperately to bridge the separations that had been imposed upon them despite being unable to guarantee the delivery of their efforts. For them, diaries were, if not life-and-death concerns, psychological and emotional tools for dealing with the disruption of intimate family relations during the Holocaust.

Unlike diarists who wrote for an audience of strangers, among them Chaim Kaplan, the authors of these letter-diaries rarely envisioned their diaries serving a political function. Diarists who wrote for the world at large sought to contribute to the exaction of justice after the war, whether through history, legal proceedings, or violent retribution. Diarists who wrote to their loved ones had arguably more modest goals in mind. Perhaps this is why so few of these diaries have been published: at first glance, they do not seem to treat the larger Holocaust themes with which we have grown familiar, in particular the theme of resistance. Yet they shed light on several aspects of Jewish life during the war, including the wartime situation of families, parents' emotional responses to sending their children

away, and how the concepts of family that people held continued to root them
in the world beyond German occupation—the world of normal life.

In showing how diaries and letters became intermeshed for some Jews during
the war, I want to revisit the question of how to define literary genres. With some
recent exceptions, literary scholars have argued that correspondence and diaries,
though closely related, are ultimately different from one another. Scholars distinguish the two on the basis of their intended audiences. Whereas it is generally
assumed that letters are written with a specific audience in mind, diaries are often
considered to be more personal documents, intended for the writer's own eyes
and affording the diarist a medium to externalize his or her inner emotional life
and potentially to experiment with styles of expression. As Isaac Disraeli wrote,
"We converse with the absent by letters, and with ourselves by diaries."[3] But an
analysis of diaries addressed to absent family members by Jewish men and women
during the Holocaust years breaks down such clear-cut distinctions. By looking
at the function of these texts as both diaries and letters—as both inner dialogues
and more public exchanges—we can analyze more specifically their complex
instrumentalities. Jewish diarists adapted preexisting forms of diaries and correspondence to fit their wartime circumstances. For this subset of diarists, diaries
served a range of functions.

First, diaries addressed to absent family members were a means of mitigating
the effects of distance, a function typically reserved for correspondence. Indeed,
scholars' analyses of nineteenth- and twentieth-century Europeans' family correspondence offer pertinent insights into these Holocaust diaries. Just as the individual act of writing a letter was also a social act that reaffirmed the coherence of
a family in the face of separation, so too diaries written by Jews to their families
functioned both as opportunities to unburden emotions and as instruments for
maintaining some semblance of family relations.[4] In the case of parents writing
to their children, through their diaries they attempted to "parent at a distance,"
as the scholar Jenny Hartley has put it.[5] Parents anticipated that, if they were
killed, their children would face an excruciating emotional struggle after the
war. They used their diaries to try to ease their children's burden of mourning.
Furthermore, diarists who wrote to their children as well as those who wrote to
other family members sought to bridge the epistemological gap created by their
wartime experiences. They recognized that the boundary separating those inside
German occupation from those outside was not merely geographical, and they
tried to inform their loved ones about the workings of this horrific world.

Second, Jews who wrote diaries for their families were drawing upon traditional uses of diaries as well. When parents counseled their children about how

to behave ethically, they were perpetuating the historical use of diaries as a moral tool. In addition, the efforts of diarists to relay news about their wartime experiences were related to the long-established function of diaries as sites for recording family history.[6] The malleability of the diary form, evident in its various uses historically, made it a convenient vehicle for people who were isolated and facing death.

Last, a discussion of family requires going beyond what the texts did or attempted to do. These diaries were more than a means of communication; they also are windows onto the meaning of family itself for these diary writers. In writing to family members, particularly children whose survival seemed assured, these diarists projected a view of the postwar future as a resumption of Jewish history and of the values of liberal enlightened society. Rather than a Jewish future devoid of content as a result of the destruction of family and community, some Jews continued to envision a return to normal life after the war.[7] Consequently, in and through their diaries, these individuals projected an image of the future that differed from that of the post-1942 news readers. As they imagined the continuity of their own families, they could envision the continuity of Jewish history. The survival of children, in particular, meant that the future would not be rendered meaningless by the Nazis, even if they could not take part in that future. Thus, like news readers, Jews who wrote diaries for their families adapted their notions of the future over the course of the war. Yet their divergent visions of the future reveal not only a range of responses among Jews, but also that people's responses were affected by their personal circumstances as well as by their understanding of the scope of the Germans' murderous actions.

SEPARATION AND POWERLESSNESS

All of the diarists I discuss in this chapter were separated from their loved ones as a result of the spread of German authority. Yet the specific circumstances that created the separations varied depending on where the diarists were located. For German Jews, the breakup of families began in 1933, following the advent of Hitler to the German chancellorship. Discriminatory measures against Jews were put into effect within the first three months of the Third Reich, and around 37,000 Jews left Germany that year. Many initially went to other European countries in the hope that the National Socialist regime would be short-lived and they would soon be able to return home. Between 1933 and 1937, almost one-quarter of German Jews left Germany, despite the difficulties posed by increasingly restrictive immigration laws in most countries to which they hoped to gain entry.

As persecution intensified in 1938, the number of émigrés rose steeply. By the end of 1939, the German Jewish population had declined to 190,000 from a high of approximately 525,000 in January 1933.[8]

Jews over the age of forty tended to stay in Germany, whereas the majority of children and adults under that age left. The age discrepancy among German Jewish émigrés is most striking when one compares the percentage of children and youth to the percentage of elderly who left Germany. By September 1939, 83 percent of German Jews between the ages of sixteen and twenty-four and 82 percent of children up to age sixteen had managed to leave Germany. In stark contrast, only 27 percent of Jews over age sixty emigrated during the same period.[9] There were a variety of reasons for this generational divide among German Jewish émigrés, from the health-related (many older men and women did not feel physically capable of making such a dramatic life change), to the professional (it was much more difficult for people, usually men, who were long established in middle-class professions to accept the social and economic demotion that necessarily followed from starting over in a new country), to the logistical (it was generally easier to secure visas for youth than for older people, and the Nazis placed barriers in the way of emigrating with one's property and savings, which also made it all the more difficult to procure visas). What this meant was that thousands of parents remained in Germany after having sent off their children and grandchildren.[10]

Parents expressed relief that their children would be spared the worsening persecution by leaving Nazi Germany. They also were tormented by their powerlessness as they watched their children set out into the unknown. Their children would have to contend with financial insecurity, life with strangers, new languages, and homesickness all alone. Willy Cohn, a *Gymnasium* teacher, medieval historian, and lifelong diary writer in Breslau, turned to his diary immediately after saying good-bye to his daughter, Ruth. They were never to see each other again. Ruth left home in September 1939 in the hope of making her way to Denmark. From Denmark, she ended up on a Youth Aliyah, a group of young Jews that emigrated to Palestine, one year later and survived the war there. Her parents and two younger sisters were deported from Breslau to Kovno in November 1941 and murdered in Fort Nine.[11] At the time of her initial departure, as she headed to the Breslau train station with her mother and sister, her father mentally accompanied her in his diary:

> Now the third child has also left home; will we ever see her again in this lifetime? One can't conceive of it. In a quarter of an hour Ruth's train leaves. [. . .] It is hard to say what one is feeling at such a moment [. . .]. But one has to accept the fact that it is for the best for the child. [. . .] That we have to release

her on her life path so prematurely and alone is what is tragic about this era; but maybe it is the best thing for her. The generations before us also became independent at this age. While I am writing these lines, she is already now sitting in the train, which will leave Breslau in a minute. Then her youth in her *Heimat* is concluded [*abgeschlossen*]. But I believe she will carry with her in life fine memories of her youth; we have always lived for the children. Now the train is already gone, and Trudi [her mother] will have cried a lot. She is the oldest daughter, and in the first years of her life she was a problem child [*Sorgenkind*], now when she could be a support for us she has to go. But one must not think of oneself, only of the child.[12]

While Cohn was not addressing his daughter in the diary, evident in this entry are the ambivalence he felt in sending her away and his feeling of powerlessness. Her departure signified a door closing, not only on her youth, but also on her life in Germany and on their intimate relationship as father and daughter. He tried, however, to block his feelings of helplessness as a parent and to focus on the practical benefits of this decision for Ruth. To reassure himself, he placed her forced and hastened entry into adulthood in the context of previous generations' coming of age. In this way, he attempted to normalize Ruth's setting out on her own even though she was only an adolescent. While Cohn did seem able to convince himself that Ruth would manage, he was less able to fight off the feeling that he and his wife might not. They would sorely miss the emotional support of their children as they struggled daily with the ever harsher restrictions imposed upon Jews. Cohn abruptly reprimanded himself for not thinking solely of his child.

Like Cohn, many parents felt their powerlessness most acutely at the time of their children's emigration. Before the Nazis came to power, Erich Frey and his wife, Elsbeth, lived in a middle-class suburb of Berlin with their two daughters, Liselott and Miriam (Marie-Anne), born in 1918 and 1922, respectively. Frey, born in 1889, was a Berlin native of the same generation as Kaplan and Dreyfus. Erich and Elsbeth Frey's two daughters emigrated from Germany before the start of the war, first Liselott to England and later Miriam to Palestine. Miriam, like Willy Cohn's daughter, Ruth, went to Palestine with the Youth Aliyah.[13] Erich Frey articulated his and his wife's inability to protect and assist their children in a poem he wrote for Miriam at the time of her emigration in August 1939. He was clearly relieved that she was leaving Germany: "It is impossible for you to live here / where the torment increases day by day." He also trusted that she would create a better life for herself in Palestine "as a free person and Jewess / with a strong will and trust in God / tilling your land in hard labor." Yet, he repeated the identical line in the first two stanzas of the poem: "All we can give you is our blessing."[14] As the refrain of the poem, this line—"All we can give you is our blessing"—conveyed his and his wife's impotence in the face of their daughter's departure. In addition to the separation, Frey's powerlessness to assure their daughters' financial well-being may have been especially painful for him (and for other middle-class German Jews). Even before his daughters emigrated, they had had to give up many of their possessions and move to a smaller apartment in Berlin-Karlshorst. What was perhaps harder to accept was that, although Frey still had a good position with the Agil real estate and mortgage brokerage firm—a job he was forced to leave on account of his being a Jew in February 1940—under the circumstances, their ability to look after their children was limited, and all they could do was sanction their independence.

The German invasion of Poland in September 1939 split up many Polish Jewish families as well. In this case the physical separations primarily resulted from two situations. The first consisted of Jews fleeing to Soviet-occupied eastern Poland from western and central Poland. During the first three months of the war, perhaps as many as three hundred thousand Jews reached eastern Poland to escape the invading German army, including many young adults who left their older parents behind. Jews also ended up in eastern Poland because Germans attempted to force them over the German-Soviet line of demarcation into Soviet-occupied Polish territory.[15] The second situation consisted of parents who hid their infants and young children in Christian homes and religious institutions, especially after the Germans began to liquidate the ghettos.

Among this second set of parents was Grete Holländer, the self-declared optimist who read newspapers in a bunker in eastern Poland later in the war.[16] Initially, Holländer's nuclear family remained intact. She, her husband, and young daughter survived the years of Soviet occupation together, having fled eastward to escape German occupation. After the Germans overran eastern Poland, however, this state of affairs did not last long. Holländer's husband was killed by the Germans, and the sole responsibility for their daughter, Sonja, fell to her. Even more than Cohn and Frey, whose children left Germany before the start of the war, Holländer realized that her daughter's life was in jeopardy in the Czortków ghetto. Soon thereafter Holländer became one of many Jewish parents throughout Europe who were lucky enough to find someone who would take in their children, and thus she joined the ranks of parents who were separated from their children.

The feelings of powerlessness and ambivalence voiced by Cohn and Frey in sending away their teenage daughters were all the more acute for parents who gave over their young children to non-Jews. After Holländer and her daughter were almost seized in an *Aktion* in November 1942, she became fixated on how to get Sonja out of the ghetto. Sonja wanted to leave, undeterred by the prospect of being separated from her mother if it meant escaping the ghetto. More than a year after Holländer had entrusted her daughter to a Ukrainian couple, she reflected on the act in her diary: "Sometimes I was sad that she did not at all regret having to part from me for an undetermined period of time, but then I said to myself, that I should be happy that she was so sensible. Other children would not go away from their mother for any price in the world and my little one longed for the day when she would finally be rescued from the ghetto."[17] When the Ukrainian couple who had agreed to shelter Sonja came to pick her up a few weeks later, "Sonja played her role superbly, spoke perfect Ukrainian after barely three weeks, prayed flawlessly in church, and appeared to have forgotten that she had recently been in the ghetto."[18] Although Holländer expressed pride in her daughter's superb acting job, her feelings were tempered by ambivalence over her daughter's dissociation from her. She wanted to keep her daughter close, but much more important to her was to try to ensure her daughter's survival. The condition of saving Sonja's life, however, was to accept her abandonment of her identity both as her daughter and as a Jew.[19]

Though Jewish parents struggled to spare their children from persecution and extermination, most were unable to do so. Approximately a million and a half of the Jews killed by the Germans were children.[20] Those parents who were fortunate enough to get their children out of German-occupied Europe still wrestled with the issue of how to care for them from a distance. As the above passages indicate, several parents adopted diary writing as a strategy to address their powerlessness and continue to perpetuate relationships with their children.

PARENTING AT A DISTANCE

Upon separation, parents like Cohn and Frey became desperate for news of their children. The historian Marion Kaplan captured parents' distress over being separated from their children by recalling the German expression from that time "children turned into letters" (*aus Kindern wurden Briefe*), which connoted that the intimate parent-child relationship had been replaced by a physically distant one in which letters served as the only point of connection.[21] Frey, for example, wrote to his daughters that "anguish and separation from you probably were the main cause of Mom's illness."[22] Under the circumstances, correspondence became exceedingly important. In their diaries, parents took care to note the receipt of any letter or postcard from their children or any news they heard about their children from a third party. Often months passed without word. Diarists

intimated their tremendous disappointment and feeling of isolation by recording when they did not receive mail as well as when they did. Cohn referred to
this sporadic correspondence as "the fate of Jewish parents in this period." He
found it to be "almost grotesque" that, as a father, he did not know how his children were faring. "For a loving father's heart," the lack of correspondence with
his children was "the worst."[23] The lack of mail reinforced his and other parents'
feeling of powerlessness.

As "children turned into letters," so too did parents turn into letters. Not only
did parents desperately await mail from their children, they also wanted to communicate their thoughts and experiences *to* their children. They wanted to inform them of their fates and those of other members of their family. As the war
expanded and became prolonged and parents' hopes of supplying information in
person after the war dimmed, the written word assumed even more importance.
At the same time, as we have seen, people could often write only postcards, and
they could write only guardedly in those cards or, when permitted, in longer letters, wary of attracting the attention of censors. A further problem was the delivery of mail, which was erratic at best. Thus, a variety of factors contributed to
the intermingling of diary and letter writing. Unable to write openly about their
experiences in letters — if they were able to communicate by post at all — many
parents began to write to their children in other forms.

Some parents wrote diaries in place of or in addition to correspondence. The
texts I refer to as letter-diaries were typically organized in dated entries, although
some were written as one long letter or as a series of letters. In these texts, parents
imagined themselves speaking to their children, although they could not receive
a reply. Writers addressed their recipients in direct speech, using the grammatical second person. Rather than attempt to get the texts to their children during
the war, they deferred delivery, frequently giving them to someone for safekeeping until after the war's end.[24]

Frey, for example, wrote to his daughters in his diary from Berlin in the spring
of 1942, when he could no longer send them mail directly. Indeed, in the first
paragraph of his letter-diary, addressed to his "Beloved children Liselott and
Miriam," he explicitly referred to the prohibition on sending letters, implying
that one motivation for his starting to write was his inability to contact his daughters in a more direct fashion.[25] Though described in the archival catalogue as a
diary, Frey's letter to his two daughters does not conform to standard expectations of a diary. It is not divided into separate dated entries, nor is it written from a
present-tense perspective. Instead, he adopted an epistolary format, writing one
long letter over a period of two months. Although he could not guarantee its
delivery, he and his wife did their utmost to ensure that Liselott and Miriam re-

ceived the letter. Indeed, within the text to his daughters, he described in detail the efforts they had made toward that end, although he was careful not to incriminate their friends by mentioning their names: "It [this report] is being written down in four copies two of which are intended for each of you. They will be given to good friends for safekeeping and mailing immediately after peaceful times have arrived and the sending of letters is permitted. This method, we believe, will make it certain that one or several copies will reach you. You may then arrange between yourselves that whoever receives a copy will mail it to the one who has received no copy at all so that she too can read it."[26] Despite their extensive efforts, he remained doubtful that any copy would reach his daughters: "Years may pass before this report will reach you, if at all."[27] His letter writing was, like Paul Celan's poetry, "a message in a bottle, sent out in the—not always greatly hopeful—belief that somewhere and sometime it could wash up on land, on heartland perhaps."[28] Like a message in a bottle, Frey's letter-writing exercise was buoyed by hope and uncertainty about who might eventually read it.

The care the Freys took to guarantee the delivery of their diary suggests how important the text was to them. Indeed, writing was parents' only means of communicating specific information as well as affection and support to their children. In this way, it became a way of "parenting at a distance," that is, of projecting an image of family continuity and proffering emotional and moral guidance.[29] Jewish parents were left with no alternative but to combine correspondence with diary writing.

In and of itself, the use of correspondence during wartime as a means of parenting is not unusual. Mary Favret, writing on British parent-child correspondence during the Napoleonic wars, Martha Hanna, writing on French family correspondence during the First World War, and Jenny Hartley, writing on British mother-child correspondence during the Second World War, have all shown the special importance letters assumed for families separated by war.[30] Hartley described how British mothers' "long-distance mothering role was to bring not just a person to the one away but a place—home—with its concomitant sense of security and identity to the reader. [. . .] Others have spoken of the world-making power of the letter; the variant we have in mothers' letters is the home-making power of the letter. In their letters mothers reproduced the kind of dailiness we find in women's fiction."[31]

During the Second World War Jewish parents conducted long-distance parenting differently from British parents and contended with different issues. Not only were Jews forced to write one-sided correspondences, but they also were unable to replicate the normalcy of home in their letters. They could not reassure their children that home continued to function as their anchor in the world because their homes and communities were in the process of being destroyed. Rather than imparting a "sense of security and identity" anchored in place and routine, therefore, Jewish parents suggested that security and identity could be located in family relationships and values. Through their writing, they reinforced family bonds and attempted to help their children with the emotional and moral struggles that lay ahead. They relied on many strategies in that effort, but key among them were efforts at communicating love and affection, creating a vision of familial continuity, and offering emotional and moral guidance.

Jewish fathers were just as likely to take on the role of correspondent as Jewish mothers. Among non-Jewish letter writers the reverse was true. Hartley found that British fathers were infrequent correspondents with sons and daughters who had been evacuated or who were on military duty, and, as a corollary, sons and daughters did not expect their fathers to write to them.[32] My evidence suggests that Jewish fathers as well as mothers were actively engaged in long-distance parenting. The circumstances created by Nazi persecution altered the long-term significance of such parenting efforts, rendering them equally pertinent to both parents.

Gender was possibly a factor in parents' writing styles. On the whole, men tried to be more dispassionate than women when writing to their children, though some were not. A twelve-year-old German Jewish girl who kept a diary while living apart from her parents in a children's home in France regularly reported on the letters she received from her parents, who had smuggled her and her brother to France in an effort to save them. Of her "Papa's" letters from Germany, she recorded, "I find that he writes more motherly than Mother. In every letter we read 'do not think that we forget you, I think of you every minute.'"[33] By contrast, the tone adopted by Frey in his letter-diary to his daughters was more the norm for fathers. For example, he tended to conceptualize what he was writing as a report rather than a letter. He made this distinction explicit at the outset when he noted, "Today is April 7, 1942. This day in itself has no special significance. It just fixes the point in time at which this letter or, to phrase it better, this report is being started."[34] Perhaps by regarding what he was writing as a report, he was better able to compose his thoughts dispassionately and with self-restraint. Certainly his tone was characterized by emotional guardedness. Marking it as a report might also have been a kind of parenting guide: a subtle warning to his daughters about the contents of his text and an indication that they should try to read it dispassionately. Furthermore, in distinguishing this form of writing from standard correspondence, he acknowledged the one-sidedness of his writing; there could be no mutual disclosure of information and affection between parents and children.

Indeed, Frey's report is very much a monologue. Within it, he failed to construct a dialogue with his daughters by imagining how they would respond.

Women tended to affect a style of greater emotional immediacy in their letter-diaries. To be sure, women's diaries to their children were often overflowing with expressions of love and concern. While conscious of the time lag between their writing and their children's receipt of the diary, they often wrote as if in conversation with their children. The diary written by Toni Ringel for her four grown children while she was in hiding with her husband, Max (Meilech), in Amsterdam conveyed tremendous emotionality. Ringel and her husband were born outside of Tarnow, in Galicia, in 1888 and 1878, respectively. They married when she was sixteen years old and an orphan. Her parents, owners of a farm with multiple servants, had died in the flu epidemic in the late nineteenth century and left their property and three children to be divided among various relatives. Ringel had been apprenticed to a hatmaker before she was married to Max. Upon being married, the couple moved to Germany and raised their four children during the pre–First World War and interwar period. Max was a produce wholesaler, an enterprising man and Talmud scholar from a well-respected Tarnow family. After his business was ruined by the inflation of the early 1920s, he moved the family from Berlin to Frankfurt am Main and started over, reestablishing a successful business. Although the entire family left Germany in 1933 for Barcelona, they ended up in different locales as a result of the outbreak of the Spanish Civil War. The parents and one son ended up in Amsterdam and thus were later subject to German domination. The other three children—their two married daughters and other son—eventually went to England and the United States.[35]

When Toni and Max Ringel went into hiding, Toni began to keep a diary. The diary's Yiddish-inflected German orthography and colloquialisms (see notes) point toward her interrupted childhood in Galicia and adult years in Germany. Like Frey, she initially expressed her intention to report on their experiences under German occupation; however, she mostly used the diary to communicate with her children. She recorded in the first entry, "I have the intention, with God's help, to write down everything that is happening around us. May the Almighty keep and protect our children and not forget us either. Our only hope is to see you again, our darling children, and to hand over to you these pages in joy and happiness, to *you* and not to strangers. We have before us a path full of sufferings and dangers. But we are not alone, God is with us. We have gone through much during the past months, and we know how to behave in the new surrounding. There will be no lack of good will, courage and adaptability."[36] Addressed

"To our Beloved Children," Ringel's diary helped her to bridge their separation. From this first entry, she alternated between writing *to* her children and writing *about* her children, indicating that the line had blurred between correspondence and diary. Prominent in this first entry was her attempt to reassure her children — and undoubtedly herself, as well — that she and her husband would manage to live through the war. Yet as the war continued and their circumstances deteriorated, she returned to this theme less frequently. Instead what became the most persistent theme was her concern for her children's well-being and her abiding parental affection. In maintaining the emotional tenor of their relationship, she was tendering a continued sense of home and of the security of their parent–child bond.

Ringel communicated her love particularly on the children's birthdays. The first of October 1942, for example, was "the birthday of our eldest daughter. Our very fondest congratulations and a happy future for our beloved daughter, her husband and dear children. May we live to derive great happiness from all our children and grandchildren. Amen. Maligold, sweetheart, I hold your picture in my hands. It is wet from kisses and tears, and now it is Papa's turn. Children, pray to God that we, who are so severely tried by fate, may see you again."[37] Ringel tried to make her diary function as maternal domesticity would in regular life. Because she could not express her affection in person or even in letters, she used her diary to reinforce family relations in the midst of separation.[38] This effort to sustain the family as a functioning unit — even if only in the form of a one-sided correspondence — became a second feature of parents' letter-diaries.

On the days when Ringel seemed to feel her children's absence most acutely, she wrote to tell them that they were as present in her and her husband's minds as ever before. Forced to parent at a distance, she did not fail to record, for example,

> the birthday of our dearly beloved daughter. All the luck in the world to her. Bettychen, my child, may you never know of sickness and worries any more. A long and happy life to all of you, our darling children and grandchildren. Amen. To a happy and healthy reunion.
>
> On days like these we feel our loneliness the most. It seems to us as if we were forgotten by God and people alike. And yet, we have no reason to sin [that is, commit suicide?]. Thank God, our most valuable treasures are safe and may the Almighty protect them. Those treasures are you, our children, and we praise and thank the good Lord. Everything else is replaceable. Today Papa awakened me at four o'clock with the question: "Do you know what special day this is?" I wanted to give the poor man a little pleasure and said: "No." You should have seen the proud expression on his face when he said: "A good thing

that at least I have not forgotten our sweet daughter's birthday." Darling, your father's blessings should come true for you and your family, Papa and Mama.[39]

In this passage, Ringel not only demonstrated her continuing love for her children, but also her role in sustaining family feeling among them all.

Significantly, Ringel's repeated expressions of affection to her children were inseparable from her religious faith. She used the diary not only to communicate with her children but also to send up prayers to God. Indeed, writing to her children worked self-reflexively. It reminded her of how fortunate she was that her children were safe, which served to dispel her fears that God had forgotten them. Thus, through her diary, in addition to communicating affection and a vision of familial continuity, she told her children that she and her husband continued to be guided by the values and commitments that had given their lives meaning before their present suffering.[40]

Many parents' diaries served the function of guiding their children, demonstrating and reinforcing the values they hoped their children would retain. Like Ringel, other parents used diary writing to convey to their children their ongoing faith in both family and God. One such parent was a German-writing Jewish woman from Prague whose name is unknown but who is referred to as "A.B." in Yad Vashem's catalog. A.B. had been a doctor's widow for over ten years before the start of the Second World War and was the mother of a grown son. She began her diary in Theresienstadt on 21 August 1942, almost two months after her transport had arrived there, and continued to record entries through her liberation and beyond, until mid-June 1945. Like other parent diarists, A.B. was separated from her son during most of the war, but in her case she was not assured of her son's safety. Her son and daughter-in-law remained in Prague until sometime in early 1944, at which time they, too, were deported to Theresienstadt. During this initial period of separation and in the absence of an uncensored postal system, A.B. started a diary in order to commune with them. Like Frey and Ringel, she addressed her children in the first lines of the diary in direct speech, as "you [*Ihr*]," indicating that they were her audience.[41]

A.B. drew on her diary as a means of overcoming the separation from her children in much the same manner as Ringel. As a religiously observant Jew, A.B. extended her thoughts to her children and offered up her prayers to God. She turned to her diary to mark significant dates, including occasional Shabbats, holidays, birthdays and wedding anniversaries, death dates and burial dates. Indeed, she began the diary on the second wedding anniversary of her son and daughter-in-law, seemingly out of a need to relay to her children that her thoughts were with them on this occasion.[42] The diary was for her a vehicle for marking this date, allowing her to externalize her thoughts. Like Ringel's, A.B.'s family life and her religious observance were interwoven, and she used the diary to give structure and meaning to the passage of time in Theresienstadt outside of the activities and routines being imposed upon her. Her diary acted as a feeble confirmation that family life continued to exist beyond Theresienstadt.

The diary also seemed to have therapeutic value for A.B. by affording her a space in which to unburden her fears that she and her children would not survive. This salutary function is borne out by the fact that even after her children were transported to Theresienstadt and reunited with her, she continued to keep the diary and to address them within it. Though the diary was originally intended to bridge the period of her separation from her children by forging a connection to them in her thoughts and on paper, writing appears to have become its own habit and an implicit tie to humanity outside the ghetto. Perhaps she gave expression in her diary to thoughts she would not voice to her children directly. Indeed, while writing continued to give her the space to commemorate holidays and death dates, most of all it allowed her to express her fear of the ceaseless transports to Poland and to record her failing health. When her children were deported from Theresienstadt on 16 October 1944, the diary again became her sole means of communicating with them. She copied into her notebook the letter she had been unable to deliver to them before their transport departed. She continued recording entries in her diary until one month after being liberated from Theresienstadt, on the day she learned her children had been killed in an extermination camp in Poland. In her last dated entry, she recorded, "This morning Paul visited me and gave me the so dreaded news that you my sweethearts will never be seen again. I don't know if I can bear this life; it is too hard for me and for what purpose? Why has God so punished me? Have I committed a crime?" [43] Diary writing had been a way of maintaining the family in the face of separation, but when the possibility of her children reading the diary in the future vanished, it ceased to serve any purpose.

The diaries of parents who were together during the war were often communal in nature, further underscoring their goal of maintaining an image of continued family wholeness. Ringel, not her husband, was clearly the designated correspondent, but his voice was nonetheless audible in her text. She frequently employed the pronoun "we" and sometimes acted as an intermediary for her husband, representing specifically his thoughts and wishes. Ringel was hardly exceptional in this respect. Frey also used the "we" voice in his text, indicating his shared experiences and sentiments with his wife: "We, Mom and I—Dad—want to report now on what happened to us since your emigration, that is since June 27, 1939 and August 21, 1939 respectively." Furthermore, he framed the reading of their report in a communal setting. He imagined them sitting around as a family after the war and reading the report together, although he recognized the likelihood that this would not take place.[44]

In part, these plural voices kept the family present in the text and maintained the semblance that both parents were offering love and guidance. At the same time, the communal nature of the diaries constitutes a further linkage between the diaries and correspondence. Contrary to the common present-day perception of letter writing as an individual undertaking, according to the historian Rebecca Earle, from the seventeenth century until well into the twentieth, letter writing and reading throughout Europe were often "an entirely social affair." Several family members might contribute to the same letter, and letters were usually passed around and read by various people.[45] Thus, correspondence itself was already a family affair, and Jewish parents integrated this feature of family correspondence into their letter-diaries.

Communal authorship was nowhere more pronounced than in the jointly written diary of Max (Marcus) and Frieda Reinach.[46] Max and Frieda began their diary on the day the Germans invaded Poland, 1 September 1939, and addressed it to their two daughters and sons-in-law in Boston and Palestine. Max was in his midsixties and Frieda in her midfifties—almost the exact same ages as the Ringels—and they had remained in Berlin after their children emigrated from Germany. The Reinachs actually took turns writing to their children, although Max contributed more entries than Frieda overall. Like a letter to which family members contributed, the Reinachs' diary was a mutual effort, one in which they each engaged as writers and as readers of each other's entries.

Although Max did not compose his entries in letter form, he made it clear he was writing the diary in the hope his children would read it someday. In the second entry of the diary, he explained, "When I attempt in this small booklet to keep track of the days and weeks to follow I do this for you, beloved children, so you shall one day understand and come to know the time in which we live, what we suffer."[47] Like Ringel and Frey, he set out to write a report of his and his wife's experiences for their children.

Whereas Max addressed his children directly, at first Frieda did not. Initially, she seemed to differentiate the diary from the letters she wrote to her children. Her first contribution to the diary in 1939 revealed the prominence of her children in her thoughts. Yet unlike Max, she referred to them in the third person, writing about them rather than to them, leaving open the question of her imagined audience. Although she wrote in the same book as her husband and was, therefore, aware that he intended the journal for their children, Frieda seemed to write more to comfort herself and, perhaps, to communicate with her husband through the medium of the written word. Maybe she was less optimistic than Max that their children would actually read it. She recorded, "3/9. Sunday [—] England declares war at 11 a.m., France at 6 p.m. Dora and Aunt Terese came for a visit, very nervous, all of us. I do not like to leave our home, only at home do I feel more or less safe. Due to the calm of father I am able to go on, but it is exceedingly difficult; the thought of our children who will worry terribly for us, does not leave me for a moment. We continue to write to them in the hope letters will reach them."[48] Interestingly, Frieda mentioned explicitly their tremendous insecurity and despair, whereas Max had only hinted at this in the previous day's entry. Max might have written more self-consciously as a result of laying claim to the audience of his children, while Frieda might have written more candidly precisely because she did not imagine her children as readers. Indeed, as Frieda's entry suggests, it had been some time since they had received confirmation that their letters were being delivered. For this reason, it might have been unusually difficult at this moment to believe that their children would one day get to read their diary. Nevertheless, Max and Frieda did not cease trying to communicate with their children. Not only did they send a series of letters that went unanswered, but they also continued to keep their diary.[49]

For Frieda, the diary did not initially function as a parenting instrument. Though she mentioned wanting desperately to reassure their children that they should not worry about their mother and father, her first entry was in no way consolatory. There was nothing reassuring in its content, nor did she seem to write specifically with them in mind as readers. In 1939, Frieda's diary entry was distinct from her correspondence with her children. By 1942, the relationship she drew between letters and diaries had changed. In the spring of 1942, though she still sent a monthly letter to her children through the Red Cross, the diary became another means of corresponding with them.

The relationship between letter writing and diary writing changed in conjunction with Frieda's dwindling expectation that they would outlast Nazi persecution. Indeed, this shift from writing about her children to addressing them directly in the diary took place over the course of one entry: "10 May 1942. Sunday 7 p.m. [—] How often do I ask myself: shall we ever be able to tell *our children* about everything we have lived through? I do not believe so, even if until now— thank heaven—we have been lucky! How many thousand Jews have been resettled [*ausgesiedelt*] (as it's nicely and obliquely called) from Germany since October 1941, how many are no longer alive because of terrible privations?" (emphasis added).[50] Frieda's wish, expressed in the first line of this entry, to describe their experiences to their children carried with it the hope that she would one day narrate their story in person. As she continued this entry, she enumerated the many family members and friends who had already been deported, repeating that she and her husband had been comparatively fortunate. Her awareness that they too would most likely be deported spelled a shift in her writing:

> I am with good reason most terrified of evacuation [*Evakuierung*], and it is a disaster that hangs over our heads at every moment. Whenever I think of it [. . .] I know: if we have to go this road, I will never see *you* again, my beloved children. How are you doing? With what tremendous concern are you thinking of us? If only you have no financial worries, that is my daily prayer. [. . .] Now you are both happily married—you, my Trude, are a mother and we cannot take part—not even through letters. Every month since December '41 we have written to you through the Red Cross, but we have still not received a line from you in reply. [. . .] Every day I hope to see your handwriting. [emphasis added][51]

It was as if at that moment—despairing for their own future—Frieda began to tell her children what she would not be able to tell them later. She began to detail her and her husband's situation in Berlin, specifically, how much weight they had lost and the precise quantities of their meager food rations. She described their work and the social isolation they suffered, unable even to meet with friends who also lived in Berlin. For a variety of reasons, people residing in the city often found it impossible to visit family or friends: the nightly curfew, the ban on using public transportation, the many streets that were declared off-limits to Jews, and the impossibility of sitting to rest anywhere en route. Once Frieda imagined that she would never have the chance to communicate with her children—either in person or in letters—she utilized her diary as a last point of connection.

Six weeks later, Frieda returned to the diary to inform her children of the new restrictions and miseries they faced. She wrote of how she and Max had agonized over whether he should return to work, if that would better protect them from "evacuation." "There is not a quiet hour," she wrote, since things changed so often and so quickly. "So now you again know a little about our lives."[52] The diary had acquired the intimacy of letters.

The communal nature of the diary and the vision of continuing family it proffered also made possible another form of communication: that between wife and husband. Max and Frieda read each other's entries and divulged their shared sentiments to their children. In his entry of 12 July 1942, for example, Max commented at the outset that he had reread his wife's last entry, and he then picked up from where she had left off.[53] On another occasion, in the last entry of the diary, Max wrote, "The aforementioned words, written by mother, come from the bottom of our heart."[54] In conveying to their children the extent of their mutual dependence and support, they also wrote for each other. When Frieda told her children that "father is a hero, he is my only support," she was also telling her husband how much he meant to her. Perhaps she was reiterating what she regularly verbalized to him; perhaps she was expressing something in writing that she rarely put into words.[55] And when Max reassured his children that he was looking after their mother, he was also telling his wife he would continue to take care of her: "Wherever we have to go, I shall always try, with the help of God, to protect and help your mother."[56] Frieda and Max were both readers and writers of the diary.

Beyond assuring their daughters that home continued to exist in their familial relationships, if not in their surroundings, the Reinachs and the Freys wanted to offer guidance to their children, both emotional and moral. Of great importance was the necessity of guiding their children through mourning. Both the Freys and the Reinachs already recognized in 1942 the horrible burden being placed on their children. They realized how difficult it would be, if they did not survive, for their children to mourn for them under conditions no one would be able to understand. They tried to release them from the burden of excessive mourning.

While Frey wished to inform his daughters of what they had suffered—his report reads like a narrative summary of the discriminatory measures imposed by the Nazi regime on the Jews between September 1939 and May 1942—his foremost concern was not to upset his daughters unduly. He expressed the wish, therefore, that they feel relief and not sadness upon learning of their parents' deaths, since it would mean their suffering had ended: "Do not be sad then [if we are no longer alive]. Read calmly through this report, which I kept as factual and sober as possible, and tell yourselves: 'Thank God, they have finished enduring!'"[57] He hoped his report would contribute to his daughters' understanding the context of their parents' deaths and to their being able to mourn appropriately.

Both Frieda and Max Reinach also anticipated the emotional burden their children would face after the war, and they tried to ease their suffering. In an entry of May 1942, Max told his children they should not mourn if he and Frieda did not survive: "If we should have the luck to survive and are allowed to spend our future years with you, beloved children, [then] our daily prayers have been listened to and accepted. [. . .] However, should this happiness to be united again with you remain a dream, do not mourn for us. You will remain our sunshine til our evening comes and until dark night surrounds us. Your childhood was happy and delightful for you and for us and memories will remain."[58] Frieda reiterated her husband's entreaty in an entry six months later. By that time, she wrote, "I can no longer believe in a reunion with you." Yet she urged them not to allow their lives to be "overshadowed" by their parents' fate and asked that they continue to live their lives in the manner in which they had been reared: "So we wish all of you, beloved children, a good future. Remain healthy, upright people as we brought you up to be [. . .] I know that you will never forget us, but do not allow your lives to be overshadowed by our destiny. You are still so young and you should not mourn."[59] Frieda and Max understood that their untimely deaths could have a lasting impact on their children's lives, and thus they expressed the wish that their children only focus on what was good from the past and otherwise look to the future.

The Freys and the Reinachs were conscious of the difference between healthy and excessive mourning.[60] When they asked their children not to be sad or not to mourn, they expressed the fear that their children would be unable to grieve and move on, in other words, that they would become "melancholic." Indeed, the letter-diaries they wrote were intended partially to aid the grieving process. Not only did they urge them not to grieve excessively, but in recording as much as possible about their experiences during these years (as well as their hopes for how their children would respond to this information), these parents recognized their children's need to know about the past in order for them to be able to move on with their lives. They provided them with the kind of information that would address their nagging questions and allow some kind of closure.

Because they realized the circumstances of their deaths would be exceptional, the Freys and the Reinachs recognized that potentially their children might fixate on the past rather than work through the past.[61] They tried, through their letter-diaries, to help their children avoid grief reactions that included confusion and obsessive review. As Frieda and Max faced deportation in the middle of October 1942, Frieda tried to leave as few unanswered questions as possible. She furnished her children with an update on the fate of every family member, to the best of her knowledge. She also recorded her parting wishes to each of her daughters, sons-in-law, and her one grandchild, whom she had never met. Finally, recognizing that her children would not know where their parents' remains were, she held out the diary as a substitute memorial: "You will never know where your parents are buried, as I know nothing of my five sisters and brothers. Perhaps this small diary will one day come into your possession and also other things of ours, who knows?"[62] Seemingly out of her concern that the lack of a burial site would render mourning more difficult, she suggested their diary could act as a *yizker bukh*, or memorial book, presaging the memorial books that served as ersatz gravestones in hundreds of Jewish communities after the war.[63] Frieda ultimately hoped their writing would facilitate the children's process of mourning and recovery.

Frey also affirmed his great concern over his daughters' well-being and attempted, by means of his diary, to take care of them. Though powerless under the present circumstances to help secure his daughters' future, he made every effort to do so. In the event he and his wife did not survive the war, which, he wrote in understated fashion, was "not improbable in view of the happenings of the last half year," he recorded detailed financial information in his report for his daughters in case of need.[64] The information included the name and address of a contact person in New York who was indebted to the Freys and the reasons for her indebtedness; precise figures of the family's financial assets as of May 1942 and the comment that such assets would be seized if they were deported; the amounts they had been forced to pay since 1938 "due to the Jewry legislation"; and lost income and pensions resulting from his premature dismissal from the Agil corporation.[65] Frey noted that such information could be of potential use if, with the end of the war and a return of the rule of law, his daughters filed a claim for restitution: "I cannot judge whether those losses of assets and income could later on be the basis for restitution claims, which you as legal heirs of my estate could assert. I am making this suggestion to you just in case such claims and requests will have to be filed at some future time."[66] Since he was unable to bequeath his assets, he imparted whatever information he could to enable his daughters to pursue financial security. Already in 1942, he considered the possibility of restitution claims being filed in the future and thought of them in terms of a legacy he was leaving for his children.

Given its attention to financial arrangements, Frey's report to his daughters was, ultimately, a type of last will and testament. Yet he did not merely devise a testament of assets; as part of his report he also left a kind of ethical will, with moral injunctions for his daughters, which demonstrated the kind of parental guidance diarists attempted to offer.[67] Though he suggested the possibility of legal recourse to recover the family's assets, he advised them to eschew restitution claims if possible: "If you should live in comfortable circumstances and have no dire need for the money, you might want to relinquish your claims, provided both of you agree. Usually only money earned by one's own efforts yields blessings. Both of you are industrious and imbued with a high sense of duty. I am convinced that both of you will do well in the world."[68] In Frey's version of why one would pursue restitution, a need for justice or revenge against a regime that had wronged him did not seem to enter the picture. Quite the opposite, in fact: money gained by that process would not place the burden of guilt on the German regime as much as it would taint his daughters by serving as proof of their dependence. The best course of action would be to wash their hands of the matter and forge their own way in the world. Indeed, the legacy he and his wife were leaving their children went beyond a claim to file for restitution. It included their upbringing, education, and strong moral sense. Despite the fact that "mankind will often offend your sense of duty and high ethical standards," he urged them to "continue on your way as destiny has ordained for you and hold on to your convictions of decency."[69] Harkening back to the earlier use of diaries as tools "to instruct the living, an edification task that pertains to mourning," Frey took this last opportunity to offer parental wisdom to his children.[70]

FILLING IN GAPS OR BRIDGING THE DIVIDE

In addition to communicating their deep and abiding affection for their children and, even more, their ongoing belief in the values of family, religion, and human decency in the face of a world gone mad, most diarists who wrote to their children or to other family members were intent on describing the horrific world of the Nazis' creation. Indeed, for some individuals, this took on the greatest importance. They wanted their children and siblings to understand both the nature of Nazi racial policy and their responses to it, recognizing that life under German occupation was utterly unlike normal life. Through their diaries, they tried to close the experiential and resulting epistemological gap between them and their loved ones.[71]

Diarists attempted to educate their loved ones, to make them literate in Jewish everyday life under German occupation. Richard Ehrlich, for example, wrote his "ghetto-letters, reminiscences for my dear son Willy Ehrlich in England" in order to enlighten his son on the various aspects of life in Theresienstadt.[72] Almost five years earlier, in March 1939, Richard and his wife, Sophie, had sent their then ten-year-old son away from Nazi Germany to safer shores. In the meantime they had been unable to emigrate and remained in Berlin until they were deported to Theresienstadt in early 1943. Like other diarists, Ehrlich combined elements of letter writing and diary writing in his "ghetto-letters." He frequently addressed his son in direct speech even though he divided his text into dated entries. For example, whenever he received a postcard from neutral Portugal with news about his son, he told his son about it: "The cards were even more valuable to us [than the accompanying gift of sardines]; they brought indirect news from you, my dear boy, to whom our thoughts and feelings are tied day and night!"[73] In Ehrlich's case, however, the "ghetto-letters" were less a continuation in diary form of his correspondence with his son than an extension of the memoirs he had been writing before being deported, a narrative in which he discussed his son's youth and what he referred to as "the history of our negative emigration." He made this connection explicit in his first entry from Theresienstadt: "Thus these 'ghetto-letters' in a certain sense constitute a resumption of my notes of that time, and everything bears an indirect correlation."[74] Ehrlich was interested in documenting his and his wife's experiences under the Third Reich, first and foremost for their son to read in the future.

Ehrlich wanted to depict a clear image of ghetto life for his son. In his first entry, he described the goal of his endeavor in the following terms: "Today, in memorable November, which has brought so much misery to us Jews, I have sufficient leisure time, on account of a mild indisposition, to begin a by now already long-intended report. These notes should convey to you, my dear boy, a picture of the situation in which we have found ourselves against our will for nearly 10 months. My 'ghetto-letters' make no claim to comprehensiveness, nor are they in the nature of things completely objective, since *I* am only capable of describing things as *I* see them and as they affect me personally."[75] Thus, Ehrlich expressed his intention to render a subjective account of their life in Theresienstadt. For this reason, he started out by describing their transport from Berlin to Theresienstadt and their initial impressions upon arriving there.

Yet it appears that presenting life in Theresienstadt as he and his wife personally experienced it proved to be a greater challenge than he had anticipated. Indeed, within the first few entries of his "ghetto-letters," he seemed to encounter several difficulties. First, although Ehrlich sought to disclose their personal experiences, he seemed to realize that the details of their lives made sense only if his son understood the general context of Theresienstadt. He now determined that it was necessary to convey that larger picture. Thus, at the start of his second entry, he advanced a new writing strategy. He explained, "Now before I continue with a description of our personal condition, I would like to give you, my dear Willy [. . .] a general picture of Theresienstadt, even though I will introduce the main account later." Now he stressed the objectivity of his account. He proceeded to describe Theresienstadt's physical structure and appearance, its administrative departments, and the size and composition of the ghetto's population. Writing from a detached vantage point, he also explained how there were regular transports that carried Jews away "from here to the East" and that these transports were much feared.[76] Despite Ehrlich's disclaimer in his first entry, his "ghetto-letters" ended up resembling a presentation of the truth of ghetto life much more than an expression of his subjectivity.

The second difficulty Ehrlich encountered in writing a subjective account of their experiences was that he found he could not write about certain of their experiences until he had attained a degree of emotional distance. Indeed, when he felt unable to distance himself from an event, he could mention it only in passing. For example, in an atypically brief entry, he wrote: "III. *Volkszählung* [or "census" of Theresienstadt inmates for the purpose of selecting people to put on transports to Poland]. I will report on this later in greater detail than I am capable of doing at the moment. The incident [of the *Volkszählung*] is so monstrous, that I first have to gain some distance from it, in order to be able to see everything in its true light."[77] What proved to be the most difficult to record was precisely what he had set out to record in his first "ghetto-letter," namely, how things "affected" him "personally" rather than a "comprehensive" picture. Attaining emotional distance turned out to be the precondition for Ehrlich's writing. It made it possible, for example, for him to describe at length the sights and sounds of the ghetto's streets, which "offer a very interesting picture."[78]

At the same time, because emotional distance was the result of adaptation, it was also a measure of the widening gap of knowledge that separated father and son. Of course, adaptation made it easier for Ehrlich to get through the days. The shock and horror he and his wife had felt when they first arrived in Theresienstadt—as well as the barrage of advice and coping strategies proffered by ghetto veterans—gave way to a feeling of familiarity: "But one quickly grew accustomed to all these strange images, which lose their horror through habit."[79] In becoming a ghetto veteran, however, he found it more difficult to see the differences that had originally been so unsettling, let alone communicate those very features that would be so unfamiliar to his son: "There would be so many oddities to report, but because things have become commonplace in our eyes, one loses one's sense of the out of the ordinary."[80] Paradoxically, then, emotional distance also presented a challenge to writing effectively for it dulled his sensitivity to the extraordinary nature of life in Theresienstadt. As Ehrlich grew accustomed to the sights and sounds peculiar to life in the ghetto, the epistemological gap between him and his son widened.

Writing to his son helped to bring them closer together. His son would learn about Theresienstadt through his diary, but, what's more, Ehrlich seemed to regain an awareness of the tragic nature of daily life in Theresienstadt in the process of recounting it. For example, he presented snapshots of life in the courtyards of the ghetto—of unclothed people out in the open washing in the fountain and of enfeebled old people standing in line for two hours, often in vain, for a ladleful of soup—which he twice described as "unforgettable." So, too, he recorded verbal expressions "unfamiliar" to their "North German ears." He commented further that morality bore an "entirely different face" in Theresienstadt than it did in "private life," referring to the necessity of smuggling to dampen one's hunger.[81] Via writing and imagining how his son would see all of this, Ehrlich retrieved his old lenses, those of the ghetto outsider. He worked to mitigate the distance between him and his son by attempting to translate the foreign nature of the ghetto.

Other people were gripped by the same concern as Ehrlich: that their family members in Allied or neutral countries would not understand their experiences

in Nazi Germany. A large part of Frey's letter to his daughters consisted of a
personal account of German anti-Jewish legislation since his daughters' emigration from Germany in 1939. Frey stressed the tremendous uncertainty with
which Jews in Germany had to cope everyday. As an admonition to his daughter
Miriam, lest she had forgotten, he recounted the events of the month prior to her
leaving for Palestine: "I just want to remind you how difficult it was to obtain the
passport on time and also how, at the last moment, several children including
you were to stay behind and wait for the next transport."[82] While he assumed that
Miriam "always will remember" the excitement of receiving final clearance for
her departure, he considered it less likely that she would recall how uncertain her
departure was up to the last minute. Perhaps he sensed that, having left Nazi Germany, a person would quickly forget the role chance played in their daily lives.
Since most of his report narrated his and his wife's extensive efforts to get out of
Germany and to cope with the barrage of anti-Jewish decrees, Frey's message was
clear. If they were "evacuated one of these days" it would be a result of their "bad
luck" and not because of their lack of effort to avoid deportation.[83] Thus, he tried
to make his daughters understand their circumstances during those years—both
the circumscription of their world and their efforts to escape Nazi Germany.

Especially for diarists writing in Poland in the wake of mass killings of Jews,
the gap between them and their loved ones in the outside world widened to
a chasm. Nevertheless, they tried to fill the breach through their diaries. They
wanted their family members to understand their experiences during what were
probably going to be the last days of their lives. During almost three weeks in July
1943, Aryeh Klonicki (Klonymus) filled ninety notebook pages in pencil for his
siblings living outside of Poland. He recorded, "In deciding to write this diary I
was motivated by the desire to leave some remembrance at least to those of my
brothers fortunate enough to be living in lands untouched by the hand of Hitler."[84] Hiding in the forest and fields with his wife, Malwina, during the last phase
of the murder of Galician Jewry, Klonicki wrote in Hebrew rather than Yiddish
so that fewer people would be able to read his writing. He explained to his siblings, "My lines to you are meant to portray the poignant characteristics of life
under Hitler."[85] His mission bore special urgency because he and his wife were
leaving behind their young son, Adam, who was born in 1942 and had been taken
in by a Christian family in the vicinity of Buczacz. The same family safeguarded
Klonicki's diary, hiding it in the ground until after the war.[86]

Klonicki realized that the terminology and characteristics of "life under Hitler" would be utterly foreign to his siblings living outside German occupation. In
order for them to comprehend his account, he tried to explain its alien compo-

nents. He introduced them to the concepts of the Judenrat and the Jewish police: "You will no doubt be astonished to learn of the existence of a creature known as a 'Jewish policeman' whose task it is to beat up Jews. In every town he [Hitler] set up a 'Judenrat' and a Jewish police force. Their function is to fulfill all his requirements. It is with their help that he collects from the Jews whatever he needs [...]. It is with their aid that men are seized and carried off to the labour camps."[87] He also described in detail what "actions" were, assuming his siblings would not only know nothing about them but also would cast doubt on their reality:

> However, a new period began with the birth of our child, a new chapter in the endless tale of Jewish suffering. I am referring to the systematic "actions" launched against the Jews. Every four or five weeks German officials embark upon this "sacred" task under the auspices of the Gestapo. These raids begin at a definite hour and terminate at a set time, lasting one or two days. The Germans go from house to house, looking for their victims in the hideouts (Schrony), which the Jews had learned to erect. From there they are ferreted out and led to the railway stations. Then they are loaded onto special wagons and sent to specified towns where the Germans have built crematoria for the purpose of burning the Jews. Their ashes are used as fertilizer in agriculture. [...] During the latest "actions" they have no longer bothered to send the Jews whom they snatched to special towns. They are put to death on the spot. The easiest places for carrying out the "actions" are the hospitals and charitable institutions for children. Here the job is very simple. They enter the hospitals and shoot at the sick people lying on their beds, whereas the children are thrown out of the windows from the top floors. This is what happened at Stanislavov. But in our vicinity they do not slay children, preferring to bury them alive (after all, why waste bullets?). You will no doubt refuse to believe this. What a happy state you are in, that you find it difficult to lend credence to such a tale. But we are no longer impressed by such occurrences. So much so that we would hardly as much as interrupt our meal if someone came and told us that our parents or children had been put to death.[88]

In this entry and others, Klonicki described the horrors being perpetrated. A graduate of the University of Vilna with a master's degree and a secondary school teacher by profession, Klonicki sought to teach his siblings this chapter of their family's history and of Jewish history more generally. He recognized how difficult it would be for them to believe the truth. Yet it was so important to him that his siblings learn about what had happened—and learn it directly from him—that he dedicated himself to the task of writing under the least propitious circumstances:

"Now that the knife of the slaughterer is resting on my throat I find it difficult to concentrate on the chronological record of events. It is not indoors that I am writing these lines, but outside in a field of wheat where I am hiding with my wife."[89]

As was the case with Chaim Kaplan, the effort to relay news about Jewish wartime experiences certainly must have been sustained by the diarists' faith in history as an arena of justice in which past events were accounted for. But these undertakings must also be seen as a way of recording family history in particular. Using diaries as a site for recording family history was common in normal life.[90] Many Jews who wrote diaries during the war hoped their children or siblings would come into possession of the diaries after the war and thereby learn about the final years or months of their lives. One final example is a woman identified only by the last name Rubinsztejnowa, who wrote a diary, in case she did not survive, for her siblings who lived outside German-occupied territory or whose fate was unknown to her.[91] Writing over a period of five months, she addressed many of the entries to "My dearest ones!" which shows yet again how intertwined diary writing and letter writing had become. Indeed, she described what she was writing as a letter: "As you see, my dears, we are still alive. Moszko and I are still alive. The rest were murdered. No one else from our family is left. No one. [. . .] I am writing this letter in case we die. If we do not survive the war [. . .] then our hosts [*gospodarze*] will send you this letter, so you will know something of our experiences under Hitler's regime."[92] As the only adult family member in Lwów who had survived up to that moment, she wanted her siblings to know what the family had suffered, but especially of the deaths of their family members: "I want to describe to you our history [*nasze dzieje*] and the sequence of our cruelly murdered loved ones' deaths. I am not a talented writer, but despite that I want to describe our sufferings and experiences to you as far as I am able."[93] As a chronicle of her family's history, her diary exhibited and reinforced the close ties among siblings.

In a sense, Rubinsztejnowa had taken up her father's charge to his children. Since "our beloved father did not live to the moment of Hitler's defeat," she was compelled to tell them in his stead.[94] She described her father's last days in the ghetto and how he had often expressed the wish to be reunited with his other children after the war and to tell them about their wartime suffering. Yet, in the wake of his death, the responsibility of recounting the family's history had become graver. Indeed on two occasions in the beginning of the diary, she caught herself "digressing" from the subject of her father and deceased siblings. Several months later, she still seemed unable to tell the story of her father's death. After writing a brief description of her father's routine during his final days in the ghetto and blurting out the date of his "so-called 'freedom'" (that is, his death) — "It was Wednesday, the 11th of Adar, 4 days before Purim" — she abruptly broke off writing for good.[95] Having discharged her duty to her deceased family members and to those still alive, perhaps she had no more motivation to write. Rubinsztejnowa seemed to bring to an end what she had set out to accomplish in her diary. Or perhaps she and her son were discovered in their hiding place and killed. The Soviets did not take over Lwów for another six months, and at that time there were only about thirty-four hundred Jewish survivors.[96]

Rubinsztejnowa wanted her siblings to understand not simply the madness of life under Hitler, but also what in particular had become of her and other relatives. Aryeh Klonicki, Erich Frey, the Reinachs, and Richard Ehrlich all wrote for this reason in addition to others. A.B. also made explicit her intention to record her experiences in the eventuality that she would be unable to tell her children about her experiences in person: "Since I know not when, whether and where we will be reunited, I would like to put my experiences and impressions in writing, in order to preserve them for you."[97] So, too, Grete Holländer, imagining she would not survive to recount it herself, hoped her daughter and other family members would one day read her account of the war: "The day before yesterday I started my notes, whether I will bring them to an end is more than doubtful. Illusions are out of place here, each moment I am in mortal danger, but I am well used to that already. Maybe tomorrow I will no longer be alive and no longer write, today I do it anyway. I need to do it, because I am unable to shout out loud, I want to write it down as long as it goes on, as long as I am alive. Maybe my little Sonja will read it one day and my people and Ilse [. . .]."[98]

In recording family history and bridging the epistemological divide, diarists attempted to maintain the continuity of their families. These efforts at filling in gaps in information and understanding were part of Jews' efforts to render their wartime experiences meaningful by ensuring that they did not remain unknown and unassimilated by their families.

FAMILY AS A SOURCE OF MEANING AND HOPE

Parents like Erich Frey and Max and Frieda Reinach wrote diaries in order to establish a further connection to their loved ones in the outside world, but diary writing also satisfied a need of the writers themselves. Writing to, for, and about families aided their emotional coping and helped assuage their feelings of loneliness. Thus, in a significant way, the benefit of diary writing was not only for future readers; diarists, too, benefited from the process of connecting mentally with their family members. Moreover, by addressing themselves to loved ones, these diarists connected with their prewar identities, which were rooted in family and community. The visions of family they held aloft and enacted in their diaries not only served to aid distant children, but also continued to anchor the diarists themselves in a world beyond that created by the Nazis. In this way, they held on to their belief that humankind would craft a brighter postwar future.

At the same time, for many diarists the centrality of their families went far beyond the texts they were writing. They made clear that the possibility that their children would survive the war kept them clinging to life. Juliusz Feurman, the father of a grown son, wrote a series of letters between July 1943 and February 1944 from a Gestapo prison cell about the experiences of Jews in the Stanislawów ghetto. A civil engineer and member of the Judenrat, he was kept alive by the local German authorities at least eight months longer than the rest of Stanislawów's Jewish residents because of his expertise in construction. Lacking knowledge of his son's whereabouts, he addressed his letters to a "dear Doctor" and asked the doctor to hold on to the letters for his son. Feurman's son had been sent outside of Lwów on a Soviet "work company" in April 1941, and Feurman had not heard from him since late June 1941, when Germany invaded the Soviet Union. Nonetheless, on the basis of news from some men who had accompanied his son as far east as Kiev, he retained the hope that he was alive in the Soviet Union.[99] Feurman explained in his letters that after the liquidation of the Stanislawów ghetto, and in the wake of his father's death in the ghetto and the murder of his wife, the only thing preventing him from committing suicide was the possibility that his son was still alive. This possibility drove him to write the series of letters before he, too, was murdered by the Germans when he was no longer needed.[100]

Like Feurman, Holländer attributed her will to live—despite the murder of her husband and family—to her daughter's continued existence. Initially, she had resigned herself to being shot and killed in a mass grave, "but then I remembered my poor child who would be left all alone and abandoned in the world and suddenly an immense will to live [*ein ungeheurer Lebenswille*] seized me. You must save yourself, I told myself, you must and you will."[101] The thought of her child, orphaned, compelled her to try and escape the liquidation of the camp in Czortków. And after she went into hiding, good news about her daughter's well-being overwhelmed the revolting circumstances of life in the bunker. On hearing that Sonja was alive and well, Holländer "forgot the unbearable heat, the plague of flies and my weakness. [. . .] Oh how badly I want to live, how impatiently I long for our liberation."[102] Her daughter gave her a reason for continuing to try to stay alive.

Many parents expressed this sentiment in their diaries. Irena Hauser, a native of Vienna who was in the Łódź ghetto, mentioned repeatedly in her diary that she was not going to commit suicide because she could not leave her son all alone.[103]

Unlike Holländer, whose husband had already been killed at the time of her writing, Hauser lived with her son and husband in the ghetto. Yet she could not trust her husband to look after their son and castigated him throughout the diary for spending money on cigarettes instead of providing food for his family. In epigrammatic fashion, she captured the straining of family relations to the breaking point that starvation and suffering wrought: "[. . .] the child cries hunger, the father [smokes] cigarettes, the mother wants to die, family life in the ghetto."[104] Hauser would have killed herself but for her son's insistence that they struggle to survive.

Beyond her attachment to her son, however, Hauser was motivated by her deep yearning to be reunited with her siblings in England and with her father, and her diary proved vital in sustaining this feeling: "In any case why don't I end it all and throw myself out the window—but I can't abandon the child and he still wants to live [and] he begs me to stay with him and the heat makes it impossible to think. Beloved brothers and sisters, I would so like to see you again and you, beloved father, where are you [?]"[105] Not only did Hauser not commit suicide, but she continued, despite being on the brink of starvation, to write a diary for and to her siblings. In one entry she commented on her amazement that she managed to go on writing.[106] Thus, it was not just the immediate demands of her son that sustained her, but the imagined communication her diary offered her as well. Without overstating the significance of diary writing for Hauser, I would suggest that the diary and the vision of family it allowed her to maintain served to connect her to the outside world and to her absent loved ones, and this in turn seemed to keep her hanging on to life by the most delicate of threads.

The ties of family bound people to life, but even more, they rendered the future meaningful. For many writers, diaries became a vehicle for expressing the greater faith in the future that they possessed because their families would survive the war. When his children's survival was secure, Lucien Dreyfus looked to the future with hope: "In this moment when my children leave the old world in search of adventure in the new, I feel that I am participating in the revolution that opens a new era. God protect us."[107] As a direct consequence of his children's escape from German-occupied Europe, he envisioned "the revolution" continuing in other places in the future instead of considering the Nazi era as the culmination of Western civilization. In a manner not unlike that of Dreyfus, Frey expressed his belief in a better future if his daughters' lives were assured. He and his wife "played that record [of one of their daughter's farewell to them at the time of her emigration] often thereby strengthening our own trust in a better future."[108] And he assured his daughters, "But you can believe us that we are attached to you with every fiber of our hearts and that we have only one wish for you: may you be healthy and happy! As far as we are concerned, our only wish is to see you again and to talk to at least one of you. We thus will be reassured that you are well and can look forward to a future that will be more beautiful and radiant than anything Jewry has ever experienced, even in its prime!"[109] Frey and Dreyfus shifted seamlessly from imagining their children's individual futures to imagining the collective future of, respectively, all Jews and all human beings. With this slippage from the individual to the collective, they framed their children's future more broadly than the "private and personal."[110] By situating it in a national framework or in a religious-humanist framework, they invested the future with tremendous meaning and thereby downplayed the significance of their own potentially premature deaths. Furthermore, because they both felt they would continue to play a role in the future through their children, their deaths took on even less importance. The continuity of family—like good news reports and faith in historical judgment—proffered a kind of hope or at least a limited acceptance of their suffering.

For many letter-diarists the various symbolic and actual implications of family became interwoven. Aryeh Klonicki demonstrated this explicitly. Like Frey, he linked his hope for humankind's future to his child. In his case, this linkage took on symbolic value in his and his wife's choice of a name for their baby boy: they named him Adam, or "human being" in Hebrew. Klonicki explained this in his diary to his brothers: "In three days, on July 8th, my son will be one year old. My son's name is Adam. I chose it for its symbolic significance. I wanted to emphasize by this that the Germans, worse than all beasts of prey yet who call themselves supermen and deny us the right to exist—will finally be conquered by human beings. Therefore I called him Adam (human being)."[111] Klonicki trusted that Nazi Germany would be defeated and that the future would usher in a return to normal life. Those who prevailed over the Germans would again structure society on the basis of principles of human decency. First and foremost in his family, then, the birth of his son symbolized for him a hoped-for return to humanist values that would follow Germany's defeat. He strove to voice that hope to his brothers in his diary, so that they might better understand his experience and his state of mind. Additionally, though, his brothers' survival also played a role in his faith in the future: "In the present situation I should be satisfied if at least our child should be able to survive. His future after the war does not really worry me, since I have left with Franka [the woman who took in his son] the addresses of Yaakov and Shalom [his brothers]. I'm convinced that when the war is over and we shall no longer be alive one of you will no doubt come here in order to investigate on the spot what has been our fate. We rely upon you to show gratitude to those who have helped us and to take suitable action against the ones who have caused us so much suffering."[112] Klonicki trusted his brothers to mete out justice after the war, and he derived comfort from the thought that justice would prevail. Yet the justice he conceptualized was a personal, familial justice: the survival of his son, the punishment by his brothers of those who had harmed them, and the compensation by his brothers of those who had tried to help. Nevertheless, like Frey and Dreyfus, he seemed to connect these personal acts to a better future overall.

These diarists wrote with hope and optimism about the postwar future. They imagined their children and grandchildren moving forward with their lives, perpetuating the values and dreams they had instilled in them. The image of their own families' continuity made it possible for them to envision the future recovery and flourishing of Jewry and of humanity as a whole. The Nazi persecution and murder of the Jews did not lead them to despair of finding meaning in human existence.

These letter-diaries proved to be the last communication that some children and siblings had with their parents and loved ones. The two brothers of Aryeh Klonicki received his diary after the war from the Gentile couple that had hidden it and who also sheltered the Klonickis' son, Adam. That couple informed the brothers that the Germans had discovered Aryeh and Malwina in hiding in January 1944 and killed them. They also divulged that Adam was still alive, but that they had given him to a convent during the war. Aryeh's brothers spent years trying to determine Adam's whereabouts. As of 1973, when the diary was published, they had been unable to find Adam despite their suspicion that he was alive and living in the Ukraine.[113]

Max and Frieda Reinach were deported from Berlin to an unknown concentration camp in eastern Europe on 26 October 1942. A few months earlier, Frieda had written doubtfully, "Whether you will ever read this little book, I do not know."[114] Nevertheless, the Reinachs continued to hope their diary would form a lasting link between parents and children. They entrusted the diary to a friend in their Berlin apartment building who promised to safeguard it by carrying it with her attached to her belt at all times. When American army forces occupied Berlin after the war, this woman asked an American G.I. to deliver it to Boston, where one of the Reinachs' daughters lived. Thus, as it turns out, their daughters did eventually receive the diary.[115]

One of the four copies Erich and Elsbeth Frey made of their report also safely reached the hands of their daughters. After Erich concluded writing his report, the couple continued to live in their one room in the "Jew House" in Berlin-Karlshorst until the spring of 1943. Erich was a laborer at a workshop for the blind and deaf-mute run by Otto Weidt, who was recognized as a "righteous Gentile" by Yad Vashem for trying to save his Jewish employees from deportation. Until the so-called *Fabrik-Aktion* of 27 February 1943, the Freys were spared deportation because he worked in a war production industry. On that day in Berlin, the Gestapo and S.S. rounded up Jewish forced laborers—men and women—from factories and workshops as well as on the streets and in their residences. Most of them were sent to various assembly camps, and from there, in the first week of March, around seven thousand Berlin Jews were deported to Auschwitz. The Freys somehow managed to evade arrest during the *Fabrik-Aktion* and went into hiding, but eventually they were caught. On 8 April 1944, exactly two years and one day after Erich began his letter to his daughters, the couple signed a "declaration of assets" at a Berlin assembly camp. They were deported to Theresienstadt on 19 April, on the 109th *Alterstransport*, or transport of the aged. Erich was deported to Auschwitz from Theresienstadt on 15 May 1944. Elsbeth may have been deported with him. Their daughters, Liselott and Miriam, never saw their parents again, but they did read their father's report.[116]

Irena Hauser, Juliusz Feurman, and Rubinsztejnowa were all killed during the war. Little information is available about their deaths and the postwar fate of their diaries. Hauser either died in the Łódź ghetto or was deported and killed in an extermination camp. Feurman was killed by the Germans after his engineering skills were no longer needed. Rubinsztejnowa's fate is unknown. I do not know if any of their diaries reached their intended audiences.

Grete Holländer and A.B. survived the war, but their children did not. Holländer was told after the war that Sonja had gotten sick with appendicitis and died. And A.B.'s son and daughter-in-law were deported from Theresienstadt, probably to Auschwitz, and killed. Learning of their children's deaths proved devastating for both mothers, destroying whatever hope for the future they had retained until the war's end. Echoing A.B.'s grief-stricken final entry of her diary (quoted earlier), Holländer recorded at the end of Yom Kippur 1944: "Since my darling is no longer alive, something in me has shattered. I have grown hard and cold like a stone. For whom else should I pray? For me? Why?"[117]

Only Toni Ringel and probably Richard and Sophie Ehrlich were reunited with their children after the war. In addition to delivering their letter-diaries, they were able to narrate their wartime experiences in person.

In those instances in which the diarists were killed but their letter-diaries reached their intended recipients after the war, the diaries do not appear to have served some of the crucial functions their authors had hoped they would. Parents writing for their children wanted to lighten their children's burdens as they faced having to establish new lives while grappling emotionally with the loss of their parents under exceptional circumstances. These diarists also tried to lessen the emotional and epistemological distance between them and their loved ones, which was created as a result of their experiences of Nazi persecution. Yet for one of Max and Frieda Reinach's daughters, her parents' diary seemed to reinforce her sense of alienation from her parents during their final years.[118] It would be surprising if this was an isolated response.

In other respects, the diaries did serve their hoped-for functions. The Frey daughters were able to file restitution claims thanks to the detailed documentation furnished by their father. Klonicki's brothers did reward those individuals who had helped Aryeh and Malwina, although they did not punish those who had betrayed them. Most important, perhaps, was the effect the diaries had on their authors rather than on their intended audience. The letter-diaries seemed to help their authors. Writing for one's children or siblings who lived abroad acted as a reminder and reinforcement of a person's connection to the outside world. Diaries mitigated some of their isolation and helped to renew their hope in a future reunion with their loved ones. For those diarists who had ceased to believe they would live to see Germany's defeat, the knowledge that younger generations of Jews—their own children—were safely abroad and in the process of establishing new lives was critical to their faith in the existence of a brighter future.

These individuals' continued faith in the future suggests that diary writing may have also functioned as a means of controlling their despair and grief in the midst of genocide. In conjuring up their families on the page for their children, they also conjured them up for themselves. By writing about what was happening to them, they could in a very small way exercise some power in the situation by defining what was being done to them and their responses. In his study of grief and nineteenth-century diaries, the psychologist Paul Rosenblatt speculated, "The act of defining may be seen as an act of controlling, delimiting, and shaping one's emotional expression. One may also be controlling emotions through distracting oneself by composing sentences, by distancing events enough in one's thoughts so that one can write about them, and by the physical act of writing."[119] The process Rosenblatt described seems relevant to these family diarists. While that distancing could render them less sensitive as reporters, the writing may have served a similar therapeutic function for them.

Yet diary writing, as we shall see, could also hinder grief control. For many Jews writing in the second half of the war who had witnessed the genocide being carried out in Poland and temporarily escaped it, diary writing seemed to reinforce their feelings of physical and epistemological distance from the outside world. As they attempted to "define" their experiences in writing, they found themselves unable to do so. Despite their best efforts, the inconceivable, incomparable, and inarticulable seemed destined to remain so. Diarists who wrote for their families rarely contemplated the potential futility of their efforts, whereas the diarists discussed in chapter 5 repeatedly despaired that their diaries would be unable to bridge the gap between them and the outside world.

5

RELUCTANT MESSENGERS

In what has become a well-known excerpt from his memoir of Auschwitz, Primo Levi described how he recited Dante from memory to a fellow inmate while retrieving the day's soup ration. After first reciting a verse in Italian, he would attempt to translate the verse into his meager French for his French-speaking companion. The effect of the poetry on Levi was profound: "For a moment I forget who I am and where I am."[1] Dante's words momentarily transported Levi beyond Auschwitz. In a later work in which Levi returned to his memory of this incident, he reflected that, in Auschwitz, "culture was useful to me." It had enabled him to transcend his circumstances, "not often, not everywhere, not for everyone, but sometimes, on certain rare occasions, precious as a precious stone, it was actually useful, and one felt almost lifted up from the ground—with the danger of crashing back down again, the pain being all the greater the higher and longer the exaltation lasted."[2] Levi recognized that culture did not serve the same function for every camp inmate, but it had helped him to connect to the world of his past, to the humanist tradition, and to his identity as a cultured individual.

Many diarists writing in less brutal circumstances than those of Auschwitz described culture in terms similar to Levi's. Reading and writing, listening to or performing music, appreciating nature, creating art, engaging in conversation—what the philosopher and literary theorist Tzvetan Todorov referred to as "the search for the truth and the search for the beautiful"—these could be "morally uplifting" activities for Jews under German occupation. They enabled individuals momentarily to transcend their horrific circumstances and to "sanctify life." Scholars have understandably valorized Jews' efforts to resist the dehumanizing effects of Nazi persecution by continuing to engage in cultural pursuits.[3]

Diary writing was one of the cultural pursuits in which Jews took part in their efforts to connect with the world beyond German occupation. In contrast to other cultural activities, however, the role of diary writing changed much more dramatically over the course of the war for many Jewish diarists. Genocide transformed the function of diary writing. The mass deportations and killings made Jews realize that the world had closed in around them and there was nothing they could do. Some diarists, as they came to believe they faced a historically unprecedented situation, found that writing about their experiences for a postwar audience made manifest their sense of the unrepresentability of their experiences, which only deepened their alienation from the outside world. Like those who wrote letter-diaries for their families, Jewish diarists who wrote with no specific audience in mind were also trying to bridge the divide between the world of German occupation and the outside world and to fill in historical gaps they feared would remain yawning cavities but for their efforts. Yet many diarists who wrote later in the war, including some who addressed their diaries to relatives, harbored tremendous doubts about being able to bridge the chasm of understanding. Furthermore, the worsening of conditions and the intensification of feelings of hopelessness during these final years made it difficult for many Jews to sustain their writing efforts or even to write at all. Throughout the war to a certain extent, but especially during this later period, diary writing became more an onerous duty than a medium of momentary forgetfulness and uplift, as Levi experienced in reciting Dante.[4]

Initially, diary writing was like other forms of culture: it mostly had a salutary effect on those who engaged in it. Indeed, this function of diary writing has been well documented by historians and literary scholars. They have described how wartime Jewish diary writing helped individuals to carve out a human space, removed from the dehumanizing circumstances of dislocation and Nazi persecution. Rachel Feldhay Brenner, in her analysis of Anne Frank's and Etty Hillesum's diaries, argued, for example, that "writing becomes a lifeline." It offered a refuge from anti-Semitic persecution and affirmed the self's existence and uniqueness in the face of measures intended to efface Jews' individual humanity. It also facilitated diarists' psychological coping by helping them to keep at bay their mounting knowledge of European Jewry's extermination. According to Brenner, for these two women, writing had a "therapeutic function."[5] David Patterson similarly suggested that the written page functioned like a listening other. The diary reflected and thereby exteriorized the self to the self, which allowed the diarist to relate to her diary as a partner in dialogue. This relationship between the writer and her diary made possible the diarist's "recovery of life." In talking to her diary, the diarist was able to see herself as a unified subject in the eyes of the other. Identity, or the integration of the self, was constituted in the relationship between self and other. As a self-reflexive process, writing perpetuated the writer's existence in a fundamental way and for Jewish diarists potentially cleared a space for the alleviation of tension.[6]

In Patterson's and Brenner's analyses, the act of diary writing during the Holocaust was understood to have been more than an act of resistance. It was a means of transcendence: it permitted a person to rise above or go beyond everyday experience. While genocide loomed on the horizon, writing served as a distancing device, which in turn acted as a reminder and reinforcement of the self's integrity and humanity. What underlies this supposition is the premise that a boundary could be demarcated between the world outside—a brutal, terror-filled world—and the world of the mind—the space and refuge of the self. Writing was a conduit to and constitutive of that private space.

Most of the diaries analyzed by Patterson, Brenner, and other scholars were written during the first three years of the war. These diarists suffered tremendously and were subject to extreme uncertainty about their fates, but they were not subjected to the degree of deprivation and sense of despair experienced by Jewish men and women who wrote in the wake of the mass killings. What is more, they wrote within a still-existing communal setting, one that supported the efforts of diarists implicitly and in some instances explicitly.[7] An analysis of diaries written in the second half of the war—by Jews in hiding, in camps, and in the Łódź ghetto before its final liquidation in the summer of 1944—reveals that diary writing affected many people differently later in the war. In the early years of the war, writing at times failed to provide moments of transcendence for Jews, ceased to function as an escape or to connect a diarist to his or her sense of self from before the war. During the later war years, however, this tendency became much more pronounced. The experiences that Jews had undergone by that time attenuated the therapeutic function of writing.

Diaries became the nagging impossibility that countered their earlier therapeutic function. Indeed, Jews who were writing diaries during the latter years of the war struggled with the relationship between their experiences and the representation of their experiences much as survivors and scholars would after the war.[8] The two questions at the heart of historiographical and theoretical discussions about the difficulties of representing the Holocaust—those of narrative construction and of the textual apprehension of the "reality" of experience—were vitally important to Jewish diarists. They, too, considered their diaries representations that transformed their experiences into the symbolic order of language, or narrative, and this realization made some diarists uneasy. Instead of a window that rendered their experiences plainly visible to others, they perceived their writing to be distanced from their experiences. Yet rather than open up a self-affirming space, the distancing reinforced their feelings of isolation from the outside world. They feared their experiences were ultimately incommunicable and would remain, therefore, incomprehensible. In this way, diarists' sense of their distance from the outside world was not merely an intellectual and ethical matter, but also had psychological and emotional ramifications.

Despite fearing that their representational efforts might be futile, many Jews continued to record their experiences. Like Edith Wyschogrod's "heterological historian," many Jews who kept diaries after 1941 wrote with a consciousness of the simultaneous "possibility" and "improbability" of language to represent their experiences.[9] Their dedication to diary writing was an expression of their abiding belief in history and human beings as well as an outgrowth of their sense of responsibility to those who had been killed and a desire for revenge. Nevertheless, because of feelings of depression and isolation, many Jews chose to discontinue writing. Many others might never have been able to bring themselves to write in the first place. When individuals felt particularly lacking in hope, writing may have made coping more difficult because it forced them to grapple with their feelings of loss and despair. Thus, writing a diary did not function as a catalyst for hope but was itself an expression of hope. Hope remained a necessary precondition to diary writing.

An examination of Jewish diarists' struggles to represent their experiences picks up on several themes I have raised elsewhere in the book. Diarists' efforts return us to the discussion of representation in chapter 1 and show how central those theoretical issues were to them. They reveal how Chaim Kaplan's faith in the justice of history was still viable, though not as solid, for diarists writing later in the war. The rupture in understanding and hope evident among the news readers discussed in chapter 3 reverberates here as well, permitting us to investigate the role diary writing played for Jews after that shift. Finally, diaries written later in the war for an unspecified audience develop the analysis of the function and meaning of diary writing presented in chapter 4 and show that these diarists also hoped their diaries would be a bridge to the outside world. Ultimately, though, this chapter is about the rending of the self, the inability of writing to repair trauma, and the struggle to articulate this experience of rupture to others.

THE DIARIES OF READERS: CULTURE AS REFUGE/CULTURE AS POLITICS

The contrast between diarists' descriptions of diary writing and other forms of culture is often striking. Most cultural activities helped some Jews to transcend the present by connecting them with a sense of self that was unaffected by Nazi persecution. In a manner reminiscent of Primo Levi, the diarist Arthur Flaum described a conversation about music he had with "a fine, quiet young man" in a German prison in Prague. They stood in a corner of the noisy room that quartered 240 Jewish prisoners in a space intended for 100 and "discussed modern music for an entire hour." That hour "lifted us out of this atmosphere for a time," and they "decided every day for one such hour to have a conversation, whenever it is possible for me to do so. Helmut thinks that we need this in order not to surrender ourselves as quickly."[10] The hour of conversation was a moment of reprieve for the two men. Even more, Helmut and Flaum believed that cultured discussion would delay, if not forestall, the demoralizing effects of life in German custody. Like reciting Dante from memory for Levi, talking about music enabled these men to recall their identities as educated, refined individuals, and this provided some defense against the oppressive atmosphere of the prison.

For many diarists, reading was the most useful cultural activity in the sense of affording escape and moral uplift. In most cases, individuals who were able to procure writing materials could also get their hands on books. Of course, their reading selection was limited. However, as Todorov argued on the basis of his study of survivors' memoirs, the content of the book did not matter as long as the writing was of a certain quality. In general, reading connected the reader to the writer of that work and, through the writer, to "the world at large."[11] Indeed, there is much evidence from diaries to support Todorov's claim. Hélène Abraham, a French Jewish woman who lived alone, in exile from Paris, in Vichy France, recorded in her diary that reading Colette in particular made her forget her loneliness: "Whenever I come into contact with one of her works, or even remember or think about the existence of that work, the barriers of solitude are momentarily abolished for me."[12] Abraham filled the pages of her diary with quotations from the books she was reading. Reading helped her connect with a world beyond her isolated, makeshift existence, to the world of her real identity and normal life. Both her extensive references to reading in her diary and the terms she used to describe the effect of reading attest to the power of literature in Abraham's diminished world.

Most references to reading by diarists described its value as that of offering insight into and escape from their present circumstances. Adam Czerniakow, the head of the *Judenrat* in the Warsaw ghetto, used literature and headache powders to find a modicum of relief from the pressures of his position. Because of the curfew, he got into bed early each night and read. In an entry from early in the war, he described his nightly routine: "When I go to bed at 9 in the evening I read. At 2 a.m. I begin to fret. And so on until 5 or 6 in the morning when I get up. Shoes."[13] Reading temporarily took his mind off his worries. He also gained perspective and hope from works of literature, as is evident in his mention of Proust: "I am reading Proust's *Within a Budding Grove*. He says: 'According to the Japanese, victory belongs to an antagonist who knows how to suffer one quarter of an hour longer.'"[14] Czerniakow seemed to derive courage from Proust's assertion that the ability to endure—a historically Jewish strength that Chaim Kaplan also commented on during the same period—would ultimately triumph. Other diarists found literature to be a valuable coping aid because of the insight it offered into their present-day existences. For two German-speaking Jewish diarists—one doing forced labor outside Theresienstadt and the other in Bergen-Belsen—one particular line of Rainer Maria Rilke's prose especially captured their feelings during the war. Vally Fink found a moment of solace during months clearing and burning branches in the Czech forest, writing, "For one hour today I forgot where I am. Rueza Behal lent me Rainer Maria Rilke's *Weise von Liebe und Tod des Cornets Christoph Rilke*—the language in it is so splendid and sincere. Rilke says so much that applies to our life today [. . .]. '*Und der Mut ist so müde geworden und die Sehnsucht so gross.*' [And the spirit is grown so weary, the longing so great.]"[15] This exact line from Rilke appeared as the epigraph of the diary of a woman in Bergen-Belsen. Although this diarist did not elaborate on what she derived from the quote, it must have meant a great deal to her to put it on the cover of her diary. Perhaps it suggested that her experience was not unique, that other people, Rilke included, had felt and been able to articulate the same feelings. Reading Rilke undoubtedly also connected both of these women to what was beautiful and praiseworthy in German and European culture.[16]

The effect of reading that diarists commented upon most frequently was one of escape, of helping them momentarily forget the present. While in the Grünberg camp, Fela Szeps looked back to the first two years of the war, when she was still living at home with her parents and siblings. "Sometimes," she wrote in her diary, "in the midst of conversation and reading one forgot about reality completely." Even in the midst of the war, "in which fear did not leave our hearts," reading in the bosom of her family could bring moments of mental escape from the outside world.[17] Moreover, there is evidence to suggest that deriving this benefit from reading was quite common. The librarian and diarist Herman Kruk conducted a study in the Vilna ghetto in the fall of 1942, and his report, entitled the "Ghetto Library and Ghetto Readers," concluded, "The book became a narcotic, a means of escape. A human being can endure hunger, poverty, pain, and suffering, but he cannot endure isolation. [. . .] The new ghetto inhabitant thus clings to the little bit of what remained from before. A reader could thus tear himself away from his oppressive isolation and in his mind be reunited with life, with his stolen freedom."[18] Reading became the primary vehicle for Jews to forget the present and connect with their past.

Before the war, reading and writing were typically related activities, both signaling a turn toward introspection.[19] During the war, however, the function of reading and diary writing became increasingly dissimilar for many Jews. As we have seen, reading became a means of mentally escaping the present by momentarily connecting with the outside world through literature. In Todorov's terms, reading was one of several examples of "the search for the beautiful." Against Todorov's contention that diary writing provided a similar moral uplift, many diarists saw the two activities as quite opposed. Even during the initial years of the war, diary writing was a less useful vehicle than reading for transcending Nazi persecution.

Occasionally, diarists explicitly contrasted what they got out of reading over against diary writing. For Grete Steiner, the German Jewish emigré in Holland who optimistically interpreted war news and chose to remain in Zeist rather than move to Amsterdam, reading seemed to be the only calming activity in her life in January 1942. Indeed, she distinguished the sense of "peace" she derived from reading with the tedium she experienced writing a diary: "I sleep poorly, [I] can't take writing about myself because it would be too long-winded [. . .]. I read a lot and find tremendous peace in it, but my nights and dreams are not good, although they could be worse. It really seems as if terrible things are in store for us in the very near future."[20] This was neither the first nor the last time Steiner referred to her disinterest in writing. She repeatedly expressed the sentiment that writing, unlike reading, was an effort: "I read a lot, but I am not in the mood to write about it; as far as my spirits are concerned I am so down, I don't feel like doing anything."[21] Although Steiner kept a diary off and on from at least as early as May 1937 until the end of March 1942, she struggled with writing. Periods lapsed without a single entry—on one occasion for longer than two years—because, as she explained, she had "lost all interest in recording so many horrors, so many disappointments."[22] Whereas reading opened up other vistas, diary writing was a pond in which her own wretched image was continually reflected: "This notebook is so monotonous and dull and colorless, like my mood."[23] With the news of deportations of Jews from other Dutch towns and her own deportation to Westerbork looming, Steiner reached the last blank page of her notebook and decided she could not bring herself to start a new one: "And with this I close this notebook, in which there is, unfortunately, nothing good or pleasant to read. The next notebook—if there is one—will first come after great changes."[24]

Vally Fink, who derived such pleasure from reading Rilke, also found it difficult to sustain her diary writing. She struggled with depression, which sapped her interest in writing, but she also felt overwhelmed by the task: "For five days I have not felt like writing because it is impossible to describe it all."[25] Later in this chapter I will explore how diarists grappled with the seeming impossibility of their writing projects. For now, I want to highlight how Fink, like Steiner, wanted her diary to pull her out of the misery of her daily existence but found that it failed to do so. As she explained, "I would like so badly to write more and something beautiful, but I am hungry, scared and worried and have so little joy that I am not capable of concentrating."[26] Diary writing did not help Fink to transcend the present.

Steiner's, Fink's, and other diarists' comments force us to reconsider grouping diary writing with other cultural activities that allowed Jews momentarily to transcend their daily existences under German occupation. It would appear that diary writing was exemplary of what Todorov referred to as "the search for the truth," whereas reading and other forms of cultural expression were also a part of "the search for the beautiful." Although they all perpetuated "the life of the mind" in extreme circumstances and were examples of individuals using culture as politics (since those participating were, without a doubt, "tak[ing] a stand against inhumanity" through their actions), there was one significant difference between diary writing and the rest: their effect on people at the time. In the case of "the search for the beautiful," explained Todorov, individuals experienced a "sense of escape" and a feeling of taking part in something greater than their individual suffering or of connecting to "the universal."[27] Indeed, diarists described their experiences of reading in just such terms. Reading brought them a measure of relief. Their encounters with literature offered a means of mental escape from inhumane conditions and thereby allowed them to reestablish contact, however fleeting, with the world outside. In this way reading connected people to a sense of self that stretched beyond the confines of German occupation.

Neither Steiner nor Fink could connect to beauty through writing, however. They both seemed to embark on writing in the expectation that it would become a creative outlet and provide moments of respite; but both were disappointed and apologetic when they found themselves unable to transcend their daily miseries in the act of writing. Thus, the meaning of diary writing did not derive from its being able to transport the diarists beyond the present and to affirm their existence as individuals. Instead, what made diaries meaningful was that they were attempts to represent the truth. Todorov contended that "to report, in all honesty, what they saw and what they felt" was experienced by some individuals as their "duty to humanity" and a way to give meaning, not to their deaths, but to their lives.[28] Indeed, many diarists felt a deep sense of responsibility and a desire to testify to a life lived. Nevertheless, diary writing exacerbated the risks faced by

Jews and proved to be logistically and emotionally difficult. As we shall see, "the search for truth" was, for some, a terrible burden and therapeutic only in an indirect way.

THE PSYCHOLOGY OF DIARY WRITING

Rather than an escape, writing was often the cause of considerable anxiety. Some diarists indicated that writing was not merely difficult under their present circumstances, but actually made it *more* challenging to contend with the present, especially after the onset of genocide. During the latter years of the war, some diarists talked about their diaries as elixirs, permitting moments of escape or helping them to relieve their consciences, but more often they described them as being deeply embedded in their horror-filled circumstances. Diary writing, therefore, stirred up emotions, and that made coping more difficult.[29]

Furthermore, after the mass shootings and deportations to death camps, many diarists found that writing did not help them sustain a connection to their prewar identities because they recognized that the world of the past no longer existed. Writing may have opened up a space for introspection, as Patterson and Brenner argued, but in so doing it could no longer restore the self's integrity and the continuity of identity. Instead, the self that was reflected back was fundamentally changed. Contemplating this rupture served only to reinforce the sense of the irretrievability of the past.

The following discussion seeks to enlarge our understanding of the psychology of diary writing during the war. On the one hand, diarists conveyed a range of motivations for writing, among them a sense of duty, a fear of the meaninglessness of Jewish suffering, a need for emotional release, a desire for revenge, and even personal vanity. On the other hand, diarists struggled with numerous anxieties that writing provoked or intensified.

FEAR OF DISCOVERY

The most literal difficulty diary writing posed was physical: if discovered, a diary would endanger the life of the writer and many others' besides. In his "Last Will and Testament" from the end of December 1942, a copy of which he placed in each crate of his personal notes and documents that he buried in the Kovno ghetto, Avraham Tory admitted that he "overcame the fear of death which is directly connected with the very fact of writing each page of my diary, and with the very collection and hiding of the documentary material. Had the slightest part of any of this been discovered, my fate would have been sealed."[30] As Tory conveyed, diary writing became incredibly stressful for diarists, who were well aware of the risk they ran by documenting their experiences. In this respect, the physical threat also had a psychological dimension.

Beyond the risk to the diarist, diaries put other people's lives in jeopardy. For this reason, when a person chose to continue or discontinue keeping a diary, he or she was also making a complex ethical decision. Jewish diarists were forced to weigh the importance of their documentary efforts to the future against the threat they posed to people's lives in the present, most of all to those who were near and dear to them. Indeed, the indefatigable diarist Victor Klemperer acknowledged in an entry from May 1941 that "certainly I also put other people at risk." He refused to stop writing, however, feeling it was a matter of "professional courage," as a scholar and contemporary observer, to record "precisely the details of such a time!"[31] Nevertheless, as the threat of house searches by the Gestapo increased, he did take steps to get his diaries out of his rooms in order to safeguard the manuscripts and to lessen the chance of their discovery. His wife, Eva, who was not Jewish, carried a few loose pages at a time—at great personal risk—to the home of their close friend. Thus, because of his "Aryan" wife, Klemperer had more opportunities to hide his diaries than others had. Yet even having this hiding place, he did not feel safe, and he briefly contemplated discontinuing his endeavor: "If necessary I shall have to stop the diary notes altogether."[32] According to Klemperer, though, this thought never lasted longer than half a day: "The relief at having manuscript pages out of the house always lasts exactly twelve hours. Then an inner sense of duty (or vanity or a feeling of emptiness) conquers the fear of death. (Hiding place of the moment: Delteil—*Joan of Arc* notes, a manuscript file from the '20s.)"[33] For Klemperer, the fear of discovery was regularly offset by other impetuses—duty, vanity, and emptiness—that spurred on his diary writing. To varying degrees, these factors were present for all Jewish wartime diarists, but the sense of duty became particularly acute during the second half of the war.

Like Klemperer, Jews in hiding who wrote diaries had to determine whether they would continue to write despite the risk it entailed. On the one hand, they felt duty-bound to make German crimes known for the sake of remembering the victims and for the pursuit of justice; on the other hand, they felt responsible to the people who were helping to save their lives. Unlike Klemperer, some diarists chose to discontinue writing. Jacob Müller, a German Jewish man in hiding in Holland, explained how, because of his concern that the Germans would discover his diary during a *Razzia*, or raid, he would have to postpone writing a full account of his wartime experiences: "Today is 12/4/42 and unfortunately I have to put off the continuation of this report until later. Recently there have been so many raids that it seems more certain to me that I will have to dispose of these sheets. If they fell into German hands with me, too many [people] would be harmed. [. . .] It is becoming more dangerous every day."[34] Müller recorded entries in his diary for another six months, but then, as he explained in 1946 in a letter that accompanied his diary, he stopped writing until after the war, when he wrote a retrospective account of the final two years of the war.[35] Writing had become too dangerous, and he decided that other people's lives were more important than his contemporaneous notes.

The risk posed to other people's lives could provoke a great deal of anxiety. A diarist in hiding in Ukraine, Dina Rathauserowa, described the dilemma of what to do with her diary, knowing it would seal the fate of the Ukrainian man who was hiding her in his cellar if it was found: "Fear seizes hold of me when I write something bad about Hitler. The fear is so strong that even while writing it does not leave me even for a second. I am constantly worried to death by these thoughts: they have discovered our bunker and we want to defend our [host]. We say that we snuck in here, that he knew nothing about it, [. . .] that we had some supplies from the forest, that we lived on them, that he is innocent. It could save him. But this diary? It will give him away, but where can it be hidden? It would be a pity to destroy it. What a shame, and yet it is something that often disturbs my peace. I will give it to [Mrs.] Pańczyszynowa, let her hide it!"[36]

As Rathauserowa confessed, writing was a source of worry for her, exacerbating her already acute sense of vulnerability and fear for her host. The writing process also seemed to lead her from one terrible thought to another. In an earlier entry, this heightening of tension forced her to cut short that day's entry: "I could not sleep last night. [. . .] Various thoughts oppressed me: maybe we will get sick, what will happen to us? Will they bury us here in the cellar? How terrible. But isn't death by the Nazis worse? I cannot write any more, my head aches."[37] Rather than unburdening her of such thoughts, thereby providing a measure of relief, writing seemed to carry her to consider the futility of their situation. Indeed two and a half months later, Rathauserowa gave her diary to Pańczyszynowa for safekeeping. Interestingly, we know this because Rathauserowa recorded at least two more entries after entrusting her diary to this woman.[38] That she chose to take it up again after delivering her diary to Pańczyszynowa suggests that, at the same time diary writing provoked anxiety, it must have also been a thread that (barely) stitched her to life. Like Klemperer, Rathauserowa struggled with the emotional benefit and detriment of diary writing. It seemed to have an existential effect, that of connecting her to life, perhaps by functioning as a listening other; however, it did not serve as a means of transcendence allowing her to forget her situation as a Jew in hiding in the spring of 1943.

The examples of Klemperer, Müller, and Rathauserowa reveal some of the countervailing forces at work in diary writing and the decisions people made as

a result of confronting them. Klemperer chose to continue his diary writing regardless of the threat it posed to him and others; Müller and Rathauserowa made
the opposite decision. Klemperer was seemingly more driven by vanity and by
the sense that words really mattered, an attitude likely stemming from his background as a philologist and lifelong diarist. He also seemed to have a better place
to hide his diary. Rathauserowa's decision to stop writing was clearly not an easy
one. In giving her diary to someone to hide and then recording more entries, she
indicated that diary writing simultaneously affirmed her sense of self and deepened her feeling of vulnerability. Diaries could be anxiety provoking as well as
therapeutic.

PHYSICAL AND MENTAL OBSTACLES

For other people, not ethical reasons but the physical or mental difficulty
of writing a diary under the circumstances overwhelmed their sense of duty to
record their experiences. Diarists' frequent references to their struggles to muster
up the energy and will to write are like indeterminate traces of the many Jews who
wanted to write but found themselves unable to do so. Indeed, a single entry by
an unknown writer from the Warsaw ghetto hints at how many Jews may never
have been able to bring themselves to write despite their deeply felt conviction
that it was their duty to do so: "I've often been asked by friends and acquaintances why I don't write something, why I don't choose some aspect of the 3-year
war and write about it as I see it. The 3-year bloodbath, after all, has caused an
upheaval in all aspects of Jewish life—there is so much to write about, let those
who come later read and know what we have suffered from the murderous occu-
pant. And indeed, my friends are right."[39] This person, as well as his extended
circle of acquaintances, recognized so vividly the critical importance of writing
that he found it necessary to account for his inactivity. To this individual, writing
did not promise an emotional release but emerged as a kind of duty: to ensure
that people in the future would learn of the Jews' suffering.

As much as this person from the Warsaw ghetto wanted to capture in writing
some aspect of the events he witnessed, the circumstances presented tremendous physical and mental obstacles. Here it is apparent how enormous were the
effort and resolve required to write: "At a time when the murderer stands, revolver
in hand, when everyone clearly sees death before his eyes, it is truly difficult to
write. It is difficult to collect one's thoughts and render an account of the three-
year war in general and the situation of the Jews in particular. How many times
have I taken a pen in hand to write when something has happened, a capture beneath my window, a cry of pain, ending in gunshot, in more Jewish blood being
spilt."[40] He believed writing constituted a significant act of resistance, and yet,

despite this deeply held belief, he could not bring himself to fulfill his duty. Writing did not enable him to transcend his circumstances.

This person also indicated that his sense of duty was so powerful it led him to attempt repeatedly to put pen to paper. Regardless of the obstacles, this unknown author "consider[s] it a sacred duty for everyone, whether capable or not, to write down everything he himself has seen, or heard from those that have seen, of the outrages committed by the barbarians in every Jewish town. It must all be recorded with not a single fact omitted." According to this author, the duty to write was incumbent upon all Jews. He wrote for the future "mourner," who would "write the elegy on present times," and for the future "avenger," who would "settle accounts." This unknown author tried to assume this "sacred duty" and forced himself to write something so that the world would "know what the murderers have done."[41]

A diarist who wrote in the Łódź ghetto during the final three months of its existence—just before almost all of the remaining sixty-eight thousand Jews in Łódź were killed in Auschwitz-Birkenau—also articulated how physically and intellectually difficult he found writing. This Polish Jewish young man recorded *in English* that, "many times I resolved; many times I began writing memoirs, diaries, but after a few entries I dropped it—it is the total lack of mental and phisical [*sic*] energy which accounts for it."[42] Nonetheless, for the brief period from 5 May until the first week of August 1944, this remarkable man sustained his diary writing in four languages—English, Hebrew, Polish, and Yiddish—in the margins of a French storybook.

Why was he able to keep up his writing during these months when he was as much as ever on the brink of starvation? Perhaps because, in these final months of the ghetto's existence, news of the Red Army's progress filled him with hope that liberation from the Germans was fast approaching, and his diary became a manifestation of his timid optimism. With a new justification for hope that he might survive the war, he seemed to turn to diary writing with a different purpose in mind. The possibility of surviving allowed him to postpone writing an account of the Jewish collective wartime experience—a project that posed seemingly insurmountable challenges—until the postwar future. He continued "dreaming, dreaming, about survival and about getting fame in order to be able to 'tell' the world, to tell and to 'rebuke,' to tell and to protest. [. . .] I dream about telling to humanity, but should I be able? Should Shakespeare be able?"[43] His yearning for fame and his fear of failing to be able to communicate Jews' experiences were issues with which he would contend after the war.

As a result, he now wrote for himself, not to fulfill his duty to others. In his first entry, he explained that "to recapitulate the past events is quite impossible so I begin with the present" and proceeded to use the diary to carve out a private space for confession. By writing in English, he could acknowledge his "terrible remorse of conscience" and feeling like "a miserably helpless criminal" over eating his sister's weekly bread ration with a degree of certainty that his admission would remain confidential.[44] He even said of his diary that it was "like a friend," suggesting it had become a listening other for him with self-affirming effect.[45] His diary opened up a space for him to unburden his conscience and fears. Nevertheless, when Hans Biebow, the German administrator in charge of the Łódź ghetto, announced to the remaining Jews in Łódź that they would be deported from the ghetto in a matter of days, this diarist unleashed a torrent of words about the futility of their suffering for the past five years and then had to leave off writing: "I cannot write more. I am terribly resigned and black-spirited."[46] Utterly hopeless, with no hope of surviving, he no longer found writing to be an affirmation of his existence.

As the Łódź ghetto diarist indicated, there were Jews who started writing diaries in the wake of mass killings for whom writing was a welcome and salutary practice despite the physical and mental obstacles. One major component of such diaries was their confessional nature. Another diarist who wrote in the second half of the war out of his need to relieve his conscience was Calel Perechodnik. As a member of the Jewish police in the provincial ghetto of Otwock, outside of Warsaw, Perechodnik watched as his wife and only child were forced on a transport to Treblinka. The incredible guilt he harbored over his family's deportation as well as over the things he had done as a Jewish policeman in the ghetto compelled him to write "a confession about my lifetime, a sincere and true confession. Alas, I don't believe in divine absolution, and as far as others are concerned, only my wife could—although she shouldn't—absolve me. However, she is no longer among the living."[47] He made clear in the very first paragraph of his "confession" that he sought to write an individual account, not a collective one. He intended to "try to describe my family's history during the German occupation. This is not a literary work; I have neither the ability nor the ambition to attempt one. It is not a history of Polish Jewry. It is a memoir of a Jew and his family."[48] Even though later in his writing Perechodnik expressed the hope that his account of the war would be "preserved and in the future will be handed down to Jews as a faithful reflection of those tragic times," this was not the driving force behind his endeavor.[49] Instead, he wrote out of his need to attain his wife's forgiveness. Despite recognizing that it was impossible to be forgiven by the deceased, he expressed at the end of his memoir his belief that, to some extent, he had atoned for his wrongdoing. He believed his memoir would be a monument to his wife, ensuring her eternal remembrance.[50] In this way, he clearly derived a great deal of therapeutic value from writing, although this version of writing-as-therapy is different from that described by Brenner and Patterson.

Perechodnik was able to sustain writing over the course of six months in 1943, but he wrote for individual, not collective, reasons. He also wrote while in hiding rather than in a ghetto or camp. Many other Jews, including those in hiding, could not. Starvation, violence, and hopelessness made it difficult for them to write, despite their deeply felt sense of duty to help preserve Jewish memory and to further the exaction of justice after the war.

LONELINESS

For many Jews, diary writing became an emotional catalyst in a negative sense as they experienced the world closing in around them. Rather than relieving their feelings, writing often deepened them. Similar to the Łódź ghetto diarist, many diarists stopped writing when their circumstances worsened to the point of hopelessness, perhaps because it prevented them from being able to shut off their thoughts. Writing may have opened a space for self-reflection, but they could not face the lonely self that their diaries were reflecting back.

For some diarists, the more alone they were, the more emotionally difficult this introspective process seemed to become. M. Landsberg, the diarist who decoded newspapers while in hiding in a cellar with Rudy in Krzemieniec, in western Ukraine, almost entirely broke off writing after his bunker mate left him alone. Rudy was apparently trying to establish contact with Jewish partisans in the region and then planned to return to the bunker. Shortly after his departure, Landsberg wrote, "It is barely a few hours since Rudy's departure and I already sense loneliness. I can't imagine how I am going to get through a longer period here by myself."[51] On the day Rudy left, 30 December 1942, Landsberg learned of the slaughter of the Jews in the nearby town of Brody and that Hitler had allegedly ordered that "in the New Year not a single Jew will be left alive on German-occupied territory."[52] His loneliness and the tumult outside combined to cause him to regret having gone along with Rudy's plan. On the following day, Landsberg recorded curtly, "Rudy did not return today" and "I slept little."[53] Following this entry, he broke off writing—merely noting the day of the week and date in a makeshift calendar he had constructed—until three months later, by which time Rudy had rejoined him. Although it is not entirely clear that he took a break from writing on account of his loneliness, certainly his isolation did not compel him to write more or even to continue writing. Perhaps the act of writing had been integrated into his daily routine in the bunker with Rudy; perhaps it had helped him to create a private space separate from Rudy, which he no longer needed when Rudy was gone. That his isolation hindered his writing suggests that writing did not provide an escape from his loneliness. It did not place him in a dialogic relationship, nor did it lift him out of the present and into the continuum of Jewish history. Writing may even have magnified his loneliness.

In the case of other diarists, the correlation between being left alone and curtailing their writing was even clearer. Fifteen-year-old Isabelle Jesion was left alone in Paris when, in mid-July 1942, her parents were taken to Drancy. For the previous ten months, Jesion had kept a diary in which she poured out her feelings of alienation and deep need for affection from, on the one hand, her French Catholic schoolmates and teachers and, on the other hand, her Jewish immigrant parents. Under normal circumstances, her diary could be read as the exhibition of a teenage girl in the throes of adolescent angst. Yet under the circumstances, this Jewish girl's confessions communicated much more than adolescent insecurity. During the period before her parents were taken to Drancy, she felt her diary was her "sole friend" and "confidante" and often turned to writing when in need of comfort: "Dear diary, when I am sad and feel abandoned, I take you up to console me."[54] Jesion addressed her diary directly, suggesting that it functioned like a listening other: "*Au revoir*, beloved diary, who listens to me and whom I love almost like a living being. Is it not my only support that never fails me; it is mute but does not mock, soothes me and seems to give me courage."[55] After her parents had been taken, however, writing in her diary seemed to have the opposite effect: it drained her of courage. "I am alone, Dear Diary," wrote Jesion, "because my parents were taken just one week ago on July 16th at 3 o'clock. I miss my parents. I am alone like Mlle. Munsch. I no longer have the courage to write or else I will cry too hard. *Adieu*, Dear Diary, Isabelle."[56] Three weeks later, she again had to cut short her writing: "I am not writing any more. I don't have the courage. No news of my parents for two weeks."[57] Initially, then, Jesion enjoyed writing and found it to be therapeutic. During the terrifying period after her parents were taken, articulating her situation in writing did not provide relief but seemed to render coping more difficult. Thus, writing functioned both ways for Jesion depending on her circumstances: as a listening other and as a reflection of her misery that only served to deepen her feelings of isolation and hopelessness. For four months, she continued to record sporadic entries but then stopped writing altogether, only resuming her diary a year and a half later, under significantly changed circumstances.[58]

The departure of a loved one silenced another diarist. Toni Ringel, one of the parents who wrote a diary for her children, broke off writing when she was left a widow while in hiding in Amsterdam. Ringel kept a diary from the end of September 1942, when she and her husband, Max, first went into hiding, until the end of March 1945, when Max died in their hiding place while holding her hand.

In the previous two months, she had taken breaks from writing when she felt particularly weak or when the news was especially dismal. In February 1945, for example, she explained, "I have not written anything for several weeks," because "there was nothing good to report."[59] After her husband died, she described the last hours of his life and concluded, "After having been together for almost forty years, in misery and happiness, I am now alone and wait for my dear children."[60] With that, she ceased writing. As discussed previously, Ringel's diary had been an expression of her and her husband's mutual love and good wishes for their children. Rather than a private act, her diary was a product of conversations with her husband, and she more often than not made reference to "we" in the course of her writing. Maybe writing served at this moment to reinforce her aloneness, and Ringel did not want to express her grief to her children but to convey her hope.

Landsberg, Jesion, and Ringel all stopped writing when they were left alone. Their diaries may have been mediums for self-reflection, but they merely reflected the diarists' feelings of loneliness and hopelessness without being able to change them. If anything, they may have exacerbated those feelings by validating them, thereby confirming the reality of the situation. Writing prevented them from being able to suppress what had happened. At these moments, the emotional difficulty of writing overwhelmed whatever forces had previously impelled them to continue to record their diaries.

TRAUMATIC MEMORIES

Jews writing diaries in the wake of the mass deportations to extermination camps often wrote about the earlier years of the war as well as their present circumstances. This process of recollection brought to the forefront of their consciousness traumatic memories from the recent past. If later diarists derived therapeutic benefit from writing, it was not generally because writing offered a means of transcending their experiences, but rather because it necessitated a painful confrontation with their experiences.

Grete Holländer, who tried to save her young daughter, Sonja, by entrusting her to a Gentile couple, struggled emotionally with writing. Nevertheless, she kept a diary for close to two years, from July 1943 when she went into hiding after having narrowly escaped the liquidation of the Czortków Lager until V-E Day, which was over a year after the Red Army had overrun the village in which she hid and "liberated" her. She wrote in pencil in the typical notebooks used by schoolchildren. Initially, she turned to writing to find an outlet for her bottomless rage. In her first entry, she described how "an unspeakable anger shook me" as she watched the four hundred women from the camp be taken away to be murdered and "the earth did not open. No, and the sun continued to shine, unconcerned."[61] In this instance and elsewhere in her diary, Holländer commented on what she perceived to be a disjuncture between the extermination of the Jews and the absence of a concomitant natural disaster. Her repeated references to this disjuncture reflected both her sense of the universal scale of this human catastrophe and her alienation from the outside world. She "wanted to scream but did not scream," and since "I cannot shout it all out, I want to write it down as long as it continues, as long as I am alive."[62] In writing, she sought to express her unremitting pain and anger.

Although diarists like Holländer, who wrote later in the war, used their diaries to vent their rage, writing did not function solely as emotional expression. Holländer wrote because she could not scream but also in order to unsettle the world's ongoing sense of normalcy and complacency in the face of the annihilation of her people. She wanted to ensure that the crimes of the Germans did not go unknown and unavenged: "The very few [Jews] who will be left [after the war] will have to avenge their murdered brothers! Revenge that shakes the world to its very foundations. Otherwise those in mass graves will know no peace."[63] For Holländer and others, writing often became associated with their responsibility to avenge the murder of their Jewish brothers and sisters. Revenge was perceived as a just response to the atrocities committed by the Germans, as a duty that surviving Jews owed to those who had been killed, and as a welcome outlet for their anger. Writing fulfilled an emotional need and constituted the first stage of this pursuit of justice. The anger and yearning for revenge among Jewish victims have not been extensively represented in the historiography, perhaps because it was a response specific to the last years of the war and the immediate postwar period, and few documents besides diaries attest to it. Jewish memoirs of the Holocaust, written under different political realities, rarely convey the deep-seated anger that Jews directed at Germans during these years.[64]

The sense of duty to further the pursuit of justice drove some diarists to go back over their experiences from earlier in the war. Yet this process of remembering could be, in the words of the writer and diarist Yitzhak Katzenelson, like "scrap[ing] these running sores."[65] Nevertheless, as part of their effort to record the horrors they had experienced, Holländer and other diarists frequently wrote about the first years of the war as well as about their current existences. They turned their gaze backward and began to create narratives about their experiences since the start of the war. These were generally narratives of naiveté and self-reproach as well as of longing for the lost Eden of family and community. At the same time, they chronicled the daily hardships of life in hiding or in camps. Thus, diarists writing in the second half of the war often conveyed a dual sense of time: retrospective and contemporaneous.[66] The contrasting of these two periods, and the recollection of the horrible experiences that intervened, was a painful process. As the opposite of repression, diaries made some individuals consider repression's therapeutic virtue.

The form that Holländer's diary took made it increasingly difficult for her to find the emotional relief she had sought in writing. She clearly delineated the two time perspectives by labeling memoir entries serially, with the title *Vergangenheit* (The Past) and consecutive numbers, and diary entries chronologically, with the day of the week and date. In this way, she underlined the diachronic divide separating now from then. In her first *Vergangenheit* entry, she elaborated upon the rupture dividing these two moments: "Now when I am writing it's July 1943. I want now to describe August 1939. Today I am homeless, alone, dirty, ragged and sentenced to death by the Germans. Today I am not allowed to move around freely and am overjoyed to have found a mouse hole in which I can hide myself. Then ——."[67] Unlike "now," in August 1939 she had had a home, a husband and daughter, had spoken no Yiddish and very little Polish, and had been unaccustomed to the "liveliness [*Lebhaftigkeit*]" of Jews from Galicia. When the war began and she and her family fled to Soviet-occupied eastern Poland, Holländer recalled having been "deeply unhappy"; however, "now, when I have to sit in the earth like a mole, without light or air, my former life seems like a lost paradise. Then, my dear Marek was alive and I was together with him and Sonja. Today he is dead and Sonja's with strange farmers."[68] In writing about the past, Holländer sought to connect the two periods. Yet she implied that writing could not forge a link between these periods of her life. Instead, it seemed to reinforce the distance separating her from her past.

Holländer's impulse to write out of her need for emotional relief came into conflict with her other motivation for writing: her sense of duty and desire for revenge. She recognized this conflict herself. Although she was determined to record the experiences that had carried her from the past to the present, she was anxious about the memories that would be churned up in the process: "I am really afraid of letting my thoughts go to the oh so distant, beautiful past. Everywhere [I turn] I encounter only dead people. Am I really still alive?"[69] By choosing to write about her experiences from before the outbreak of the war, Holländer would conjure memories she otherwise tried hard to repress: "You try to push away from yourself the thoughts of all the horrors that you have seen, lived through and heard. You simply do not want to think about it, that none of the people are there anymore with whom, a short time ago, you lived, spoke, hoped and were afraid. Sometimes you manage it [not to think about it], but often, at night, all the memories come and inundate our pained minds like an unstoppable flood. You cannot fight it, you lie there and break out in a cold sweat from every pore."[70] Writing brought her nighttime thoughts into her days. Indeed, when she reached the moment in her *Vergangenheit* narrative when she had to describe her husband's death, she found herself temporarily unable to continue: "And then the terrible day arrived that stole my Marek from me. Since then two years have gone by and I have had to look death in the eye more than once. Nevertheless my hand does not want to obey by writing and cold shudders go up my spine when I recall all the details again."[71] At this moment in particular, writing did not function as an escape for Holländer but recalled the trauma of her husband's loss even more vividly.

For the previous five months, until the end of November 1943, Holländer had typically written a couple of *Vergangenheit* entries every week. Now she avoided writing a *Vergangenheit* installment for an entire month, although she continued to record regular diary entries. When she resumed her retrospective narrative, she numbered the new installment the same as the last in order to underline that she was conscious of having interrupted her last entry. Her still-present agitation in writing about Marek's death was attested to by her open admission at the beginning of the entry and by her seemingly unconscious switch of verb tense in the middle of her description: "It is so difficult for me, I have hesitated for so long, but if I want to continue with my report, I have to describe the events that made me lonely. [. . .] Mother, Genia and I, with tears, pleas, entreaties and eventually with money, tried to persuade the policeman not to take Marek. But that one only shook his head. I *can* do nothing at all, before the front door *stands* a man from the Gestapo with other prisoners. He already saw that man" (emphasis added).[72] At the point where Holländer shifted to the present tense, she seemed to relive her experience of utter powerlessness to do anything to save her husband. And yet, once she had forced herself to record this account of the moment Marek was taken away, Holländer was able to continue her *Vergangenheit* entries as before. Perhaps, as painful as it was, recounting this episode had a therapeutic effect on her. If in this case writing opened up a space for healing, it was not as a refuge from experiences, however, but as an almost unbearable encounter with them.

Yitzhak Katzenelson, the acclaimed poet, playwright, and educator, also forced himself to record what he could of Jewish wartime experiences in a diary he kept for several months in 1943 in the German internment camp in Vittel, France. After escaping to the "Aryan" side of Warsaw during the final liquidation of the ghetto, in April 1943, eight months after his wife and two of his sons had been deported and killed, he obtained Honduran passports for himself and his one remaining son. They were sent to Vittel to await a prisoner exchange that never took place. Like Holländer, Katzenelson was trying to lock away memories. He found that writing about certain of his experiences imperiled his ability to maintain his sanity: "I shall not recount what I saw on that day of Mila,[73] for fear that I shall go insane. I have not attempted to recall it to memory for almost a year. It lies there, buried deep, deep within my soul, and I dare not conjure it up before my eyes. There it lies buried together with my madness and I shall not attempt to disinter it. If I disturb this bundle that lies buried within me, then madness will surely seize hold of me."[74] Writing furnished Katzenelson with an outlet for his anger, but it also posed a risk in that it might force him to confront experiences he could not possibly work through. Writing contradicted his need to repress his memories.

During the second half of the war, some diary writing became interconnected with memoir writing about the first half of the war. As a result, whatever emotional release diary writing provided was counterbalanced by the difficulty of recounting traumatic experiences. Those experiences created a permanent rupture, severing the past from the present. Writing could not mend the breach.

"BROKEN" SELF

Fela Szeps struggled with diary writing because it prevented her from shutting off her thoughts. Like Holländer, Szeps did not find writing to be an emotional burden at the outset, but in time and to the extent that it reflected her new, irrevocably changed self and world, it became one. Nevertheless, she kept a diary for most of the three years she spent in the Grünberg camp with her younger sister, Sabina.[75] In an early entry, in April 1942, she described writing as a deeply felt need and desire: "Many times one wants to take up a pencil to do something and write something about what lies deep in one's heart, what bothers us and subconsciously [sic] and doesn't leave us in peace."[76] A student of psychology at the University of Warsaw before the war, Szeps turned to diary writing in the first place in the expectation it would be a therapeutic practice. She sought to unload her "deepest" feelings—"some sort of bitterness" that "the heart stows away in its deepest depths"—of which she may not have even been conscious.[77] She did indeed seem to think of a diary as an other that would mutely listen to her, permitting her to assuage the negative feelings that tormented her.

To this personal motive for writing a diary Szeps added a collective one: it constituted a form of resistance. Among the women she spoke with in the camp, "there is much talk about diaries, everyone believes that there is a lot to record about things that don't happen every day (in normal life), things that we would not have believed could exist on earth."[78] Creating a written account of the world gone mad was intended for the future, when the world would return to normal. Thus, diary writing was not only an act of defiance, but also an expression of hope: "Now it is difficult to collect one's thoughts and yet it would be useful to describe what we are living through here [because] one day it will be historical evidence, for I don't doubt that one day things will be otherwise, better, but I do doubt whether I will live to see it."[79] Whether or not she would witness its demise, she believed that the Hitlerian universe would fall apart. Her diary would serve as her contribution to humanity's brighter future. Like Kaplan, she had faith that justice would prevail in the courts of history.

Convinced, as Szeps was, that the world would right itself, she hesitated nevertheless when it came to the question of whether Jews would recover from the trauma of their wartime experiences. She occupied herself in her diary with the question, would the self be changed? She wondered, "Many times I ask myself whether, one day, when we return to normal circumstances, we will have normal human desires, aspirations, wider interests, worries and joys, whether we will be capable of getting over camp habits."[80] In 1942, still clinging to the hope that she would be reunited with her parents and brother after the war, she alternated between believing that she and others in the camp had been permanently changed and that they would return to normal:

> Days, weeks go by, everything follows its course, and yet, and yet what changes [have taken place] in our life, in our hearts! Superficially we appear to be at peace, as we attend to our duties as usual, we work, eat, look after everything that is essential for our comfort. Superficially! Because inside, inside is a burning, terrible wound! Because only inside, every single one, all alone is living through a cruel tragedy! I step through life like in a dream, a cruel dream, and like in a dream something subconscious commands me to believe that it will pass, that it will immediately end, that it is not after all real life, only a dream, a nightmare, which will come to an end and return to reality.[81]

During her first year in the camp, Szeps vacillated on the issue of whether they had changed as people as a result of their wartime experiences. On the one hand, she conveyed how deeply she and other Jews had been wounded. She portrayed the self as divided into internal and external halves, and the external self was "superficial" because it failed to reveal their real suffering inside. On the other hand, Szeps portrayed the world of the camp—the world that had inflicted their wounds—as unreal. If it could pass like a dream, then assumably her prewar self could be restored, deeply shaken but not scarred. Writing seemed to help her counteract the effects of the camp on her self. It helped her to connect mentally with life outside the camp.

In time, writing, for Szeps, lost its capacity to aid her in forging a link to the outside world and her earlier self. The longer Szeps was in the Grünberg camp, the more she adapted to the reality of it. Yet it still "seemed to me that this was not reality, it was a dream, that in a moment I would wake up. But the dream keeps going."[82] She continued to feel that the world of the camp was entirely separate from the world outside, that they were temporally and spatially noncontiguous. However, she experienced a reversal in her perception of these two worlds. Now, life in the camp "seems to me that this is an eternity, and the other [life] was only a dream and such a life like the present one has existed for ever."[83] Now it was the outside world—her past and her future—that had become unreal. Writing could no longer help her conjure the outside world vividly enough to sustain her grasp on its reality. It could not counteract the effects of the camp on her self. She felt herself becoming someone different in the process of adapting to camp life, and writing only reflected that difference between her former and present selves.

When she learned of the almost certain deaths of her parents—"home, parents, everything has evaporated into smoke as if it had never existed"—her hope that the war would prove to be a temporary interruption of their lives was shattered.[84] Her parents had been deported, her family's home destroyed, "nothing is left that reminds me of my childhood, my past [. . .]."[85] In 1942, she could still hope to recover her home and family after the war. One year later, she wrote that, though she continued to carry out her "physiological functions," she was living a "broken" existence. She had to forget that she had "once claimed a right to youth," that she had had desires and longings, and that she had "dreamt and made plans" for the future.[86] In needing to forget that she was once young and had dreams and desires, she implied that the dimensions of her identity from before the war—her youth, idealism, and independence—had been subsumed by the experience of being a Jew under the Nazis. The destruction of her past made it impossible for her to imagine a future. She and other Jews in the camp did not believe that "freedom [. . .] was meant for us. We can no longer imagine what normal free life looks like, we have the impression that that which is not real for us doesn't exist, that it is something abstract."[87] Writing could not connect her to a space and time outside the camp because, for Jews, that space no longer existed. It had been permanently destroyed.

Cut off as Szeps was from the world outside, her diary became the record of her struggle with remembering and forgetting. As she was being taken away from Dąbrowa, her mother's last words to her were "to remember." Though her mother did not mean to do so, she had planted a "curse" on them, Szeps wrote. As if speaking directly to her mother, she wailed, "Mama, your words that you wanted us to heed became a curse for us." To remember, she wrote, "tears pieces from my soul," and she asked her mother in her diary why her "farewell words" were not the opposite: "to forget about everything, [. . .] to be unthinking creatures."[88]

For Szeps, the act of writing seemed to be part of the responsibility of remembering. It dragged her out of an "unthinking" state and forced her to ponder the horrors of the present. In so doing, she inevitably contrasted her present existence with the world that was destroyed and the future that was closed to them. In December 1943, she voiced a desire to stop writing: "Oh, how very, very badly would I like to have nothing more to write." [89] To stop writing would have meant the war had ended. Yet as long as the war continued, she did not feel she had any choice but to continue with the diary. In January 1944 she repeated, "I was anxious to finish this diary by now but world events don't want to accommodate my wishes." [90] By the end of her second year in Grünberg camp, Szeps wrote grudgingly and unwillingly. Nevertheless, writing and remembering were duties she could not neglect for the sake of her family and her people.

Many Jews during the war, especially those who remained alive in 1943 and after, shared her sense that writing was a burdensome duty. Katzenelson echoed Szeps when he opined in a September 1943 entry in his Vittel diary, "Oh, would that I were a *Shochet* [ritual slaughterer] and not a writer. Of all my brother writers and poets, I alone survive. [. . .] My survival is, of course, only for the time being." [91] Although not a professional writer like Katzenelson, Szeps also felt saddled with the duty to record Jews' wartime experiences. And, too, she experienced a tension between her duty to the Jewish collectivity to remember and the personal anguish it caused her. [92]

For many Jews writing diaries in the second half of the war, the search for the truth did not bring transcendence, however much they were convinced of the importance of their efforts. Writing could not restore a sense of continuity with their prewar selves but instead made manifest the trauma that was still far from over. For this reason, diary writing was rarely useful in the sense meant by Levi. More often, in the midst of the mass murder of Jews, it forced Jewish diarists to contemplate the world they had lost and the hopelessness of their situations.

DIARY WRITING AS A PROJECT DESTINED TO FAIL?

Reflecting upon their changed selves and existences was not the goal of writing for many Jewish diarists, but by writing about their own and other Jews' wartime experiences they found themselves unable to avoid engaging in this self-reflexive process. Diaries showed their writers that which they did not want to see — or see again. At the same time, many diarists were disturbed by the potential of their diaries to be distorting mirrors. They sensed that the written texts they were in the process of creating *mis*represented their experiences, but they felt incapable of using language to greater effect. Especially for Jews writing from 1942 on, what they had lived through was so horrific, so lacking in historical precedent, that they feared no one who had not directly experienced the atrocities would be able to comprehend them. This struggle with representation constituted an epistemological problem for diarists, requiring them both to confront the issue of how to understand the reality before them and to translate that reality for others. In the process, Jewish diarists became all the more conscious of the chasm they believed existed between them and the outside world.

Diarists attempted to bridge the divide by means of the written word, yet feared their efforts would fail, which only made them feel more isolated. One central component of their fear of failing was that no one who had not witnessed such horrors firsthand would believe their descriptions. As Abraham Lewin deplored in an entry of his diary, written toward the end of the great deportation from the Warsaw Ghetto, "Those who are far away cannot imagine our bitter situation. *They will not understand and will not believe* that day after day thousands of men, women and children, innocent of any crime, were taken to their death. And the handful of those remaining after nine weeks is in mortal danger and, it seems, can expect the same fate. Almighty God! Why did this happen? And why is the whole world deaf to our screams?" (emphasis added).[93] Part of Lewin's concern over not being believed may have stemmed from the prevalence of hyperbolic war propaganda and the general suspicion of the written word that it bred. But most of all he indicated that those far away in the future would not believe such descriptions because what was then occurring constituted an unprecedented reality. His concern that readers might not trust his account of atrocities was shared by many diarists and later memoirists. Even the perpetrators were acutely aware of the unbelievability of the crimes they were committing. As Levi said, "It is important to emphasize how both parties, victims and oppressors, had a keen awareness of the enormity and therefore the noncredibility of what took place in the Lagers—and, we may add here, not only in the Lagers, but in the ghettos, in the rear areas of the Eastern front, in the police stations, and in the asylums for the mentally handicapped."[94]

Beyond convincing future readers to trust their accounts, diarists struggled with other aspects of writing. Katzenelson, for example, sensed he had failed to convey adequately the extermination of his people, and this only further compounded the misery of diary writing for him and made him question whether he should continue with it. After recording three months of entries, he wondered, "Shall I continue to record the annihilation of a whole nation, my nation? For what I have so far recorded is as naught. My most terrible dread I have as yet not touched upon. Shall I perhaps deal with it now as I go along? And yet perhaps I shall not continue at all." Despite the effort he had put into his diary, he was discouraged by how incomplete it remained. At the same time, it was with the greatest trepidation that he contemplated writing about some of the events he had witnessed. Yet even if he were to set down those experiences in writing, he went on to imply that his record would never achieve the desired wholeness. As an extension of his "broken" self, his writing could not help but be fragmentary as well: "For this pen of mine, wherewith I have written most of these notes, has become a living part of me. This pen, too, is broken, like myself, like my soul, like everything within me."[95] Katzenelson seemed to desire that his text capture fully what Jews had been made to suffer. Yet he could not breathe such life into his words, just as he could not restore his self to wholeness.

Jews who were neither professional writers like Katzenelson nor experienced diarists frequently reread parts of their diaries and were chagrined by the sum of their efforts. After only one week of writing, Holländer read over her description of the liquidation of the Czortków camp and reproached herself for failing to capture the experience: "I had wanted to describe accurately the *Aktion* in the Czortków camp. Now I see that I failed to do it. I have barely portrayed one tenth of the atrocious experience."[96] Her disappointment compelled her to begin the serialized memoir section of her diary, hoping that perhaps she would be able to communicate better what she had lived through if she started with the beginning of the war instead of in the middle. A diarist from the Stanislawów ghetto, Eliszewa, also registered her disappointment with her writing after rereading a prior entry about her hopes and dreams: "When, after writing, I read it over, it appears to me that everything [I write] is very naïve and absurd." In contrast to Holländer, Eliszewa felt she had no choice but to continue writing as she had until then since "this is my way of thinking." "Completely irrespective of this discovery," she went on, "I will still record my thoughts, but I will not read them over immediately."[97] She opted to stop rereading her diary rather than write in a manner that did not come naturally to her. She accepted that she might be misunderstood by others, whereas Holländer still hoped she could make her readers understand her experiences as she herself saw them. Rubinsztejnowa, who wrote a letter-diary to her siblings from a hiding place in Lwów, knew without rereading her writing that she would not be able to capture what she had lived through. In her diary, she told them, "What I describe to you in this letter will not be one thousandth part of how it really was."[98]

It is common for diarists in general—not only Jewish diarists from the Holocaust—to express feelings of inadequacy as writers. Typically, diarists convey the hope that they will improve as writers with practice.[99] Unlike average diarists, however, Jewish diarists writing in the wake of mass deportations and killings suggested that it was not a question of their becoming better writers. On the contrary,

they did not seem to believe they would ever be capable of recording their experiences, nor did they feel responsible for the inadequacy of their writing. They
felt that their experiences were potentially indescribable, even to the most gifted
elegist. From one diary to the next, Jewish men and women expressed this sentiment. Abraham Lewin, writing in the wake of the great deportation from the
Warsaw ghetto, insisted, "Our language has no words with which to express the
calamity and disaster that has struck us."[100] Rathauserowa, in hiding in November 1942, wrote, "No, no pen, no writer will be able to describe what we are
living through."[101] Malwina Klonicki, in hiding with her husband in an open
field in Galicia in the summer of 1943, confided, "But it seems to me that even
the most talented author will fail to give a full authentic account of our lives
under the present circumstances."[102] Brandla (Bronka) Siekierkowa, in hiding
in Mińsk Mazowiecki in 1942 or 1943, grieved, "We are so sad, so hopeless, and
so ill that no pen can succeed in describing it."[103] Zielenziger, in Bergen-Belsen
in September 1944, declared, "No one is capable of putting it all into words."[104]
And the diarist who wrote in four languages from the Łódź ghetto ruminated in
entries from July and May 1944: "If I should be a poet I should say that my heart
is like the stormy ocean, my brains a bursting volcano — my soul like . . . Forgiveness I am no poet. And the greatest of poets is to[o] poor a fellow in word even
to hint, only to allude at what we passed, and are presently passing by. Never has
any human being been put into such a state of 'the profundis' as we have been.
[. . .] to describe what we pass through is a task equal to that of drinking up the
ocean or embracing the universe."[105] These diarists believed that Jews' suffering
surpassed the limits of language to represent it.

Believing their experiences to be unprecedented in history, several diarists
tried to coin new words or used existing words in new ways in order to portray their dehumanized state. Holländer stumbled over describing what Jews had
been doing during the prior two years as "living": "Living? No, one can't describe it as such. Vegetating!"[106] Other diarists also employed the metaphor of
"vegetating" to refer to their physical and emotional states. Eliszewa described
how, at night, she "has the opportunity for adequate reflection on my present
life. I doubt very much whether it is possible to call this a life. Vegetation? Not
that either."[107] A writer from Gurs described the inmates of that Vichy-run camp
as "human-plants [*Menschenpflanze*]."[108] The diarist writing in four languages
from Łódź coined the term "Gettonian" for ghetto inhabitants, distinguishing
them from humans living in normal circumstances and implying that the conditions of life in the ghetto had changed people's values.[109] He also set off words
like "life" in quotation marks in order to highlight that he was using the word in
an extraordinary way. Szeps remarked upon the misuse of the word "tragedy" by

someone else in the camp to refer to their experiences. Its deployment caused her and others to "laugh maliciously and cynically. No, it isn't a tragedy, a term doesn't yet exist for it [. . .]."[110] Despite her criticism of this person's application of the term "tragedy" to describe what they were living through, she could not help using the word "tragic" to describe scenes from the camp in an entry one week later. By contrast, it was precisely because of the unprecedented nature of their experiences that Oskar Rosenfeld, writing in the Łódź ghetto, believed "tragedy" to be most appropriate: "And why tragedy? Because the pain does not reach out to something human, to a strange heart, but is something incomprehensible, colliding with the cosmos, a natural phenomenon like the creation of the world."[111] All of these diarists' ruminations on language anticipated Levi's speculation that, "if the Lagers had lasted longer a new, harsh language would have been born."[112]

Diarists struggled not only with specific terms, but also with narrative possibilities. The issue of creating linkages between individual events confronted diarists from the second half of the war to a far greater extent than it had diarists from the first half of the war. Earlier diarists had also often vented their frustration with their literary abilities. They, too, had felt they could not faithfully represent in language the experiences they were undergoing. Moreover, as Chaim Kaplan expressed after not writing for almost a week, "The sheer volume and number of impressions leaves me without the literary power to record and organize them."[113] For later diarists, the quantity and quality of impressions accumulated over the course of the war rendered their task all the more overwhelming. Indeed, as we have seen, many of them struggled to depict what had occurred during the previous years as well as their daily existences under German occupation. Thus, unlike earlier writers, some diarists from the second half of the war also became the first memoirists of this period, as in the case of Holländer. Writing a retrospective account of the preceding war years raised different representational issues from writing a contemporaneous account. Landsberg addressed this difference directly: "Parallel to the diary, I intend to begin writing my history covering the period from the memorable first of July 1941, the day the Germans invaded Krzemieniec, until the present moment. This part of my memoirs presents more difficulties than the diary because, even aside from the need to reconstruct from memory all the events in chronological order, there still remains the problem of form that can be neither as simple nor as trite as a diary. It [that is, the chronological account] smacks of something that smells like literature and that's precisely why I am filled with dread and anxiety that I won't manage to do it."[114] While Landsberg oversimplified diary writing, ignoring the ways in which a diary also involves narrative construction, he was attuned to the complexity of writing a memoir. He was concerned that a retrospective account was mediated by memory and risked being contrived. To Landsberg, only a skilled writer could produce a decent memoir whereas a diary was a genre accessible to every man and woman. Landsberg was not the only diarist who was preoccupied with the implications of narrative form.

Szeps also mulled over the complexity of writing a retrospective account as compared to a contemporaneous one. In contrast to Landsberg, she initially suspected that writing about the recent past would pose fewer problems than writing about the present: "I will not write after all about current matters: they are too fresh to be able to describe them properly. Rather I will write starting from the beginning of our captivity, [since] maybe I will be able to write more accurately about the past than the present. [. . .] I will try to describe everything chronologically, but I do not remember precise dates [. . .]."[115] Szeps regarded chronological distance to be an advantage, affording the possibility of attaining greater perspective thanks to time's passage. Two months later, however, she had also become cognizant of the shortcomings of a more distanced, retrospective account. During the intervening months, she had neglected to continue recording entries and was worried that in her retrospective account of that period "it will be possible for everything to be depicted chronologically and accurately, but it will lack the desperate scream of one's heart. The spasmodic sobs of one's soul. The tremendous, tremendous longing bordering on insanity. The moments when those dark clouds would block the horizon and there was no glimmer of hope for us and the moments when hope would unfurl its bright wings and would show us the bright and beautiful world of the future: those falls and upward flights."[116] Szeps did not doubt that her retrospective account would scrupulously render the facts, even if she could not recall "precise dates"; yet she feared that the emotional depths and heights would be a gaping hole in her narrative. If it did not convey her emotions, her diary would fail to depict completely the reality of her experiences and of the period as a whole. Thus, unlike Landsberg, she was attuned to the deficiencies of both perspectives and generally elected to write about her feelings at the risk of losing context.

Holländer, too, feared she was not managing to convey the experience of being a Jew during the war. In an entry from the first week of her diary, she admitted her "great predilection for adventure novels" and explicitly—and sarcastically— identified her wartime experiences with that genre of writing: "Life has done me the favor and bestowed upon me the most improbable adventure."[117] Nevertheless, she also seemed to derive courage and hope from that identification. The adventure metaphor imparted a kind of normalcy to her circumstances, as if now she was a protagonist in one of those stories, and this sentiment became a way for her to understand what she was living through. Indeed, Holländer was prone to using sensational, suspenseful language to depict her real-life "adventure." She cut off installments of her *Vergangenheit* narrative at cliff-hanger moments, for example, with loud knocking at the door, and used hackneyed metaphors, describing someone's lips as "turning white" with fear or her heart becoming "cold as ice."[118] She recognized the suspense value of her experiences and employed literary devices to embellish them. Well versed in the adventure genre, she modeled her story on that particular form.

At the same time, Holländer noted that the model did not quite fit. Jews' wartime experiences were both more extreme than fictional adventure stories and full of terror instead of thrills: "The kitschiest adventure film, the craziest sensationalist novel is boring compared with our present life. If someone were to film it all, it would be the most interesting, sit on the edge of your seat film! For us it is only horrible, since it is unfortunately the bitterest reality [and] means the fight for our bare existence."[119] She emphasized how different the perspective of the Jewish insider was from that of the outsider. For Jews, their experiences were far removed from a generic adventure, perhaps especially because the heroes of adventure stories always survive.

Holländer not only made explicit the point about how ill-fitting the adventure genre was, but also illustrated it in the character profiles of herself and the two other Jews in hiding with her. Although she portrayed herself in her first diary entry as the heroine of an adventure story, she later represented herself and the others as moles living in the ground. After two months of writing, she reread what she had written and, ever conscious of telling a story to an imagined future reader, saw that she had "forgotten the most important thing": "to describe accurately us three moles." Holländer realized she had neglected to provide character portraits of her story's main protagonists and proceeded to enumerate, one at a time, each person's sex, facial characteristics, eye color, age, hair color, height, outstanding physical features, profession, and personality. In all of these portraits and in the description of their bunker that followed, she clearly derived pleasure from writing. At the same time, her sarcastic tone in these descriptions—for example, characterizing the bunker's furnishings as possessing "a modern functionalism [*die moderne Sachlichkeit*]"—suggested that, although she found it necessary to set the stage for her story, she was also parodying this literary device as inappropriate to the content of her description.[120] She tried to show that, ultimately, Jews' experiences should not be understood as an adventure.

Holländer was concerned that the readers of her diary would not be able to empathize with Jewish wartime experiences. As a Jew, she believed she had a completely different perspective from even the Poles who hid her. When her Polish hosts had to sleep in the bunker for several nights with their Jewish stowaways in order to hide from Ukrainians who had been killing Poles in the vicinity, they still did not feel as vulnerable and terrorized as Holländer and her two bunker mates: "No one will understand what indescribable agony we endure. For Polda [one of their Polish hosts] the business [of hiding] was a good joke. Our every nerve shook with fear and we listened with bated breath to every noise from outside."[121] Polda found hiding, as a novelty and successful subterfuge, to be thrilling. By contrast, Holländer and the other Jews, who had already been in the bunker for seven months and whose only chance for surviving the war meant remaining in the bunker until the war's end, were deeply frightened. Even at this moment when Poles and Jews hid in the bunker together, they did not have the same reactions. Thus, Holländer inferred that it would be impossible for people who had not lived under German occupation at all to understand.

Holländer and other diarists did not fear that their experiences would remain unknown by the outside world but that they would never be assimilated by anyone else. Holländer was confident that "when this horrible war finally ends, surely thousands of books will be written. But I do not believe that anyone who has not experienced it firsthand could feel a fraction of the incomprehensible horror, of the uninterrupted terror, the helplessness, and the powerless rage in which we have, already for over two years, Lived? No [. . .] Vegetated!"[122] Szeps expressed the same doubts that people outside would ever comprehend their experiences: "No one will understand it who hasn't himself lived through it. No one will have the slightest conception of how it is if they do not see it with their own eyes or live through several days with us. There is no expression of words to define, to describe our life."[123] So, too, in a letter dated 24 August 1943, written from Westerbork, the way station for Dutch Jews waiting to be deported to the killing centers in Poland, Etty Hillesum was skeptical that either she or any other Jew would be able to communicate the complexity of Jewish life and wartime experiences to "the outside world."[124] In depicting human society beyond Westerbork's barbed wire as the outside world, she alluded to the fissure that she believed existed between Jews inside the camp and those outside. Although she attempted to bridge that divide by means of the written word, she feared her writing would not be successful. Hillesum and other diarists assumed that aspects of this history which they perceived, as its victims and eyewitnesses, would not be accessible to readers in the future.[125]

Many diarists did not believe their efforts to communicate their experiences would bridge the chasm of understanding between them and the outside world. At the same time, they regarded the written word as extraordinarily powerful even if it was ultimately an insufficient medium. "They could only be banal words," Katzenelson wrote, "the benumbed emotions of the mere shadow of what was once a Jew. At times my conscience prods me for my slackness in recording things that should not be buried alive and consigned to oblivion. There should be no cloaking of utterance, no deceit, not a single word should be concealed. It is, however, not slackness on my part. I am seized with mental nausea as I scrape these running sores day by day. It depresses and maddens me. It will also depress and madden whosoever will read these memorials."[126] On the one hand, Katzenelson believed that words were merely "banal." But on the other hand, he recognized that even banal words would have the power to "depress and madden" those who would read them in the future. Representing the seemingly unrepresentable was a vitally important enterprise. The knowledge imparted through diaries would not redeem the deaths of millions of Jews, but it would ensure that others would know something of Jews' experiences.

This sense of unrepresentability presented Jewish diarists with the paradox of embarking on a quest that seemed doomed to fail. Nevertheless, having recognized its potential futility, they insisted on continuing, however reluctantly. Writing about their experiences for a postwar audience was an expression of their commitment to humanity, which endured even with their firsthand knowledge of the potential of human beings to perpetrate evil. They recognized that the tools of human civilization—among them language and history—were equivocal, capable of being used for good and for evil, yet they wrote diaries in the hope that one day people would again use them to foster understanding. As a contributor to the *Oyneg Shabbes* underground archives wrote in the wake of the mass deportation of Jews from the Warsaw ghetto to Treblinka, "The desire to write is as strong as the repugnance of words. We hate them, because they too often served as a cover for emptiness or meanness. We despise them, for they are pale in comparison with the emotions tormenting us. And yet, in the past the word meant human dignity and was man's best possession—an instrument of communication between people."[127] In representing their experiences in diaries, some Jews continued to hope that those experiences would be rendered meaningful to others.

Only a small number of Jews who wrote diaries after the onset of genocide found the kind of solace and self-affirmation in writing that diarists like Chaim Kaplan had found earlier. On the contrary, they felt it contributed to an awareness that their selves and their world had been irreparably broken. What was more, writing could not help them repair the trauma. Thus, their diaries made more evident the hopelessness of their predicament, which made it even harder to cope with. These individuals realized that future readers of their diaries would not have had direct experience of the Germans' exterminatory actions. Trying to write for outsiders made them acutely conscious of the epistemological distance that separated them from their readers in the outside world. This sense of distance injected their diaries with even greater significance, making them the only possible means of bridging the chasm. At the same time and despite their best efforts, diarists did not believe that anyone who had not undergone the same experiences would be able to understand the sights and feelings to which they had been subjected.

Even as they despaired of the efficacy of the representations they were creating and despite often finding the process of writing to be excruciating, Jews continued to record their experiences. Conscious of the incommensurability of language and narrative to directly represent their experiences, diarists nonetheless struggled to render the difference between representation and reality productive. They insisted that futility or despair be offset by the hope that something of the reality of their experiences would be imparted in and through their diaries.[128]

Did Jewish diarists succeed or fail in representing the Holocaust? But what would success have looked like? To wring sorrow from words? To put death on the page? Yet, the fact that Jewish men and women contended with the conundrum of representability is highly significant, indicating that the struggle of representation was itself part of their experience. In this way, Jewish diarists from the Holocaust certainly managed to represent one aspect of their experience: their struggles with representation. Doubting the capacity of representation was one facet of what they underwent as a whole, and the evidence of that experience is indeed visible throughout the pages of their diaries.

The question of the limits of representation was part of diarists' larger effort to comprehend their own deaths and the unimaginable killing of their entire people. They struggled to make use of existing epistemological and conceptual frameworks to understand their experiences and, in so doing, to render them meaningful. Through their diaries, they made it incumbent upon humanity to continue that struggle.

CONCLUSION: "A STONE UNDER HISTORY'S WHEEL"

In their diaries, Jewish men and women left evidence of their struggles to understand something that had never been conceived of before: the regime-sanctioned extermination of an entire people. For them, the world was now fundamentally different, different in its suppositions as well as in the material circumstances to which they were daily subjected. In and through their diaries, they responded to the staggering psychical and physical changes. They reoriented themselves vis-à-vis the past and replotted their part in the future. And the diaries they created turned out to be not a separate and particular cultural response, but an integral part of other cultural responses—literary, theological, historical, familial—to Nazi persecution.

In studying Jewish diaries from this period, I have aimed to move beyond abstraction while sustaining a thoroughgoing analysis of the personal reactions of individuals who lived in a moment of radical disarray. Diaries shed light on the effect that Nazi exterminatory policies had on specific people and, through them, on their families and communities. In so doing, they allow us to move from the broad and often overly simplified picture of the Holocaust and its victims to dozens of individual snapshots. Through these multiple stories, a new challenge emerges, that of categorizing the ranges of victims' experiences. I have proposed one way: through the various strategies of interpretation that individuals employed to comprehend what was happening to them. By focusing on Jews' epistemological and meaning-making approaches, commonalities and differences among the victims become apparent, commonalities and differences that are not based solely on their prewar identities or on their wartime experiences. The categories proposed in this book help to illuminate aspects of the complexity of Jewish wartime life that are not simply about Jews' shared victimhood or their nationality.

By looking at a body of material larger than the so-called canonical or widely known published diaries, I have shown that diary writing was a broader phenomenon among Jews during the war. Jewish diarists, while all literate, ranged widely in economic and social position and in education. What is more, the writing of these diaries represented a social, intellectual, and cultural phenomenon that not only linked Jews from all over Europe to one another, but also reflected their connection to prevalent European cultural practices. Diary writing was not merely a *Jewish* response to persecution in the sense that it drew solely upon the traditional Jewish value invested in the written word and in the importance of remembrance. It was also a modern European practice that sought to accomplish a range of goals: perpetuating the values of Western civilization, especially historical justice, in the face of Nazi barbarism; pointing toward the theological meaning of human history; bequeathing information to future generations of family and strangers; parenting children at a distance; ensuring posthumous fame for the diarist; and furthering the diarist's own development as a self-reflective individual.

What this catalogue suggests is that if there was a common Jewish experience during the war it was the personal struggle to believe and conceptualize the horror of genocide. Jews suffered in different ways in camps or ghettos and in various nations. Those differences, to a large degree, are diverse forms of victimhood. In tracing the interpretive efforts of Jews, however, one captures the active efforts they made to understand. And in these projects of intellectual agency, Jews are revealed to be not only victims but also meaning makers. Diarists, in particular, also held in common the effort to translate their experiences and transmit them to others. In so doing, they attempted to empower themselves within the tremendous constraints imposed upon them. They tried to stave off the fear that nothing would remain of their lives and worlds by rendering their experiences meaningful to themselves and to future readers.

This form of empowerment offered no guarantee of success, as diarists themselves were aware. For one, diarists could not insure the preservation of their diaries. They also continued to struggle to retain a clear sense of identity. Diary writing has typically been portrayed as a means of self-preservation in the midst of dehumanizing conditions. Yet, as this book has shown, diary writing could be self-effacing as well as self-legitimating. As they wrote, diarists often kept in their heads the image of an audience of strangers from the outside world reading their diaries. As the extermination progressed, diarists became less able to believe their readers would truly understand their experiences. This developing sense of alienation from the outside world had an impact on their efforts at self-assertion. Indeed, some Jewish diarists wrote about the "self" in ways that suggest that the distinction scholars draw between "selfhood" and "subjectivity" is not merely academic. Diarists' references over the course of the war to their sense of self indicate that they moved from feeling like unified individuals to being the subjects of forces that determined their experiences of subjectivity.

Beyond alienation, however, diaries focus attention on Jewish emotion more generally. Importantly, tracking the transformation of people's emotions in the Holocaust from hope into despair and anger underscores the changing nature of Jewish experience during the war. As texts written contemporaneously with the unfolding of genocide, these diaries enlarge our perspective of the Holocaust by calling attention to the importance of time—the period of the Holocaust—in addition to place—the ghettos and camps. Some of the diarists writing in the second half of the war in Poland may not have undergone the horrors of life in the camps, but they struggled nevertheless with the shattering of their worlds and their selves. Thus, physical conditions were not the sole factor determining whether individuals could construct narrative identities that were continuous with their prewar identities and that connected them to the future.[1] That these men and women knew their families and communities had been killed and thus that there could be no return to normal life after the war was another aspect of their dehumanization. Similarly, for many diarists the challenge of interpreting Nazi actions altered dramatically after 1942 as evidence of massive atrocities became impossible to deny.

The hybrid nature of Jews' wartime diaries also reveals something particular about the situations Jews were in during the war and their understanding of their position. The lack of uniformity in Jews' diaries could also be analyzed as reflecting Jewish wartime diversity and the changes in Jews' understandings of what was happening to them and their prognoses for the future. To that end, I have tried to keep the diaries themselves in view throughout the chapters of this book rather than read through them as if they were windows onto Jews' experiences. By focusing on the function of diary writing for diarists—as solace, epistemological bridges, parenting instruments, therapeutic and anxiety-provoking devices—I wanted to bear in mind how the perspectives of Jews' experiences offered by diaries are mediated perspectives and necessarily affected by an individual's reason for writing a diary as well as by the relationship an individual developed to diary writing over time. These inevitably shaped the content of the diary and are clues to what diarists were not able or willing to write about.

Clearly, my thinking about mediated perspectives arises out of the theoretical discussions of the late twentieth century. And while this study has connected Jewish diary writing during the Holocaust—and Jewish Holocaust history—to the larger narrative of European history in the nineteenth and twentieth centuries, it also looks forward. It reveals the genesis of issues that would become central to postwar thought, including the relationship of memory to history, the concept of a fragmented self, the potential impossibility of mourning trauma, and the moral fallibility of Western science and democracy. The issue I have addressed most extensively is whether the Holocaust "probes the limits of representation." This book has demonstrated that many of the men and women who wrote diaries, particularly those who wrote in the wake of the mass shootings and deportations to death camps, were centrally concerned with a version of this question. In tracing the relationship between experience and representation for Jewish men and women who recorded contemporaneous notes about their wartime experiences I connect their struggles with those of postwar scholars. Indeed, much of what diarists struggled with anticipated scholars' later intellectual quandaries. Diarists feared that a caesura had been formed between the Germans' Jewish victims and the outside world, and scholars have indeed questioned their own ability to imagine and to empathize with experiences of suffering that bear no relation to normal life. A few diarists also projected into the future that historians would face an overwhelming task in trying to explain the motives of the perpetrators, and, again, they were right in their predictions. What is more, scholars' oft-professed uncertainty over rendering the Holocaust as historical narrative unintentionally repeats diarists' own apprehension about their writing efforts.[2] As Jews attempted to make sense of the genocide of their people, they wrestled with whether the events they were living through were ultimately unrepresentable for any writer, no matter how talented. They also tried to anticipate what effect the diaries they were in the process of creating would have on future readers. Diarists' reflections on this and other issues show that such questions were deeply meaningful to people at the time—and not only subsequently to scholars. In this respect, diary material makes theory more accessible. It also has the potential of adding new considerations to current theoretical discussions.

Yet in other respects what was befalling diarists was "unimaginable" in a different sense than for later scholars. On an obvious level, this was because diarists directly experienced this history. But also the difference stems from diarists' and scholars' divergent vantage points on this history and the concomitant perceptions of reality that those vantage points have made possible. With the passage of time, historians have clearly gained the wisdom of hindsight and accumulated knowledge. Indeed, historians' sense that their historical narratives have failed to capture the essence of the Holocaust in all its complexity could be regarded as a direct result of their accumulated knowledge. Historians have attempted, on the one hand, to capture the scale of the Holocaust, which generally has entailed devoting less attention to its human element. On the other hand, when they have focused on the impact of such suffering on individuals, it can result in a narrowing of focus, which, in turn, can lead to a neglect of the event's magnitude. There is in addition the challenge, rarely taken up by historians, of wrestling with the perpetrators' extreme inhumanity and the victims' extreme suffering in the same historical work.[3] These challenges of scale and focus have been central to historians' questioning of the appropriateness of different narrative forms.

Jewish diarists had no way to piece together the scale of what was occurring. Few had access to information that would have enabled them to relate what was happening in one community or region to what was happening to Jews throughout Europe. At the same time, their lack of perspective is part of the history of how European Jews from the 1930s and 1940s perceived reality. And, inevitably, much that they thought and felt and did has been lost to history. Thus, we know more than they knew, and we know less. In reading their diaries, we learn much about a past that we are already familiar with.

In the final analysis, it seems appropriate to regard these diarists more as sophisticated thinkers than as unknowing subjects. Beyond anticipating many postwar dilemmas, diarists, in spite of not understanding fully, were fully cognizant that what they were living through bore tremendous significance. Although diarists lacked an awareness of the full magnitude of the Nazi genocidal operation, the destruction they experienced firsthand was sufficient to provoke the conviction that they stood at the threshold of a new era in history.[4] Indeed, diary writers' perception that, however inscrutable its meaning, their suffering was nonetheless significant undergirds their writing. As Cypora Zonszajn attested to in the diary she kept in the Siedlce ghetto after temporarily surviving the deportations from Siedlce to Treblinka with her eleven-month-old daughter, "The situation is so horrible that it is hard to understand and hard to picture what is going on." Nevertheless, despite not understanding how it all fit together and not knowing what sense could be made of the different pieces of information she had gathered through direct experience and secondhand channels, much less the larger meaning that could be derived from Jews' mass murder, she wrote her diary with the fierce determination to "let these words be the living witnesses to those who lived these horrors in these tragic times."[5] Zonszajn's and others' diaries attest to how worldly-wise the writing and thinking of these individuals were despite their isolation and horrific living conditions.[6]

Jews' diary writing testifies to the ethical possibility of hope that Edith Wyschogrod figured in the "heterological historian." Hope acquired the force of meaning for individuals who wanted to help ensure that what they had lived through would never be repeated—that humanity would learn from their experiences—but who also wanted to ensure that being oriented toward the future would involve simultaneously remembering the past. They did not envision their project of writing the future's past as redemptive, as being able to offset in some way the loss of Jewish life and potential, or as optimistic, as suggesting that good would ultimately prevail over evil in the world. Instead, it was an ethical project, undertaken with open-eyed awareness of its possibility and improbability. Many of the diaries quoted in the preceding pages convey this combination of hope, the exigency of justice, and unbounded sorrow. It is also powerfully expressed by a person whose identity is unknown, who wrote a report, "The Last Stage of Resettlement is Death," after the mass deportation from the Warsaw ghetto:

> We want to believe that there is some sense in still being alive among the shambles, among human hyenas and jackals who live by stripping the dead. These documents and notes are a remnant resembling a clue in a detective story. [. . .] We are noting the evidence of the crime. This will no longer be of any help to us. The record must be hurled like a stone under the history's wheel in order to stop it [sic]. That stone has the weight of our knowledge that reached the bottom of human cruelty. It contains the memory of mothers crazed with pain after losing their children: the memory of the cry of little children carried away without overcoats, in summer clothes and barefooted, going on the road to death and crying with innocent tears, not grasping the horror of what was happening to them, the memory of the despair of old fathers and mothers, abandoned to their fate by their adult children, and the memory of that stony silence hanging over the dead city, after the sentence, passed upon 300 thousand persons, had been carried out.
>
> Perhaps this material should be gathered in order to find a reply to the questions: what caused such monstrosity, how did it happen that individuals were found executing these orders, carrying away these children and murdering hundreds of thousands of civilians? Awareness of the following truth should guide the hand and mind that will create the new mold of reality: this city that is silent today and its deserted streets will yet return to life, though the people who have gone away from here will live no more.[7]

NOTES

PREFACE

1. Information about the death march is from the testimony given by Genia Halina Tengler as told to Vladimir Jeřábek, "Report about the women's death march and the establishment of a burial site in Volary for the victims of this march," Acc. 1995.A.332, folder 2, United States Holocaust Memorial Museum [hereafter USHMM]; Adela Kestenberg Manheimer, Acc. 1999.A.0253, USHMM; Szewa Szeps, testimony, File 2728, RG 03, Yad Vashem Archives [hereafter YVA]; and Goldhagen, *Hitler's Willing Executioners*, 333–34. I first read Fela Szeps's diary in 1998 in YVA. In 2002, it was translated into Hebrew and published as Fela Szeps, *Ba-lev ba'arah ha-shalhevet: yomanah shel Felah Sheps, mahaneh ha'avodah Grinberg*, ed. Belah Guterman, trans. Aleksander Netser (Jerusalem: Yad Vashem, 2002).

2. "War diary of life in hiding became world bestseller," Home Pages, *Guardian*, 5 July 2002, 3 (accessed 22 August 2005 on LexisNexis).

1. HISTORICAL AND THEORETICAL CONSIDERATIONS

1. "Zeszyt Nr. 1

Prośba

Komukolwiek w ręce przypadkowo ten pamiętnik wpadnie proszony jest usilnie *aby* go nie odrzucić, ani nie zniszczyć.

W razie niemożności dostarczyć go pod adresem—uprzejmie jest proszony oddać go w powołane ręce, aby przyszły historyk mógł zaczerpnąć prawdziwe dane oświetlające choć częściowo owe straszne nasze czasy, pełne mordu, pożogi, krwi, i łez niesłychanych w dziejach świata, cierpień narodu bezbronnego. Z chaosu, we mgle spowitej, wypłyną kontury prawdziwej niesłychanej zbrodni, która ohydą i niesłychanym wstrętem przejmie najzatwardzialsze nawet serca i wieczną hańbą okryją ich wykonawców." Kalman Rotgeber, manuscript and typed copy, notebook 1, p. 1, File 990, RG 033, Yad Vashem Archives [hereafter YVA].

2. Rotgeber numbered the notebooks 1 through 24, but since he skipped number 13, technically there are only 23 notebooks.

3. In the Warsaw ghetto alone, Emanuel Ringelblum estimated that perhaps hundreds of Jews kept diaries, although the vast majority of them were lost or destroyed in the massive deportation of Warsaw's Jews to Treblinka, which began on 22 July 1942, and in the demolition of the ghetto by the Nazis following the ghetto uprising in April 1943. Ringelblum, "O.S.," in Kermish, *To Live With Honor and Die With Honor!*, 18.

4. On the importance of Jewish memories in light of the Nazis' intention to control knowledge of the past, see LaCapra, *Representing the Holocaust*, 64; Young, "Memory and Monument," in Hartman, *Bitburg in Moral and Political Perspective*, 103–13.

5. Jerome Brunner, "The Autobiographical Process," 162.

6. Ursula von Kardorff, "Vom Tagebuch," *Deutsche Allgemeine Zeitung*, 9 November 1942, no. 534/535, Literarische Rundschau section, quoted in zur Nieden, "Aus dem vergessenen Alltag der Tyrannei," in Heer, *Im Herzen der Finsternis*, 110, 207 n.1.

7. Leleu, *Les Journaux Intimes*, 237.

8. Studies on World War II diaries include Bluhm, *Das Tagebuch zum Dritten Reich*; zur Nieden, *Alltag im Ausnahmezustand*; Boal, *Journaux Intimes Sous L'Occupation*. Most notably, David Roskies makes this argument about the place of Holocaust diaries within Jewish literature in *Against the Apocalypse*. I return to this issue later in the chapter. On the complexity of European Jewish identity in this period, there are interesting parallels with the memoirs from Harvard University's "My Life in Germany" series. See Liebersohn and Schneider, "Editors' Introduction," in *"My Life in Germany Before and After January 30, 1933,"* especially 29.

9. Bernstein, *Foregone Conclusions*, 37. Bernstein argues that the creation of this "undifferentiated category" of Jews is the result of our projecting what we know to have happened onto the study of the past, a process he refers to as "backshadowing."

10. Barbara Rosenwein, "Worrying about Emotions in History," 821, 823. Rosenwein also points out that Febvre was not the first historian to look at emotions. Huizinga preceded him in his *The Waning of the Middle Ages* (1919).

11. Adam Gopnik expressed a similar idea in *New Republic* 196 (1987), 33, quoted in LaCapra, *History and Memory after Auschwitz*, 142 n. 6.

12. Wisse, *The Modern Jewish Canon*, 203.

13. Lawrence L. Langer makes a similar point in several essays. See Langer, *Admitting the Holocaust*, especially chapter 2, "Beyond Theodicy: Jewish Victims and the Holocaust," and chapter 3, "A Tainted Legacy: Remembering the Warsaw Ghetto."

14. Hillesum, Letter dated 24 August 1943 and entry of 28 July 1942, in *An Interrupted Life*, 353, 195.

15. Scott, "The Evidence of Experience," 796. See also Jo Burr Margadant, "Introduction," in Margadant, *The New Biography*, in which she contends that many historians have avoided taking "a radical postmodern epistemological position" while still utilizing "a method of analysis that recognizes the constructed nature of our conscious selves and views of others" (8). For a discussion of the influences on and goals of the study of "Ego-documents," see Schulze, "Ego-Dokumente: Annäherung an den Men-

schen in der Geschichte?" in Schulze, *Ego-Dokumente*, 11–30. Jeremy D. Popkin has suggested that this historiographical shift toward individual experience and away from "generalizations about the collective experience of any group" is also borne out by the recent spate of historians' autobiographies that have been published in France, the United States, and elsewhere to a lesser degree. He also calls attention to a common critique of microhistorical studies: "The evidence is never complete and conclusive enough to answer all our questions about life in the past." See Popkin, "Historians on the Autobiographical Frontier," par. 10.

16. For example, see Chartier, *Forms and Meanings*; Dauphin, Lebrun-Pézerat, and Poublan, "Une correspondance familiale au XIXe siècle;" and their *Ces bonnes lettres*.

17. My work is indebted to that of several scholars whose reading of diaries and memoirs and testimonies has proved deeply influential on my own. The first and foremost is Lawrence Langer, *Holocaust Testimonies*, whose work on oral testimonies taught me the importance of listening for unexpected—and sometimes undesired—messages from those sources. Other notable recent works in English or in English translation that focus on Jewish experiences during the Third Reich and the Holocaust include Aschheim, *Scholem, Arendt, Klemperer*; Brenner, *Writing as Resistance*; Engelking-Boni, *Holocaust and Memory*; Felstiner, *To Paint Her Life*; Friedländer, *Nazi Germany and the Jews*; Kaplan, *Between Dignity and Despair*; Mankowitz, *Life between Memory and Hope*; Ofer and Weitzman, eds., *Women in the Holocaust*; Patterson, *Along the Edge of Annihilation*; Poznanski, *Jews in France during World War II*; Roseman, *A Past in Hiding*; Shapiro, ed., *Holocaust Chronicles*; and Tec, *Resilience and Courage*.

18. Young, "Between History and Memory," 56. See also Kathleen Canning's discussion of "experience, as the rendering of meaning, [which] is inextricably entwined with the notion of agency," in "Feminist History after the Linguistic Turn," 377.

19. Young, *Writing and Rewriting the Holocaust*, 26.

20. See Hilberg, "Reflections: The Victims," chap. 10 in *The Destruction of the European Jews*, vol. 3, 1030–44; Arendt, *Eichmann in Jerusalem*, 5, 10–12.

21. For example, see Bauer, *The Jewish Emergence from Powerlessness*. Gutman's *The Jews of Warsaw* was originally published in Hebrew in 1977. For a pithy discussion of the historiography on Jewish resistance, see Michman, "Jewish Resistance during the Holocaust and its Significance: Theoretical Observations," part VI in *Holocaust Historiography: A Jewish Perspective*, 217–48. The historiographical portrayals of armed resistance from the 1960s and 1970s differed from earlier Israeli leftist writing on and commemoration of the Shoah, which had pitted the vast majority of "submissive" diaspora Jews, who supposedly failed to do anything in the face of the Nazi threat, against the tiny minority of Jewish "fighters," who were regarded as the embodiment and predecessors of Zionism's heroic settler-soldiers. This linkage was made explicit, for example, by the Israeli minister of culture and education in the 1950s and the first chairman of Yad Vashem, Benzion Dinur, who said in 1954 during a Knesset debate on the Holocaust and Heroism Memorial Act—Yad Vashem that the "War of Independence" in 1948 was a "direct continuation" of the armed struggles of the ghetto

fighters, partisans, and Jewish Allied Brigades. Dinur, "From the Knesset Debate over the 'Holocaust and Heroism Act—Yad Vashem'" (in Hebrew), *Yediot Yad Vashem* 1 (30 April 1954): 2–3, quoted in Kenan, *Between Memory and History*, 44.

22. Samuel David Kassow discusses this controversy in "Vilna and Warsaw, Two Ghetto Diaries: Herman Kruk and Emanuel Ringelblum," in Shapiro, *Holocaust Chronicles*, 204–6. These two positions emerged in a slightly different form during the war itself, in the Vilna ghetto, where there was a debate over the appropriateness of performing theater "in a graveyard," as the Vilna ghetto diarist Herman Kruk phrased it in his entry of 17 January 1942. Kassow noted that Kruk slowly changed his mind and, in subsequent months, became less critical toward theater. Kruk, 17 January 1942, *The Last Days of the Jerusalem of Lithuania*, 174.

23. Gutman, "The Political Underground in the Warsaw Ghetto," chap. 4 in *The Jews of Warsaw*, 119–54. For an excellent articulation of this more complex notion of resistance, see Tec, *Resilience and Courage*, 261. Many Holocaust survivors have long believed that armed struggle was the outgrowth of moral and spiritual resistance rather than its antithesis. See Kenan, *Between Memory and History*, 27–28. But Langer has continued to question the notion of "cultural resistance," asking, "How much of the origin of a phrase like 'cultural resistance to genocide' springs from what I have called 'our desire to redesign hope from the shards of despair'? [. . .] The intent of culture, we may assume, is to preserve and enrich intellectual, moral, and spiritual existence. The purpose of genocide is to destroy physical life. The weapons of each are entirely different, and certainly unequal." Langer, "Cultural Resistance to Genocide," chap. 5 in *Admitting the Holocaust*, 52.

24. I borrow "ghetto scribes" from the chapter title, "Scribes of the Ghetto," chap. 8 in Roskies, *Against the Apocalypse*. In his most recent work, Bauer revised his definition of Jewish resistance from twenty years prior in order to include individual actions within the concept of *Amidah*. See Bauer, "Jewish Resistance—Myth or Reality?" chap. 6 in *Rethinking the Holocaust*, 119–42. I discuss Bauer's concept of *Amidah* at greater length in chapter 3.

25. Bauer makes this point in *Rethinking the Holocaust*, 163–64. The question of the timing of the Final Solution is intensely debated among historians. This debate offers a fascinating look at the historian's craft, specifically the challenges of interpreting a range of historical documents. Among others, see Burrin, *Hitler and the Jews*, 115–47; Gerlach, "The Wannsee Conference, the Fate of German Jews, and Hitler's Decision in Principle to Exterminate all European Jews," 759–812; Browning, *Nazi Policy, Jewish Workers, German Killers*, 26–57; and Browning, *The Origins of the Final Solution*, 316. A collection of essays that encapsulates German scholars' recent research findings on German occupation in eastern Europe has been published in English. See Ulrich Herbert, ed., *National Socialist Extermination Policies*. Bauer connects these research findings to the question of evaluating Jewish resistance in *Rethinking the Holocaust*, 25, as does Michman in *Holocaust Historiography*, 222.

26. Hunt, "Introduction: History, Culture, and Text," in *The New Cultural History*, 17.

27. For example, see Brenner, *Writing as Resistance*; Patterson, *Along the Edge of Annihilation*; and Scharf, "Literature in the Ghetto in the Polish Language." Steven E.

Aschheim makes a similar point in his essay on Victor Klemperer, although the question of agency is not the essay's focus. See Aschheim, *Scholem, Arendt, Klemperer*, 80.

28. Kagle and Gramegna, "Rewriting Her Life," in Bunkers and Huff, *Inscribing the Daily*, 43.

29. Aharon Appelfeld emphasizes that diary writing was a "last effort" at self-preservation rather than an effective means of maintaining the integrity of the self. Appelfeld, "Individualization of the Holocaust," in Shapiro, *Holocaust Chronicles*, 4–5.

30. Michman, "Understanding the Jewish Dimension of the Holocaust," in Frankel, *The Fate of the European Jews, 1939–1945*, 240, 228–31.

31. Roskies argues, "The greater the catastrophe, the more the Jews have recalled the ancient archetypes." Roskies, *Against the Apocalypse*, 13. See also Mintz, *Hurban*, x; Young, *Writing and Rewriting the Holocaust*, 19–20.

32. Langer, "On Writing and Reading Holocaust Literature," in *Art from the Ashes*, 4–5. So, too, Patterson argues that "the Holocaust diary" is "in a category of its own." See Patterson, *Along the Edge of Annihilation*, 21. On the politics of genres, see Celeste Schenck, *All of a Piece: Women's Poetry and Autobiography*, discussed in Podnieks, *Daily Modernism*, 10.

33. Wisse, *The Modern Jewish Canon*, 197.

34. This does not apply to Patterson's notion of "the Holocaust diary," which sets diaries apart from other types of texts produced during the Holocaust. Patterson, *Along the Edge of Annihilation*, 16. Sara R. Horowitz also distinguishes between diaries and memoirs, suggesting that ghetto writers bore witness "with a strange confidence" missing from postwar memoirs, in "Voices from the Killing Ground," chap. 3 in *Voicing the Void*, 54. This sense of confidence diminished for diarists writing later in the war, as I show in chapter 5. Diarists who were writing throughout the war, however, contended with different issues than memoirists, and thus they contextualized events differently. Essentially, diarists were writing themselves into an unknown future. By contrast, memoirists possessed knowledge of the fate of European Jewry as well as of the fact that the Nazis were ultimately unable to ensure that the Final Solution remained a secret. What is more, there exist entirely different possibilities for action in and through the process of writing a diary versus a memoir. If, as Paul Ricoeur has argued, "truth is time-dependent" in narratives, then diarists wrote in a state of what he called "prefiguration" and "figuration," when the goal of narrative is to understand and to respond on the basis of one's understanding; memoirists' retrospective point of view, or "refiguration," leads to the reordering of the significance of events based on their knowledge of outcomes. Whereas a memoir's story is "pulled toward its future," that of the diary is "pushed onward by its past." Paul Ricoeur, *Time and Narrative*, vol. 1, trans. Kathleen McLaughlin and David Pellauer (Chicago: University of Chicago Press, 1984), discussed in Martin, *Recent Theories of Narrative*, 66, 72–76.

35. One major exception is Aschheim's analysis of Klemperer in *Scholem, Arendt, Klemperer*.

36. In France, diaries' educational function was institutionalized as of 1880 in the newly created public secondary schools for girls. By the turn of the twentieth century in Germany, reading manuals for classes in *Gymnasien* contained excerpts from early diaries.

Philippe Lejeune, "The 'Journal de Jeune Fille' in Nineteenth-Century France," in Bunkers and Huff, *Inscribing the Daily*, 115–17; Boerner, *Tagebuch*, 52. The popularity and exercise of diary writing seem to have substantially changed in the nineteenth and twentieth centuries. The fact that bound blank journals began to be commercially produced in England in 1816 with the year or, in some cases, the dates printed on the books' pages reveals that diary writing had become a common practice, at least among the educated middle and upper classes. Beginning in the 1830s but especially from midcentury onward, the posthumous publication of writers', artists', and intellectuals' diaries became common practice, among them the diaries of Maine de Biran, Benjamin Constant, Byron, Goethe, Stendhal, Jean-Paul, Herder, Novalis, Michelet, Amiel, and Delacroix. During the same period, bourgeois families began to publish the complete or partial diaries of their deceased daughters, some of which became bestsellers. These volumes regularly included a hagiography of the deceased by the family or a priest and served both as a memorial to the dead and guide to the living. These diaries resembled the Pietist and Puritan diaries of the seventeenth century, which were part of a regime of self-observation, obedience, and self-development with an eye fixed on one's relationship to God. Although the heyday of these diaries was the third quarter of the nineteenth century, they continued to be influential after the First World War. Additionally, with the publication of Marie Bashkirtseff's diary in 1887 in France and in translation elsewhere in Europe soon thereafter, the public's interest in reading diaries and the diarist's tone acquired new dimensions. Before Bashkirtseff's, the diaries of nineteenth-century figures that had reached publication were by prominent persons. Bashkirtseff was an ordinary person, a French-Russian artist who died of tuberculosis at age twenty-four. What was remarkable about her diary was not merely that it was published, but that, as she explicitly stated in her diary, she had written it with publication in mind and envisioned gaining posthumous fame by means of its publication. Moreover, according to Philippe Lejeune, her diary was "a complete subversion of the 'moral order' diary, a proud claim to self-value, a commitment to revealing the truth, a message for future readers instead of reserve, indirect hints, and the distant looming of private life." By the twentieth century, European diarists often mentioned reading other people's diaries. Lejeune, "The 'Journal de Jeune Fille' in Nineteenth-Century France," 119, 109–17; Girard, *Le Journal Intime*, ix–xiii, 35, 61–66; Bryant, "Revolution and Introspection," 260–61; Podnieks, *Daily Modernism*, 16, 21, 24–25; Weintraub, "Autobiography and Historical Consciousness," 821–48; Rosenblatt, *Bitter, Bitter Tears*, 8; Boerner, *Tagebuch*, 51–55; Fothergill, *Private Chronicles*, 17–18; von Greyerz, "Religion in the Life of German and Swiss Autobiographers (Sixteenth and Early Seventeenth Centuries)," in von Greyerz, *Religion and Society in Early Modern Europe*, 228–30.

37. Bauer, *Rethinking the Holocaust*, 127.

38. Lang, "Is It Possible to Misrepresent the Holocaust?" 85.

39. Saul Friedländer's use of the term "closure" has psychological, ethical, and political connotations beyond the strictly rhetorical. See his *Memory, History, and the Extermination of the Jews of Europe*, 131–33. Langer makes a similar argument in his pathbreaking work on Holocaust oral testimonies: "We need to search for the inner

principles of *in*coherence that make these testimonies accessible to us" (*Holocaust Testimonies*, 16–17). For additional discussions of the questions raised by the Holocaust for historical narrative, see Friedländer's introduction and the essays by Perry Anderson, "On Emplotment: Two Kinds of Ruin"; Christopher Browning, "German Memory, Judicial Interrogation, and Historical Reconstruction: Writing Perpetrator History from Postwar Testimony"; Amos Funkenstein, "History, Counterhistory, and Narrative"; Carlo Ginzburg, "Just One Witness"; Martin Jay, "Of Plots, Witnesses, and Judgments"; Dominick LaCapra, "Representing the Holocaust: Reflections on the Historians' Debate"; Eric L. Santner, "History beyond the Pleasure Principle: Some Thoughts on the Representation of Trauma"; and Hayden White, "Historical Emplotment and the Problem of Truth," in Friedländer, *Probing the Limits of Representation*. On the need to develop different categories of analysis, see Friedländer's "Some Aspects of the Historical Significance of the Holocaust," 5. For an attempt to theorize "counterrationality" as a new category of analysis, see Diner, "Historical Understanding and Counterrationality: The *Judenrat* as Epistemological Vantage," in Friedländer, *Probing the Limits of Representation*, 128–42.

40. Friedlander, *Memory, History, and the Extermination of the Jews of Europe*, 131.

41. Alexandra Zapruder critiques this redemptive reading of Anne Frank's diary in her "Introduction" to *Salvaged Pages*, 5. On people's tendency to find "rhetorical consolation" in testimonies, see Langer, *Holocaust Testimonies*, x–xi.

42. Thus, I would challenge Girard's contention that a presentation of a large mass of diary material can proceed *either* thematically *or* chronologically. See his *Le Journal Intime*, xxi.

43. On the issue of how to present diary material in a way that replicates the experience of reading diaries, see Lejeune, *Le Moi des demoiselles*. In this book, Lejeune sandwiches eight chapters consisting of his analyses of individual diaries with his own diary, which he kept while researching and writing *Le Moi des demoiselles*. As Lejeune describes it in a later article, "The book is a patch-work showing the work of research in progress, and showing what a gripping, but also difficult task it is to read a journal." Lejeune, "The Practice of the Private Journal: Chronicle of an Investigation (1986–1998)," in Langford and West, *Marginal Voices, Marginal Forms*, 196.

44. For an earlier discussion of the influence of literary theory on history, see John E. Toews, "Intellectual History after the Linguistic Turn: The Autonomy of Meaning and the Irreducibility of Experience," 879–907. Canning reminds historians that the terms "poststructuralism" and "linguistic turn" encompass several different fields of criticism, including literary theory, linguistic theory, philosophy, cultural and social anthropology, new historicism, and gender studies. Historians subsume these different fields under the terms "poststructuralism" and "linguistic turn" in order to denote the idea that has been central to historians, namely, that they need to examine the workings of representation—both in the sources they study and in their own creation of historical narratives. Canning, "Feminist History after the Linguistic Turn," 369–70.

45. Wyschogrod, *An Ethics of Remembering*, 3.

46. Braun, "The Holocaust and Problems of Historical Representation," 196.

47. Lang, "Is It Possible to Misrepresent the Holocaust?" 88. On the debate between

"positivist" and "relativist" history in relation to the historical representation of the Holocaust, see Young, "Toward a Received History of the Holocaust." The ethical dimension of this debate about the historical representation of the Holocaust has been underlined by Michael Dintenfass, who argued that it is impossible for the Holocaust to serve as a test case of "the knowability of the past if it defies our comprehension." On the contrary, according to Dintenfass, we have "conflat[ed] the cognitive with the ethical," and "the way forward from here is for all the participants in the conversation about historiographical theory to accept the prominence of the Holocaust in historiographical controversy after the linguistic turn as irrefutable evidence of the centrality of questions of good and evil to the historical enterprise and to begin to consider the study of the past as a project of the should and the ought as well as the did and the was." Dintenfass, "Truth's Other," 19–20.

48. Michael Bernard-Donals and Richard Glejzer reach a similar conclusion with one difference. Whereas I would contend that diarists appear to be quite conscious of what was happening to them while it was happening, they draw on Cathy Caruth's notion of trauma to argue that even the victim "doesn't have access to the event (she doesn't remember it) because she was not fully conscious at the time of its occurrence" (*Between Witness and Testimony*, xii). For a detailed discussion of this issue with respect to Abraham Lewin's Warsaw ghetto diary, see chapter 2 of their book, and Bernard-Donals's article on the same subject, entitled "History and Disaster." For a full elaboration of Caruth's notion of the referential limits of "a history of trauma," see her "Unclaimed Experience."

49. To Scott, "the productive quality of discourse" is a corollary to the notion that "'experience' and language" are inseparable. See Scott, "The Evidence of Experience," 792–93. This notion that "material reality is a force that pressures and destabilizes the discursive domain" has also been put forth by Judith Walkowitz, as discussed in Canning, "Feminist History after the Linguistic Turn," 380.

50. Wyschogrod, *An Ethics of Remembering*, xii, 3.

51. Ibid., 242.

52. "Proximity" is a term of Emmanuel Levinas, as quoted in ibid., 9.

53. Kagle, *American Diary Literature*, 15.

54. Ibid.

55. Jerome Brunner proposed that a text "can be written in one genre and interpreted by its readers in another." Brunner, "The Autobiographical Process," 163.

56. Fothergill, *Private Chronicles*, 48.

57. Blodgett, *Centuries of Female Days*, 7.

58. Felicity A. Nussbaum, "Toward Conceptualizing Diary," in Olney, *Studies in Autobiography*, 129. One recent exception is Marcus Moseley, who makes a counterargument for the value of retaining the generic paradigm of autobiography as defined along the lines laid out by Lejeune. See Moseley, "Jewish Autobiography," 19–21.

59. Dauphin, Lebrun-Pézerat, and Poublan, *Ces bonnes lettres*, 161. Scholars who have argued that correspondence, although a "neighboring genre," is ultimately different from diaries because correspondents have a specific audience in mind include Leleu,

Les Journaux Intimes, 237; Girard, *Le Journal Intime,* 20; Fothergill, *Private Chronicles,* 30.

60. H. Porter Abbott quoted in Bunkers and Huff, "Issues in Studying Women's Diaries," 11.

61. Fothergill, *Private Chronicles,* 30. Fothergill excluded from his study what he called "public" diaries (16). Gusdorf characterized them as *journaux externes.* Gusdorf quoted in Girard, *Le Journal Intime,* 6. Girard accepted Gusdorf's differentiation and excluded them from his study of *journaux intimes.*

62. Bloom, "'I Write for Myself and Strangers,'" in Bunkers and Huff, *Inscribing the Daily,* 23–24; Fothergill, *Private Chronicles,* 39–40; Podnieks, *Daily Modernism,* 37.

63. For the idea of bourgeois certainty, see Fussell, *Great War and Modern Memory,* 21.

64. Lewin, 16 September 1942, *A Cup of Tears,* 181.

2. HISTORIANS AND MARTYRS

1. Kaplan, 1 September 1939, *Scroll of Agony,* 19. Unless otherwise indicated, all quotations from Kaplan's diary are taken from the published English translation of Kaplan's Hebrew-language diary, translated by Abraham Katsh. See my "Note on Translations" above for a discussion of how Katsh's translation is differentiated from the newly translated passages (which were left out of the English edition but included in the published Hebrew edition). The author gratefully acknowledges Zvi Ben-Dor Benite and Amos Goldberg for their help reading and translating the Hebrew entries. Those additional entries provide critical evidence in support of the chapter's argument. Both the Hebrew and English published editions of Kaplan's diary are missing entire notebooks from the original diary. The most recent English edition is missing notebook 10, which covers 14 April to 4 October 1941. The Hebrew edition (1966) consulted here is missing notebooks 10 and 11, which extends the missing entries to 3 May 1942. In addition to the published editions, I consulted the handwritten copies of notebooks 10 and 11 in the Moreshet Archives.

2. Kaplan, 14 September 1939, *Megilat yisurin,* 21. Translated by Zvi Ben-Dor Benite. The published English translation of this sentence reads, "I will write a scroll of agony in order to remember the past in the future [לתקופת חיי העתידה]" (Kaplan, *Scroll of Agony,* 30). This new translation better reflects Kaplan's initial intention to keep his diary for himself, to read after the war was over.

3. Kaplan, 5 September 1939, *Scroll of Agony,* 25. The biographical information on Kaplan is from Katsh, introduction to Kaplan, *Scroll of Agony,* 12–14; Gutman, foreword to Kaplan, *Scroll of Agony,* 5.

4. Katsh, undated nine-page memorandum [in Hebrew], File D.2.470.3, Moreshet Archives.

5. Lucien Dreyfus, 28 December 1942, *Cahier* D, diary, manuscript, RG 10.144*07, Lucien Dreyfus collection, United States Holocaust Memorial Museum [hereafter USHMM].

6. Dreyfus, 20 December 1940, *Cahier* A, RG 10.144*04, USHMM. The biographical

information on Dreyfus is from Joseph Bloch, "In Memoriam Lucien Dreyfus," [Periodical Unknown and n.d.] in Folder "General Information on Lucien Dreyfus," RG 10.144*10, Dreyfus collection, USHMM.

7. Roskies, *Against the Apocalypse*, 200.

8. *Le pogrome froid* is Dreyfus's term, 13 December 1935, RG 10.144*03, USHMM. In addition to his articles in *La Tribune Juive*, Dreyfus published an article on 15 March 1926, entitled "Théorie Française du Sionisme," in *Menorah*, 84–85.

9. "Les principes religieuse incommodent dans les périodes d'euphorie, mais rassurent d[an]s les périodes de crises." Dreyfus, 25 January 1940, first half of notebook, RG 10.144*06, USHMM. Dreyfus started this notebook in 1936, then restarted and renumbered it with a new page one and the heading "*Mémoires, Cahier* C" on 15 June 1942. Perhaps he did this because stationery was in short supply.

10. Kaplan's view contradicts Yosef H. Yerushalmi's suggestion in *Zakhor* that Jewish historiography bears a problematic relationship to Jewish memory.

11. Reeve Robert Brenner's research in the 1970s into Israeli survivors' theological responses to the Holocaust based on interviews with 708 survivors revealed that "*53 percent of all survivors — more than half the survivor community — consciously and specifically asserted that the Holocaust affected or, to a certain extent, modified their faith in God.* Of these, 72 percent can be said to have turned away from faith in God. [. . .] Included among these are survivors who claimed their religious faith had been weakened by the Holocaust; others who had lost their faith entirely; and those for whom belief in a personal God had been displaced by belief in an impersonal God idea." Brenner, *The Faith and Doubt of Holocaust Survivors*, 103. Brenner's research was largely confirmed by Helmreich, *Against All Odds*, 237–47. In the first of his many works on theology after the Holocaust, Richard Rubenstein wrote, "After Auschwitz many Jews did not need Nietzsche to tell them that the old God of Jewish patriarchal monotheism was dead beyond all hope of resurrection. [. . .] Even the existentialist leap of faith cannot resurrect this dead God after Auschwitz." Rubenstein, *After Auschwitz*, 227, 238. For an interesting reading of Rubenstein that posits his theology as less revolutionary than it appeared to be in the 1960s and 1970s, see Braiterman, *(God) After Auschwitz*, 87–111.

12. Around 5 percent of the Israeli survivors polled by Brenner in the 1970s testified to having gone from being atheists to religious believers as a result of their experiences during the Holocaust, which represents an even more profound shift than than that of Dreyfus. Brenner, *The Faith and Doubt of Holocaust Survivors*, 119.

13. On Orthodox faith and observance during and in the wake of the Holocaust, see Abramson, "Deciphering the Ancestral Paradigm: A Hasidic Court in the Warsaw Ghetto"; Greenberg, "Ultra-Orthodox Reflections on the Holocaust"; Greenberg, "The Theological Letters of Rabbi Talmud of Lublin, Summer and Fall 1942"; Kirschner, *Rabbinic Responsa of the Holocaust Era*; Michman, "'In Faithfulness Thou Hast Afflicted Me' (Psalms 119:75)—Remarks on Trends in Religious Faith during the Holocaust," in *Holocaust Historiography*, 285–99; Rudavsky, *To Live with Hope, To Die with Dignity*, esp. 69–80; Zimmels, *The Echo of the Nazi Holocaust in Rabbinic Literature*; and excerpts by Bernard Maza, Ignaz Maybaum, Sha'ar Yashuv Cohen,

Hayyim Kanfo, and Yosef Roth, in Cohn-Sherbok, *Holocaust Theology*, 93–105. One additional unpublished article informed my analysis in this chapter: Greenberg, "Jewish Religious Practice Through the War: God, Israel and History."

14. The best-known works are Horkheimer and Adorno, *Dialectic of Enlightenment*; Kren and Rappoport, *The Holocaust and the Crisis of Human Behavior*; and Bauman, *Modernity and the Holocaust*.

15. As Dominick LaCapra wrote, "Especially for victims, trauma brings about a lapse or rupture in memory that breaks continuity with the past, thereby placing identity in question to the point of shattering it. But it may raise problems of identity for others insofar as it unsettles narcissistic investments and desired self-images, including—especially with respect to the Shoah—the image of Western civilization itself as the bastion of elevated values if not the high point in the evolution of humanity." LaCapra, *History and Memory after Auschwitz*, 9.

16. Mendelssohn, *The Jews of East Central Europe Between the Wars*, 20–21; Lichten, "Jewish Assimilation in Poland," in Abramsky et al., *The Jews in Poland*, 115.

17. Kaplan, 24 November 1939, *Scroll of Agony*, 75–76. Kaplan critiqued the chairman of the Judenrat, Adam Czerniakow, for his Polish patriotism in his entry of 9 March 1941, *Scroll of Agony*, 254. He also expressed tremendous rancor toward Jewish converts to Christianity, for example, in the entry of 30 November 1939, *Scroll of Agony*, 78–79.

18. Kaplan, 1 August 1940, *Scroll of Agony*, 174.

19. Kaplan, 2 July 1942, ibid., 366.

20. Dreyfus, 1 January 1926, RG 10.144*02, USHMM; L[ucien]. D[reyfus]., *La Tribune Juive*, 9 July 1937, 425. The Zionist movement in Alsace was better organized and more widely supported than elsewhere in France before the war. Poznanski, "Le Sionisme en France pendant la Deuxième Guerre mondiale: développements institutionnels et impact idéologique," in Bensimon and Pinkus, *Les Juifs de France*, 194, 215 n.9; Raphaël and Weyl, "La double demeure: les juifs d'Alsace et le sionisme," in *Regards nouveaux sur les juifs d'Alsace*, 271.

21. "Ne pouvons nous avoir des âmes juives, parlant la langue français?" Dreyfus, 17 September 1925, RG 10.144*02, USHMM.

22. Caron, *Between France and Germany*, 9.

23. "La France est une nation libre par instinct et libératrice par vocation héréditaire. [. . .] Le destin de la France a voulu que ce pays répondît à l'appel de la vocation séculaire qui sans cesse l'invite à combattre et à vaincre pour la défense de la civilisation et de la liberté." Dreyfus, 10 November 1927, RG 10.144*02, USHMM. His French nationalism, like that of Jews in France in general, was based on a "liberal vision of the state," which was revitalized in the wake of the Dreyfus Affair when supporters of the Third Republic took pains to defend the rights of Jews. Caron, *Between France and Germany*, 188. In defending France's right to use aggression in order to spread its universalist message, Dreyfus put forth an argument that dated back to the expansionist wars waged by the revolutionary army against the forces of counterrevolution in the eighteenth century. On the "perverse effects" of this interweaving of Republic and *Patrie*, see Agulhon, *The French Republic*, 14.

24. "La France est restée jeune. Elle est restée la patrie de la liberté, la terre des penseurs

et des soldats de l'Europe, toujours débout, héros invincibles à leur poste de péril et d'honneur, apparemment incapables de se reposer tant qu'il y aura sur le globe ravagé et sous le ciel orageux la barbarie de l'injustice humaine. Tous les persécutés, nos co-religionnaires et les autres, ceux de Berlin et ceux de Rome, tous mettent leurs su-prêmes espérances en ce pays généreux et courageux [. . .]. Tous, ils prient avec nous que la France demeure." L[ucien]. D[reyfus]., "Quatorze Juillet 1939," *La Tribune Juive,* 14 July 1939, 429.

25. The full passage reads: "Même émancipée il y a une vie juive. Les générations qui surent s'émanciper, surent prendre part à la culture de leur temps et l'enrichir des idéals juifs. Allons-nous laisser périr cet effort? Ceux-là trahissent le judaïsme, qui à notre époque veulent se dépouiller de l'idéal juif dans l'intérêt d'une assimilation complète. Ceux-là trahissent le judaïsme qui nous disent qu'on ne peut mener une vie juive dans un milieu non-juif." Dreyfus, 17 September 1925, RG 10.144*02, USHMM.

26. Caron, *Between France and Germany,* 189.

27. In this respect, Dreyfus responded differently from his French coreligionists. For most French Jews, their faith in the state to act as protector and inculcator of liberal values was not shattered the way it was for German Jews. On this point, see Caron, *Between France and Germany,* 192–93. The notion of "moral and cultural security" was sug-gested by Ruth R. Wisse's analysis of Anne Frank in *The Modern Jewish Canon,* 220.

28. According to the historians Michael R. Marrus and Robert O. Paxton, this law "as-signed, on the basis of race, an inferior position in French civil law and society to a whole segment of French citizens and noncitizens and foreigners living on French soil." Marrus and Paxton, *Vichy France and the Jews,* 3.

29. This idea was implied in Dreyfus's entry of 20 December 1940 and elaborated in his entry of 12 October 1941, *Cahier* B, RG 10.144*05, USHMM.

30. "Le guerrier, l'homme d'État représente le type le plus élevé du genre humain; il est supérieur au penseur qui ne connaît pas l'action." Dreyfus, 20 December 1940, *Cahier* A, RG 10.144*04, USHMM. Dreyfus used the catchword of his epoch—"action"—to describe the realm of the warrior. Revolutionary syndicalists and nationalists on the extreme right and left of the political spectrum in France frequently called for action as part of their political philosophies. According to the historian Zeev Sternhell, they sought "to create a new world—virile, heroic, pessimistic, and puritanical" and glorified violence as the means to overturn the current world order. Unlike many of his contemporaries, however, Dreyfus emphasized the need for humility, not virility, among warriors and believers. Dreyfus was neither fascinated by violence nor did he hold "manly virtues" in high esteem. Sternhell, *Neither Right nor Left,* 11, 257.

31. "[La religion] est une arme essentielle dans la lutte pour l'existence. Elle ne donne pas seulement une consolation à ceux qui sont éprouvés, tenaillés par les peines et les misères quotidiennes, elle offre un port et une récompense à la fidelité, à la patience, à la soumission et à toutes les autres vertus guerrières. Depuis toujours, les philoso-phes qui comptent, les hommes d'État qui ont tracé les bases d'un nouvel ordre se sont opposés à l'impiété et ont respecté les cultes." Dreyfus, 20 December 1940, *Cahier* A, RG 10.144*04, USHMM. Dreyfus's critique of liberalism and his call for a strong executive were prevalent among French politicians of the right and left during the

interwar years. See Weber, *The Hollow Years*, 117–22. Dreyfus's critique of secularism could be viewed as part of the larger concern with decadence and moral decline that concerned French thinkers from the late 1890s through the 1930s. See Sternhell, *Neither Right nor Left*, 66–89, 213–65.

32. Looking back from the vantage point of the war, Dreyfus realized that "civic equality inscribed in law was not in [people's] consciences [l'égalité civique inscrite dans le code ne l'était pas dans les consciences]." Dreyfus, 31 May 1942, *Cahier* B, RG 10.144*05, USHMM. Dreyfus's view that the masses were impressionable and would be easily swayed by emotions, which were fundamentally irrational, was the mainstream thinking on emotions and the masses from the 1940s to the 1960s. See Rosenwein, "Worrying about Emotions in History," 822–23.

33. Dreyfus's critique of rationalism and science differed considerably from that of the antirationalist intellectuals who emerged in the 1890s, such as Georges Sorel, Maurice Barrès, Henri Bergson, and even Emile Durkheim. In opposition to liberalism and democracy, they created a new "theory of political conduct" to connect the individual to society and fundamentally challenged the philosophical foundations of the Republic in the social sciences and humanities. See Sternhell, *Neither Right nor Left*, 32–34; Wright, *France in Modern Times*, 286–87.

34. "La vérité est que la science, idole des Européens cultivés depuis plus d'un demi-siècle, s'est élevé sur les ruines amoncelées par les démolisseurs des croyances et des principes politiques reçus." All preceding quotations in this paragraph from Dreyfus, 20 December 1940, *Cahier* A, RG 10.144*04, USHMM.

35. Dreyfus plainly expressed this idea in his prewar entry of 20 June 1925, RG 10.144*02, USHMM. This sentiment was hardly unique to Dreyfus. In 1915, Romain Rolland had written, "They believed in Reason as the Catholics believed in the Blessed Virgin." Rolland quoted in Hobsbawm, *The Age of Empire*, 262.

36. "On ne peut persuader les gens qui ne partagent pas vos opinions [. . .] La plupart des gens acceptent les idées qui leur plaisent, qui s'adaptent facilement à leur tempérament, très peu d'hommes se règlent sur des idées acquises par des raisonnements fondés." Dreyfus, 20 December 1940, *Cahier* A, RG 10.144*04, USHMM.

37. Dreyfus contrasted "l'universalité . . . de l'esprit français" with the German "nationalisme éliminatoire." Dreyfus, 8 March 1942, first half of journal, RG 10.144*06, USHMM. He also mentioned the "French spirit" and French universalism elsewhere in his diary in entries of 26 March 1942, *Cahier* B, 10.144*05, USHMM; 4 August 1942, *Cahier* D, RG 10.144*07, USHMM.

38. Dreyfus, 20 December 1940, *Cahier* A, RG 10.144*04, USHMM. Here again one can see how, consciously or unconsciously, Dreyfus made use of the language of his epoch. His "ideal of the warrior and the believer" strikes a chord with what Sternhell aptly described as "a morality of warriors and monks" among those on the extreme right and left. Whereas for those on the extreme right and left this morality was connected to an exclusive vision of supposed racial difference and hygiene, for Dreyfus it was to be an ecumenical movement, designed to draw in whoever shared the principles. Sternhell, *Neither Right nor Left*, 11–12.

39. The second Statut des Juifs made the quota system that had been established in 1940

much stricter and added a host of additional fields to the list of professions from which Jews were entirely excluded. Paxton, *Vichy France*, 178–79.

40. The entire sentence reads, "La propagande nazie profitait des misères de l'après-guerre pour s'introduire dans les milieux jusqu'ici fermés à la haine antijuive et le succès du patron de Berchtesgaden ne s'explique que par la complicité de toute la bourgeoisie européenne qui partageait ses antipathies ou les exploitait." Dreyfus, 16 March 1941, *Cahier* A, RG 10.144*04, USHMM.

41. Dreyfus, 14 May 1941, *Cahier* B, RG 10.144*05, USHMM.

42. "Après qu'un pays a abandonné la religion, il ne cultivera pas non plus les vertus qui créent et conservent les grands puissances." Dreyfus, 20 March 1942, *Cahier* B, RG 10.144*05, USHMM. On the Riom trial, see Michel, *Le Procès de Riom.*

43. The entire passage reads, "J'avais l'impression que ceux qui mesurent les choses avec les raisonnements logiques ne voient pas loin, succombent à des arguments spécieux et s'adonnent d'autant plus facilement à des convictions qu'ils croyaient ne pas avoir et pu[?] naissaient tout de même dans leur subconscient grâce à des propagandes ou des espoirs venus du dehors. On les appelle les gens de bonne foi. C'est qu'ils n'ont pas la foi. Celui qui a la foi ne consulte pas les choses passagères de la vie moins la logique qui s'adapte à toutes les circonstances mouvantes, mais se tient à la foi qui donne à la vie une direction, une règle et une terme qui dicte toutes les convictions et toutes les espérances." Dreyfus, 11 April 1941, *Cahier* A, RG 10.144*04, USHMM.

44. Dreyfus, 28 April 1941, *Cahier* A, RG 10.144*04, USHMM.

45. Dreyfus, 6 July 1942, *Cahier* C, RG 10.144*06, USHMM. He recorded the news about the murder of seven hundred thousand Jews in Poland in an entry of 4 July 1942, *Cahier* C, RG 10.144*06, USHMM. Dreyfus did not cite his source for this information. The BBC first broadcast news of the killing of Jews on 2 July 1942. It is also possible that Dreyfus read a pamphlet passed around Nice by anonymous women, saying that seven hundred thousand Jews in Poland had been shot, drowned, or killed by gas. The pamphlet, cited by Mary Felstiner, urged the French to help their Jewish neighbors. "Circular enclosed in dispatch from American Consulate in Nice to U.S. Embassy in Vichy," NARA, RG 59, Box 18, 841.1-Jews, cited in Felstiner, *To Paint Her Life*, 192, 269 n. On the dissemination of news to the west about the extermination of Polish Jewry, see Stola, "Early News of the Holocaust from Poland," 1–27. Against Yisrael Gutman and David Engel, Stola argues that the Polish government-in-exile did not purposely suppress news of the killings of Polish Jewry.

46. "Ce qu'on peut reprocher aux Américains? Ce qu'on peut leur reprocher aujourd'hui encore. Ils n'ont pas envoyé les bateaux pour établir dans le centre des États-Unis quelques 5 à 600.000 juifs polonais, allemands et français, ce qui aurait bien soulagé la situation générale sans alourdir l'essor de l'agriculture et l'industrie d'un pays de plus de 120 millions d'âmes. Les juifs sont loin d'être justes, les autres le sont encore moins. Ceux-ci ou assassinent ou n'empêchent pas les assassinats." Dreyfus, 4 July 1942, *Cahier* C, RG 10.144*06, USHMM.

47. Dreyfus, 4 July 1942, *Cahier* C, RG 10.144*06, USHMM.

48. "Le déclin de l'idée religieuse a facilité l'explosion de la haine antijuive et la catastro-

phe de cette guerre. [. . .] Ce qui ne s'accorde pas avec la science et la raison humaine peut tout de même être indispensable à la vie en société. On n'a qu'à établir que la science et la raison ont en elles-mêmes des tendances destructives et cette réflexion vous conduit à la nécessité de reconnaître une autorité." Dreyfus, 6 July 1942, *Cahier* C, RG 10.144*06, USHMM.

49. Dreyfus's view of science and reason powerfully resonates with the writing of other thinkers, most famously in the thesis of Horkheimer and Adorno that civilization and barbarism stand in dialectical relationship to one another within "enlightenment." Indeed, according to Horkheimer and Adorno, "not merely the ideal but the practical tendency to self-destruction has always been characteristic of rationalism, and not only in the stage in which it appears undisguised" (*The Dialectic of Enlightenment*, xvi–xvii). See also Bauman, *Modernity and the Holocaust*, 12.

50. Kaplan criticized the Poles in numerous entries; among the most potent from early in the war are 5 September and 7 October 1939, *Scroll of Agony*, 25–26, 47–48.

51. Kaplan, 2 March 1941, *Scroll of Agony*, 248.

52. Dreyfus did sometimes wonder about the extent of France's complicity with Nazi Germany. After Vichy promulgated its second Statut des Juifs, Dreyfus recorded, "What is difficult to say is up to what point the government wanted to identify with the injunctions of the conqueror. [Ce qui est difficile à dire c'est jusqu'à quel point le g[ouvernemen]t a bien voulu s'identifier avec les injonctions du vainqueur]." Dreyfus, 18 June 1941, *Cahier* B, RG 10.144*05, USHMM.

53. Kaplan, 1 September 1939, *Scroll of Agony*, 19.

54. Yerushalmi, *Zakhor*, 87, and on history as a response to tragedy, see 34–39, and chap. 3, "In the Wake of the Spanish Expulsion."

55. This is a different argument from the one made by James Young, who interpreted Kaplan's use of Hebrew as evidence of his desire "to locate events in the sanctified linguistic sphere of scripture, rabbinical disputation, and covenant" (*Writing and Rewriting the Holocaust*, 27). Young's contention does not take into consideration Kaplan's long-standing personal commitment to the use and vitality of Hebrew as a modern spoken language. Kaplan's Hebrew-language school taught Hebrew as a spoken language. Furthermore, as a public speaker at Zionist gatherings in the Warsaw ghetto, Kaplan elected to deliver his speeches in Hebrew when all of his fellow speakers used Yiddish.

56. Kaplan, 1 September 1939, *Scroll of Agony*, 19. On the traditional Jewish concept of history, see Yerushalmi, *Zakhor*, 5–26, 31–52.

57. Kaplan, 1 September 1939, *Scroll of Agony*, 20. See also his entries of 5 and 14 September 1939.

58. What I am arguing is a literary-archetypal viewpoint other scholars have argued is historical. For example, David Roskies wrote that the Nazis' employment of images from the past in their persecution of the Jews made all Jews into historians because they sought and found historical analogies to their present suffering (*Against the Apocalypse*, 202). I would argue that this "search for archetypes" is precisely not historical because it regards the present, not in its particularity, but as a return to the past.

59. Kaplan, 19 May 1942, *Scroll of Agony*, 334.

60. Kaplan, 4 February 1940, ibid., 116. In this entry, Kaplan also criticized his fellow Jews, describing them as "the prisoners of hope [אסירי התקווה]" because they incorrectly doubted that forced labor decrees would be put into effect. Translated by Amos Goldberg.

61. Kaplan, 13 October 1939, ibid., 49–50. "Worthless [חדל אישים]" was omitted from this sentence in the English published edition of the diary. Translated by Amos Goldberg. See also Kaplan's entry of 5 November 1939, in which he compares the "horrible persecutions of the Middle Ages" to the "Nazi inquisition" and claims that "even a tyrant of the Middle Ages would have been ashamed to publicize [such sadistic torture]" as that committed by the Nazis (64).

62. Kaplan, 1 December 1939, ibid., 80. Interestingly, the discrepancy Kaplan observed between Nazi ideology and anti-Jewish actions during the first two years of the war became central to historians' debates about whether Hitler had intended to exterminate the Jews all along or whether the Final Solution developed during the war itself as a functional strategy for dealing with the Jews. For a concise summary of the debate between Intentionalists and Functionalists, see Marrus, *The Holocaust in History*, 31–51. Another Polish Jewish man fully anticipated this historiographical debate in his memoir of 1946, writing, "It is not yet clear whether all of the horrible murders came about according to a systematic plan worked out previously, or whether they came about gradually, i.e., the appetite grew with the meal. But this I shall leave for future writers and historians." Bernard Rechnitz, "Diary," English translation of Polish original, RG 02.069, USHMM, 3.

63. See Kaplan's extended discussion of the physiological, psychological, and scientific dimensions of Nazi anti-Jewish hatred in his entry of 10 March 1940, *Scroll of Agony*, 129–30.

64. Kaplan, 26 October 1939, *Megilat yisurin*, 65–66; *Scroll of Agony*, 58. Translated by Amos Goldberg and Zvi Ben-Dor Benite. The published English translation of the first sentence reads, "Individuals will be destroyed, but the Jewish community will live on."

65. Kaplan, 5 November 1939, *Megilat yisurin*, 73. This passage was omitted from the English published edition, probably because of its derogatory reference to the Jews of Yemen and Iran. Translated by Zvi Ben-Dor Benite.

66. His response to the forced labor decree is in Kaplan, 14 January 1940, *Scroll of Agony*, 102. "Its own martyrology": Kaplan, 18 March 1940, ibid., 132.

67. Kaplan, 16 January 1940, ibid., 104.

68. The restrictions imposed in Russia in 1887 on Jewish attendance in *Gymnasia* and universities propelled many younger Jews westward for their education, especially to Berlin and Vienna. Modern historical scholarship made its way back to Poland in the years before World War I. See Myers, *Re-Inventing the Jewish Past*, 34 n. 93, 35–36; Roskies, "Landkentenish," in Shapiro, *Holocaust Chronicles*, 12; Eisenbach, "Jewish Historiography in Interwar Poland," in Gutman et al., *The Jews of Poland Between Two World Wars*, 453; Dawidowicz, *The Golden Tradition*, 48. On the wide-ranging intellectual impact of the emergence of a modern historical consciousness in the nine-

teenth century, see Schorsch, "The Emergence of Historical Consciousness in Modern Judaism," 413–37.

69. Myers, *Re-Inventing the Jewish Past*, 16–20, 32; Eisenbach, "Jewish Historiography in Interwar Poland," 459–60; Penslar, *Shylock's Children*, 158–60.

70. Roskies, *Against the Apocalypse*, 135; Roskies, "Landkentenish," 12; Dobroszycki, "YIVO in Interwar Poland," in Gutman et al., 494, 498–99. On the origins of the "Polish method" of sponsoring essay contests in order to gather autobiographical materials for the study of social phenomena and personal experience, see Markiewicz-Lagneau, "L'autobiographie en Pologne," 591–93. On the influence of this method on Max Weinreich, YIVO's research director, see Soyer, "Documenting Immigrant Lives at an Immigrant Institution," 219–20. For an analysis of the relationship between autobiographical writing, reading, and concepts of individualism within Jewish society in eastern Europe during the interwar period, see Moseley, "Life, Literature: Autobiographies of Jewish Youth in Interwar Poland," 1–51. A volume of the YIVO collection of youth autobiographies from the interwar period was recently published in English: Shandler, ed., *Awakening Lives*.

71. Quoted in Dobroszycki, "YIVO in Interwar Poland," 508.

72. Roskies, *Against the Apocalypse*, 200. On the "historical diaries" of Ringelblum and Herman Kruk from the Vilna ghetto, see Kassow, "Vilna and Warsaw, Two Ghetto Diaries," in Shapiro, *Holocaust Chronicles*, 171–215. Roskies also described Ringelblum's and Kruk's diaries as historically oriented.

73. Kaplan, 26 October 1939, *Scroll of Agony*, 58. A diarist who expressed the same sentiment as Kaplan, writing for "the researchers of our generation" and insisting that he neither "understated" nor "overstated" anything, was Rabbi Aharonson of Konin. See Farbstein, "Diaries and Memoirs as a Historical Source," 121–22.

74. Roskies, "Landkentenish," 13–14.

75. Kaplan, 20 February 1940, *Scroll of Agony*, 121.

76. Kaplan, 30 November 1939, ibid., 79.

77. The phrase belongs to Yerushalmi, *Zakhor*, xiv.

78. In his prewar journalism, his critique of historians is articulated most unabashedly in his article "Mais ce juif horrible, c'est Hitler," *La Tribune Juive*, 5 May 1939, 269.

79. The quotation is from Leopold von Ranke, "On the Relations of History and Philosophy (A Manuscript of the 1830s)," in Iggers and von Moltke, *The Theory and Practice of History*, 30. In this French historians emulated Leopold von Ranke despite the fact that Germany was France's enemy throughout these years. On post-Sedan history in France, see Dosse, "The Prehistory of the *Annales*," chap. 1 in *New History in France*; Wright, *France in Modern Times*, 80.

80. "L'histoire et les historiens se plaisent, comme les conservateurs de musée, à changer les objets de place, à modifier la manière d'observer et le point de vue d'où l'on observe, et surtout à renouveler les étiquettes. C'est leur science à eux, et ils s'imaginent que les autres croient comme eux que des personnes intelligentes prennent leur occupation amusante et nulle pour une activité scientifique. L'histoire n'a rien à voir à la science." Dreyfus, 23 June 1942, *Cahier C*, RG 10.144*06, USHMM.

81. "The truth": Dreyfus, 10 June 1942, *Cahier C*, RG 10.144*06, USHMM. "Depuis

longtemps je considère les contemporains comme les seuls bons juges des hommes et des choses: ils n'ont pas besoin d'attendre les découvertes des historiens qui dépouillent les archives." Dreyfus, 25 May 1943, *Cahier* D, RG 10.144*07, USHMM.

82. Kaplan, 26 January 1940, *Scroll of Agony*, 109.

83. Kaplan, 3 February 1940, ibid., 115.

84. Kaplan, 14 March 1941, ibid., 257; *Megilat yisurin*, 467. Translated by Zvi Ben-Dor Benite and Amos Goldberg.

85. "On peut douter des historiens, mais pas contester l'histoire. Elle éclaire de son flambeau la route où va l'humanité. Sans elle nous n'éviterions aucun précipice ni ne saurions trouver aucun gué." It is unclear if this was a quotation of the adventure travel writer Pierre Benoit or if this was Dreyfus's commentary on a piece of Benoit's. Dreyfus, 1 August 1935, RG 10.144*03, USHMM.

86. Dreyfus, 24 June 1942, *Cahier* C, RG 10.144*06, USHMM.

87. "Le sacrifice de soi-même est l'acte sublime du juif exposé aux coups des assassins." Dreyfus, 12 June 1942, *Cahier* B, RG 10.144*05.

88. On *Kiddush Ha-Hayim*, the sanctification of life, and *Kiddush Ha-Shem*, the sanctification of God's name or martyrdom, see Rudavsky, *To Live with Hope*, 5–9, 13–26.

89. Kaplan, 5 October 1939, *Scroll of Agony*, 46.

90. Kaplan, 3 February 1940, *Megilat yisurin*, 162. Translated by Zvi Ben-Dor Benite and Amos Goldberg. These lines were omitted from the English published edition. Kaplan was hardly alone in questioning God's righteousness. Greenberg discusses this response among Orthodox Jews in "The Theological Letters of Rabbi Talmud of Lublin, Summer and Fall 1942," 117–21; and in his unpublished paper "Jewish Religious Practice Through the War: God, Israel and History."

91. Kaplan, 12 April 1940, *Scroll of Agony*, 139; *Megilat yisurin*, 219. The inserted sentences, omitted from the English edition, were translated by Amos Goldberg.

92. Kaplan, 14 October 1940, *Scroll of Agony*, 209; *Megilat yisurin*, 362–63. The inserted sentences, omitted from the English edition, were translated by Amos Goldberg.

93. Kaplan, 15 October 1940, *Scroll of Agony*, 209–10.

94. Kaplan, 31 January 1940, ibid., 111.

95. Kaplan, 26 October 1939, ibid., 57–58.

96. Pinnock, *Beyond Theodicy*, 11.

97. Kaplan, 2 October 1940, *Scroll of Agony*, 202–3.

98. Kaplan, 26 December 1940, ibid., 234–35; *Megilat yisurin*, 417. The parts of this entry quoted here and omitted from the English published edition were translated by Zvi Ben-Dor Benite.

99. Kaplan, 10 October 1941, *Scroll of Agony*, 268–69.

100. See Kaplan, 1 August and 15 August 1940, ibid., 174–75, 182.

101. Katsh, undated nine-page memorandum [in Hebrew], File D.2.470.3, Moreshet Archives. Translated by Amos Goldberg.

102. Kaplan, 14 December 1939, *Scroll of Agony*, 87.

103. Katsh, Introduction to Kaplan, ibid., 14.

104. Kaplan, 13 November 1941, ibid., 278.

105. Kaplan, 5 October 1939, ibid., 46.

106. Kaplan, 5 September 1940, ibid., 192.

107. "C'est pour échapper à la nécessité de voir autour de moi un amas inextricable de contradictions et de méchancetés humaines qui dirigent le cours des choses." Dreyfus, 18 June 1941, *Cahier* B, RG 10.144*05, USHMM.

108. "Ces idées correspondent à mon tempérament et si je m'occupe dans ces cahiers de peu de choses autres que le principe dernier de l'homme, c'est que la reste de ce qui préoccupe les miens, même la guerre, ne sont rien vis-à-vis du problème posé par la Bible. Il y a un Dieu qui punit et qui récompense. [. . .] je ne chercherai pas à convaincre les opposants, mais j'entends conserver intactes les traditions spirituelles qui remontent jusqu'au Sinaï." Dreyfus, 18 June 1941, *Cahier* B, RG 10.144*05, USHMM.

109. Yerushalmi, *Zakhor*, 8.

110. The most visible postwar proponent of this view was Rabbi Yoel Taitelbaum, the leader of the ultra-Orthodox Satmar movement, who published *And It Pleased Moses* (*Vayo'el Moshe*) in 1952, cited in Funkenstein, "Theological Responses to the Holocaust," chap. 9 in *Perceptions of Jewish History*, 307–8.

111. Dreyfus, 18 June 1941, *Cahier* B, RG 10.144*05, USHMM. In an article of December 1938, Dreyfus also contemplated Jewish assimilation and its effects, contending, "Our effort to take part in European culture and to enrich the Jewish ideal has suffered a resounding defeat. [Notre effort de prendre part à la culture européene et de l'enrichir d'un idéal juif a subi une défaite éclatante.]" However, at that time he repudiated any suggestion to the effect that the current trials suffered by Jews were God's punishment for assimilation: "To the one who asks why heaven sent us these extraordinary trials, we respond that one must be well-initiated in the decisions and designs of providence in order to want to explain or interpret divine will manifesting itself in History. [À celui qui nous demande pourquoi le ciel nous envoie ces épreuves extraordinaires, nous répondons qu'il faut être bien initié dans les décisions et les desseins de la providence pour vouloir expliquer ou interpréter la volonté divine se manifestant dans l'Histoire.]" L[ucien]. D[reyfus]., "Au carrefour," *La Tribune Juive*, 23 December 1938, 781.

112. "Celui qui croit que le Ciel (fait) crée aussi le mal selon le mot du prophète ne voit dans l'action du fuehrer que la chose devenue nécessaire aux juifs. On leur rappelle leur origine, leur histoire, leur vocation oubliées dans l'abandon de toutes les traditions au profit d'un assimilation en dernier lieu irréalisable." Dreyfus, 26 October 1941, *Cahier* B, RG 10.144*05, USHMM.

113. Dreyfus, 26 October 1941, *Cahier* B, RG 10.144*05, USHMM.

114. "Les juifs des pays occidentaux se croyaient en sécurité derrière le rempart des législations qui n'exprimaient cependant pas les volontés populaires, mais des mesures d'ordre idéologique des gouvernements avancés. [. . .] Maintenant ils ne retrouvent pas la chemin du retour. La leçon de la guerre ne change pas leur mentalité." Dreyfus, 16 March 1941, *Cahier* A, RG 10.144*04, USHMM.

115. Dreyfus, 14 May 1941, *Cahier* B, RG 10.144*05, USHMM.

116. Dreyfus, 13 May 1943, *Cahier* D, RG 10.144*07, USHMM.

117. Dreyfus, 27 May 1943, *Cahier* D, RG 10.144*07, USHMM.

118. "Je suis moi-même la matière de mon livre. Ce mot de Montaigne est bien trouvé, mais ne va pas encore assez loin. Il aurait tranquillement pu dire que le livre, la phrase

même que nous écrivons ou pensons contribue à nous faire connaître à nous-mêmes et aux autres. Nous parlons toujours de nous-mêmes, a dit Anatole, quand nous n'avons pas la force de nous taire." Dreyfus, 20 October 1942, *Cahier* D, RG 10.144*07, USHMM.

119. "Cette période-ci est terrible et terriblement intéressante. [. . .] Je remercie le ciel de m'avoir fait vivre à cette époque et de m'avoir favorisé du don de comprendre cette époque." Dreyfus, 27 June 1941, *Cahier* B, RG 10.144*05, USHMM.

120. "Israël reste le témoin de la préhistoire qui prépare les temps messianiques et qui est encore loin de se terminer." Dreyfus, 27 June 1941, *Cahier* B, RG 10.144*05, USHMM.

121. Preceding quotations from Dreyfus, 18 July 1941, *Cahier* B, RG 10.144*05, USHMM.

122. Dreyfus, 2 December 1941, *Cahier* B, RG 10.144*05, USHMM.

123. Kaplan, 19 November 1940, *Scroll of Agony*, 225.

124. Kaplan, 29 November 1940, ibid., 229; *Megilat yisurin*, 403. The inserted sentences, omitted from the English edition, were translated by Amos Goldberg.

125. Kaplan, 2 February 1942, *Scroll of Agony*, 296–97.

126. Kaplan, 7 [*sic*] April 1942, ibid., 312–13. Although the date at the top of the entry is the seventh of April, it should read the seventeenth of April. According to Walter Laqueur, the news about Lublin was so alarming to Kaplan and to others because "Lublin was Poland proper; furthermore, this was precisely the place where most (or all) East European Jews were to be 'resettled.' " Before these March reports about Lublin, there had been reports in Warsaw that spoke of the killings in Chełmno and of the murder of four hundred thousand Lithuanian Jews. These reports tended to be greeted in Warsaw with the contention that what was taking place in eastern Poland and Lithuania would not be dared in Warsaw because the Jewish population was too large and it was the center of the country. Laqueur, *The Terrible Secret*, 127.

127. Kaplan, 7 June 1942, *Scroll of Agony*, 347–48. The italicized phrases are different translations from the English published edition. Translated by Amos Goldberg.

128. Kaplan, 7 [*sic*] April 1942, ibid., 314.

129. Kaplan, 26 July 1942, ibid., 384.

130. In his entry of 16 May 1942 he wrote, "What do they argue about in the ghetto? About whether the downfall will come quickly, during this summer, or next summer. As usual, there are those who rush the end and those who put it off. But this is not the main point. What concerns us is whether we will live to see that debacle. Alfred Rosenberg has stated explicitly: 'The Jews are awaiting the end of the war; but the Jews will not live to see it. They will pass from the earth before it comes!' Vilna, Kovno, Lublin, Slonim, and Novogrudok have proved that the Nazi may be relied upon to keep his word." Kaplan, ibid., 334.

131. Kaplan, 23 July 1942, ibid., 382.

132. Kaplan, ibid., 383. The italicized phrase is a different translation from the English published edition. Translated by Amos Goldberg.

133. "‏אין זאת כי אם אין אלוהים לישראל‎!" Kaplan, 2 August 1942, ibid., 396; *Megilat yisurin*, 559. Omitted sentence translated by Amos Goldberg.

134. Kaplan, 4 August 1942, *Scroll of Agony*, 400.

135. Dreyfus placed little value in the importance of individuals: "It is impossible to ex-

aggerate how unimportant people are. [. . .] In my already long life I have maybe seen half of a half-dozen important persons [Il est impossible de s'exagérer le peu d'importance des gens. [. . .] Dans ma vie déjà longue j'ai peut-être vu la moitié d'une demi-douzaine de personnes importantes]." Dreyfus, 26 August 1943, *Cahier* G, RG 10.144*08, USHMM.

136. Dreyfus, 16 March 1941, *Cahier* A, RG 10.144*04, USHMM.

137. "On parle de 700.000 juifs tués en Pologne et environs. Ce chiffre n'est pas nécessairement exagéré. En proportions des juifs dispersés sur le globe ce n'est pas autant qu'à l'époque des persécutions de Chmelniki." Dreyfus, 4 July 1942, *Cahier* C, RG 10.144*06, USHMM.

138. L[ucien]. D[reyfus]., "Les revendications de la Pologne et le malaise juif," *La Tribune Juive,* 17 December 1935, 777. On the "depth" of feeling of east European Jews, see Dreyfus's entry of 22 March 1941, *Cahier* A, RG 10.144*04, USHMM. On Jewish martyrdom during the Middle Ages, see his entry of 12 June 1942, *Cahier* B, RG 10.144*05, USHMM.

139. After the first report in July 1942 about the murder of seven hundred thousand Polish Jews, Dreyfus mentioned several other reports in his diary about killings of Jews. It is not clear from his diary whether he read the reports in newspapers, heard them on the radio, or attained them by some other means. In December 1942, he learned of more massacres of Jews in Poland, "for certain of thousands, and of a million? What do I know?" Dreyfus, 1 December 1942, *Cahier* D, RG 10.144*07, USHMM. Almost three weeks later, the news of even more mass killings of Polish Jews was accompanied by a report on the murder of eighty-five thousand Jews in Yugoslavia. Dreyfus, 20 December 1942, *Cahier* D, RG 10.144*07, USHMM.

140. "À Nice l'atmosphère est lourde, par une chaleur plus forte que d'ordinaire, et par des bruits qui remplissent les têtes de l'arrestation et l'expédition des étrangers dans des camps et en Allemagne où l'on les envoie comme travailleurs. Impossible d'avoir des précisions, mais il y a des faits qui justifiant des appréhensions et qui contribuent à faire déprécier notre pays. [. . .] On dit que la même atmosphère règne à Marseille. De Paris viennent des bruits alarmants, les Allds auraient demandé 20000 ouvriers juifs, valides, on sépare les familles d'une façon barbare. Tout cela est incontrôlable, mais la nervosité de la population juive est grande." Dreyfus, 23 August 1942, *Cahier* C, RG 10.144*06, USHMM.

141. Throughout the fall of 1942, he was occupied full-time with helping foreign Jews who faced deportation. He spent his days trying to find hiding places for Jewish refugees and to help those who had already been arrested by the police. See Dreyfus, 23 August 1942, *Cahier* C, RG 10.144*06; 24 August, 26 August, 8 September, 15 September, and 5 October 1942, *Cahier* D, RG 10.144*07, USHMM.

142. Dreyfus, 25 November 1942, 16 March 1943, *Cahier* D, RG 10.144*07, USHMM.

143. Dreyfus's response confirms Mary Felstiner's argument that there were no sources in the Nice region which could have contributed to "a conceptual grasp of genocide" among Jews living there during the war. Felstiner, *To Paint Her Life,* 191.

144. Dreyfus, 28 December 1942, *Cahier* D, RG 10.144*07, USHMM.

145. Felstiner, *To Paint Her Life,* 161–65; Poznanski, *Jews in France during World War II,*

386–90, 407–10; Dreyfus, 25 December, 28 December 1942, 4 February, 15 February, 10 March, 19 April, 12 May, and 7 June 1943, *Cahier* D, RG 10.144*07, USHMM.

146. Ironically, in a 1938 entry, he had reflected on the difference between knowledge and understanding. Thinking back to the murder of the Austrian archduke in July 1914, he remembered how "we knew about it, but we moved on. We only believed it when, one month later, we read the mobilization order. It is not enough to know in order to believe. You have to see something with your own eyes; then you believe. [On le savait, mais on passait. On le croyait seulement lorsqu'un mois plus tard, on lut l'ordre de mobilisation. Il ne suffit pas de savoir pour croire. Il faut avoir vu de ses yeux; alors on croit.]" Dreyfus, 31 May 1938, first half of notebook, RG 10.144*06, USHMM.

147. "Ce sont là des réflexions d'un homme qui ne craint rien, qui a beaucoup vu et qui a un jugement d'autant plus serein que ses enfants sont sauvés." Dreyfus, 4 July 1942, *Cahier* C, RG 10.144*06, USHMM.

148. "Tout le monde vit dans l'anxiété, à l'exception de moi. Quand on a renoncé à regarder son existence comme le contre du monde, on n'a plus peur de rien. Mes enfants sont sauvés." Dreyfus, 8 October 1942, *Cahier* D, RG 10.144*07.

149. "Mais mon calme dans l'angoisse [. . .] ne s'explique que par la certitude de me survivre par mes chers établis en Amérique. À mon age, on a montré ce qu'on est, ce qu'on a et ce qu'on peut. Si je dois renoncer à les revoir, la satisfaction d'avoir être souvent et longtemps entouré par eux me consolera. Si les Allds. abrègent mon existence, ils auront la satisfaction d'avoir eu un peu martyr. Dieu les bénira et ils continueront à rester parmi les premiers en Israël." Dreyfus, 27 February 1943, *Cahier* D, RG 10.144*07, USHMM.

150. "Des âmes de feu, capables d'animer de leur souffle et de leur foi la croisade contre la barbare germanique." Dreyfus, 20 November 1939, first half of journal, RG 10.144*06, USHMM.

151. "Le sacrifice de soi-même est l'acte sublime du juif exposé aux coups des assassins." Dreyfus, 12 June 1942, *Cahier* B, RG 10.144*05, USHMM.

152. See Eidelberg, trans. and ed., *The Jews and the Crusaders.*

153. "S'il est écrasé, une légende sacrée l'entourera éternellement dans la mémoire de la postérité." Dreyfus, 17 November 1927, RG 10.144*02, USHMM. He reiterated and extended this idea in his article "Ce que nous apprennent les juifs du moyen âge," *La Tribune Juive,* 31 December 1937, 810.

154. "Ce qui constitue le héros, c'est d'avoir été victime de qqe grande tragédie et d'avoir supporté avec courage sa disgrace. [. . .] Quand on espère qqchose de très grand, on puise dans la beauté du but le courage de braver les obstacles." Dreyfus, 7 July 1931, RG 10.144*03, USHMM.

155. The Milice were a French paramilitary organization led by Joseph Darnand that emerged out of the Légion Française des Combattants. In 1943 the Milice became an independent organization that assisted the SS in rounding up Jews, stepping in when the French police forces became increasingly indifferent. The Milice also helped the Germans fight the French Resistance. See Marrus and Paxton, *Vichy France and the Jews,* 335; Soucy, *French Fascism,* 53. On Darnand, see Burrin, *France Under the Germans,* 438–46.

156. "Jeudi 16. Des bruits alarmants se répandent. À Nice, il y a des arrestations en quan-
tité, dans les rues, dans les hôtels, dans les villas de la promenade des Anglais. Ce
sont les Allds. aidés par les gens de la milice qui procèdent sans pitié. On ne sait pas
que faire. Il y a une chose à faire: avoir la confiance que D. aidera. Après tout, j'ai dé-
passé la soixantaine, et mes enfants se consoleront héroïquement d'avoir eu un père
martyr." Lucien Dreyfus, 16 September 1943, *Cahier* G, RG 10.144*08, USHMM.

157. Twenty-nine people from Dreyfus's transport were alive in 1945, among them two
women. In his first mention of Drancy, he referred to it as "Drance (Seine)": Dreyfus, 15 August 1942, *Cahier* C, RG 10.144*06, USHMM. Dreyfus never mentioned
Auschwitz, or the name of any other camp in Poland. We know he was deported from
Drancy to Auschwitz because his name appeared on a transport list for convoy no. 62
to Auschwitz, reprinted in Klarsfeld, *Memorial to the Jews Deported from France 1942–
1944.* That transport list contained two men with the name "Lucien Dreyfus," one of
whom was definitely the diarist since the birthplace and birth year match his. In the
case of documents of labor assignments from Drancy, a "Lucien Dreyfus" is mentioned in two instances, but it is impossible to ascertain if the reference was to the diarist or to a different man with the same name. See *Note de Service* No. 164, 20 October
1943, Drancy, DLXII-163, Centre de documentation juive contemporaine [hereafter
CDJC], Paris; *Note de Service* No. 169, 30 October 1943, Drancy, DLXII-169, CDJC.

158. Gutman, "Warsaw," in Laqueur, *The Holocaust Encyclopedia,* 690, 694; Engelking
and Leociak, *Getto Warszawskie,* 689.

159. On the concept of a trilingual polysystem, see Shmeruk, "Hebrew-Yiddish-Polish: A
Trilingual Jewish Culture," in Gutman et al., *The Jews of Poland Between Two World
Wars,* 285–311. See the discussions of Kaplan's diary in Young, *Writing and Rewriting
the Holocaust,* 27, 35–36; Wisse, *The Modern Jewish Canon,* 195, 198–202. Roskies
analyzed the changes in Jewish consciousness in the ghettos, arguing that there were
three identifiable stages. Still, he grouped Kaplan apart from "historical diarists" like
Emanuel Ringelblum and Herman Kruk, thereby deemphasizing the incredible historical awareness displayed by Kaplan and his fundamental questioning of biblical archetypes and faith to confer meaning on Jewish suffering. Roskies, *Against the Apocalypse,* 200, 209–11.

160. One famous example will have to suffice by way of contrast. Like Dreyfus, the *Annales*
historian and fellow Alsatian Jew, Marc Bloch, tackled the question of who bore responsibility for France's defeat by Nazi Germany in June 1940. In his "Statement of
Evidence," *Strange Defeat,* Bloch posed the question, "On whom or on what should
the blame be laid?" He assigned blame to many parties in French society. He believed
that salvation—meaning the liberation of France—depended on the more energetic
pursuit of rational knowledge: "Salvation can be ours only on condition that we set
our brains to work with a will, in order that we may *know* more fully, and get our imagi-
nations moving to a quicker tempo." In contrast to Dreyfus, however, Bloch reavowed
his faith in France. Bloch's critical assessment of French politicians, the military, intellectuals, and the bourgeoisie did not shake his proud identification as a Frenchman.
Three years later, in his famous testamentary statement, written after the promulgation of Vichy's anti-Jewish laws and the beginning of the roundups of Jews, Bloch

declared himself "a stranger to all credal dogmas, as to all pretended community of life and spirit based on race, I have, through life, felt that I was above all, and quite simply, a Frenchman." Bloch, *Strange Defeat*, 25, 149; Bloch, "The Testamentary Instructions of Marc Bloch," in *Strange Defeat*, 178. See also Fink, *Marc Bloch*; Friedländer, "Marc Bloch and Ernst Kantorowicz," in Barnavi and Friedländer, *Les Juifs et le XXe siècle.*

161. Mintz, *Hurban*, 4.

3. NEWS READERS

1. Becker, *Jakob the Liar*, 84. Since Becker was a child in the Łódź ghetto during the war, it is generally assumed that the ghetto depicted in *Jakob the Liar* was a fictive version of Łódź. Indeed, a group of illegal radio listeners existed in the Łódź ghetto, although it is not absolutely certain that Becker knew about them during the war. The historian Hanno Loewy, for one, questions whether he did. See Loewy and Bodek, "Vorwort: Les vrais riches. . .," in *"Les Vrais Riches,"* 32. For a sensitive analysis of Becker's *Jakob the Liar*, see Roskies, *Against the Apocalypse*, 191–92. For an insightful biography of Becker, see Gilman, *Jurek Becker.*

2. So many books have been written on the subject that what follows is just a sampling. For a documentation of the German press and radio during the Third Reich, see Wulf, *Presse und Funk im Dritten Reich.* For the history of the German press during the Third Reich, see Hale, *The Captive Press in the Third Reich*; Frei and Schmitz, *Journalismus im Dritten Reich.* On the workings of Nazi wartime propaganda, see Baird, *The Mythical World of Nazi War Propaganda, 1939–1945*; Herzstein, *The War that Hitler Won.* For a history of the German Jewish press under the Nazi regime, see Freeden, *The Jewish Press in the Third Reich*; Diehl, *Die jüdische Presse im Dritten Reich.* Yisrael Gutman provides a concise overview of the underground newspapers printed in the Warsaw ghetto that were recovered after the war in his *The Jews of Warsaw*, 146–54. On the French press under German occupation, see Burrin, *France Under the Germans*, 372, 374–75, 390–91, 394, 399–401, 420–21. For a documentation of the Jewish underground press in France during the German occupation, see Rayski, "La presse des organizations juives de résistance de la MOI face à l'extermination et au secret qui l'entourait," in Courtois and Rayski, *Qui savait quoi?*, 122–228.

3. For example, see Laqueur, "The Jews in Nazi-occupied Europe: Denial and Acceptance," chap. 5 in *The Terrible Secret*, 123–56; Engel, "'Will They Dare?'" in Shapiro, *Holocaust Chronicles*, 71–82.

4. Bauer, *Rethinking the Holocaust*, 120.

5. *Ibid.*, 26, 120. See discussion in chapter 1 on the timing of the Final Solution.

6. Kaplan, 16 May 1942, *Scroll of Agony*, 334.

7. To scrutinize Jews' actions and to evaluate them on the basis of their outcome, namely, whether they led to death or survival, in the words of Michael André Bernstein, "drains all meaningful reality [. . .] from the lives of the people being described." In this quotation, Bernstein referred specifically to the expectation imparted in many works about the Holocaust that Jews should have been more prescient than their historical con-

temporaries and foreseen what was coming. Bernstein, *Foregone Conclusions*, 17. On reading as an active form of consumption, see de Certeau, *The Practice of Everyday Life*, 169.

8. In Germany during the last two decades of the nineteenth century, daily newspaper reading expanded beyond its largely middle-class audience of midcentury. Fritzsche, *Reading Berlin 1900*, 20, 50–60. In Russia during the same period, mass circulation journalism came into being, as did a mass audience of readers from the lower classes. Balmuth, *Censorship in Russia*, 95–96. So, too, in France during the last third of the nineteenth century a mass press sprang up, and "news and newsworthiness began to matter more than before." Weber, *France*, 27. On the power of a women's reading public in changing Jewish society in the nineteenth century, see Parush, *Reading Jewish Women*.

9. Hobsbawm, *The Age of Empire*, 87; Fritzsche, *Reading Berlin 1900*, 20, 50–61; Schwartz, "Setting the Stage: The Boulevard, the Press and the Framing of Everyday Life," chap. 1 in *Spectacular Realities*. For a compact overview of the "reading revolution" in nineteenth-century Germany, see Nipperdey, *Germany from Napoleon to Bismarck*, 520–26.

10. Anderson, *Imagined Communities*, 35–36.

11. By the mid–nineteenth century, the majority of German Jews lived in urban areas. Aschheim, *Brothers and Strangers*, 7; Freeden, *The Jewish Press in the Third Reich*, 21–24, 47; Diehl, *Die jüdische Presse im Dritten Reich*, 14–20, 23. The Yiddish press was by far the most extensive Jewish press in Poland and Lithuania throughout the 1920s and 1930s. In Vilna alone on the eve of the Second World War there were five Yiddish dailies. Shmeruk, "Hebrew-Yiddish-Polish: A Trilingual Jewish Culture," in Gutman et al., *The Jews of Poland Between the Two World Wars*, 304–9.

12. Weber, *The Hollow Years*, 128.

13. "Täglich 3 mal kehrt sich die ganze Weltlage um." Grete Steiner, 27 September ["abends"] 1938, first notebook, diary from Scheveningen, Holland, manuscript, File 1064, Lohamei Ha'Ghetaot [hereafter LHG].

14. Text of the *Schriftleitergesetz* of 4 October 1933, quoted in Hale, *The Captive Press in the Third Reich*, 86.

15. Jelavich, "Metamorphoses of Censorship in Modern Germany," in Lehmann, *Culture and Politics in Nineteenth- and Twentieth-Century Germany*, 12.

16. Hale, *The Captive Press in the Third Reich*, 255–57, 274–83. For the fate of different segments of the German press, e.g., the liberal democratic press, the confessional press, and others, see Frei and Schmitz, *Journalismus im Dritten Reich*, 39–120.

17. Klemperer, 19 July 1942, *I Will Bear Witness, 1942–1945*, 104.

18. Geissmar, 28 July [1943], [Poem] No. 241, "Theresienstädter Tagebuch," photocopy of manuscript, File ME 182, Leo Baeck Institute Archives [hereafter LBI]. The question of truth was a central concern, and not only in direct relation to news reading. The title of a lecture given at Theresienstadt less than a year later, "Truth and Untruth from Theater and Film," suggests that Jews were contemplating these questions in different contexts or trying to discuss these issues without doing so in a more direct and dangerous manner. The lecture "Wahres und Unwahres von Bühne und Film"

was mentioned in the diary of Richard Ehrlich, 26 April 1944, "The History of Our Negative Emigration," manuscript, File ME 1101, Richard A. Ehrlich Collection, LBI.

19. Laqueur, *The Terrible Secret*, 105, 129, 165.

20. Dobroszycki, ed., *The Chronicle of the Łódź Ghetto*, xxxix, and entry of 10–24 March 1941, 35.

21. Dobroszycki, ed., 22 July 1941, ibid., 66, and 5–12, 20 July 1941, 63, 64.

22. Dobroszycki, ed., 1–5 January 1942, ibid., 109, 109 n. 3.

23. Rosenfeld, 28 August 1942, *In the Beginning Was the Ghetto*, 118; Dobroszycki, ed., March, 16 April, 18 June 1942, *The Chronicle of the Łódź Ghetto*, 135, 147, 206.

24. Dobroszycki, ed., 9 May 1944, ibid., 484.

25. Beneš and Tošnerová, *Pošta v ghettu Terezín*, 82.

26. Mechanicus, 18 November 1943, *Year of Fear*, 192.

27. "Wczoraj ciocia zalewając się łzami, przyniosła list od swego syna z Italii. Czyni wyrzuty, dlaczego nie zawiadomiono go wcześniej o chorobie ojca. W swej naiwności wyznaje, że byłby przyjechał ratować ojca (w paszczę lwa). Prosi, żeby zanieść kwiaty za grób. (Jaka nieznajomość naszych stosunków). [. . .] To jest zresztą całkiem naiwne ale ma się potrzebę by nawet w tej formie powiedzieć [. . .] jak nam miodowo." Eliszewa, 23 December 1941, diary from Stanislawów, typed copy, File 267, Reel 39, RG 02.208M, ŻIH Memoir Collection 302, United States Holocaust Memorial Museum Archives [hereafter USHMM]. The diary of Eliszewa, also referred to as Elsa Binder, was published in English translation in Zapruder, *Salvaged Pages*, 301–28.

28. Gutman, *The Jews of Warsaw*, 111–12.

29. Laqueur, *The Terrible Secret*, 165. Jews' coding of messages in Hebrew was used in tsarist times as well. See Roskies, *Against the Apocalypse*, 167.

30. Beneš and Tošnerová, *Pošta v ghettu Terezín*, 78.

31. "Delatin 17. Mai 1942

    Lieber Onkel

    Die Karte vom 5.II habe erhalten. Von unsere ganzen vamilie [sic] bin nur ich und mein jüngerer Bruder Artur gebliben [sic]. Wir haben müssen von unsere heim aus-ziehen uns [sic] befunden uns in Delatyn ohne welche Mittel zum Leben. Wenn Euch möglich wären uns mit etwas zu helfen wären wir sehr dankbar dafür. Bitte an uns nicht zu fergesen [sic]. Ich sand meine Frau und Kind wie auch Artur grüssen Sie Lieber Onkel und Tante herzlichst.

    Herman"

    Herman Kraminer to Mendel Schorr, Delatyn, 17 May 1942, RG 0.75, File 363, Yad Vashem Archives [hereafter YVA].

32. Szeps, 19 April, 26 May, 28 June 1942, diary from Grünberg Schlesien Lager, manu-script and typed copy, File 747, RG 033, YVA.

33. Starościak, *Żydzi w Dąbrowie Górniczej*, 21.

34. J. Izrael Kalmowich to Fela Sara Scheps, Dombrowa, 11 March 1943, and J. Izrael Kalmowich to Fela Sara Scheps, Dombrowa, [illegible day] April 1943, both in RG 033, File 747, YVA.

35. See, for example, the postcards sent from Dombrowa, 3 and 29 June 1943, in Acc. 1995.A.1043, USHMM; the postcards sent to Grünberg, 24 August 1942, in Acc.

1997.A.0406, USHMM; and the postcards and letter from Dombrowa to Grünberg, 25 February, 27 March, 10 April 1942, in Acc. 1999.A.0255, USHMM.

36. Laqueur, *The Terrible Secret*, 129–30.

37. "8 August 1943

Liebe Freunde,

Wir sind nicht mehr in Theresienstadt, sondern sind alle vier hier heute angekommen. Wir sind alle gesund und grüssen sich alle herzlichst.

Eure,

Helene"

Helene Faltin to Robert Schalek, Arbeitslager Birkenau, 8 August 1943, RG 075, File 371, YVA; Beneš and Tošnerová, *Pošta v ghettu Terezín*, 152–59.

38. In Holland from July 1942 until October 1943, seventeen hundred letters and postcards were received from people who had been deported to camps in Poland. Laqueur, *The Terrible Secret*, 153.

39. Frieda Reinach, 10 May 1942, diary by Frieda and Max Reinach from Berlin, manuscript and English translation, Acc. 1999.A.0215, USHMM. Not my translation.

40. Hämmerle, "'You let a weeping woman call you home?,'" in Earle, *Epistolary Selves*, 154.

41. Kaplan, 2 August 1942, *Scroll of Agony*, 397.

42. "Über den Bestimmungsort mehrerer Transporte ist man noch heute im Unklaren, da Nachrichten von diesen Transportteilnehmern noch nicht eingegangen sind. Es handelt sich hierbei um November-Transporte, sodass die hiesigen Angehörigen seitdem ohne jede Nachricht über ihre Angehörigen sind." Erich Frey, diary, in Kreutzer, *"Die Gespräche drehten sich auch vielfach um die Reise,"* 101. English translation from Frey, "The Diary of Erich Frey," English translation only, RG 10.041*03, Alfred H. Elbau papers, USHMM.

43. Isabelle Jesion, 10 and 31 August, 12 September 1942, diary from Paris, manuscript, File 2131, LHG. Most Jews in Drancy were later deported to Auschwitz, as happened to Dreyfus and his wife.

44. "Ob sie noch am Leben sind? Wir haben seitdem von keinem mehr etwas gehört." Jacob (Köbes) Müller, 10 December 1942, diary from Holland, typed copy, ME 1028, LBI. Unfortunately, the original copies of the diary have been lost. Müller prepared the diary in three copies, retaining one for himself and giving a copy each to his uncle in England and brother in New York after the war. All three of these have gone missing. What remains is a copy of the original, prepared by Müller's cousin and donated to the Leo Baeck Institute Archives. Gerald Weiss, e-mail message to author, 14 November 2004.

45. "Wo sind all die Menschen geblieben, die mir näher und ferner standen und von hier fortkamen!—Ob man je wieder etwas von ihnen hören wird?" Caecilie Lewissohn, 1 January 1944, diary from Berlin, manuscript, Box 42, ME 388, LBI.

46. The desperation to find out what awaited German Jews sent to Łódź is especially evident in the October, November, and December 1941 entries of Victor Klemperer's diary. See Klemperer, *I Will Bear Witness, 1933–1941*, 440, 441, 444, 446.

47. Dina Rathauserowa, 10 December 1942, diary from Peczeniżynie, manuscript and

typed copy, File 633, RG 033, YVA. The German term *Aktion* and the Polish translation *Akcja*, which, in a military context, referred to a campaign, action, or operation,
was applied by Nazi perpetrators to connote the rounding up and deportation of Jews
from towns and cities to kill them. This euphemism, like *die Endlösung der Juden-
frage* ("the Final Solution to the Jewish Question"), was intentionally ambiguous and
deceptive. When diarists referred to an *Akcja* having taken place in their town, they
seemed to mean the violent roundup of Jews, which was accompanied by torture and
murder. In diarists' use of the term it was often implied that the specific fates of the
Jews were unknown.

48. During the war, Holländer's name was Margarete (Grete) Bolchower. When she re-
married after the war, she changed her name to Holländer. Holländer herself donated
a typed copy of her diary to YVA. Since the original is not available, it is possible that
Holländer edited the diary in some fashion after the war. Bearing that in mind, it is
still a remarkable document of the period.

49. "Dauernd kamen sogar Nachrichten, dass sie man in dieser und jener Stadt gesehen
habe. Boten kamen, die Grüsse übermittelten und Geldsendungen und Briefe mit-
nahmen. Natürlich waren diese Nachrichten ausnahmslos gefälscht, oder fingiert.
[. . .] Dadurch glaubte man noch längere Zeit an Seifenblasen und gab die Hoffnung nicht auf." Holländer, Vergangenheit Nr. 28, written 22–23 November 1943,
diary from bunker near Czortków in Galicia, typed copy, File 774, RG 033, YVA.

50. Ehrlich, 12 November 1943, ME 1101, LBI.

51. Titelman, 14 May 1941, [Notes], in Kermish, *To Live With Honor and Die With
Honor!*, 73.

52. Hebrew entry of 9 July 1944, diary from the Łódź ghetto written in the margins of a
French storybook, *Les Vrais Riches*, File 1032, RG 03, YVA. Author unknown. Translated from the Hebrew by Dorota Wach. This diary has been published in German
translation in an edition edited by Hanno Loewy and Andrzej Bodek. A substantial
portion of this diary has been published in English translation as well in Zapruder,
Salvaged Pages, 361–94.

53. "Wieści, chcę wieści, wieści od których żywiej biją serca, pałają oczy, zaciskają się
pięści bezsilnie a dość silne jeszcze [. . .] Wieści te, siłą serca przewrażliwioną imagi-
nacją doszukują się w niedopowiedzianych słowach, odczytują z twarzy nowo-
przebyłych, odszyfrowują je w słowach drukowanych i pisanych." Szeps, 5 July 1943,
File 747, RG 033, YVA.

54. I am indebted to Debora Silverman for this analysis.

55. Szewa Szeps, testimony, File 2728, RG 03, YVA, 6.

56. See Bernhard Kolb, 19–24 June 1943, typed copy, P.III.h. (Theresienstadt) 520,
Wiener Library Collection, Tel Aviv University; A.B., 18 April 1945, diary from
Theresienstadt, microfilm of manuscript, File 13, RG JM, YVA; Ehrlich, 22 April 1945,
ME 1101, LBI.

57. Szeps, 5 April and 28 June 1942, File 747, RG 033, YVA.

58. Brandla (Bronka) Siekierkowa, 29 June 194[?], diary from Mińsk Mazowiecki, manuscript and typed copy, File 123, Reel 21, RG 02.208M, ŻIH Memoir Collection 302,
USHMM.

59. "Man ist vollkommen abgeschlossen von der Aussenwelt, hört und sieht nichts vom Krieg als den ganzen Tag die SS-Leute, die scheinend noch an einen Sieg Deutschlands glauben, so selbstbewusst ist ihr Auftreten. Ich denke, dass man sie auch im Unklaren darüber lässt, was draussen vorgeht und wie es an der Front steht. In Westerbork haben wir durch Zeitungen, Radio u[nd] Berichten von ausserhalb des Lagers noch einiges erfahren und der Zustand gab uns allen Grund optimistisch über die Dauer des Krieges zu sein. Aber hier??? Ich denke, dass es für uns ganz plötzlich und unverhofft zu Ende sein wird." Keller and Horwitz, 31 March 1944, diary from Bergen-Belsen, typed copy, File 7, RG 033, YVA.

60. Keller and Horwitz, 17 March 1944, File 7, RG 033, YVA.

61. Freeden, *The Jewish Press in the Third Reich*, 6.

62. Klemperer, 28 September 1943, *I Will Bear Witness, 1942–1945*, 264.

63. Katzenelson, 23 July 1943, *Vittel Diary*, 58.

64. Consonant with anti-Semitic perceptions of Jews as devious and skilled conspirators, the German guards also asked Müller for news because they believed Jews were better at "reading between the lines." Furthermore, what this example underscores is that it was not only Jews who were left in the dark about news, and neither were they the only ones trying to figure out what was happening in the war. This dimension of news reading was not uniquely Jewish. Müller, ME 1028, LBI, 9.

65. "Die deutsch. Berichte in den hiesigen Zeitungen sind Tragi-komisch. Auch wenn man nicht durch engl. Berichte informiert würde, könnte man alles Wichtige herauslesen." Steiner, 5 December 1941 and 11 January 1942, third notebook, File 1064, LHG.

66. Kramer (née Schwarz), 1–2 February 1944, diary from Żołkiew, manuscript, Object ID No. 1994.95.2a-e, Collections Division, USHMM. All quotations are from the English translation of the diary from a private collection. My thanks to Alexandra Zapruder for sharing the English translation of this diary with me.

67. "Sie dürfen doch nur bringen, was die Deutschen ihnen geben, und das ist manchmal sehr bedeutungsvoll." Steiner, 11 January 1942, third notebook, File 1064, LHG. "So hofft man, dass man wieder einen Tag der Befreiung näher ist." Steiner, 21 November 1941, third notebook, File 1064, LHG.

68. Steiner, 8 December 1941, third notebook, File 1064, LHG.

69. *Zerlegen* carries a mechanical and scientific meaning, but does not have the figurative sense that the English *dissecting* has. Steiner, 26 September 1938, first notebook, and 21 November 1941, third notebook, File 1064, LHG.

70. After the war, Klemperer published his linguistic analysis of the language of the Third Reich in a book by the same name. *LTI: Notizbuch eines Philologen* was originally published in 1957 in Halle and was published in English translation as *The Language of the Third Reich: LTI—Lingua Tertii Imperii: A Philologist's Notebook* in 2001.

71. Klemperer, 8 July 1942, *I Will Bear Witness, 1942–1945*, 96. On 6 July 1940, Klemperer recorded that there were "new deterrent sentences for 'moral traitors' who listen to foreign broadcasting stations—eight years imprisonment, whole families in prison." Klemperer, 6 July 1940, *I Will Bear Witness, 1933–1941*, 346.

72. M. Landsberg, diary from hiding in Krzemieniec, two notebooks, manuscript and

typed copy, File 1099, RG 033, YVA. The first notebook of this diary contains a hand-written calendar in the left column of each page and writing in the right column, alongside the dates. It is unclear, however, if the dates on the left side of the page correspond in each and every instance to the date of an individual entry. In the second notebook, there are twenty pages of text that precede thirty-one pages of dated entries. The longer discussion of newspapers I analyze here is contained within the section of that notebook that is not organized by dated entries. Nevertheless, this discussion appears to have been recorded on or shortly after the date of the newspaper he cited, 21 November 1942. For all undated entries, I include the page number from the original manuscript. Information about Krzemieniec and Benjamin Landsberg is from *Encyclopedia Judaica*, 1997 CD-Rom edition, s.v. "Kremenets."

73. The phrase "flashes of objectivity [*przebłyski rzeczowości*]" is from an entry in the second notebook dated 25 November 1942, File 1099, RG 033, YVA.

74. "Po przeczytaniu komunikatu zaczynamy go 'tłumaczyć' na 'swój' język. Wiemy więc: że na Kaukazie wojska sowieckie atakują, że w Stalingradzie niemcom również idzie 'jak krew z nosa,' że nad Donem inicjatywa jest w rosyjskim ręku, [. . .] że . . w ogóle jest dobrze. My mamy już 'swój' klucz, którym się posługujemy przy czytaniu niemieckich gazet." Landsberg, [n.d.], second notebook, File 1099, RG 033, YVA, 12. Klara Kramer also mentioned tracking the Russians' progress on a map. See Kramer, 3 January 1944, Object ID 1994.95.2a-e, Collections, USHMM.

75. Though he did not characterize it as such, his method calls to mind the "'decoding' method" of interpreting dreams described (and rejected) by Freud, "as a kind of cryptography in which each sign can be translated into another sign having a known meaning in accordance with a fixed key." Freud, *The Interpretation of Dreams*, 130.

76. "Tak, tak! Coraz to bardziej utwierdzamy się w przekonaniu, że gazety trzeba umieć czytać." Landsberg, 29 November 1942, second notebook, File 1099, RG 033, YVA.

77. Kaplan, 18 November 1939, *Scroll of Agony*, 72.

78. Zonszajn, diary from Siedlce ghetto, original manuscript and English translation, Rachel Ben Shaul Collection. Not my translation. I am indebted to Suzy Snyder for showing me a copy of this diary and to Gal Ben Shaul for allowing me to quote from it. Information about Siedlce from *Encyclopedia Judaica*, 1997 CD-Rom edition, s.v. "Siedlce."

79. "Die Zeitungen sind jetzt Rätseln mit 7 Siegeln, aus denen man absolut nicht klug werden kann. Eine Flut von Berichten, die sich gegenseitig widersprechen und was wirklich passiert, das wissen die Götter." Holländer, 16 September 1943, File 774, RG 033, YVA. Her mention of the Polish paper is from 5 August 1943.

80. "Eben kam Jozek zurück und brachte eine kaum glaubliche Nachricht: Italien soll endlich kapituliert haben. Er hörte es von einem Volksdeutschen, der ein Radio besitzt. [. . .] Wir sind leider schon so oft grausam enttäuscht worden, dass ich nichts glaube, ehe es nicht in der Zeitung steht." Holländer, 9 September 1943, File 774, RG 033, YVA. The Italian armistice did occur that week on 3 September 1943.

81. "Je länger die Sache dauert, desto verwirrter werden wir." Holländer, 14 March 1944, File 774, RG 033, YVA.

82. Klemperer, 27 July 1943, *I Will Bear Witness, 1942–1945*, 249.

83. Ringelblum, [undated entry], *Notes from the Warsaw Ghetto*, 299.

84. "Czy byłoby tak, czy nie było, mniejsza o to, ale same słowa dodają otuchy, są warte miliony." Siekierkowa, 22 June [1943?], File 123, Reel 21, RG 02.208M, ŻIH Memoir Collection 302, USHMM.

85. The first quotation reads: "ale ktoby to jadł, kiedy są gazety." And the second: "'Czy znajdą nas?' 'Czy dożyjemy?' 'Kiedy wojna się skończy i jak?'" Landsberg, second notebook, File 1099, RG 033, YVA, 10–11, 15.

86. This function of news is also attested to by Bernard Rechnitz in his memoir of the war. Rechnitz described how he and his wife "lived in the center of the city [Wieliczka, Poland] and so a lot of acquaintances gathered at our house every day and we carried on political and strategic discussions and analyzed the leading stories in the papers, in order to find hints of a German defeat." Rechnitz, "Bernard Rechnitz Diary," English translation only, RG 02.069, USHMM, 44.

87. "Die Strasse ist gleichzeitig Nachrichtenzentrum wo Gerüchte und Informationen ausgetauscht und kommentiert werden, sie ist Börse und Marktplatz, wo man irgendwelche Kostbarkeiten, z.B. ein Stück Brot oder gar ein Viertel PfundFett [. . .] erwerben kann, sie ist voll von Abenteuern und Geheimnissen [. . .]—sie ist Erholung, Abwechslung und Lebensventil des Lagers, alles in einem." Hans J. Steinitz, "Das Buch von Gurs: ein Weissbuch über das südfranzöische Interniertenlager Gurs," typed coped, File 19, Box 8, RG 04.072, USHMM.

88. Kaplan, 5 September 1940, *Scroll of Agony*, 192; *Megilat yisurin*, 324–25. The inserted sentences, omitted from the English edition, were translated by Zvi Ben-Dor Benite.

89. "So behauptete sich auch in dieser abnormen Situation wieder der bekannte Optimismus und Lebenswille unserer Glaubensgenossen!" Ehrlich, 12 November 1943, ME 1101, LBI.

90. "Ich habe immer eine grosse Vorliebe für Abenteuerromane gehabt. Das Leben hat mir den Gefallen getan und mir selbst die unwahrscheinlichsten Abenteuer beschert. Aber ich bin eine unverbesserliche Optimistin. Vielleicht gelingt es mir doch, mich durchzuschmuggeln." Holländer, 30 July 1943, File 774, RG 033, YVA.

91. Ringelblum, 18 May 1941, *Notes from the Warsaw Ghetto*, 178.

92. The whole sentence reads, "Vielleicht ist es gerade er [der Optimismus], der uns immer wie der Halt, und uns dieses Leben erträglich macht." Flaum, diary from Prague, Sosnowiec, Haifa, manuscript, File 25, RG 033, YVA, 40 verso.

93. Ringelblum, 26 September 1940, *Notes from the Warsaw Ghetto*, 55.

94. Kaplan, 7 June 1942, *Scroll of Agony*, 347.

95. Ringelblum, 8 May 1942, *Notes from the Warsaw Ghetto*, 261.

96. Kramer, 3 February 1944, Object ID 1994.95.2a-e, Collections, USHMM. Not my translation.

97. "Jak Ty się zapytam czy nie jestem za naiwna, czy nie żyję zanadto w świecie złudzeń? Ale nie istnieje dla mnie inny świat. Ludzie żyjący w takich warunkach [. . .] przechodzą po rzeczywistości omackiem, marzenia są dla nas pełnią życia." Copy of a letter written by Fela Szeps to "Mój drogi braciszku! [my dear brother]," Grünberg Schlesien camp, [undated], 5 pages, File 747, RG 033, YVA, 2.

98. "Selbstverständlich wurde auch sehr viel über die Kriegslage und die Zukunft der

Juden debattiert, wobei meistens ein Optimismus zu Tage trat, der an Naivität grenzte. Wehe dem, der es wagte anderer Meinung zu sein; derjenige wurde als Pessimist und Miessmacher verschrieen und war nirgends gern gesehen." Ehrlich, 12 November 1943, ME 1101, LBI.

99. "Der einzige, der skeptisch, allen Gerüchten gegenüber steht ist Dr. Bohrer. Ein polnischer Journalist, der in Prag für verschiedene grosse polnische Blätter geschrieben hat [. . .] er versammelt jeden Abend eine grossere Anzahl Leute um sich und halt Vorträge meist über das Thema: der Civilist als Internierter. Seine Ausführungen haben meist einen pessimistischen Unterton. [. . .] Obwohl ich persönlich ein Gegner von Verbreitungen solchen pessimistischen Ansichten bin, von Leuten, die über dem Niveau der Anderen stehen, habe ich den Doktor sehr gern." Flaum, File 25, RG 033, YVA, 15 recto.

100. On this point and the specific role played by Zionist Youth Movements during the Shoah, see Gutman, "The Youth Movement as an Alternative Leadership in Eastern Europe," in Cohen and Cochavi, *Zionist Youth Movements during the Shoah*, 14.

101. Holländer, 30 July 1943, 29 January, 12 March, 5 February, 13 February 1944, File 774, RG 033, YVA.

102. Klemperer, 24 July 1940, *I Will Bear Witness, 1933–1941*, 349.

103. "Ich schwanke so zwischen Hoffnung und Depression und weiss selbst nicht, wie mir zu Mute [sic] ist." Flaum, 41 recto-41 verso. "Es beginnt wieder das selbe Spiel." Flaum, File 25, RG 033, YVA, 21 recto.

104. Klemperer, 2 September 1941, *I Will Bear Witness, 1933–1941*, 428.

105. Ringelblum, 11 May 1941, *Notes from the Warsaw Ghetto*, 173–74.

106. Titelman, 14 May 1941, [Notes], in Kermish, *To Live With Honor and Die With Honor!*, 74.

107. Even in Auschwitz, Primo Levi described their moods as vacillating between hope and despair, though he did not link this "state of mind" specifically to news reading. Philip Roth, "A Conversation with Primo Levi," in Levi, *Survival in Auschwitz*, 180–81.

108. My use of the word "tactics" is drawn from de Certeau, *The Practice of Everyday Life*, xii–xix, 30, 37.

109. "Ich glaube nun nicht, dass Deutschland noch mehr als 3 Monate zusammenhält." Steiner, 22 December 1941, third notebook, File 1064, LHG.

110. "Deutschland ist eigentlich schon geschlagen [. . .]." Steiner, 10 December 1941, third notebook, File 1064, LHG.

111. "Man kann die Zukunft nicht sehen, zu viel Vorsorge kann uns grade in die Gefahr bringen. Wir warten hier ruhig ab, was kommt. [. . .] Wir sind trotz aller Erfolge der Jap. u. Misserfolge der Engl. u. Americk. sehr guter Hoffnung auf ein baldiges Ende." Steiner, 17 February 1942, third notebook, File 1064, LHG.

112. Klemperer reported on the same piece of news about "Hitler taking over supreme command." He was, however, more circumspect than Steiner in his interpretation of its implications. Undoubtedly, it was a "turnabout" for Germany and "a terrible sign of uncertainty, especially as the defeat in the East is hardly concealed anymore, that in Africa is plain to the whole world." In order to assess the significance of this decisive moment, he paid close attention, as was his practice, to the language Hitler used:

"Hitler's proclamation to the army is a model example of LTI [the language of the Third Reich]. Excessive piling up of the Barnum superlatives, underneath it uncertainty, fear. *Fanatical* twice. The form corresponds to the veiled, in part mysterious content. For consideration: A few weeks ago the Russians were officially 'annihilated.' Now they are to be annihilated in the spring." The combination of Hitler's most recent utterances in LTI and the news about Hitler becoming supreme commander convinced Klemperer that Hitler would suffer defeat. Unlike Steiner, however, Klemperer's optimism on this front was clouded by his fear that Hitler's demise would not come soon enough: "Certainty: *He* will fall. Uncertainty: (1) When? (2) Before we do?" At this juncture, Klemperer surmised that Germany's eventual defeat might not ensure that the Jews would be saved. By late 1941, however, it was no longer possible for Jews to emigrate legally from Germany. He evaded being deported to Riga, Auschwitz, or Theresienstadt like the rest of Dresden's Jews because he was married to a non-Jew and because the Allied firebombing of Dresden occurred three days before he was supposed to be deported in February 1945. All quotations in this paragraph are from Klemperer, 23 December 1941, *I Will Bear Witness, 1933–1941*, 452. Martin Chalmers, "Preface: The Lives of Victor Klemperer," in *I Will Bear Witness, 1933–1941*, vii.

113. According to Raul Hilberg, around 102,000 of the prewar Dutch Jewish population of about 140,000 were killed. The largest two groups of Dutch Jews who survived were 8–9,000 Jews who had intermarried and about the same number of Jews in hiding. Though Steiner had been married to a non-Jew, she was widowed by the time the war started. Hilberg, *The Destruction of the European Jews*, vol. 2, 593–94.

114. In this entry, Eliszewa mentioned the twelfth of October without specifying what had taken place on that date. She wrote about this massacre at greater length on 12 January 1943, the three-month anniversary, and returned to the subject in several entries thereafter. She estimated that twelve thousand Jews were killed that day, whereas Hilberg cites the figure of ten thousand people killed. See Hilberg, *The Destruction of the European Jews*, vol. 2, 496.

115. "Wyczorajsza gazeta podała, że 'wódz' objął naczelne dowództwo armiją [sic]. Żydzi wyciągają stąd najdalej idące i najpomyślniejsze wnioski. Otóż: Hitler widząc swoją bliską klęskę, i gwałtowne cofanie swojej niezwyciężonej dotychczas armii, chcąc [. . .] jako też całe dowództwo zgrupować w jednym ręku, sam podjął się tej misji." Eliszewa, 24 December 1941, File 267, Reel 39, RG 02.208M, ŻIH Memoir Collection 302, USHMM.

116. "Bo jeżeli za Sowietów kwestja pracy była sprawą chleba, dziś jest ona dla Żydów kwestją 'być albo nie być.'" Eliszewa, 24 December 1941, File 267, Reel 39, RG 02.208M, ŻIH Memoir Collection 302, USHMM.

117. Eliszewa, 5 January 1942, File 267, Reel 39, RG 02.208M, ŻIH Memoir Collection 302, USHMM.

118. Hilberg, *The Destruction of the European Jews*, vol. 2, 496; Zapruder, *Salvaged Pages*, 306, 464 n. 5.

119. One diarist in hiding in Lwów described the irony of people paying small fortunes in the ghetto to be assigned to ten hours of hard labor a day. She, too, had believed that work would shelter her from extermination, and for that reason she had labored dili-

gently in a workshop. Rubinsztejnowa, 30 January and 7 February 1944, diary from Lwów, typed copy, File 116, Reel 20, RG 02.208M, ŻIH Memoir Collection 302, USHMM.

120. Jacob Müller recorded the following on 4 December 1942 from his hiding place in Holland: "And when I have to think of my fellow Jews [*Glaubensgenossen*] who will be deported to Poland in total uncertainty and most likely will never return, I feel like a prince in a fairy tale." Müller, ME 1028, LBI. Richard Ehrlich in Theresienstadt recorded on 12 January 1944, "When one considers that in Poland it must be much worse, we have to be very content with our situation." Ehrlich, ME 1101, LBI. On 1 December 1942, Victor Klemperer commented on this type of thinking by Jews who concluded that their situation was favorable in comparison to Jews in Poland: "It is quite deplorable that this imprisonment is already considered to be halfway good fortune. It is not Poland, it is not a concentration camp! One does not quite eat one's fill, but one does not starve. One has not yet been beaten. Etc., etc." Klemperer, *I Will Bear Witness, 1942–1945*, 171–72.

121. In Holland, for example, where it is estimated some twenty-five thousand Jews did go into hiding, only around eight to nine thousand of them survived the war. Hilberg, *The Destruction of the European Jews*, vol. 2, 593–94.

122. Holländer, 27 November 1943, File 774, RG 033, YVA.

123. "Jasno oddajemy sobie sprawozdanie, że nikt się nie zostanie przy życiu, że pod koniec bardzo możliwe zrobią nam wspólny grobowiec, jak dziewczęta mówią, zamurują [nam] drzwi wpuszczą gaz, łóżka będą naszemi grobami, szafki pomnikami nasze nazwisko przyszłość odszuka według numeracji." Szeps, 28 February 1943, File 747, RG 033, YVA.

124. On this moment of recognition that the Germans clearly intended to destroy all Jews, see Letter written by Julian Feurman to "Kochany Panie Doktorze! [Dear Doctor!]," Stanislawów, July 1943, File 135, Reel 23, RG 02.208M, ŻIH Memoir Collection 302, USHMM; Rubinsztejnowa, 23 January 1944, File 116, Reel 20, RG 02.208M, ŻIH Memoir Collection 302, USHMM; Peretz Opoczyński, 5 September 1942, "Warsaw Ghetto Chronicle," in Kermish, *To Live With Honor and Die With Honor*, 104.

125. Klemperer, 27 October 1942, *I Will Bear Witness, 1942–1945*, 158. Ten days before, Klemperer mentioned the transfer of two women "to Auschwitz, which appears to be a swift-working slaughterhouse," but he in no way indicated knowledge of the means employed to kill Jews or that killing Jews was the goal, not the by-product, of deporting them. Klemperer, 17 October 1942, *I Will Bear Witness, 1942–1945*, 155.

126. "K. pisała, że na froncie dobrze. W Brodach idzie rzeź. Podobno jest rozkaz H., że do Nowego Roku ani jednego Żyda ma nie być na teranach okupanych przez Niemców." Landsberg, 30 December 1942, File 1099, RG 033, YVA.

127. Klonicki, 7 July 1943, *The Diary of Adam's Father*, 39.

128. Two days later, Kramer corrected herself. In this case, the "converts" were arrested for black marketeering, not for being Jewish. Kramer, 5 November 1943, Object ID 1994.95.2a-e, Collections, USHMM. Not my translation.

129. "Wprawdzie polityczne wiadomości są bardzo dobre, ale ich klęska zwala się na nasze

głowy, Judenvernichtung na ukończeniu." Szeps, 28 February 1943, File 747, RG 033, YVA.

130. "Für die [Juden] ist der Krieg schon verloren." Holländer, 1 September 1943, File 774, RG 033, YVA.

131. Klemperer, 21 November 1942, *I Will Bear Witness, 1942–1945*, 168.

132. Toni Ringel, end of February 1945, "Diary of a Jewish Mother," File ME 894, Leo Baeck Institute [hereafter LBI]. In the file is only an English translation of the diary, which I quoted here. The original manuscript is in a private collection. Ringel wrote in a Yiddish- and Dutch-inflected German, as is evident in the original of this entry and in subsequent entries I quote in notes, particularly in chapter 4: "Die Lage ist wohl fevendert maar wir denken an andere dingen als Politik wir sind Tood gewonte Mentshen u. haben hunger u. es feilt an allem."

133. Letter written by Berta to Carolina Knoch Taitz, from the Riga ghetto, undated, letter 9, RG 05.004*01, Carolina Taitz papers, USHMM. These letters were written in Latvian. I am quoting from the English translation in the file.

134. Perechodnik, written between 26 July and 1 August 1943, *Am I a Murderer?*, 187. On the problems with the English edition of Perechodnik's diary, see Engel, "On the Bowdlerization of a Holocaust Testimony."

135. "Mein Liebes, wie hatten wir auf diesen Augenblick gehofft, und nun soll das ganze Leben durch alles von mir allein bezwungen werden." Frau Zielenziger, 13 November 1944, P.III.h (Bergen-Belsen) 1118, Wiener Library Collection. According to *In Memoriam: Nederlandse oorlogsslachtoffers*, her husband, Kurt Zielenziger, died on 19 July 1944.

136. "Wyjadę, wyjadę z G, do domu—dokąd? do domu? Do którego domu, gdzie ja mam dom? Do kogo pojadę? [. . .] Samobójstwo nie mam odwagi popełnić, jakaś podświadoma świadomość pragnie we mnie żyć, żyć.! A z drugiej strony nie wyobrażę sobie tego życia, tej przyszłości bez mych drogich bliskich." Szeps, 6 September 1943, File 747, RG 033, YVA.

137. "7 Monate sitzen wir im Bunker. Was erwarten und erhoffen wir eigentlich?" Holländer, 20 February 1944, File 774, RG 033, YVA.

138. Mermall, "Narrative and Diary of Mr. Gabriel Mermall," English translation only, RG 02.008, USHMM, 78. This is a strange hybrid text, part diary, part testimony. Because the file contains only the English translation, it is difficult to discern where the wartime diary ends and where the postwar testimony begins. For this reason, I have made limited use of the text.

139. Katzenelson, 20 August 1943, *Vittel Diary*, 150.

140. "A może to wcale nie jest początkiem nowego tylko końcem byłego?" Szeps, 7 March 1943, File 747, RG 033, YVA.

4. FAMILY CORRESPONDENTS

1. My approach to diaries as bearing symbolic as well as instrumental meanings is borrowed from Roger Chartier, preface to Dauphin, Lebrun-Pézerat, and Poublan, *Ces*

bonnes lettres, 12–14; Dauphin, Lebrun-Pézerat, and Poublan, "Une correspondance familiale au XIXe siècle," in Bossis, *La lettre à la croisée de l'individu et du social*, 126.

2. In her study of family correspondence during the Napoleonic wars, Mary A. Favret argued that letters marked the distance between correspondents, while attempting to bring correspondents closer together. See Favret, "War Correspondence: Reading Romantic War," 174.

3. Isaac Disraeli (1766–1848), father of Benjamin Disraeli, *Curiosities of Literature*; quoted in *Oxford English Dictionary*, 2nd ed., s.v. "diary." The OED's first definition of *diary* reads, "A daily record of events or transactions, a journal; specifically, a daily record of matters affecting the writer personally, or which come under his personal observation." Leleu, *Les Journaux Intimes*, 237; Girard, *Le Journal Intime*, 20; Fothergill, *Private Chronicles*, 30. A recent study that seeks to tear down the walls between genres is Podnieks, *Daily Modernism*. Lynn Z. Bloom challenges the notion that diaries are private documents in "'I Write for Myself and Strangers': Private Diaries as Public Documents," in Bunkers and Huff, *Inscribing the Daily*, 23–37.

4. Dauphin, Lebrun-Pézerat, and Poublan, "Une correspondance familiale au XIXe siècle," 133.

5. Hartley, "'Letters are *everything* these days,'" in Earle, *Epistolary Selves*, 186–87.

6. Gebhardt, *Das Familiengedächtnis*, 58–59; Lejeune, "The 'Journal de Jeune Fille' in Nineteenth-Century France," in Bunkers and Huff, *Inscribing the Daily*, 109, 115–20; Podnieks, *Daily Modernism*, 26.

7. The Theresienstadt diary of Philipp Manes was also written in the hopes that it would reach his four children, all of whom escaped to safety before the war. I learned of the diary's existence only after writing this chapter, so no analysis is contained therein. For a description of the diary, which is located in the London branch of the Wiener Library, see Klaus Leist, "Philipp Manes: A Theresienstadt Chronicle," *Journal of Holocaust Education* 6, no. 2 (1997): 36–70.

8. Strauss, "Jewish Emigration from Germany—Nazi Policies and Jewish Responses (I)," 326; Kaplan, *Between Dignity and Despair*, 73; Friedländer, *Nazi Germany and the Jews*, vol. I, 317, 393 n. 21, 15.

9. Strauss, "Jewish Emigration from Germany," 318. A comparable percentage of working-age adults (twenty-five- to thirty-nine-year-olds) emigrated during the same years: 80 percent.

10. The issue of why people emigrated is incredibly complex, and I furnish only the briefest of explanations here. For a sensitive and thorough treatment of the gender and generational differences among German Jewish émigrés, see Kaplan, *Between Dignity and Despair*, 62–73, 116, 129–44.

11. Information about the fate of Ruth Cohn and her family is from Atzmon-Cohn, "Vorwort," in Cohn, *Als Jude in Breslau 1941*, 9; Laqueur, "Three Witnesses," 261–62.

12. "Nun ist das 3. Kind auch aus dem Hause gegangen; wird man es in diesem Leben noch einmal wiedersehen? Man kann das nicht ausdenken. In einer Viertelstunde geht Ruths Zug. [. . .] In einem solchen Augenblick kann man schwer sagen, was man empfindet [. . .]. Aber man muss sich damit abfinden, dass es zum Besten des Kindes ist. [. . .] Dass wir sie schon frühzeitig auf ihren Lebensweg allein entlassen müssen,

das ist das Tragische dieser Zeit; aber vielleicht das Beste für sie. Auch die Generationen vor uns sind ja in diesem Alter selbständig geworden. Während ich diese Zeile schreibe, wird sie nun schon im Zuge sitzen, der in einer Minute Breslau verlässt; dann ist ihre Jugend in ihrer Heimat abgeschlossen; aber ich denke, dass sie an ihre Jugendzeit eine schöne Erinnerung im Leben mitnehmen wird; wir haben ja immer für die Kinder gelebt. Nun ist der Zug schon heraus, und Trudi wird sehr geweint haben. Es ist die älteste Tochter, und im ersten Jahre ihres Lebens war sie ein Sorgenkind, jetzt wo sie uns schon Stutze sein könnte, muss sie hinaus. Aber man darf nicht an sich denken, nur an das Kind." Willy Cohn, 16 September 1939, diary from Breslau, manuscript, Notebook 90, Box 2, RP 88, Central Archives for the History of the Jewish People, Hebrew University, Jerusalem [hereafter CAHJP]. Yad Vashem possesses a typed copy of Cohn's diaries. See Willy Cohn, File 260, RG 01, Yad Vashem Archives [hereafter YVA].

13. Frey, diary, in Kreutzer, *"Die Gespräche drehten sich auch vielfach um die Reise"*; and "The Diary of Erich Frey," English translation only, RG 10.041*03, Alfred H. Elbau papers, United States Holocaust Memorial Museum Archives [hereafter USHMM]. Information on the Frey family is in "Introduction to Frey's Diary," RG 10.041*03, Alfred H. Elbau papers, USHMM, 2. This translation and all subsequent translations from Frey's diary come from the USHMM translation. The original German, published in Kreutzer's hard-to-find volume, is quoted in the notes.

14. Frey, "A Farewell to Our Dear Marie-Anne, 21 August 1939," RG 10.041*03, USHMM, 4A. This poem was not reproduced in Kreutzer, *"Die Gespräche drehten sich auch vielfach um die Reise."*

15. According to Maciej Siekierski's analysis of Polish Jewish and non-Jewish refugees to eastern Poland in the fall of 1939, around 30 percent of the approximately 600,000 refugees either returned to their homes or emigrated farther east as the war continued. Of the remaining refugees in eastern Poland, the Soviets deported 80 percent, including 198,000 Jews. Siekierski, "The Jews in Soviet-Occupied Eastern Poland at the End of 1939: Numbers and Distribution," in Davies and Polonsky, *Jews in Eastern Poland and the USSR, 1939–1946*, 112–13.

16. Margarete (Grete) Holländer, diary from bunker near Czortków in Galicia, typed copy, File 774, RG 033, YVA. For more information about Holländer and her diary, see chapter 3.

17. "Manchmal war ich traurig darüber, dass sie es gar nicht bedauerte, auf unbestimmbare Zeit von mir fortzumüssen, aber dann sagte ich mir, dass ich glücklich darüber sein mussten, dass sie so vernünftig war. Andere Kinder wären um keinen Preis der Welt von der Mutter weggegangen und meine Kleine sehnte den Tag herbei, der sie endlich aus dem Ghetto befreien sollte." Holländer, Vergangenheit Nr. 50, written between 12 and 14 March 1944, File 774, RG 033, YVA.

18. "Sonja spielt ihre Rolle ausgezeichnet, sprach nach kaum 3 Wochen perfekt ukrainisch, betete in der Kirche tadellos und schien vergessen zu haben dass sie noch vor kurzen im Ghetto gewesen war." Holländer, Vergangenheit Nr. 50, written between 12 and 14 March 1944, File 774, RG 033, YVA.

19. The eagerness Sonja displayed with respect to leaving the ghetto and leaving her

mother sheds light on the corollary of parents' inability to protect their children: children's feelings of vulnerability and their attempts to seek protection from adults other than their parents. Fifteen-year-old Isabelle Jesion wrote in her diary in Paris about a dream she had had in which she was in a concentration camp without her parents. In the dream one of her favorite schoolteachers, who was not Jewish, expressed a willingness to adopt Isabelle. Without a second thought for her parents, Isabelle replied, "I accept gladly [*J'accepte joyeusement*]." Isabelle Jesion, 9 January 1942, first notebook, manuscript, File 2131, Lohamei Ha'Ghetaot [hereafter LHG]. On children's vulnerability and seeking the protection of adults other than their parents, also see the memoir of Sarah Kofman, *Rue Ordener, Rue Labat*, trans. Ann Smock (Lincoln: University of Nebraska Press, 1996).

20. Nili Keren, "Children," in Laqueur, *The Holocaust Encyclopedia*, 115.

21. Kaplan, *Between Dignity and Despair*, 117.

22. Frey, "Diary," RG 10.041*03, USHMM, 8. The original reads, "Diese [Drangsal], sowie die Trennung von Euch, waren wohl die Hauptursache von Muttis Erkrankung." Frey, diary, in Kreutzer, *"Die Gespräche drehten sich auch vielfach um die Reise,"* 95.

23. Cohn, 6 August 1940, Notebook 98, Box 3, and 29 September and 13 September 1939, Notebook 90, Box 2, RP 88, CAHJP.

24. Kaplan described this practice, although she did not explore the genre dimensions, in *Between Dignity and Despair*, 191–92.

25. Frey, "Diary," RG 10.041*03, USHMM, 3; Frey, diary, in Kreutzer, *"Die Gespräche drehten sich auch vielfach um die Reise,"* 93.

26. Frey, "Diary," RG 10.041*03, USHMM, 3. The original reads, "Er wird in vier Exemplaren niedergeschrieben, von denen je 2 für einen Jeden von Euch bestimmt sind. Sie werden guten Freunden zur Aufve[r]wahrung übergeben, um sofort abgesandt zu werden, sobald friedliche Zeiten gekommen sind und die Versendung der Briefe zulässig ist. Hierdurch glauben wir, die Gewissheit zu schaffen, dass das eine oder andere Exemplar in die Hände einer von Euch gelangt. Dann könnt Ihr Euch gegenseitig verständigen, einer der anderen ihr Exemplar zum Lesen zusenden, falls dieselbe noch nichts erhalten hat." Frey, diary, in Kreutzer, *"Die Gespräche drehten sich auch vielfach um die Reise,"* 93.

27. Frey, "Diary," RG 10.041*03, USHMM, 3. The original reads, "Bis Ihr jedoch überhaup[t] diesen Bericht erhalten werdet, können Jahre vergehen." Frey, diary, in Kreutzer, *"Die Gespräche drehten sich auch vielfach um die Reise,"* 93. It is unclear whether Frey's letter-diary, written between 7 April and 10 May 1942, was based on an earlier, missing diary he had begun in June 1939. The epilogue accompanying the translation of the diary in the USHMM file states that the diary addressed to his daughters was "based on a detailed and precise diary covering a period from June 27, 1939 to May 10, 1942." But Frey did not mention any other diary in his 1942 text. At the same time, Frey did record precise dates of events from the preceding years, lending credence to the possibility that he referred to notes of some kind while writing. The issue of whether Frey wrote another, earlier diary is significant in considering his motivations for writing. One thing is clear: he did not go to the same trouble to ensure the survival of his

earlier diary or notes, if they did indeed exist, as he did for the letter-diary addressed to his daughters. See "Epilogue [to diary]," RG 10.041*03, USHMM, 39–40.

28. Celan, "Speech on the Occasion of Receiving the Literature Prize of the Free Hanseatic City of Bremen," in *Selected Poems and Prose of Paul Celan*, 396.

29. The phrase "mothering at a distance" is Jenny Hartley's in " 'Letters are *everything* these days,' " 186.

30. Favret, "War Correspondence," 173; Hanna, "A Republic of Letters," par. 1–4, 20–45; Hartley, " 'Letters are *everything* these days,' " 183.

31. Hartley, " 'Letters are *everything* these days,' " 186.

32. ibid., 185–86. Podnieks also described how recording family chronicles and maintaining familial networks often fell to women. See Podnieks, *Daily Modernism*, 26.

33. Susan Warsinger (née Hilsenrath), 10 August 1941, diary from Château de Morelles, France, original manuscript and English translation, Acc. 2000.127, USHMM. Not my translation.

34. Frey, "Diary," RG 10.041*03, USHMM, 3. The original reads, "es ist heute der 7. April 1942. Der Tag an sich hat keine wesentliche Bedeutung. Er soll nur den Zeitpunkt feststellen, anwelchem dieser Brief,—oder, besser gesagt, dieser Bericht—begonnen wird." Frey, diary, in Kreutzer, *"Die Gespräche drehten sich auch vielfach um die Reise,"* 93.

35. Information about the Ringel family is included in pages accompanying the diary in Toni Ringel, "Diary of a Jewish Mother," English translation only, ME 894, Leo Baeck Institute Archives [hereafter LBI]. The original diary is in a private collection.

36. Ringel, 25 September 1942, "Diary of a Jewish Mother," ME 894, LBI. This translation and all subsequent translations from Ringel's diary come from the LBI translation. The original reads as follows (I have not altered her orthography or punctuation in this entry or in subsequent entries): "Ich habe mir vorgenomen s.g.w. alles auf zu schreiben was rund um unser Leben sich abschpielt. Möge der Almächtiger unsere Kinder behütten u. Beschützen und auch uns nicht fergessen. Unsere einzige Hofnung ist eich meine Herzens Kinder widerzusehen in Glück und Freude sollen wir eich dise Blätter ibereichen und Nicht Fremde Mentschen. Wir gehen einen Schwehren Leidens weg, vohller gefaren entgegen. Maar wir wir sind nich allein den [ha shem] ist mit uns. Wir haben die lätzte Monate fiel mit gemacht und wissen ganz genau wie wir uns in der Neuer Umgebung zu ferhalten haben. An gutten willen Tapferkeit und anpasungsfeukeit soll es nich fehle." Ringel, 25 September 1942, diary, original manuscript, private collection.

37. Ringel, 1 October 1942, ME 894, LBI. The original reads, "Der Geburtstag unserer Eltesten Tochter. Unsere Heisse Glückwüntsche und eine Glückliche zukunft für unsere Herzens Tochter mit Ihren l. Mann und Geliebten Kinderen[.] wir sollen nach Gross Nachis erleiben von allen unseren Kinderen u. Klein Kinderen umein[.] Malunciu süs Leben ich halte dein Bild in Meine Hände das Bild ist nass von Kissen u. Tränen u. jetzt comt Papa an die Bürt. Kinderschen Böttet Gott das wir shwer geprüften eich noch widersehen sollen." Ringel, 1 October 1942, diary, original manuscript, private collection. Grete Holländer also wrote to her daughter on the occasion of her sixth birthday: "Morgen ist Jom-Kipur und Sonjas 6. Geburtstag. Mein geliebtes

Töchterchen! Ich werde dich nicht ans Herz drücken und Dir alles Gute wünschen können. Höchstwahrscheinlich hast Du gar keine Ahnung von Deinem Ehrentage. Aber mit allen meinen Gedanken will ich bei Dir sein und mein heissestes Flehen will ich zu Gott senden, dass er Dich behüte und beschütze und dass die Stunde unseres Wiedersehens nicht mehr allzu fern sein möge!" Holländer, 8 October 1943, File 774, RG 033, YVA.

38. Dauphin, Lebrun-Pézerat, and Poublan refer to this commitment between correspondents to overcome absence by means of the written word as the "epistolary pact" (*Ces bonnes lettres*, 131).

39. Ringel, 31 January 1943, ME 894, LBI. The original reads, "Unser Heisgeliebtes Kinds Geburtstag. Ein Süs Glück auf Ihr Leben[.] Betyschen Mein Kind du solst mir von jetzt ab nie von Keine Krankheiten u. nie wissen was Sorgen sind. Ein lang u. Glücklich Leben für für [sic] eich alle Unsere Herzens Kinder u. Kinderskinder umein. Ein Gesuntes u. Glückliches widersehen.

Ihn solchene Tage wie heute empfinden wir unsere Einsamkeit am Schlimsten. wir komen uns vor als ob [ha shem] die Mäntschen uns fergessen haben. Und doch haben wir noch kein Grund zu sindigen den unsere Kostbarste Shätzer haben wir in sicherheit gebracht [ha shem] soll sie uns beschützen dafür danken u. Leben wir [ha shem] den unsere Schätzer seid Ihr Kinder. Andere Dinge sind zu ersetzen. Auch heute wekte mich Papa mit selber Frage um 4 Uhr ob ich wüste was heute wäre um den Armen Mentschen ein Plisier zu tuhn sagte ich Nein[.] Ihr hettet dises stolze Gesicht sehen müssen morgens was für ein Glück das ich nicht auch wie du unser süse Tochters Geburtstag fergessen habe. Herzens Tochter die Wüntsche von deinem Fater sollen für dich u. deine Familie in erfülung kommen. Mama u. Papa." Ringel, 31 January 1943, diary, original manuscript, private collection.

40. Tzvetan Todorov described how caring for others under extreme circumstances could work self-reflexively; it could have the effect of renewing one's own strength. See Todorov, *Facing the Extreme*, 89.

41. Indeed, A.B. remarked in her first entry that she was unable to correspond with her children in letters. Though they were allowed to write cards daily, such cards could only be "pro forma," to confirm receipt of packages. A.B., 21 August 1942, diary from Theresienstadt, microfilm copy of manuscript, File 13, RG JM, YVA.

42. A.B., 21 August 1942, File 13, RG JM, YVA.

43. "Heute Vormittag war Paul bei mir und brachte mir die so gefürchtete Nachricht, Euch meine Geliebten nie mehr wieder zu sehen. Ob ich das Leben ertragen werde, weiß ich nicht; es ist zu schwer für mich u. wozu? Warum hat mich Gott so gestraft? Habe ich etwas verbrochen?" A.B., 16 June 1945, File 13, RG JM, YVA.

44. Frey, "Diary," RG 10.041*03, USHMM, 4, 3; Frey, diary, in Kreutzer, "*Die Gespräche drehten sich auch vielfach um die Reise*," 93.

45. Earle, "Introduction: Letters, Writers and the Historian," in Earle, *Epistolary Selves*, 7. And see Dauphin, Lebrun-Pézerat, and Poublan, *Ces bonnes lettres*, 124–30, 167–71; Hämmerle, "'You let a weeping woman call you home?,'" in Earle, *Epistolary Selves*, 162.

46. Frieda and Max Reinach, diary, 1939–42, manuscript and English translation, Acc. 1999.A.0215, USHMM.

47. Max Reinach, 2 September 1939, Acc. 1999.A.0215, USHMM. Not my translation.

48. Frieda Reinach, 3 September 1939, Acc. 1999.A.0215, USHMM. Not my translation.

49. Whether circumstances surrounding the outbreak of war made Frieda feel even more vulnerable than before remains unclear. They might have felt a heightened nervousness during the first week of the war. Less than a week before Germany invaded Poland, ration cards for food were introduced in Germany, imposing further hardships on Jews, whose allotments were substantially curtailed. A curfew was introduced for Jews in Germany within days after the start of the war, forbidding Jews to be on the streets after 8 p.m. in winter, 9 p.m. in summer. Furthermore, during the same week, the Gestapo required the *Reichsvereinigung der Juden in Deutschland* [the Central Association of Jews in Germany], an organization that formally came into being on 4 July 1939 under the auspices of the Gestapo, to register all Jews between the ages of 16 and 55. Grüner, *Judenverfolgung in Berlin 1933–1945*, 68.

50. Frieda Reinach, 10 May 1942, Acc. 1999.A.0215, USHMM.

51. Frieda Reinach, 10 May 1942, Acc. 1999.A.0215, USHMM.

52. Frieda Reinach, 20 June 1942, Acc. 1999.A.0215, USHMM.

53. Max Reinach, 12 July 1942, Acc. 1999.A.0215, USHMM. Not my translation.

54. Max Reinach, 22 October 1942, Acc. 1999.A.0215, USHMM. Not my translation.

55. Frieda Reinach, 20 October 1942, Acc. 1999.A.0215, USHMM. Not my translation.

56. Max Reinach, 22 October 1942, Acc. 1999.A.0215, USHMM. Not my translation.

57. Frey, "Diary," RG 10.041*03, USHMM, 3. The original reads, "dann seid nicht traurig. Lest den Bericht, der möglichst sachlich und nüchtern gehalten ist, in Ruhe durch und sagt Euch: 'Gottlob, sie haben es überstanden!'" Frey, diary, in Kreutzer, *"Die Gespräche drehten sich auch vielfach um die Reise,"* 93.

58. Max Reinach, beginning of May 1942, Acc. 1999.A.0215, USHMM. Not my translation.

59. Frieda Reinach, 20 October 1942, Acc. 1999.A.0215, USHMM.

60. The Freys and the Reinachs may not have been familiar with psychoanalysis but the distinction they drew between healthy and excessive mourning resembles that made by Sigmund Freud, "Mourning and Melancholia" (1917), *The Standard Edition of the Complete Psychological Works of Sigmund Freud*, 237–60. For a discussion of Freud's essay in the context of psychology and the post-Freudian psychological literature on grief, see Rosenblatt, *Bitter, Bitter Tears*, 32–40.

61. The Freys' and the Reinachs' intuition about the difficulty of mourning anticipated Dominick LaCapra's writing on "working through" the history and memory of the Holocaust. LaCapra has suggested that historical and artistic works on the Holocaust that obsessively relive the past "should be countered by the effort to work it [the past] through in a manner that would, to whatever extent is possible, convert the past into memory and provide a measure of responsible control over one's behavior with respect to it and to the current demands of life. For example, the isolation and despair of melancholy and depression, bound up with the compulsively repeated reliving of

trauma, may be engaged and to some extent countered by mourning in which there is a reinvestment in life, as some critical distance is achieved on the past and the lost other is no longer an object of unmediated identification." LaCapra, *History and Memory after Auschwitz*, 110.

62. Frieda Reinach, 20 October 1942, Acc. 1999.A.0215, USHMM.

63. On *yizker bikher*, see Kugelmass and Boyarin, *From a Ruined Garden*; Horowitz, "Reading and Writing During the Holocaust as Described in *Yisker* Books," in Rose, *The Holocaust and the Book*, 128–42. A new bibliography of *yizker bikher* in the British Library was recently compiled by Ilana Tahan: *Memorial Volumes To Jewish Communities Destroyed in the Holocaust* (London: British Library, 2004).

64. Frey, "Diary," RG 10.041*03, USHMM, 3; Frey, diary, in Kreutzer, *"Die Gespräche drehten sich auch vielfach um die Reise,"* 93.

65. Frey, "Diary," RG 10.041*03, USHMM, 36–37; Frey, diary, in Kreutzer, *"Die Gespräche drehten sich auch vielfach um die Reise,"* 105.

66. Frey, "Diary," RG 10.041*03, USHMM, 37–38. The original reads, "Ob aus diesen Vermögens- und Einnahme-Ausfällen später einmal Regressansprüche hergeleitet werden können, aus denen Ihr als gesetzliche Erben meines Nachlasses geltend machen könnt, vermag ich nicht zu beurteilen. Wenn dereinst eine Anmeldung derartiger Forderungen und Ansprüche verlangt wird, soll Euch hiermit ein Hinweis gegeben werden." Frey, diary, in Kreutzer, *"Die Gespräche drehten sich auch vielfach um die Reise,"* 105.

67. On Jewish ethical wills, see Natalie Zemon Davis, "Fame and Secrecy," in Cohen, *The Autobiography of a Seventeenth-Century Venetian Rabbi*, 56–58. Alan Mintz discusses how early modern Jewish ethical wills influenced nineteenth-century Jewish autobiographies in *"Banished from their father's table."*

68. Frey, "Diary," RG 10.041*03, USHMM, 38. The original reads, "Solltet Ihr aber in guten Lebensverhältnissen leben und das Geld nicht unbedingt brauchen, so könnt Ihr auch, wenn Ihr Beide darüber einig seid, darauf verzichten. Segen bringt meist nur selbstverdientes Geld. Ihr seid Beide fleissig und voller Pflichtgefühl. Ich bin davon überzeugt, dass Ihr Beide gut durch die Welt kommen werdet." Frey, diary, in Kreutzer, *"Die Gespräche drehten sich auch vielfach um die Reise,"* 105.

69. Frey, "Diary," RG 10.041*03, USHMM, 38. The original reads, "Euer Gerechtigkeitssinn und Eure hohe ethische Einstellung wird Euch manche Enttäuschung an der Menschheit bereiten, doch Ihr wisst ja, man ist Kummer nur zu sehr gewöhnt. [. . .] Geht weiter Euren Weg, den Euch das Schicksal bereitet hat, und behaltet Eure anständige Gesinnung." Frey, diary, in Kreutzer, *"Die Gespräche drehten sich auch vielfach um die Reise,"* 105.

70. Lejeune, "The 'Journal de Jeune Fille' in Nineteenth-Century France," 109.

71. Wars generally open an epistemological divide between those who are fighting and those who are not, and it is common for people to write letters in order to bridge the two worlds of home and front. What was unusual in this case was that both worlds belonged to the realm of "civilian" life and that diaries were being used rather than letters. On the epistemological gap between letter writers on the front and at home, see Favret, "War Correspondence," 175, 180–81; Hanna, "A Republic of Letters," par. 42.

72. I found this Theresienstadt diary in the collections of two different archives. At the Leo Baeck Institute in New York I read the original diary, written in pencil in a notebook, entitled by Ehrlich, "The History of Our Negative Emigration," manuscript, Richard A. Ehrlich Collection, LBI Archives, ME 1101. At Yad Vashem, I found a typed copy of the diary called "Aufzeichnungen aus Theresienstadt," typed copy, File 74, RG 02, Wiener Library Collection, YVA. Since the original manuscript does not contain numbered pages and the entries of the diary can be quite lengthy, I cite the date of the entry as well as the page number appearing in the typed copy of the diary from the YVA. Ehrlich, 9 November 1943, File 74, RG 02, YVA, 1.

73. "Die Karten waren uns aber noch wertvoller, brachten sie uns doch indirekt Nachricht von Dir, mein geliebter Junge, mit dem unser Denken und Fühlen Tag und Nacht vollkommen Verknüpft ist!" Ehrlich, 13 November 1943, File 74, RG 02, YVA, 12.

74. "So bilden diese 'Ghetto-Briefe' in gewissem Sinne eine Fortsetzung meiner damaligen Niederschrift und alles hat auch einen indirekten Zusammenhang." Ehrlich, 9 November 1943, File 74, RG 02, YVA, 1.

75. "Heute, am denkwürdigend 9. November, der soviel Unglück über uns Juden gebracht hat, habe ich wegen einer kleinen Indisposition genügend Musse, um mit einem schon lange beabsichtigten Bericht zu beginnen. Diese Aufzeichnungen sollen Dir, mein lieber Junge, ein Bild der Situation vermitteln, in der wir uns unfreiwillig seit nahe zu 10 Monaten befinden. Meine "Ghetto-Briefe" erheben keinen Anspruch auf Vollständigkeit sind auch naturgemäss nicht vollkommen objektiv gehalten, da *ich* [sic] ja die Dinge nur so zu schildern vermag, wie *ich* [sic] sie sehe und wie sie auf mich persönlich wirken." Ehrlich, 9 November 1943, File 74, RG 02, YVA, 1.

76. "Ehe ich nun, in der Schilderung unseres persönlichen Ergehens fortfahre, möchte ich Dir, mein lieber Willy, [. . .] ein allgemeines Bild von Theresienstadt geben, wenn ich auch die hauptsächlichste Darstellung erst später einflechten werde." Ehrlich, 10 November 1943, File 74, RG 02, YVA, 3.

77. The entire entry for this date is only two sentences. It reads, "11. November 1943 III. Volkszählung. Hierübur werde ich später ausführlicher berichten, als ich es im Moment tun könnte. Das Ereignis ist so ungeheuerlich, dass ich erst Distanz bekommen muss, um alles im richtigen Licht sehen zu können." Ehrlich, 11 November 1943, File 74, RG 02, YVA, 5. When, only a couple of days later on 14 November, he did write about the Volkszählung, he launched into the story without further ado but concluded with the remark that "this strange census will be forever unforgettable to each of the over 30,000 participants. One can hardly believe that a person can bear such an abundance of suffering." ([. . .] wird wohl jedem der über 30,000 Teilnehmer dieser merkwürdigen Volkszählung für immer unvergesslich bleiben!—Es ist kaum zu glauben, welche Fülle von Leid der Mensch tragen kann!) Ehrlich, 14 November 1943, File 74, RG 02, YVA, 16.

78. Ehrlich, 12 November 1943, File 74, RG 02, YVA, 10.

79. "Aber schnell gewöhnte man sich auch an all diese eigenartigen Bilder, die durch die Gewohnheit ihre Schrecken verloren." Ehrlich, 12 November 1943, File 74, RG 02, YVA, 10.

80. "Es wäre noch soviel Merkwürdiges zu berichten, aber dadurch, dass in unseren Au-

gen die Dinge alltäglich wurden, verliert man den Sinn für das Aussergewöhnliche." Ehrlich, 13 November 1943, File 74, RG 02, YVA, 12.

81. Ehrlich, 13 November 1943, File 74, RG 02, YVA, 12–13.

82. Frey, "Diary," RG 10.041*03, USHMM, 4. The original reads, "Ich erinnere Dich nur daran, wie schwer es war, den Pass noch rechtzeitig zu erhalten, ferner, dass in letzter Stunde mehrere Kinder, darunter auch Du, bis zum nächsten Transport zurückbleiben sollten." Frey, diary, in Kreutzer, *"Die Gespräche drehten sich auch vielfach um die Reise,"* 93.

83. Frey, "Diary," RG 10.041*03, USHMM, 36; Frey, diary, in Kreutzer, *"Die Gespräche drehten sich auch vielfach um die Reise,"* 105.

84. Aryeh Klonicki, 5 July 1943, *The Diary of Adam's Father*, 21.

85. Klonicki, 11 July 1943, ibid., 57. Klonicki explicitly addressed his choice of Hebrew over Yiddish: "Finally I wish to remark on my choice of language. You will no doubt find several mistakes of syntax, style or grammar in my diary. Four years have already gone by since I have last made use of Hebrew. I did not want to write in Yiddish so that it should not be too easy for strangers to read." Klonicki, 11 July 1943, ibid., 57–58.

86. Details about the condition of the diary and the circumstances under which it was written and preserved are from the preface to ibid., 9–13.

87. Klonicki, 7 July 1943, ibid., 40.

88. Klonicki, 5 July 1943, ibid., 23–25.

89. Klonicki, 5 July 1943, ibid., 21.

90. In addition to the references in note 6 above on diaries as family chronicles, Peter Fritzsche has written about nineteenth-century middle-class households in Europe and the United States becoming repositories of their own family memories (*Stranded in the Present*, 183).

91. Rubinsztejnowa, diary in hiding in Lwów, microfilm of manuscript and typed copy, File 116, Reel 20, RG 02.208M, ŻIH Jewish Memoir collection 302, USHMM.

92. "Jak widzicie moi kochani, że jeszcze żyjemy. Ja i Moszko jeszcze żyjemy. Reszta wymordowana. Nikogo z naszych najbliższych nie ma. Nikogo. [. . .] Piszę ten list na wypadek naszej śmierci. Gdybyśmy wojny nie przeżyli, [. . .] to nasi gospodarze prześlą Wam ten list, byście choć trochę poznali nasze przejścia pod reżymem Hitlera." Rubinsztejnowa, 12 September 1943, File 116, Reel 20, RG 02.208M, USHMM.

93. "Chcę Wam opisać nasze dzieje i kolejność śmierci okrutnie zamordowanych naszych najdroższych. Nie mam talentu pisarskiego, ale chcę Wam mimo to opisać wedle moich sił ogólnie nasze męki i przeżycia." Rubinsztejnowa, 12 September 1943, File 116, Reel 20, RG 02.208M, USHMM.

94. The entire passage reads, "Nasz kochany Tato mówił bardzo często o Was i marzył o tym, by po wojnie do Was pojechać i opowiadać Wam o przebytych strasznych nieludzkich cierpieniach. Stało się jednak inaczej. Nie dożył nasz kochany Tato chwili klęski Hitlera." Rubinsztejnowa, 1 February 1944, File 116, Reel 20, RG 02.208M, USHMM.

95. Rubinsztejnowa, 9 February 1944, File 116, Reel 20, RG 02.208M, USHMM.

96. Encyclopaedia Judaica, s.v. "Lwów."

97. "Da ich nicht weisst, wann, ob und wo, es ein Wiedersehen giebt, möchte ich meine Erlebnisse u. Eindrücke zu Papier bringen, um sie für Euch zu erhalten." A.B., 21 August 1942, File 13, RG JM, YVA.

98. "Vorgestern begann ich meine Aufzeichnungen, ob ich sie beenden werde, ist noch mehr als fraglich. Illusionen sind hier nicht am Platze, ich schwebe jeden Augenblick in Lebensgefahr, aber daran bin ich schon gewöhnt. Vielleicht werde ich morgen nicht mehr sein und nicht mehr schreiben, heute tue ich es aber. Ich muss es tun, also ich dies alles nicht herausschreien darf, will ich es niederschreiben solange es geht, solange ich lebe. Vielleicht wird es doch einmal meine kleine Sonja lesen und meine Menschen und Ilse [. . .]." Holländer, 25 July 1943, File 774, RG 033, YVA.

99. I found this document in two different versions in YVA and in the USHMM's microfilm of the ŻIH Jewish Memoir Collection. See Julius Feierman [*sic*], diary from Stanislawów, manuscript and typed copy, File 778, RG 033, YVA; and Julian Feurman [*sic*], diary from Stanislawów, typed copy, File 135, Reel 23, RG 02.208M, ŻIH Jewish Memoir Collection 302, USHMM. My discussion here primarily draws from the USHMM file, 1–2.

100. Feurman, File 135, Reel 23, RG 02.208M, USHMM, 1.

101. "Aber dann erinnerte ich mich an mein armes Kind, dass dann ganz allein und verlassen auf der Welt bleiben müsste und plötzlich erfasste mich ein ungeheurer Lebenswille. Du musst dich retten, sagte ich mir, du musst und du wirst." Holländer, 23 July 1943, File 774, RG 033, YVA.

102. "Ich vergass die unerträgliche Hitze, die Fliegenplage und meine Mattigkeit. Am liebsten hätte ich ein Freudentänzchen gemacht, nur fehlte mir der Platz und die Kraft dazu. Oh wie sehr will ich nun leben, wie ungeduldig ersehne ich unsere Befreiung." Holländer, 11 January 1944, File 774, RG 033, YVA. On 28 May 1944, seven weeks after liberation, Holländer learned that Sonja was dead and that Jozek, the Polish farmer who hid her and gave her the positive report on Sonja, had fabricated this story.

103. Irena Hauser, diary from the Łódź ghetto, microfilm of manuscript, File 299, Reel 42, RG 02.208M, ŻIH Jewish Memoir Collection 302, USHMM.

104. "[. . .] das Kind weint Hunger, der Vater Zigaretten, die Mutter will sterben, das Familienleben ins Getto." Hauser, 15 July 1942, File 299, Reel 42, RG 02.208M, USHMM.

105. "So oder so warum mache ich nicht Schluß beim Fenster heraus—doch ich kann das Kind nicht lassen u. es will noch leben er bittet mich so beim ihm zu bleiben u. die Hitze nimmt einem den Verstand. Liebe Geschwister ich wollte Euch gerne nochmals sehen u. Du lieber Vater wo seid Ihr [?]" Hauser, 19 August 1942, File 299, Reel 42, RG 02.208M, USHMM.

106. Hauser, 21 August 1942, File 299, Reel 42, RG 02.208M, USHMM.

107. "En ce moment où mes enfants quittent le vieux monde pour chercher aventure dans le nouveau, je sens que je participe à la révolution qui ouvre une ère nouvelle. Dieu nous protège." Dreyfus, 8 June 1942, *Cahier* B, Diary, manuscript, RG 10.144*05, Lucien Dreyfus collection, USHMM.

108. Frey, "Diary," RG 10.041*03, USHMM, 4; Frey, diary, in Kreutzer, "*Die Gespräche drehten sich auch vielfach um die Reise,*" 93.

109. Frey, "Diary," RG 10.041*03, USHMM, 3–4. The original reads, "Ihr könnt uns aber glauben, dass wir mit jeder Faser unseres Herzens an Euch hängen und dass wir für Euch nur den einen Wunsch haben, Euch gesund und glücklich zu wissen. Für uns selbst haben wir nur den einen Wunsch, Euch, — oder wenigstens Eine von Euch, wiederzusehen und zu sprechen, damit wir die Gewissheit haben, dass es Euch gut geht und dass Ihr eine Zukunft vor Euch habt, die schöner und strahlender ist, als je das Judentum in seiner Blütezeit zu verzeichnen hatte!" Frey, diary, in Kreutzer, *"Die Gespräche drehten sich auch vielfach um die Reise,"* 93.

110. "Private and personal" is Hartley's phrase in her analysis of a similar process at work in a soldier's last letter to his mother. See Hartley, "'Letters are *everything* these days,'" 192.

111. Klonicki, 5 July 1943, *The Diary of Adam's Father,* 21.

112. Klonicki, 11 July 1943, ibid., 57.

113. Indeed, the second part of the published edition of Aryeh Klonicki's diary is a documentation of their efforts to ascertain Adam's fate. See "Adam, Where Art Thou?" in ibid., 83–109.

114. Frieda Reinach, 20 June 1942, Acc. 1999.A.0215, USHMM. Not my translation. Indeed, Frieda took precautions lest the diary not reach her daughters and end up in the wrong person's hands. When describing a woman who was an "angel" to them and gave them extra food, she left a blank space instead of writing the woman's name. Frieda Reinach, 10 May 1942, Acc. 1999.A.0215, USHMM.

115. This information is contained in a letter written by one of the Reinachs' daughters to her grandsons explaining the origins of the diary. This letter accompanies the diary in Acc. 1999.A.0215, USHMM.

116. Specific information about the fate of the Freys is from the introduction and epilogue to diary, RG 10.041*03, USHMM, 2, 39–40. On the *Fabrik-Aktion,* see Grüner, *Judenverfolgung in Berlin 1933–1945,* 88–89, 101; Kwiet, "Nach dem Pogrom," in Benz, *Die Juden in Deutschland 1933–1945,* 592–96. During the *Fabrik-Aktion,* those Jews who were classified as *Mischlinge* or as *Mischehe* — married to "Aryans" — were separated from the other Jews and sent to assembly camps on Rosenstrasse and Grosse Hamburger Strasse in Berlin. After an extraordinary weeklong protest demonstration by "Aryan" wives demanding the release of their spouses, the Gestapo freed the Jews in mixed marriages. See Stoltzfus, *Resistance of the Heart.*

117. "Seit mein Liebling nicht lebt, ist etwas in mir zerbrochen. Ich bin hart und kalt wie ein Stein geworden. Für wen sollte ich auch beten? Für mich? Wozu?" Holländer, 27 September 1944, File 774, RG 033, YVA. Holländer described the cause of Sonja's death in her letter to P.T., Naharia, September 1978, File 774, RG 033, YVA.

118. See the notes by Ilana Schwartz that accompany the diary, esp. note 18, in Acc. 1999.A.0215, USHMM.

119. Rosenblatt, *Bitter, Bitter Tears,* 107.

5. RELUCTANT MESSENGERS

1. Primo Levi, *Survival in Auschwitz,* 103.

2. Levi, *The Drowned and the Saved,* 138–39. Among survivors who did not share Levi's

view of the usefulness of culture in the camps was Jean Améry. See his *At the Mind's Limits*, 7.

3. Todorov, *Facing the Extreme*, 92. See Bauer's discussion of the concept "sanctification of life" in *Rethinking the Holocaust*, 120–28.

4. Little work has been done in general on the question of how the process of diary writing affects the writer of a diary. For an analysis of the range of psychological functions that diary writing can have for diarists, see Wiener and Rosenwald, "A Moment's Monument: The Psychology of Keeping a Diary," in Josselson and Lieblich, *The Narrative Study of Lives*, 30–58; and Rosenblatt, *Bitter, Bitter Tears*.

5. Brenner, *Writing as Resistance*, 135. Similarly, in his analysis of the diary of Victor Klemperer, Steven Aschheim contended that diary writing "was literally life-saving" for Klemperer: "The very act of diarizing provided him with a refuge, an outlet, consolation, meaning." Aschheim, *Scholem, Arendt, Klemperer*, 80. Susanne zur Nieden made a similar argument about diaries as a coping mechanism and form of escape in her article "Aus dem vergessenen Alltag der Tyrannei," in Heer, *Im Herzen der Finsternis*, 115. Rafael F. Scharf described poetry writing in the Polish ghettos as an "instrument of resistance. . . . Writing or merely listening to poetry offered a breath of air, a momentary escape from the reality roundabout. It was a kind of healing magic." Scharf, "Literature in the Ghetto in the Polish Language," in Shapiro, *Holocaust Chronicles*, 33. This argument about writing's therapeutic effect is hardly restricted to studies of the Holocaust. Many scholars investigating women's diaries have also made the argument that diaries have a therapeutic function for women diarists. See articles by Harriet Blodgett, Steven E. Kagle and Lorenza Gramegna, Judy Simons, and Trudelle H. Thomas in Bunkers and Huff, *Inscribing the Daily*. Interestingly, despite such claims, psychologists have found that, though they "expected diary-keepers to have some benefit, or be the same, but they were the worst off. [. . .] You are probably much better off if you don't write anything at all." Elaine Duncan, quoted in News, In Brief, *New Scientist*, 11 September 2004, 15.

6. Patterson, *Along the Edge of Annihilation*, 40. In Patterson's and Brenner's analyses, the *distance* between the diarist and the diary enabled the individual self to endure the Nazi assault on Jewish humanity. For James Young, it was *proximity* rather than distance, identification rather than sympathetic otherness that characterized the relationship between Holocaust diarists and their diaries; however the effect was the same. Young contended that diarists saw "their words as extensions of themselves, the link between words and events seems quite literally *self*-evident: that which has touched the writer's hand would now touch the reader." Young claimed that diarists wrote in the belief that their writing was unmediated. Nevertheless, he described the working of diaries on the authorial self in much the same terms as other scholars: "Writing not only affirms the writer's existence, but it also ensures their literary existence afterwards. By converting their experiences into written texts, the writers become self-sustaining and self-perpetuating." According to Young, diarists asserted their subjectivity in the present by writing themselves into the future. Although Young did not describe this process in dialogic terms, his notion of writing as "self-sustaining" seems quite similar to Patterson's idea that a diarist "recovered life" in and through the practice of writ-

ing. Both notions lay stress on the existential and individually redemptive capacity of writing. Young, *Writing and Rewriting the Holocaust*, 24, 38.

7. Lawrence Powell has written about this process in reference to Holocaust survivors bearing witness after the war (*Troubled Memory*, 19).

8. Diarists did not see "their words as extensions of themselves," as James Young argued. In this respect, diarists shared what Young characterized as survivors' uneasiness with the written word. While Young problematized the effect of writing on survivors, he neglected to do the same for wartime diarists. The survivor, according to Young, "fears the Derridean suggestion that 'things come into existence and lose existence by being named,' but he finds solace in the Hegelian corollary that there is 'simultaneous sacrifice of existence to the word and consecration of existence by the word.'" Young, *Writing and Rewriting the Holocaust*, 38. The scholarly discussion about the challenge posed by the Holocaust to historical representation was elaborated in chapter 1.

9. Wyschogrod, *An Ethics of Remembering*, 242.

10. "Es tat sehr wohl sich mal eine Zeit aus dieser Atmosphäre herauszuheben. Wir haben daraufhin beschlossen jeden Tag eine solche Stunde einzuschalten, wenn es mir irgend möglich ist. Helmuth meint, man braucht das, damit man sich nicht so schnell ergibt." Arthur Flaum, [undated entry], diary from Prague, Sosnowiec, and Haifa, manuscript, File 25, RG 033, Yad Vashem Archives [hereafter YVA], 12 verso.

11. Todorov, *Facing the Extreme*, 92.

12. "Toujours le contact d'une oeuvre d'elle, même le souvenir ou la pensée de l'existence de cette oeuvre, ont momentanément aboli pour moi les barrières de la solitude." Hélène Abraham, 21 May 1941, manuscript, No. 4 (xxiv), Carton III, Hélène Abraham Collection, Occidental Manuscripts, Bibliothèque Nationale de France, Richelieu, 34 recto.

13. Czerniakow, 20 November 1939, *The Warsaw Diary of Adam Czerniakow*, 91.

14. Czerniakow, 28 May 1940, ibid., 155.

15. "Für 1 Stunde vergass ich heute wo ich bin. Rueza Behal borgte mir Rainer Maria Rilkes *Weise von Liebe und Tod des Cornets Christoph Rilke* — die Sprache ist so prachtvoll und gerade darin sagt Rilke so vieles, das für unser heutige Leben passt [. . .]. 'Und der Mut ist so müde geworden und die Sehnsucht so gross.'" Vally Fink, 21 April 1942, typed copy, No. 552, RG P.III.h (Theresienstadt), Wiener Library Collection, Tel Aviv University, 8. A copy of Fink's diary can also be found in File 444, RG 02, YVA. The translation of Rilke is from his *Lay of the Love and Death of Cornet Christoph Rilke*, trans. B. J. Morse (Vienna: Amandus-Edition, 1945), 8.

16. Frau Zielenziger, diary from Bergen-Belsen, typed copy, No. 1118, RG P.III.h (Bergen-Belsen), Kurt Zielenziger Papers, Wiener Library Collection, Tel Aviv University.

17. "Nieraz wśród rozmowy i czytania zapominało się zupełnie o rzeczywistości. [. . .] Życie w którym lęk nie opuszczał nasze serca [. . .]." Fela Szeps, February 1943, diary from Grünberg Schlesien Lager, manuscript and typed copy, File 747, RG 033, YVA

18. Kruk, "Library and Reading Room in the Vilna Ghetto, Strashun Street 6," in Rose, *The Holocaust and the Book*, 192. As Kruk noted, literature did not function solely as an escape, although that was its most common function in the ghetto. For those who tried to continue to engage with serious literature, reading could be an exhaust-

ing pursuit. David Sierakowiak, a teenage boy who wrote a diary in the Łódź ghetto, described reading as the central element of his efforts to continue his education. But he found reading to be a strenuous pursuit under starvation conditions: "In exchange for my old books I bought a history of Hebrew literature, two Hebrew short stories by Breuer, *Jeremiasz* in Hebrew by Lazarus, and an article in Yiddish by Żytlowski on the theory of Marxism. I still want to read and to study. I borrow books, make plans and have projects, but there is nothing that I can turn into tangible reality. I used to blame it all on the winter, but it's quite warm now, and those winter obstacles are gone. Unfortunately, hunger is the real reason for my 'laziness.'" Sierakowiak struggled to keep up his reading. His diary writing seemed to require less exertion, perhaps because he did not connect writing with his autodidacticism. Indeed, he rarely skipped a day's entry. Sierakowiak, 17 April 1942, *The Diary of Dawid Sierakowiak*, 154–55.

19. Marcus Moseley noted this association between reading, writing, and turning inward in his study "Autobiographies of Jewish Youth in Interwar Poland." He wrote, "The act of reading is almost invariably with a marked turn to introspection [*sic*], a turn associated with the discovery of a language with which to depict the inner self. It is thus no coincidence that the initiation into literature is often accompanied by the decision to write a journal." Moseley, "Life, Literature: Autobiographies of Jewish Youth in Interwar Poland," 7.

20. "Ich schlafe schlecht, mag nicht über mich schreiben, weil es zu weitläufig würde [. . .]. Ich lese viel und finde ganz schöne Ruhe darin, nur die Nächte und die Träume sind nicht schön, obwohl diese schlimmer sein könnten. Es ist mir doch so, als ob Schlimmes in ganz naher Zukunft vor uns liegt." Grete Steiner, 31 January 1942, in Zeist, Holland, manuscript, third notebook, File 1064, Lohamei Ha'Ghetaot [hereafter LHG].

21. "Ich lese viel, habe aber keine Lust darüber zu schreiben, da ich geistig in einem 'Tief' bin und zu gar nichts Lust habe." Steiner, 19 January 1942, third notebook, File 1064, LHG.

22. "Ich verlor die Lust so viel Schrecken, so viel Enttäuschungen aufzuschreiben." Steiner, 19 November 1941, third notebook, File 1064, LHG.

23. "Dies Heft ist so eintönig und lust- und geistlos, wie mir zu Mute ist." Steiner, 21 December 1941, third notebook, File 1064, LHG.

24. "Und hiermit schliesse ich diese Heft, in dem leider nichts Gutes u[nd] Erfreuliches zu lesen ist. Das nächste Heft—wenn eines kommt—kommt erst nach grossen Veränderungen." Steiner, 28 March 1942, third notebook, File 1064, LHG.

25. "5 Tage hatte ich keine Lust etwas zu schreiben, denn beschreiben kann man das alles gar nicht." Fink, 6 May 1942, typed copy, No. 552, RG P.III.h (Theresienstadt), Wiener Library Collection, 10.

26. "Ich möchte so gerne mehr und Schöneres schreiben, aber ich habe Hunger, Angst und Sorgen und so wenig Freude, dass ich nicht fähig bin mich zu konzentrieren." Fink 22 May 1942, No. 552, RG P.III.h (Theresienstadt), Wiener Library Collection, 114.

27. Todorov, *Facing the Extreme*, 96–97.

28. Ibid.

29. Rosenblatt discussed how diary writing could be a hindrance as well as an aid to controlling grief (*Bitter, Bitter Tears*, 110–11).

30. Tory [formerly Golub], "Last Will and Testament," end of December 1942, in *Surviving the Holocaust*, 168. Another diarist, Rabbi Aharonson of Konin, also described the tortuous dilemma of wanting to write because it was a "duty" but fearing doing so because of the "possible consequences of this act if it were discovered." Farbstein, "Diaries and Memoirs as a Historical Source," 122.

31. Klemperer, 27 May 1941, *I Will Bear Witness: 1933–1941*, 386–87.

32. Klemperer, 4 December 1941, ibid., 447.

33. Klemperer, 25 June 1942, *I Will Bear Witness: 1942–1945*, 86.

34. "Heute ist der 4.12.42 und leider muss ich die Fortsetzung dieses Berichtes auf spätere Tage verschieben. In letzter Zeit kommen so viele Razzias vor, dass es mir sicherer erschient, wenn ich diese Bogen verschwinden lasse. Wenn sie mit mir in deutsche Hände fallen, würden zuviele in Mitleidenschaft gezogen. [. . .] Es wird eben täglich gefährlicher." Jacob (Köbes) Müller, 4 December 1942, diary from Holland, typed copy, ME 1028, Leo Baeck Institute Archives [hereafter LBI], 25–26. See chapter 3, n. 44 for information about the original diary.

35. Jacob (Köbes) Müller, Letter written by Müller accompanying diary and memoir, dated "Amsterdam, 1946," ME 1028, LBI.

36. "Lęk mnie ogarnia gdy piszę coś złego o Hitlerze. Lęk jest tak silny, że nawet w czasie pisania nie opuszcza mnie ani na chwilę. Ciągle zadręczają mnie myśli takie: odkryli nasz bunkier i chcemy naszego Wasyla bronić. Mówimy, żeśmy się tu zakradli, że on o tym nie wiedział, [. . .] że mieliśmy trochę prowiantów z lasu, że tym się żywimy, że on jest niewinny. Byłaby jego ratować. A ten pamiętnik? Ten go zdradzi, a więc gdzie go ukryć. Szkoda mi go zniszczyć. Szkoda, a jednak to jest coś, co mi często zamąca spokój. Dam go Pańczyszynowej, niechaj ona go schowa!" Dina Rathauserowa, 22 March 1943, diary from Peczeniżynie, manuscript and typed copy, File 633, RG 033, YVA. According to a letter written by Rathauserowa's sister in 1960, the manuscript copy of the diary was not in her sister's handwriting. Rathauserowa's sister speculated that the diary was, indeed, her sister's but was recopied by the woman who tried to rescue Rathauserowa, Pani Pańczyszyn. She suspected that parts of the diary were deliberately edited but never learned more about the story of the diary. She received the diary from the Jewish Commission in Katowice in 1946. Thus one can only conjecture that the diary may have been edited to a greater or lesser degree. However, because I do not analyze passages in the diary that treat what would have been sensitive subjects, I have proceeded under the assumption that the passages I have cited were unlikely to have been altered. Rathauserowa's sister's letter can also be found in File 633, RG 033, YVA.

37. "Nie mogłam w nocy spać. [. . .] Różne myśli dręczyły mnie: może zachorujemy, co będzie z nami? Zakopią nas tu w piwnicy? Jakie to straszne. Ale czy śmierć z rąk hitlerowca nie jest gorszą? Nie mogę więcej pisać, głowa boli." Rathauserowa, entry called "12-th day in the cellar [*12-ty dzień w piwnicy*]," File 633, RG 033, YVA.

38. In Rathauserowa's last entry, dated 22 May 1943, she mentioned that the Jewish family

in hiding at the neighboring farm had been found and killed and that the farmer hiding her wanted her to leave. I do not know the circumstances of her death.

39. "Introduction," in Kermish, *To Live With Honor and Die With Honor!*, 22.

40. Ibid., 22.

41. Ibid., 24.

42. English entry of 15 May 1944, diary from the Łódź ghetto written in the margins of a French storybook, *Les Vrais Riches*, File 1032, RG 03, YVA. Author unknown. This diary has been published in German translation as *"Les Vrais Riches" Notizen am Rand: Ein Tagebuch aus dem Ghetto Łódź (Mai bis August 1944)*, ed. Hanno Loewy and Andrzej Bodek. A substantial portion of this diary has also been published in English translation. See "Anonymous Boy: Łódź Ghetto," in Zapruder, *Salvaged Pages*, 361–94.

43. English entry of 11 June 1944, ibid.

44. English entry of 5 May 1944, ibid.

45. "Pamiętnik to niby przyjaciel": Polish entry of 26 June 1944, ibid.

46. English entry of 3 August 1944, ibid.

47. Perechodnik, *Am I a Murderer?*, xxi. As noted in chapter 3, there are significant problems with the English language edition of this diary. See Engel, "On the Bowdlerization of a Holocaust Testimony."

48. Perechodnik, *Am I a Murderer?*, xxi.

49. Ibid., 155.

50. Ibid., 191–92.

51. "Jest zaledwie kilka godzin po odejściu Rudego a już odczuwam samotność. Nie wyobrażam sobie, jakbym tu sam przez dłuższy okres wytrzymał." M. Landsberg, 30 December 1942, second notebook, diary from hiding in Krzemieniec, manuscript and typed copy, File 1099, RG 033, YVA.

52. "Podobno jest rozkaz H., że do Nowego Roku ani jednego Żyda ma nie być na teranach okupowanych przez Niemców." Landsberg, 30 December 1942, second notebook, File 1099, RG 033, YVA.

53. "Rudy dzisiaj, nie wrócił. [. . .] Spałem mało." Landsberg, 31 December 1942, second notebook, File 1099, RG 033, YVA.

54. "Cher journal car quand je suis triste et me sens délaissée, je te prends pour me consoler." Isabelle Jesion, 24 February 1942, first notebook, manuscript, File 2131, LHG.

55. "Au revoir, Journal aimé, que m'écoute et que j'aime presque comme un être vivant. N'est-il pas mon seul soutien qui ne me manque jamais, il est muet mais non moqueur, me soulage et semble me donner du courage." Jesion, 20 March 1942, first notebook, File 2131, LHG.

56. "Je suis seule, Cher Journal car mes parents ont été pris juste il y a 1 semaine le 16 juillet à 3 heures. Je m'ennuie de mes parents. Je suis seule comme Mlle. Munsch. Je n'ai plus le courage d'écrire sinon je vais pleurer trop fort. Adieu, Cher Journal, Isabelle." Jesion, 23 July 1942, second notebook, File 2131, LHG.

57. "Je n'écris pas plus. Je n'en ai pas le courage. Pas de nouvelles de mes parents depuis 2 semaines." Jesion, 10 August 1942, second notebook, File 2131, LHG.

58. In the intervening period, Jesion joined the Jewish Scout movement, led by Robert "Castor" Gamzon, and took up residence at the "centre internat de Vauquelin."

59. Ringel, entry dated "end of February, 1945," "Diary of a Jewish Mother," English translation only, File ME 894, LBI. Not my translation. The entire sentence in the original reads, "Ich habe einige wochen nichts geschriben den ich hatte nichts guttes oder was besseres als bis jetzt zu berichten [*sic*]." Ringel, "Ende Februar 1945," diary, manuscript, private collection.

60. Ringel, last entry [n.d], File ME 894, LBI. Not my translation. The entire sentence in the original reads, "Nach zirka 40 Järiger Ehe die wir zusamen in Leid u. Freud [marschieren?] ich bin Allein und warte auf meine Hertzlns Kinder [*sic*]." Ringel, [n. d.], diary, manuscript, private collection.

61. "Und die Erde öffnet sich nicht. Nein, auch die Sonne schien unbekümmert weiter. [. . .] ein namenloser Zorn schüttelte mich." Margarete (Grete) Holländer, 23 July 1943, diary from near Czortków in Galicia, typed copy, File 774, RG 033, YVA. Information about the form the original manuscript took is from a letter written by Grete Holländer to P.T., Naharia, September 1978, File 774, RG 033, YVA.

62. "Ich wollte schreien und schrie nicht." Holländer, 23 July 1943, File 774, RG 033, YVA. "Also ich dies alles nicht herausschreien darf, will ich es niederschreiben solange es geht, solange ich lebe." Holländer, 25 July 1943, File 774, RG 033, YVA.

63. "Die Wenigen aber, die bleiben werden, müssen ihre ermordeten Brüder rächen! Rächen, dass die Welt in ihren Grundfesten erbebt. Sonst werden die in den Massengräbern keine Ruhe finden." Holländer, 30 July 1943, File 774, RG 033, YVA.

64. There were several incidents of riots and violent outbursts by Jews in the Displaced Persons camps in Germany in the mid to late 1940s. Severin Hochberg, "DPs, Germans, and Americans: Riots in DP Camps 1945–49" (paper presented at the annual meeting of the Association for Jewish Studies, Washington, D.C., December 2001). Other examples of diarists for whom writing became associated with revenge include Rubinsztejnowa, 12 September 1943, diary from Lwów, microfilm of manuscript and typed copy, File 116, Reel 20, RG 02.208M, ŻIH Memoir Collection no. 302, United States Holocaust Memorial Museum [hereafter USHMM]; Yitzhak Katzenelson, 15 and 18 August 1943, *Vittel Diary*, 126–29, 188–89. Cypora Zonszajn also wrote about her desire for revenge in her diary from Siedlce ghetto, Rachel Ben Shaul Collection.

65. Katzenelson, 21 July 1943, *Vittel Diary*, 47.

66. There also exist memoirs which mix in diary entries. Consider, for example, the "Story of Ten Days" at the end of Primo Levi's *Survival in Auschwitz*, 141–57.

67. "Jetzt schreiben wir Juli 1943. August 1939, will ich nun beschreiben. Heute bin ich heimatlos, allein schmutzig, abgerissen und von den Deutschen zum Tode verurteilt. Heute darf ich mich nicht frei bewegen und bin überglücklich, ein Mäuseloch gefunden zu haben, in dem ich mich verstecken darf. Damals ———" Holländer, Vergangenheit Nr. 1, written between 30 July and 2 August 1943, File 774, RG 033, YVA.

68. "Jetzt, da ich wie ein Maulwurf in der Erde sitzen muss, ohne Licht und Luft, erscheint mir mein damaliges Leben wie ein verlorenes Paradies. Damals lebte mein guter Marek und ich war mit ihm und mit Sonja zusammen. Heute ist er tot und

Sonja bei fremden Bauern." Holländer, Vergangenheit Nr. 2, written between 2 and 3 August 1943, File 774, RG 033, YVA.

69. "Ich fürchte mich direkt davor, meine Gedanken in die ach so ferne, schöne Vergangenheit zu lassen. Überall begegne ich nur Toten. Lebe ich überhaupt noch?" Holländer, 31 October 1943, File 774, RG 033, YVA.

70. "Man bemüht sich, die Gedanken an all das Furchtbare, das man gesehen, miterlebt und gehört hat, von sich zu schieben. Man will einfach nicht daran denken, dass niemand von den Menschen mehr da ist, mit denen man vor Kurzem noch zusammengelebt, gesprochen, gehofft und gefürchtet hatte. Manchmal gelingt es einem, aber oft in der Nacht kommen alle Erinnerungen und überschwemmen wie eine unaufhaltsame Flut unser gequältes Gehirn. Dagegen kann man sich nicht wehren, man liegt und kalter Angstschweiss bricht aus allen Poren." Holländer, 4 September 1943, File 774, RG 033, YVA.

71. "Und so kam der furtbare [sic] Tag, der mir meinen Marek nahm. Seither sind zwei Jahre verflossen und ich habe mehr als einmal, dem Tod ins Auge blicken müssen. Trotzdem will die hand mir beim Schreiben nicht gehorchen und kalte Schauer laufen mir über den Rücken, wenn ich mir wieder alle Einzelheiten ins Gedächtnis zurückrufe." Holländer, Vergangenheit Nr. 30, written between 27 and 29 November 1943, File 774, RG 033, YVA.

72. "So schwer es mir fällt, so lange ich auch gezögert habe, muss ich doch, wenn ich meinem Bericht fortfahren will, die Ereignisse beschreiben, die mich einsam gemacht haben. [. . .] Mutter, Genia und ich versuchten mit Weinen, Bitten, Beschwörungen und schliesslich mit Geld, den Polizisten dazu zu bewegen, Marek nicht mitzunehmen. Aber dieser schüttelte nur den Kopf. Ich *kann* garnichts machen, vor der Haustür *steht* ein Herr von der Gestapo mit anderen Gefangenen. Er hat diesen Herrn bereits gesehen" (emphasis added). Holländer, Vergangenheit Nr. 30, written between 20 and 25 December 1943, File 774, RG 033, YVA.

73. Number 18 Mila was the location of the Warsaw ghetto bunker that sheltered the leaders of the Jewish Fighting Organization, or Ž.O.B., and around one hundred other people during the last stage of the Warsaw ghetto uprising in April-May 1943. Gutman, *The Jews of Warsaw, 1939–1943*, 395.

74. Katzenelson, 20 August 1943, *Vittel Diary*, 163.

75. Fela Szeps, diary, poems, and letters from the Grünberg Schlesien camp, manuscript and typed copy, File 747, RG 033, YVA.

76. "Nieraz się chce wziąść ołówek coś robić i coś napisać co leży w głębi serca, w nas nurtuje i podświadomie i nie daje spokoju." Szeps, 5 April 1942, File 747, RG 033, YVA.

77. The entire sentence reads, "Bo nieraz tylko serce w swojej najgłębszej głębi chowa jakąś urazę do tej i szuka jakie kość ujęcia dla swego nieokreślonego bólu i może jej ten ołówek przyniesie." Szeps, 5 April 1942, File 747, RG 033, YVA.

78. "Mówi się wiele o dzienniku, każdy uważa, że jest moc do zapisywania o rzeczach, które nie codzień się dzieją (w życiu normalnym), rzeczy w które nie wierzyłyśmy że bywają na świecie." Szeps, 5 April 1942, File 747, RG 033, YVA.

79. "Teraz trudno zebrać myśli a przecież przydałoby się wszystko opisać co tutaj przeżywamy, będzie to kiedyś historyczny dowód, nie wątpię bowiem, że kiedyś będzie inaczej, lepiej, ale wątpię czy ja to dożyję." Szeps, 26 May 1942, File 747, RG 033, YVA.

80. "Nieraz zadaję sobie pytanie czy kiedyś, gdy wrócimy do normalnych warunków, będziemy mieć normalne ludzkie pragnienia, dążenie, szersze zainteresowania, zmartwienia i uciechy, czy potrafimy wyzbyć się lagrowych przyzwyczajeń." Szeps, 5 April 1942, File 747, RG 033, YVA.

81. "Mijają dnie, tygodnie, wszystko idzie swoim trybem, a jednak, a jednak jakie zmiany w naszym życiu, w naszych sercach! Powierzchownie wydajemy się spokojne, jak zwykle spełniamy nasze obowiązki, pracujemy, jemy, dbamy o wszystko co nam jest potrzebne do wygody. Powierzchownie! bo wewnątrz, wewnątrz jest piekąca, straszliwa rana! Bo tylko wewnątrz, każdy z osobna, sam jeden przeżywa okrótne [sic] tragedje! Stąpam przez życie jak we śnie, okrótnym śnie i jak we śnie coś podświadomego każe mi wierzyć, że to przeminie, że to zaraz się skończy, że to jest przecież nie prawdziwe życie, tylko sen, zmora, który minie i wróci do realności." Szeps, 6 September 1942, File 747, RG 033, YVA. This image of the self divided appeared in other diaries as well. See, for example, Rubinsztejnowa, 12 September 1943, File 116, Reel 20, RG 02.208M, ŻIH Collection, USHMM.

82. "Zdawało mi się, że to nie rzeczywistość, sen, że zaraz nastąpi przebudzenie. A sen trwa nadal." Szeps, February 1943, File 747, RG 033, YVA.

83. The whole sentence reads, "Stuk, stuk, stuk dwa lata dopiero, a mnie się zdaje że to już wieczność, że tamto było tylko snem a takie życie jak teraz wiodłam od zawsze." Szeps, 19 April 1943, File 747, RG 033, YVA. Other diarists used similar terms to describe the contrast between their present existences and their past lives. Brandla (Bronka) Siekierkowa wrote in the diary she kept while in hiding in Poland that she could not figure out if her present existence was real: "I don't know—is it a dream or reality?" She commented that it was impossible to represent the magnitude of the tragedy that had befallen them. They had lain down to sleep like human beings and woken up without anything: without the right to live, without a roof over their heads, suddenly like cattle under assault. She had lost everyone and everything that was dear to her. Siekierkowa, 19 June [1943], diary from Mińsk Mazowiecki, manuscript and typed copy, File 123, Reel 21, RG 02.208M, ŻIH Collection, USHMM. Landsberg contrasted his unreal, nightmare-filled world in hiding with the real world that non-Jews populated outside. In the outside world, there was day and night, the sun and moon, rain and snow. In his and Rudy's world, it was eternal night. Their world was also populated with people who no longer existed. He described how he would close his eyes and a film would replay constantly of people gone mad with despair, of blood, of people now dead with whom he exchanged greetings. Landsberg, 21 November 1942, second notebook, File 1099, RG 033, YVA

84. "Dom, rodzice wszystko uleciało dymem jakby nic nie istniało." Szeps, February 1943, File 747, RG 033, YVA.

85. "Nic mi się nie zostanie co przypomni mi moje dzieciństwo, przeszłość [. . .]." Szeps, 7 March 1943, File 747, RG 033, YVA.

86. Szeps, 28 February 1943, File 747, RG 033, YVA.

87. "Wolność [. . .] nie dla nas przeznaczona. Już nie możemy sobie wyobrazić jak wygląda normalne wolne życie, mamy wrażenie że to co nie jest dla nas rzeczywiste nie istnieje, że to jest czemś abstrakcyjnem." Szeps, 31 December 1943, File 747, RG 033, YVA.

88. "I poprzez nawoływania innych słyszałam jej ostatnie słowa 'dzieci pamiętajcie, pamiętajcie.' Nie wiem co chciała właściwie przez to powiedzieć. Ale Twe słowa matko któremi chciałaś się nam przysłużyć stały się dla nas przekleństwem. O wszystkiem, wszystkich pamiętamy i to rwie żywe kawały z mej duszy. Czemu matko Twe słowa pożegnalne nie były: zapomnijcie, zapomnijcie o wszystkiem, [. . .] bądźcie bezmyślnemi stworami." Szeps, [n.d.] July 1943, File 747, RG 033, YVA.

89. "Och jak bardzo bardzo bym chciała już nic nie mieć do pisania." Szeps, 31 December 1943, File 747, RG 033, YVA.

90. "Pragnęłam już zakończyć ten dziennik ale dzieje światowe nie chcą sprzyjać moim pragnieniom." Szeps, 23 January 1944, File 747, RG 033, YVA.

91. Katzenelson, 5 September 1943, *Vittel Diary*, 216.

92. At the close of one entry, Szeps described her diary as but one small "particle," or snippet, "from the life of a girl" and "one small page from the great book of mankind. [To mała cząsteczka z życia dziewczyny roku 1939–43go. To jedna mała karteczka z wielkiej księgi ludzkości!]" Szeps, July 1943, File 747, RG 033, YVA.

93. Lewin, 21 September 1942, *A Cup of Tears*, 183.

94. Levi, *The Drowned and the Saved*, 12. Lewin attempted to render that reality in a credible fashion by recording myriad concrete details. In so doing, his strategy betrayed his instinct that, as Jean Améry contended, "when an event places the most extreme demands on us [. . .] there is no longer any abstraction and never an imaginative power that could even approach its reality." Améry, *At the Mind's Limit*, 25–26. On the suspicion bred by propaganda, a letter written by a captain in the U.S. Fifth Army Division upon visiting Dachau just after it was liberated, in April 1945, is quite revealing. He wrote, "I visited the German concentration camp at Dachau. You've probably read about it in the newspapers, but I want to put here in writing what I actually saw, so that you will know that the horror of what was described in the paper is not propaganda." Arthur Peternel to Collie, "A Letter from Dachau," 29 April 1945, in Brostoff, with Chamovitz, *Flares of Memory*, 288.

95. Both quotes in this paragraph are from Katzenelson, 27 August 1943, *Vittel Diary*, 187.

96. "Ich habe die Aktion im Czortkower Lager genau beschreiben wollen. Nun sehe ich, dass es mir nicht gelungen ist. Ich habe kaum den 10. Teil des grauenhaften Erlebnisses dargestellt." Holländer, 30 July 1943, File 774, RG 033, YVA.

97. "Gdy po napisaniu czytam to jeszcze raz wydaje mi się to wszystko bardzo naiwne i niedorzeczne. Ale to przecież mój sposób myślenia [. . .] Zupełnie niezależnie od tego odkrycia będę moje myśli dalej zapisywała, ale nie będę ich odrazu odczytywała." Eliszewa, 27 December 1941, diary from Stanisławów, File 267, Reel 39, ŻIH Memoir Collection no. 302, USHMM.

98. "To co Wam w tym liście opiszę, nie będzie w tysiącznej części takie, jakie było w rzeczywistości." Rubinsztejnowa, 19 September 1943, File 116, Reel 20, RG 02.208M, ŻIH Collection, USHMM.

99. Blodgett, *Centuries of Female Days*, 22.

100. Lewin, 29 December 1942, *A Cup of Tears*, 232.

101. "Nie, żadne pióro, żaden literat nie potrafi tego opisać, co my przeżywamy." Rathauserowa, 19 November 1942, File 633, RG 033, YVA.

102. Letter by Malwina Klonicki in Klonicki, *The Diary of Adam's Father*, 72.

103. "Jest nam tak smutno, tak beznadziejne, tak źle, że żadne pióro tego opisać nie zdoła." Siekierkowa, 30 June 194[?], File 123, Reel 21, RG 02.208M, ŻIH Collection, USHMM.

104. "Niemand ist fähig, das alles in Worten auszudrücken." Zielenziger, 29 September 1944, RG P.III.h (Bergen-Belsen) No. 1118, Wiener Library Collection.

105. English entries of 29 July and 31 May 1944, *Les Vrais Riches*, File 1032, RG 03, YVA.

106. "Leben? Nein, so kann man dass nicht bezeichnen. Vegetieren!" Holländer, 30 July 1943, File 774, RG 033, YVA.

107. "[. . .] mam sposobność dostatecznego rozmyślania nad moim obecnem życiem. Bardzo wątpię, czy można to nazwać życiem.—Wegetacja? I to nie." Eliszewa, 3 January 1942, File 267, Reel 39, ŻIH Collection, USHMM.

108. Dr. Neter, "Camp de Gurs," report from Gurs (summer 1943), original, File 210, RG 033, YVA, 4.

109. Oskar Rosenfeld, also writing in the Łódź ghetto, remarked, "In the decrees (proclamations) the phrase 'ghetto inhabitant'! A particular race!—," which suggests that the four-language diarist likely derived "Gettonian" from the Germans' use of a similar phrase in their decrees. However, this anonymous diarist seemed to use the term differently from the Germans, referring less to the notion of racial difference and more to the fact that Jews' experiences of daily life in the ghetto had changed them. Rosenfeld, 2 October 1942, *In the Beginning Was the Ghetto*, 138.

110. "śmiejemy się złośliwie i cynicznie. Nie to nie jest tragedją, na to jeszcze niema określenia [. . .]." Szeps, 14 July 1943, File 747, RG 033, YVA.

111. Rosenfeld, [n. d.], *In the Beginning Was the Ghetto*, 106.

112. Of the inadequacy of language, Levi commented, "Just as our hunger is not that feeling of missing a meal, so our way of being cold has need of a new word. We say 'hunger,' we say 'tiredness,' 'fear,' 'pain,' we say 'winter' and they are different things. They are free words, created and used by free men who lived in comfort and suffering in their homes." Levi, *Survival in Auschwitz*, 112–13. Diarists' efforts to coin new words to describe their experiences could be seen as a phenomenon related to the attempt to find a word to conceptualize the extermination of European Jewry in its entirety. This effort began before the end of the war, in a publication of 1944 by the Polish Jewish lawyer Raphael Lemkin. Lemkin coined the word *genocide* since, as he put it, "new conceptions require new terms." Lemkin, *Axis Rule in Occupied Europe*, 79. Clearly, the terms *Holocaust* and *Shoah* are additional examples of the need to expand the existing lexicon to refer to the Nazi extermination of European Jewry. On the implications of the different names used to refer to that event, see Young, *Writing and Rewriting the Holocaust*, 85–89.

113. Kaplan, 26 November 1940, *Scroll of Agony*, 226.

114. "Równolegle z dzienniczkiem mam zamiar, zacząć spisywać swe dzieje za okres od

pamiętnego 1 lipca 1941, dnia wkroczenia Niemców do Krzemieńca do chwili obecnej. Ta część pamiętników nastręcza mi więcej trudności od dzienniczka, bo pomijając potrzebę odtwarzania w pamięci wszystkich wypadków w porządku chronologicznym pozostaje jeszcze problem formy, która nie może być tak prosta i szablanowa [sic] jak w dzienniczku. Zakrawa już na coś, co pachnie literaturą i dlatego właśnie napawa mnie strachem i obawą, że sobie nie dam rady." Landsberg, 21 November 1942, second notebook, File 1099, RG 033, YVA.

115. "Nie będę już zresztą pisała o bieżących sprawach, zbyt są one świeże by można je należnie opisać, lepiej ja będę pisała z początku naszej niewoli, może potrafję dokłaniej pisać o przeszłości niż teraźniejszości. [. . .] Postaram się wszystko chronologicznie opisywać, ale dokładnych dat nie pamiętnam [. . .]." Szeps, 28 June 1942, File 747, RG 033, YVA.

116. "Będzie może chronologicznie dokładnie wszystko opisane, ale brak tam będzie rozpaczliwy krzyk serca. Spazmatyczne łkania duszy. Przeogromna, przeogromna tęsknota granicząca z obłędem. Chwile, kiedy te ciemne chmury zasłaniały horyzont i nie było już dla nas iskierki nadziei i chwile kiedy nadzieja rozwijała swoje jasne skrzydła i pokazywała nam świat przyszłości jasny i piękny, te upadki, wzloty!" Szeps, 23 August 1942, File 747, RG 033, YVA.

117. "Das Leben hat mir den Gefallen getan und mir selbst die unwahrscheinlichsten Abenteuer beschert." Holländer, 30 July 1943, File 774, RG 033, YVA.

118. Holländer, Vergangenheit Nr. 47 (written between 28 February and 8 March 1944) and Nr. 24 (written between 7 and 9 November 1943), File 774, RG 033, YVA.

119. "Der kitschigste Abenteuerfilm, der verdrehteste Sensationsroman, ist langweilig, vergleichen mit unserem jetzigen Leben. Wenn man das alles filmen würde, wäre es ein atemberaubender, hochinteressanter Film! Für uns ist es nur furchtbar, da es ja leider bitterste Wahrheit, Kampf um das nackte Leben bedeutet." Holländer, 14 December 1943, File 774, RG 033, YVA.

120. Holländer, 19 and 22 September 1943, File 774, RG 033, YVA.

121. "Niemand wird verstehen, was für unbeschreibliche Qualen wir litten. Für Polda war die Sache ein gelungener Spass. Uns zitterte jeder Nerv und wir lauschten mit angehaltenen Atem auf jedes Geräusch von aussen." Holländer, 31 January 1944, File 774, RG 033, YVA.

122. "Aber ich glaube nicht, dass jemand, der es nicht selbst miterlebt hat, nur einen Bruchteil des unfassbaren Grauens wird erfühlen können, des ununterbrochenen Schreckens, der Hilflosigkeit und ohnmächtigen Wut, in welcher wir nun schon seit über zwei Jahren. Leben? Nein, [. . .] Vegetieren!" Holländer, 30 July 1943, File 774, RG 033, YVA.

123. "Nie zrozumie tego nikt, kto sam tego nie przeżył. Nie będzie nikt miał najmniejszego wyobrażenia jak on jest, gdy tego na własne oczy nie obejrzy, choć kilka dni nie przeżyje z nami. Brak wyrażeń słów by określić, opisać nasze życie." Szeps, 5 April 1942, File 747, RG 033, YVA.

124. Etty Hillesum, Letter dated 24 August 1943, in *An Interrupted Life* and *Letters from Westerbork*, 353.

125. This argument runs counter to Cathy Caruth's contention that "for history to be a his-

tory of trauma means that it is referential precisely to the extent that it is not fully perceived as it occurs; or to put it somewhat differently, that a history can be grasped only in the very inaccessibility of its occurrence." Caruth, "Unclaimed Experience," 187.

126. Katzenelson, 21 July 1943, *Vittel Diary*, 47–48.

127. "The Last Stage of Resettlement Is Death," anonymous report written after the mass deportation of Jews from the Warsaw ghetto, in Kermish, *To Live With Honor and Die With Honor!*, 704.

128. Their extensive efforts at documentation and preservation strongly counter Robert Braun's conclusion that it is "futile to speak about the 'reality' of the past as an object of study." Robert Braun, "The Holocaust and Problems of Historical Representation," 175.

CONCLUSION. "A STONE UNDER HISTORY'S WHEEL"

1. Funkenstein, "The Incomprehensible Catastrophe: Memory and Narrative," in Josselson and Lieblich, *The Narrative Study of Lives*, 24.

2. Bauer, *Rethinking the Holocaust*, 15–18. On narrativizing the Holocaust, see essays by Hayden White, Saul Friedländer, Christopher Browning, Perry Anderson, Amos Funkenstein, Carlo Ginzburg, and Martin Jay in Friedländer, *Probing the Limits of Representation*.

3. A rare instance is Friedländer, *Nazi Germany and the Jews*, vol. 1.

4. Chaim Kaplan expressed this conviction in the first wartime entry of his diary, quoted in chapter 2. Emanuel Ringelblum wrote in a similar fashion, "To my mind, however, all this search for historical analogy is beside the point. History *does not* repeat itself. Especially now, now that we stand at the crossroads, witnessing the death pangs of an old world and the birth pangs of a new. How can our age be compared with any earlier one?" Ringelblum, [undated entry], *Notes from the Warsaw Ghetto*, 300. The distinction between significance and meaning was suggested by Mikhail Iampolski in "Community of the Loners: Arendt and Benjamin on Kafka" (lecture, Williams College, Williamstown, Mass., 6 November 2003).

5. Zonszajn, diary from Siedlce ghetto, Rachel Ben Shaul Collection. Not my translation.

6. I am indebted to Thomas A. Kohut for this insight, which poses a strong contrast to the letters written by German soldiers in Stalingrad. See Kohut and Reulecke, "'Sterben wie eine Ratte, die der Bauer ertappt,' Letzte Briefe aus Stalingrad."

7. "The Last Stage of Resettlement Is Death," anonymous report written after the mass deportation of Jews from the Warsaw ghetto, in Kermish, *To Live With Honor and Die With Honor!*, 704.

BIBLIOGRAPHY

DIARIES — UNPUBLISHED

Note: A title in quotation marks indicates that it is the archive's, not the author's.

ARCHIVES NATIONALES, PARIS, FRANCE

Kohn, Georges. Drancy, 1941–44. Drancy: Folder IVa, no. 6, F/9/5579.
Mandel, Georges. Fonds Georges Mandel, cote 544 AP: Journal de Buchenwald, 1943–44.

BIBLIOTHÈQUE NATIONALE, PARIS, FRANCE

Abraham, Hélène. Aix-en-Provence, Paris, 1940–46. Manuscrits Occidentales, Richelieu.
  Fonds Hélène Abraham, carton III, nos. 4 (xxiv)–7 (xxvii).

CENTRE DE DOCUMENTATION JUIVE
CONTEMPORAINE, PARIS, FRANCE

Persitz, Hélène. Death march from Auschwitz to Ravensbruck, 1945. DCCCV-3, doc. 5.

BEIT LOHAMEI HAGHETAOT (GHETTO FIGHTERS' HOUSE),
D.N. WESTERN GALILEE, ISRAEL

Glück, Irena. Kraków, 1940–42. File 1853.
Jesion, Isabelle. Paris, 1941–44. File 2131.
Steiner, Grete. Scheveningen, Zeist, 1937–42. File 1064.

CENTRAL ARCHIVES FOR THE HISTORY OF THE JEWISH PEOPLE,
HEBREW UNIVERSITY OF JERUSALEM, ISRAEL

Cohn, Willy. Breslau, 1939–41. RP 88, Boxes 2–3, Notebooks 90–107.

MASSUA (INSTITUTE FOR THE STUDY OF THE HOLOCAUST),
KIBBUTZ TEL YITZHAK, ISRAEL

Diary of group of girls in Peterswaldau Lager, 1943. T 9–8.

MORESHET ARCHIVES, GIVAT HAVIVA, ISRAEL

Unknown author. Diary from Łuck, 1941–43. D.2.179.

"Le Livre de la Vie." Group diary written by members of Hashomer Hatzair and Hechalutz in Brittany, France, 1942. D.2.266.

Kaplan, Chaim Aron. Notebooks 10 and 11, Warsaw, 1941–42. D.2.470.1.

Szlengel, Władysław. "What I Read to the Dead," Warsaw, 1943. D.2.267.

WIENER LIBRARY, TEL AVIV UNIVERSITY, ISRAEL

Fink, Vally. "Tagebuch," 1942. P.III.h. (Theresienstadt) Nr. 552.

Kolb, Bernhard. "Excerpt from a Diary," 1943. P.III.h. (Theresienstadt) Nr. 520.

Schüller, Nora. "Tagebuchnotizen," Holland, 1940. P.III.d. Nr. 539.

Spies, Gerty. "Tagebuchfragment aus Theresienstadt," 1944. P.III.h. (Theresienstadt I) Nr. 232.

Zielenziger, [Frau]. "Tagebuch der Frau Zielenziger," 1944. Kurt Zielenziger Papers. P.III.h. (Bergen-Belsen) Nr. 1118.

YAD VASHEM ARCHIVES, JERUSALEM, ISRAEL

Unknown author. Łódź ghetto diary written in Yiddish, Polish, Hebrew, and English in the margins of a French storybook, *Les Vrais Riches*, 1944. 03/1032.

Unknown author. Diary of a mother with two daughters in Steindamm and Brussels, 1935–40. 033/79.

Unknown author. Diary of a man in hiding in Brzeżany. 033/1373.

A. B. Theresienstadt, 1942–45. JM/13.

Berman. Lwów, 1941–42. 033/1916.

Block, Elisabeth. Bavaria, 1937–42. 033/2406.

Bosak, Abraham. Plaszów, 1943–44. 033/1218.

Feierman, Juliusz. Stanislawów, 1943. M.49-ŻIH/M.49.P/135.

Flaum, Arthur. Prague, Sosnowiec, Haifa, 1939–43. 033/25.

Gold. Lwów, 1941–42. 033/1916.

Holländer, Margarete. Near Czortków, 1943–45. 033/774.

H.S. Lwów, 1941. 033/1916.

Keller, Arnold, and Hans Horwitz. Bergen-Belsen, 1944. 033/7.

Koptowna, Maria. Białe Rawska, 1942–44. 033/334 and JM/2810.

Landsberg, M. Krzemieniec, 1942–43. 033/1099.

Magsamen, Albert. Brussels, Tournai, Le Vigeant, Beauvoir, St. Cyprien, Gurs, 1940–41. "Camp de Gurs—Temoignange B-1." 09/267.

Marcuse, Günther. Gross-Breesen, 1942–43. 033/1033.

Markiwicz, Irena. Kraków area, 1942–45. 016/P-96.

Neter, Dr. "Camp de Gurs," 1943. 033/210.

Okonowski, Sewek. Warsaw. 033/1092.

Perechodnik, Calel. Warsaw, 1943. 033/426.

Rathauserowa, Dina. Peczeniżynie, 1942–43. 033/633.

Rotgeber, Kalman. Warsaw, 1943. 033/255 and 033/990.

Schmidt, Leokadia. Warsaw, 1943–44. 033/1521.

Szeps, Fela. Grünberg Schlesien Lager, 1942–44. 033/747.

Turkel, Simon. Kopyczynce, Skałat, 1943–44. 033/722.

van den Berg, M. S. Belgium, 1940–45. 02/527.

LEO BAECK INSTITUTE, NEW YORK

Amann, Paul. Sables d'Olonnes, Brittany, 1939–40. ME 740/2, AR 7157.VI.B.

Ehrlich, Richard. Theresienstadt, 1943–45. Richard A. Ehrlich Collection. "The History of Our Negative Emigration." ME 1101.

Geissmar, Rudolf. "Theresienstadter Tagebuch," 1943. ME 182.

Judas, Karl Kurt. Pfingsten. Carl Jaburg Collection. "Karl Kurt Judas' Diary," 1941. AR 10067, A 37/2.

Lewissohn, Caecilie. Berlin, 1943–44. ME 388, Box 42.

Müller, Jacob. Holland, 1942–43. ME 1028.

Pick, Ella. "My Mother's Diary," Vienna, Prague, 1920–42. ME 1039.

Ringel, Toni. "Diary of a Jewish Mother," Amsterdam, 1942–45. ME 894.

UNITED STATES HOLOCAUST MEMORIAL MUSEUM,
WASHINGTON, D.C.

Unknown author. "Pamiętnik 12 letniej dziewczynki z Łódzkiego getta. [Diary of a 12-year-old girl from the Łódź ghetto.]" 1944. ŻIH Memoir Collection 302, RG 02.208M, Reel 2, File 9.

Unknown author. Diary of a girl in the Łódź ghetto, 1942. ŻIH Memoir Collection 302, RG 02.208M, Reel 8, File 86.

Unknown author. Warsaw, 1943. ŻIH Memoir Collection 302, RG 02.208M, Reel 36, File 228.

Binder, Elsa [Eliszewa]. Stanislawów, 1941–42. ŻIH Memoir Collection 302, RG 02.208M, Reel 39, File 267.

Dreyfus, Lucien. Strasbourg, Nice, 1925–43. Lucien Dreyfuss collection, RG 10.144.

Feurman, Julian. Stanislawów, 1943. ŻIH Memoir Collection 302, RG 02.208M, Reel 23, File 135.

Frey, Erich. Berlin, 1939–42. Alfred H. Elbau papers, "The Diary of Erich Frey," RG 10.041*03.

Hasenfuss, Chaim. Warsaw, 1939–41. ŻIH Memoir Collection 302, RG 02.208M, Reel 26, File 157.

Hauser, Irena. Łódź ghetto, 1942. ŻIH Memoir Collection 302, RG 02.208M, Reel 42, File 299.

Jakub. Warsaw, 1939–44. ŻIH Memoir Collection 302, RG 02.208M, Reel 17, File 110, and Reel 18, File 110.

Kramer, Klara. Żołkiew, 1942–44. Collections Division, Object ID No. 1994.95.2a-e.

Mermall, Gabriel. Carpathian Mountains, 1944. "Narrative and Diary of Mr. Gabriel Mermall," RG 02.008.

Reinach, Frieda, and Max. Berlin, 1939–42. Acc. 1999.A.0215.

Rubinsztejnowa. Lwów, 1943–44. ŻIH Memoir Collection 302, RG 02.208M, Reel 20, File 116.

Siekierkowa, Brandla. Mińsk Mazowiecki, 1942–45. ŻIH Memoir Collection 302, RG 02.208M, Reel 21, File 123.

Steinitz, Hans J. "Das Buch von Gurs: ein Weissbuch über das südfranzöische Interniertenlager Gurs," 1940–42. RG 04.072.

Warsinger, Susan. Chateau de Morelles, France, 1941. Acc. 2000.127.

Zysman, Jozef. Warsaw, 1944. ŻIH Memoir Collection 302, RG 02.208M, Reel 20, File 114.

PRIVATE COLLECTIONS

Ringel, Toni. Amsterdam, 1942–45. Private collection.

Zonszajn, Cypora. Siedlce, Poland, 1942. Rachel Ben-Shaul Collection.

DIARIES — PUBLISHED

"Les Vrais Riches" Notizen am Rand: Ein Tagebuch aus dem Ghetto Łódź (Mai bis August 1944). Edited by Hanno Loewy and Andrzej Bodek. Leipzig: Reclam Verlag Leipzig, 1997.

The Chronicle of the Łódź Ghetto, 1941–1944. Edited by Lucjan Dobroszycki. Translated by Richard Lourie, Joachim Neugroschel, et al. New Haven: Yale University Press, 1984.

"Anonymous Boy: Łódź Ghetto." In *Salvaged Pages: Young Writers' Diaries of the Holocaust.* Collected, edited, and introduced by Alexandra Zapruder. New Haven: Yale University Press, 2002.

"Anonymous Girl: Łódź Ghetto." In *Salvaged Pages: Young Writers' Diaries of the Holocaust.* Collected, edited, and introduced by Alexandra Zapruder. New Haven: Yale University Press, 2002.

Biélinky, Jacques. *Journal, juillet 1940–décembre 1943.* Edited, annotated, and introduced by Renée Poznanski. Paris: Cerf, 1992.

Binder, Elsa. "Stanisławów, Poland." In *Salvaged Pages: Young Writers' Diaries of the Holocaust.* Collected, edited, and introduced by Alexandra Zapruder. New Haven: Yale University Press, 2002.

Cohn, Willy. *Als Jude in Breslau 1941.* Edited by Joseph Walk. Gerlingen: Bleicher Verlag, 1984.

Czerniakow, Adam. *The Warsaw Diary of Adam Czerniakow: Prelude to Doom.* Edited by Raul Hilberg, Stanislaw Staron, and Josef Kermisz. Translated by Stanislaw Staron et al. New York: Stein and Day, 1971.

Flinker, Moshe. *Young Moshe's Diary: The Spiritual Torment of a Jewish Boy in Nazi Europe.* Jerusalem: Yad Vashem, 1971.

Frank, Anne. *The Diary of a Young Girl: The Definitive Edition.* Edited by Otto H. Frank and Mirjam Pressler. Translated by Susan Massotty. New York: Anchor Books Doubleday, 1995.

Frey, Erich. Diary in *"Die Gespräche drehten sich auch vielfach um die Reise, die wir alle antreten müssen": Leben und Verfolgtsein der Juden in Berlin-Tempelhof. Dokumenta-tion.* Edited by Michael Kreutzer. Berlin: Wichern-Verlag, 1988.

Grunberg, Albert. *Journal d'un coiffeur juif à Paris sous l'Occupation.* With an introduc-tion by Laurent Douzou. Annotated by Jean Laloum. Paris: Les Éditions de l'Atelier and Les Éditions Ouvrières, 2001.

Herzberg, Abel. *Between Two Streams: A Diary from Bergen-Belsen.* Translated by Jack Sant-cross. New York: I. B. Tauris in association with The European Jewish Publication So-ciety, 1997.

Hillesum, Etty. *An Interrupted Life* and *Letters from Westerbork.* Translated by Arnold J. Pomerans. New York: Henry Holt, 1996.

Kaplan, Chaim A. *The Warsaw Diary of Chaim A. Kaplan.* Rev. ed. With a foreword by Yisrael Gutman. Edited and translated by Abraham I. Katsh. Bloomington: Indiana Uni-versity Press in association with the United States Holocaust Memorial Museum, 1999.

———. *Megilat yisurin: yoman Geto Varshah 1 be-September 1939–4 be-August 1942.* Edited by Abraham Isaac Katsh, Nachman Blumental, Bernard Mark. Tel Aviv: Am Oved, and Jerusalem: Yad Vashem, 1966.

Katzenelson, Yitzhak. *Vittel Diary.* Translated by Myer Cohen. Ghetto Fighters' House, [n.d.].

Klemperer, Victor. *Ich will Zeugnis ablegen bis zum letzten: Tagebücher 1933–1945.* 2 vols. Berlin: Aufbau-Verlag, 1995.

———. *I Will Bear Witness: A Diary of the Nazi Years, 1933–1941.* Translated by Martin Chalmers. New York: Random House, 1998.

———. *I Will Bear Witness: A Diary of the Nazi Years, 1942–1945.* Translated by Martin Chalmers. New York: Random House, 1999.

Klonicki, Aryeh. *The Diary of Adam's Father: The Diary of Aryeh Klonicki (Klonymus) and His Wife Malwina with Letters Concerning the Fate of Their Child Adam.* Translated by Avner Tomaschoff. Beit Lohamei Haghetaot and Hakibbutz Hameuchad Publishing House, 1973.

Korczak, Janusz. *Ghetto Diary.* Translated by Jerzy Bachrach and Barbara Krzywicka (Ved-der). New York: Holocaust Library, 1978.

Kruk, Herman. *The Last Days of the Jerusalem of Lithuania: Chronicles from the Vilna Ghetto and the Camps 1939–1944.* Edited and introduced by Benjamin Harshav. Trans-lated by Barbara Harshav. New Haven: Yale University Press, 2002.

Lambert, Raymond-Raoul. *Carnet d'un témoin, 1940–1943.* Annotated and introduced by Richard Cohen. Paris: Fayard, 1985.

Laqueur, Renate. *Bergen-Belsen Tagebuch, 1944–1945.* Translated by Peter Wiebke. Han-nover: Fackelträger-Verlag, 1983.

Lewin, Abraham. *A Cup of Tears: A Diary of the Warsaw Ghetto.* Edited by Antony Po-lonsky. Translated by Christopher Hutton. Oxford: Basil Blackwell in association with Institute for Polish-Jewish Studies, 1988.

Marcuse, Günther. "The Diary of Günther Marcuse: The Last Days of the Gross-Breesen Training Center." Edited, translated, and annotated by Joseph Walk. *Yad Vashem Studies* 7 (1970): 159–81.

Mechanicus, Philip. *Year of Fear: A Jewish Prisoner Waits for Auschwitz.* Translated by Irene R. Gibbons. New York: Hawthorn Books, 1968.

Opoczyński, Peretz. "Warsaw Ghetto Chronicle." In *To Live With Honor and Die With Honor! . . . Selected Documents from the Warsaw Ghetto Underground Archives "O.S." ["Oneg Shabbath"]*, edited by Joseph Kermish. Jerusalem: Yad Vashem, 1986.

Perechodnik, Calel. *Am I a Murderer? Testament of a Jewish Ghetto Policeman.* Edited and translated by Frank Fox. Boulder: Westview Press, 1996.

Redlich, Gonda. *The Terezin Diary of Gonda Redlich.* Edited by Saul S. Friedman. Translated by Laurence Kutler. Lexington: University Press of Kentucky, 1992.

Ringelblum, Emanuel. *Notes from the Warsaw Ghetto: The Journal of Emanuel Ringelblum.* Edited and translated by Jacob Sloan. New York: McGraw Hill, 1974.

Rosenfeld, Oskar. *In the Beginning Was the Ghetto: Notebooks from Łódź.* Edited by Hanno Loewy. Translated by Brigitte M. Goldstein. Evanston, Ill.: Northwestern University Press, 2002.

Roubičkova, Eva. *We're Alive and Life Goes On: A Theresienstadt Diary.* Translated by Zaia Alexander. New York: Henry Holt, 1998.

Rudashevski, Yitzhak. *The Diary of the Vilna Ghetto, June 1941–April 1943.* Edited and translated by Percy Matenko. Beit Lohamei Haghetaot and Hakibbutz Hameuchad Publishing House, 1973.

Sebastian, Mihail. *Journal, 1935–1944, The Fascist Years.* Annotated and introduced by Radu Ioanid. Translated by Patrick Camiller. Chicago: Ivan R. Dee in association with the United States Holocaust Memorial Museum, 2000.

Sierakowiak, Dawid. *The Diary of Dawid Sierakowiak: Five Notebooks from the Łódź Ghetto.* Edited by Alan Adelson. Translated by Kamil Turowski. New York: Oxford University Press, 1996.

Szajn, Eugenia Lewin. *Aufzeichnungen aus dem Warschauer Ghetto, July 1942 bis April 1943.* Translated by Roswitha Matwin-Buschmann. Leipzig: Reclam Verlag Leipzig, 1994.

Titelman, Nehemiah. [Notes]. In *To Live With Honor and Die With Honor! . . . Selected Documents from the Warsaw Ghetto Underground Archives "O.S." ["Oneg Shabbath"]*, edited by Joseph Kermish. Jerusalem: Yad Vashem, 1986.

Tory, Avraham. *Surviving the Holocaust: The Kovno Ghetto Diary.* Edited and introduced by Martin Gilbert. Annotated by Dina Porat. Translated by Jerzy Michalowicz. Cambridge: Harvard University Press, 1990.

OTHER UNPUBLISHED PRIMARY SOURCES

Drancy, Notes de Service, DLXII-163–169, Centre de documentation juive contemporaine.

Faltin, Helene. Postcard to Robert Schalek, dated 8 August 1943, from Arbeitslager Birkenau, RG 075, File 371, Yad Vashem Archives.

Fink, Vally. "Von Theresienstadt bis London." P.III.h. (Theresienstadt) No. 554, Wiener Library Collection, Tel Aviv University.

Kraminer, Herman. Postcard to Mendel Schorr, dated 17 May 1942, from Delatyn, RG 075, File 363, Yad Vashem Archives.

Jesion, Monsieur and Madame. Postcards to their daughter, Isabelle, July and August 1942, from Drancy, DCLXXVI-1 (nos. 3, 7, 8), Centre de documentation juive contemporaine.

Manheimer, Adela Kestenberg. Testimony, Acc. 1999.A.0253, United States Holocaust Memorial Museum.

"R." Letter to "L.H.," dated 9 February 1942, from Piaski ghetto, Arc. Ms. Var. 469, Arno Nadel Archive, The Jewish National and University Library, Hebrew University of Jerusalem.

Szeps, Szewa. Testimony, 03/2728, Yad Vashem Archives.

Taitz, Carolina Knoch. Letters from the Riga ghetto, Carolina Taitz papers, RG 05.004*01, United States Holocaust Memorial Museum.

Tengler, Genia Halina. "Report about the women's death march and the establishment of a burial site in Volary for the victims of this march," Acc. 1995.A.332, folder 2, United States Holocaust Memorial Museum.

SECONDARY LITERATURE

Abramson, Henry. "Deciphering the Ancestral Paradigm: A Hasidic Court in the Warsaw Ghetto." In "Ghettos 1939–1945: New Research and Perspectives on Definition, Daily Life, and Survival," Symposium Presentations Series. Washington, D.C.: Center for Advanced Holocaust Studies at the United States Holocaust Memorial Museum, 2005.

Agulhon, Maurice. The French Republic, 1879–1992. Translated by Antonia Nevill. Cambridge, Mass.: Blackwell, 1995.

Aly, Götz. 'Final Solution': Nazi Population Policy and the Murder of the European Jews. Translated by Belinda Cooper and Allison Brown. New York: Oxford University Press, 1999.

Améry, Jean. At the Mind's Limits: Contemplations by a Survivor on Auschwitz and Its Realities. Translated by Sidney Rosenfeld and Stella P. Rosenfeld. Bloomington: Indiana University Press, 1980.

Anderson, Benedict. Imagined Communities: Reflections on the Origin and Spread of Nationalism. Rev. ed. New York: Verso, 1991.

Appelfeld, Aharon. "Individualization of the Holocaust." In Holocaust Chronicles: Individualizing the Holocaust through Diaries and Other Contemporaneous Personal Accounts, edited by Robert Moses Shapiro. Hoboken, N.J.: Ktav, 1999.

Arad, Gulie Ne'eman. "'Nazi Germany and the Jews': Reflections on a Beginning, a Middle and an Open End." History and Memory 9, no. 1/2 (1997): 409–33.

Arad, Yitzhak. Belzec, Sobibor, Treblinka: The Operation Reinhard Death Camps. Bloomington: Indiana University Press, 1987.

———. Ghetto in Flames: The Struggle and Destruction of the Jews in Vilna in the Holocaust. [Hoboken, N.J.]: Ktav, 1981.

Arendt, Hannah. Eichmann in Jerusalem: A Report on the Banality of Evil. Rev. ed. New York: Penguin, 1994.

Aschheim, Steven E. *Brothers and Strangers: The East European Jew in German and German Jewish Consciousness, 1800–1923*. Madison: University of Wisconsin Press, 1982.

———. *Culture and Catastrophe: German and Jewish Confrontations with National Socialism and Other Crises*. New York: Macmillan, 1996.

———. *Scholem, Arendt, Klemperer: Intimate Chronicles in Turbulent Times*. Bloomington: Indiana University Press published in association with Hebrew Union College-Jewish Institute of Religion in Cincinnati, 2001.

Baird, Jay W. *The Mythical World of Nazi War Propaganda, 1939–1945*. Minneapolis: University of Minnesota Press, 1974.

Balmuth, Daniel. *Censorship in Russia, 1865–1905*. Washington, D.C.: University Press of America, 1979.

Bankier, David. *The Germans and the Final Solution: Public Opinion under Nazism*. Cambridge, Mass.: Basil Blackwell, 1992.

Barker, Francis. *The Tremulous Private Body: Essays on Subjection*. Ann Arbor: University of Michigan Press, 1995.

Bartov, Omer. *Murder in Our Midst: The Holocaust, Industrial Killing, and Representation*. New York: Oxford University Press, 1996.

Bauer, Yehuda. *A History of the Holocaust*. New York: F. Watts, 1982.

———. *The Jewish Emergence from Powerlessness*. Toronto: University of Toronto Press, 1979.

———. *Rethinking the Holocaust*. New Haven: Yale University Press, 2001.

Bauman, Zygmunt. *Modernity and the Holocaust*. Ithaca: Cornell University Press, 1989.

Becker, Jurek. *Jakob the Liar*. Translated by Leila Vennewitz. New York: Harcourt Brace Jovanovich, 1975. Reprint. New York: Plume, 1999.

Beneš, František, and Patricia Tošnerová. *Pošta v ghettu Terezín / Die Post im Ghetto Theresienstadt / Mail Service in the Ghetto Terezín, 1941–1945*. Prague: Profil dům Filatelie, 1996.

Bernard-Donals, Michael, and Richard Glejzer. *Between Witness and Testimony: The Holocaust and the Limits of Representation*. Albany: State University of New York Press, 2001.

Bernard-Donals, Michael. "History and Disaster: Witness, Trauma, and the Problem of Writing the Holocaust." *CLIO* 30, no. 2 (2001): 143–68.

Bernstein, Michael André. *Foregone Conclusions: Against Apocalyptic History*. Berkeley and Los Angeles: University of California Press, 1994.

Bienenstock, Berta Stein. "Analysis of Jewish Religious Observance in Nazi-occupied Europe during World War II, 1939–1945." Ph.D. diss., New York University, 1991.

Bloch, Marc. *Strange Defeat: A Statement of Evidence Written in 1940*. Translated by Gerard Hopkins. New York: W. W. Norton, 1968.

Blodgett, Harriet. *Centuries of Female Days: Englishwomen's Private Diaries*. New Brunswick: Rutgers University Press, 1988.

Bloom, Lynn Z. "'I Write for Myself and Strangers': Private Diaries as Public Documents." In *Inscribing the Daily: Critical Essays on Women's Diaries*, edited by Suzanne L. Bunkers and Cynthia A. Huff. Amherst: University of Massachusetts Press, 1996.

Bluhm, Lothar. *Das Tagebuch zum Dritten Reich: Zeugnisse der Inneren Emigration*. Bonn: Bouvier Verlag, 1991.

Boal, David. *Journaux Intimes Sous L'Occupation*. Paris: Armand Colin Éditeur, 1993.

Boerner, Peter. *Tagebuch*. Stuttgart: J. B. Metzlersche Verlagsbuchhandlung, 1969.

Braiterman, Zachary. *(God) After Auschwitz*. Princeton: Princeton University Press, 1998.

Braun, Robert. "The Holocaust and Problems of Historical Representation." *History and Theory* 33, no. 2 (1994): 172–97.

Breitman, Richard. *The Architect of Genocide: Himmler and the Final Solution*. New York: Knopf Random House, 1991.

Brenner, Michael. *The Renaissance of Jewish Culture in Weimar Germany*. New Haven: Yale University Press, 1996.

Brenner, Rachel Feldhay. *Writing as Resistance: Four Women Confronting the Holocaust*. University Park: Pennsylvania State University Press, 1997.

Brenner, Reeve Robert. *The Faith and Doubt of Holocaust Survivors*. New York: Free Press-Macmillan, 1980.

Brostoff, Anita, ed. *Flares of Memory: Stories of Childhood during the Holocaust*. With Sheila Chamovitz. Oxford: Oxford University Press, 2001.

Browning, Christopher. *Nazi Policy, Jewish Workers, German Killers*. Cambridge: Cambridge University Press, 2000.

———. *The Origins of the Final Solution: The Evolution of Nazi Jewish Policy, September 1939–March 1942*. Contributions by Jürgen Matthäus. Lincoln and Jerusalem: University of Nebraska Press and Yad Vashem, 2004.

Brunner, Jerome. "The Autobiographical Process." *Current Sociology* 43, no. 2/3, Issue on Biographical Research (1995): 161–77.

Bryant, David. "Revolution and Introspection: The Appearance of the Private Diary in France." *European Studies Review* 8, no. 2 (1978): 259–72.

Bunkers, Suzanne L., and Cynthia A. Huff. Introduction to *Inscribing the Daily: Critical Essays on Women's Diaries*, edited by Suzanne L. Bunkers and Cynthia A. Huff. Amherst: University of Massachusetts Press, 1996.

Burleigh, Michael. *The Third Reich: A New History*. New York: Hill and Wang, 2000.

Burleigh, Michael, and Wolfgang Wipperman. *The Racial State: Germany, 1933–1945*. Cambridge: Cambridge University Press, 1991.

Burr, Ann Robeson. *The Autobiography: A Critical and Comparative Study*. Boston: Houghton Mifflin, 1909.

Burrin, Philippe. *France Under the Germans: Collaboration and Compromise*. Translated by Janet Lloyd. New York: New Press, 1996.

———. *Hitler and the Jews: The Genesis of the Holocaust*. Translated by Patsy Southgate. London: Edward Arnold, 1994.

Canning, Kathleen. "Feminist History after the Linguistic Turn: Historicizing Discourse and Experience." *Signs* 19, no. 2 (1994): 368–404.

Caron, Vicki. *Between France and Germany: The Jews of Alsace-Lorraine, 1871–1918*. Stanford: Stanford University Press, 1988.

Carpi, Daniel. *Between Mussolini and Hitler: The Jews and the Italian Authorities in France and Tunisia*. Hanover, N.H.: University Press of New England, 1994.

Caruth, Cathy. "Unclaimed Experience: Trauma and the Possibility of History." *Yale French Studies*, no. 79, *Literature and the Ethical Question* (1991): 181–92.

Celan, Paul. "Speech on the Occasion of Receiving the Literature Prize of the Free Hanseatic City of Bremen." In *Selected Poems and Prose of Paul Celan*, translated by John Felstiner. New York: W. W. Norton, 2001.

Chartier, Roger. *Forms and Meanings: Texts, Performances, and Audiences from Codex to Computer*. Philadelphia: University of Pennsylvania Press, 1995.

Clendinnen, Inga. *Reading the Holocaust*. Cambridge: Cambridge University Press, 1999.

Cohen, Nathan. "Diaries of the *Sonderkommandos* in Auschwitz: Coping with Fate and Reality." In *Yad Vashem Studies* 20 (1990): 273–312.

Cohen, Yerachmiel. "The Jewish Community of France in the Face of Vichy-German Persecution: 1940–1944." In *The Jews in Modern France*, edited by Frances Malino and Bernard Wasserstein. Hanover, N.H.: University Press of New England for Brandeis University Press, 1985.

Cohn-Sherbok, Dan, ed. *Holocaust Theology: A Reader*. New York: New York University Press, 2002.

Culley, Margo, ed. *A Day at a Time: The Diary Literature of American Women from 1764 to the Present*. New York: Feminist Press at the City University of New York, 1985.

Daladier, Edouard. *Prison Journal, 1940–1945*. Edited by Jean Daladier and Jean Daridan. Translated by Arthur D. Greenspan. Boulder: Westview Press, 1995.

Dauphin, Cécile, Pierrette Lebrun-Pézerat, and Danièle Poublan. *Ces bonnes lettres: Une correspondance familiale au XIXe siècle*. Paris: Albin Michel, 1995.

———. "Une correspondance familiale au XIXe siècle." In *La lettre à la croisée de l'individu et du social*, edited by Mireille Bossis. Paris: Éditions Kimé, 1994.

Davis, Natalie Zemon. "Fame and Secrecy: Leon Modena's *Life* as an Early Modern Autobiography." In *The Autobiography of a Seventeenth-Century Venetian Rabbi: Leon Modena's Life of Judah*, edited and translated by Mark R. Cohen. Princeton: Princeton University Press, 1988.

Dawidowicz, Lucy. *The Golden Tradition: Jewish Life and Thought in Eastern Europe*. Syracuse: Syracuse University Press, 1996.

———. *The War Against the Jews, 1933–1945*. New York: Bantam Books, 1975.

de Certeau, Michel. *The Mystic Fable*. Translated by Michael B. Smith. Chicago: University of Chicago Press, 1992.

———. *The Practice of Everyday Life*. Translated by Steven F. Rendall. Berkeley and Los Angeles: University of California Press, 1984.

Des Pres, Terence. *The Survivor: An Anatomy of Life in the Death Camps*. New York: Washington Square Press, 1976.

Didier, Béatrice. *Le Journal Intime*. Paris: Presses Universitaires de France, 1976.

Diehl, Katrin. *Das jüdische Presse im Dritten Reich: Zwischen Selbstbehauptung und Fremdbestimmung*. Tübingen: Max Niemeyer Verlag, 1997.

Diner, Dan. "Historical Understanding and Counterrationality: The *Judenrat* as Epistemological Vantage." In *Probing the Limits of Representation: Nazism and the "Final Solution,"* edited by Saul Friedländer. Cambridge: Harvard University Press, 1992.

Dintenfass, Michael. "Truth's Other: Ethics, the History of the Holocaust, and Historiographical Theory after the Linguistic Turn." *History and Theory* 39, no. 1 (Feb. 2000): 1–20.

Dobroszycki, Lucjan. "YIVO in Interwar Poland: Work in the Historical Sciences." In *The Jews of Poland Between Two World Wars*, edited by Yisrael Gutman, Ezra Mendelsohn, Jehuda Reinharz, and Chone Shmeruk. Hanover, N.H.: University Press of New England, 1989.

Dosse, François. *New History in France: The Triumph of the Annales*. Translated by Peter V. Conroy, Jr. Urbana: University of Illinois Press, 1994.

Earle, Rebecca. Introduction to *Epistolary Selves: Letters and Letter-Writers, 1600–1945*, edited by Rebecca Earle. Aldershot, England: Ashgate, 1999.

Eidelberg, Shlomo, ed. and trans. *The Jews and the Crusaders: The Hebrew Chronicles of the First and Second Crusades*. Madison: University of Wisconsin Press, 1977.

Eisenbach, Artur. "Jewish Historiography in Interwar Poland." In *The Jews of Poland Between Two World Wars*, edited by Yisrael Gutman, Ezra Mendelsohn, Jehuda Reinharz, and Chone Shmeruk. Hanover, N.H.: University Press of New England, 1989.

Engel, David. "On the Bowdlerization of a Holocaust Testimony: The Wartime Journal of Calek Perechodnik." *Polin* 12 (1999): 316–29.

———. "'Will They Dare?': Perceptions of Threat in Diaries from the Warsaw Ghetto." In *Holocaust Chronicles: Individualizing the Holocaust through Diaries and Other Contemporaneous Personal Accounts*, edited by Robert Moses Shapiro. Hoboken, N.J.: Ktav, 1999.

Engelking-Boni, Barbara. *Czas przestał dla mnie istniec: analiza doświadczania czasu w sytuacji ostatecznej*. Warsaw: Wydawn. IFiS PAN, 1996.

———. *Holocaust and Memory: The Experience of the Holocaust and Its Consequences*. Edited by Gunnar S. Paulsson. Translated by Emma Harris. London: Leicester University Press in association with the European Jewish Publication Society, 2001.

Engelking, Barbara, and Jacek Leociak. *Getto Warszawskie: przewodnik po nieistniejącym mieście*. Warsaw: Wydawnictwo IFiS PAN, 2001.

Ezrahi, Sidra Dekoven. "Representing Auschwitz." *History and Memory* 7, no. 2 (1996): 122–54.

Farbstein, Esther. "Diaries and Memoirs as a Historical Source—The Diary and Memoir of a Rabbi at the 'Konin House of Bondage.'" Translated by Naftali Greenwood. *Yad Vashem Studies* 26 (1998): 87–128.

Favret, Mary. "War Correspondence: Reading Romantic War." *Prose Studies: History, Theory, Criticism* 19, no. 2 (1996): 173–85.

Felman, Shoshana, and Dori Laub. *Testimony: Crises of Witnessing in Literature, Psychoanalysis, and History*. New York: Routledge, 1992.

Felstiner, Mary Lowenthal. *To Paint Her Life: Charlotte Salomon in the Nazi Era*. New York: HarperCollins, 1994.

Fink, Carole. *Marc Bloch: A Life in History*. Cambridge: Cambridge University Press, 1989.

Fothergill, Robert A. *Private Chronicles: A Study of English Diaries*. New York: Oxford University Press, 1974.

Freeden, Herbert. *The Jewish Press in the Third Reich*. Providence: Berg Publishers, 1993.

Frei, Norbert, and Johannes Schmitz. *Journalismus im Dritten Reich*. Munich: C. H. Beck Verlag, 1989.

Freud, Sigmund. *The Interpretation of Dreams.* Translated by James Strachey. New York: Avon Books, 1965.

———. "Mourning and Melancholia." 1917. In *The Standard Edition of the Complete Psychological Works of Sigmund Freud,* translated by James Strachey. Vol. 14. London: Hogarth Press, 1957.

Friedländer, Saul. "Marc Bloch et Ernst Kantorowicz." In *Les Juifs et le XXe siècle: Dictionnaire critique,* edited by Élie Barnavi and Saul Friedländer. Paris: Calman-Lévy, 2000.

———. *Memory, History, and the Extermination of the Jews of Europe.* Bloomington: Indiana University Press, 1993.

———. *Nazi Germany and the Jews.* Vol.1, *The Years of Persecution, 1933–1939.* New York: HarperCollins, 1997.

———. *Reflections of Nazism: An Essay on Kitsch and Death.* Translated by Thomas Weyr. New York: Harper & Row, 1984.

———. "Some Aspects of the Historical Significance of the Holocaust." The Philip M. Klutznick International Lecture, Institute of Contemporary Jewry, Hebrew University of Jerusalem, 1977.

———, ed. *Probing the Limits of Representation: Nazism and the "Final Solution."* Cambridge: Harvard University Press, 1992.

Fritzsche, Peter. *Reading Berlin 1900.* Cambridge: Harvard University Press, 1996.

———. *Stranded in the Present: Modern Time and the Melancholy of History.* Cambridge: Harvard University Press, 2004.

Funkenstein, Amos. "The Incomprehensible Catastrophe: Memory and Narrative." In *The Narrative Study of Lives,* vol.1, edited by Ruthellen Josselson and Amia Lieblich. Newbury Park and London: SAGE Publications, 1993.

———. *Perceptions of Jewish History.* Berkeley and Los Angeles: University of California Press, 1993.

Fussell, Paul. *The Great War and Modern Memory.* New York: Oxford University Press, 1975.

Gebhardt, Miriam. *Das Familiengedächtnis: Erinnerung im deutsch-jüdischen Bürgertum 1890 bis 1932.* Stuttgart: Franz Steiner Verlag, 1999.

Gerlach, Christian. "The Wannsee Conference, the Fate of German Jews, and Hitler's Decision in Principle to Exterminate All European Jews." *Journal of Modern History* 70 (December 1998): 759–812.

Gilman, Sander. *Jurek Becker: A Life in Five Worlds.* Chicago: University of Chicago Press, 2003.

Girard, Alain. *Le Journal Intime.* Paris: Presses Universitaires de France, 1963.

Goldhagen, Daniel Jonah. *Hitler's Willing Executioners: Ordinary Germans and the Holocaust.* New York: Knopf, 1996.

Greenberg, Gershon. "Jewish Religious Practice Through the War: God, Israel and History." Research paper presented at the International Institute for Holocaust Research at Yad Vashem, Jerusalem, Israel, April 2001.

———. "The Theological Letters of Rabbi Talmud of Lublin, Summer and Fall 1942." In "Ghettos 1939–1945: New Research and Perspectives on Definition, Daily Life, and Survival," Symposium Presentations Series. Washington, D.C.: Center for Advanced Holocaust Studies at the United States Holocaust Memorial Museum, 2005.

———. "Ultra-Orthodox Reflections on the Holocaust: 1945 to the Present." In *Contemporary Responses to the Holocaust*, edited by Konrad Kwiet and Jürgen Matthäus. Westport, Conn.: Praeger, 2004.

Grüner, Wolf. *Judenverfolgung in Berlin 1933–1945: Eine Chronologie der Behördenmassnahmen in der Reichshauptstadt.* Berlin: Stiftung Topographie des Terrors, 1996.

Gusdorf, Georges. "Conditions and Limits of Autobiography." In *Autobiography: Essays Theoretical and Critical*, edited and translated by James Olney. Princeton: Princeton University Press, 1980.

Gutman, Yisrael. *The Jews of Warsaw, 1939–1943, Ghetto, Underground, Revolt.* Translated by Ina Friedman. Bloomington: Indiana University Press, 1982.

———. "Warsaw." In *The Holocaust Encyclopedia*, edited by Walter Laqueur. New Haven: Yale University Press, 2001.

———. "The Youth Movement as an Alternative Leadership in Eastern Europe." In *Zionist Youth Movements during the Shoah*, edited by Asher Cohen and Yehoyakim Cochavi. Translated by Ted Gorelick. New York: Peter Lang, 1995.

Hale, Oron. *The Captive Press in the Third Reich.* Princeton: Princeton University Press, 1964.

Halperin, Irving. *Messengers from the Dead: Literature of the Holocaust.* Philadelphia: Westminster Press, [n.d.].

Hämmerle, Christa. "'You let a weeping woman call you home?' Private Correspondences during the First World War in Austria and Germany." In *Epistolary Selves: Letters and Letter-Writers, 1600–1945*, edited by Rebecca Earle. Aldershot, England: Ashgate, 1999.

Hanna, Martha. "A Republic of Letters: The Epistolary Tradition in France during World War I." In *American Historical Review* 108, no. 5 (2003): 45 pars. <http://www.history cooperative.org/journals/ahr/108.5/hanna.html> (19 January 2005).

Hartley, Jenny. "'Letters are *everything* these days': Mothers and Letters in the Second World War." In *Epistolary Selves: Letters and Letter-Writers, 1600–1945*, edited by Rebecca Earle. Aldershot, England: Ashgate, 1999.

Heer, Hannes, ed. *Im Herzen der Finsternis: Victor Klemperer als Chronist der NS-Zeit.* Berlin: Aufbau-Verlag, 1997.

Helmreich, William B. *Against All Odds: Holocaust Survivors and the Successful Lives They Made in America.* New Brunswick: Transaction Publishers, 1996.

Herbert, Ulrich. "Extermination Policy: New Answers and Questions about the History of the Holocaust in German Historiography." In *National Socialist Extermination Policies: Contemporary German Perspectives and Controversies*, edited by Ulrich Herbert. New York: Berghahn Books, 2000.

Herzstein, Robert Edwin. *The War that Hitler Won: The Most Infamous Propaganda Campaign in History.* New York: G. P. Putnam's Sons, 1978.

Hilberg, Raul. *The Destruction of the European Jews.* Rev. and def. ed. New York: Holmes and Meier, 1985.

Hobsbawm, Eric. *The Age of Empire, 1875–1914.* New York: Vintage Books, 1989.

Hochberg, Severin. "DPs, Germans, and Americans: Riots in DP camps 1945–49." Paper presented at the annual meeting of the Association for Jewish Studies, Washington, D.C., December 2001.

Horkheimer, Max, and Theodor W. Adorno. *Dialectic of Enlightenment.* Translated by John Cumming. 1944. Reprint, with a new preface, Frankfurt am Main: S. Fischer Verlag, 1969; New York: Continuum, 1997.

Horowitz, Rosemary. "Reading and Writing During the Holocaust as Described in *Yisker Books.*" In *The Holocaust and the Book: Destruction and Preservation,* edited by Jonathan Rose. Amherst: University of Massachusetts Press, 2001.

Horowitz, Sara. *Voicing the Void: Muteness and Memory in Holocaust Fiction.* Albany: State University of New York Press, 1997.

Hunt, Lynn. Introduction to *The New Cultural History,* edited by Lynn Hunt. Berkeley and Los Angeles: University of California Press, 1989.

Jelavich, Peter. "Metamorphoses of Censorship in Modern Germany." In *Culture and Politics in Nineteenth- and Twentieth-Century Germany,* edited by Hartmut Lehmann. Occasional Paper 8. Washington, D.C.: German Historical Institute, 1992.

Johnson, Eric A. *Nazi Terror: The Gestapo, Jews, and Ordinary Germans.* New York: Basic Books, 1999.

Kagle, Steven E. *American Diary Literature, 1620–1799.* Boston: Twayne, 1979.

Kagle, Steven E., and Lorenza Gramegna. "Rewriting Her Life: Fictionalization and the Use of Fictional Models in Early American Women's Diaries." In *Inscribing the Daily: Critical Essays on Women's Diaries,* edited by Suzanne L. Bunkers and Cynthia A. Huff. Amherst: University of Massachusetts Press, 1996.

Kaplan, Marion A. *Between Dignity and Despair: Jewish Life in Nazi Germany.* New York: Oxford University Press, 1998.

Karay, Felicja. "The Social and Cultural Life of the Prisoners in the Jewish Forced Labor Camp at Skarzysko-Kamienna." *Holocaust and Genocide Studies* 8, no. 1 (1994): 1–24.

Katz, Adam. "The Closure of Auschwitz but Not Its End: Alterity, Testimony, and (Post)-Modernity." *History and Memory* 10, no. 1 (1998): 59–98.

Kassow, Samuel David. "Vilna and Warsaw, Two Ghetto Diaries: Herman Kruk and Emanuel Ringelblum." In *Holocaust Chronicles: Individualizing the Holocaust through Diaries and Other Contemporaneous Personal Accounts,* edited by Robert Moses Shapiro. Hoboken, N.J.: Ktav, 1999.

Kenan, Orna. *Between Memory and History: The Evolution of Israeli Historiography of the Holocaust, 1945–1961.* New York: Peter Lang, 2003.

Keren, Nili. "Children." In *The Holocaust Encyclopedia,* edited by Walter Laqueur. New Haven: Yale University Press, 2001.

Kermish, Joseph, ed. *To Live With Honor and Die With Honor! . . . Selected Documents from the Warsaw Ghetto Underground Archives "O.S." ["Oneg Shabbat"].* Jerusalem: Yad Vashem, 1986.

Kershaw, Ian. *Popular Opinion and Political Dissent in the Third Reich, Bavaria 1933–1945.* Rev. ed. New York: Oxford University Press, 2002.

Kirschner, Robert, trans. and ed. *Rabbinic Responsa of the Holocaust Era.* New York: Schocken Books, 1985.

Klaiber, Theodor. *Die deutsche Selbstbiographie: Beschreibungen des eigenem Lebens, Memoiren, Tagebücher.* Stuttgart: J. B. Metzlersche Verlagsbuchhandlung, 1921.

Klarsfeld, Serge. *Vichy-Auschwitz: Le rôle de Vichy dans la solution finale de la question juive en France.* 2 vols. Paris: Fayard, 1983–85.

Klemperer, Victor. *The Language of the Third Reich: LTI—Lingua Tertii Imperii: A Philologist's Notebook.* Translated by Martin Brady. London: Athlone Press, 2001.

Kohut, Thomas A., and Juergen Reulecke. "'Sterben wie eine Ratte, die der Bauer ertappt,' Letzte Briefe aus Stalingrad." In *Stalingrad: Ereignis, Wirkung, Symbol,* edited by Juergen Foerster. Munich: Piper Verlag; 1992.

Kren, George M., and Leon Rappoport. *The Holocaust and the Crisis of Human Behavior.* New York: Holmes and Meier, 1980.

Kruk, Herman. "Library and Reading Room in the Vilna Ghetto, Strashun Street 6." Translated by Zachary M. Baker. In *The Holocaust and the Book: Destruction and Preservation,* edited by Jonathan Rose. Amherst: University of Massachusetts Press, 2001.

Kugelmass, Jack, and Jonathan Boyarin, eds. and trans. *From a Ruined Garden: The Memorial Books of Polish Jewry.* New York: Schocken Books, 1983.

Kwiet, Konrad. "Nach dem Pogrom: Stufen der Ausgrenzung." In *Die Juden in Deutschland 1933–1945,* edited by Wolfgang Benz. Munich: C. H. Beck, 1988.

LaCapra, Dominick. *History and Memory after Auschwitz.* Ithaca: Cornell University Press, 1998.

———. *Representing the Holocaust: History, Theory, Trauma.* Ithaca: Cornell University Press, 1994.

———. "Rethinking Intellectual History and Reading Texts." In *Modern European Intellectual History: Reappraisals and New Perspectives,* edited by Dominick LaCapra and Steven L. Kaplan. Ithaca: Cornell University Press, 1982.

Lang, Berel. "Is It Possible to Misrepresent the Holocaust?" *History and Theory* 34, no. 1 (1995): 84–89.

Langer, Lawrence L. *Admitting the Holocaust: Collected Essays.* New York: Oxford University Press, 1995.

———. *Holocaust Testimonies: The Ruins of Memory.* New Haven: Yale University Press, 1991.

———. "On Writing and Reading Holocaust Literature." In *Art from the Ashes: A Holocaust Anthology,* edited by Lawrence L. Langer. New York: Oxford University Press, 1995.

Laqueur, Walter. *The Terrible Secret: Suppression of the Truth about Hitler's 'Final Solution.'* Boston: Little, Brown, 1980.

Lejeune, Philippe. *"Cher cahier . . ."* Paris: Éditions Gallimard, 1989.

———. "The 'Journal de Jeune Fille' in Nineteenth-Century France." Translated by Martine Breillac. In *Inscribing the Daily: Critical Essays on Women's Diaries,* edited by Suzanne L. Bunkers and Cynthia A. Huff. Amherst: University of Massachusetts Press, 1996.

———. *Le Moi des demoiselles: Enquête sur le journal de jeune fille.* "La couleur de la vie" series. Paris: Seuil, 1993.

———. "The Practice of the Private Journal: Chronicle of an Investigation (1986–1998)." In *Marginal Voices, Marginal Forms: Diaries in European Literature and History,* edited by Rachael Langford and Russell West. Amsterdam: Rodopi, 1999.

Leleu, Michèle. *Les Journaux Intimes.* Paris: Presses Universitaires de France, 1952.

Levi, Primo. *The Drowned and the Saved.* Translated by Raymond Rosenthal. New York: Vintage Books, 1989.

———. *Survival in Auschwitz.* Translated by Stuart Woolf. New York: Collier Books, 1961.

Liberles, Robert. "Diaries of the Holocaust." *Orim* 1, no. 2 (1986): 35–47.

Lichten, Joseph. "Jewish Assimilation in Poland, 1863–1943." In *The Jews in Poland,* edited by Chimen Abramsky, Maciej Jachimczyk, and Antony Polonsky. Oxford: Basil Blackwell, 1986.

Liebersohn, Harry, and Dorothee Schneider, eds. *"My Life in Germany Before and After January 30, 1933": A Guide to a Manuscript Collection at Houghton Library, Harvard University.* Philadelphia: Transactions of the American Philosophical Society 91, no. 3 (2001).

Longerich, Peter. *Politik der Vernichtung: eine Gesamtdarstellung der nationalsozialistischen Judenverfolgung.* Munich: Piper, 1998.

Loewy, Hanno, and Andrzej Bodek. Foreword to *"Les Vrais Riches" Notizen am Rand: Ein Tagebuch aus dem Ghetto Łódź (Mai bis August 1944),* edited by Hanno Loewy and Andrzej Bodek. Leipzig: Reclam Verlag Leipzig, 1997.

Lyotard, Jean-François. *The Differend: Phrases in Dispute.* Translated by Georges Van Den Abbeele. Minneapolis: University of Minnesota Press, 1988.

Mahrholz, Werner. *Deutsche Selbstbekenntnisse: Ein Beitrag zur Geschichte der Selbstbiographie von der Mystik bis zum Pietismus.* Berlin: Furche Verlag, 1919.

Mallon, Thomas. *A Book of One's Own: People and Their Diaries.* New York: Ticknor and Fields, 1984.

Mankowitz, Ze'ev. *Life between Memory and Hope: The Survivors of the Holocaust in Nazi Germany.* Cambridge: Cambridge University Press, 2002.

Margadant, Jo Burr. Introduction to *The New Biography: Performing Femininity in Nineteenth-Century France,* edited by Jo Burr Margadant. Berkeley and Los Angeles: University of California Press, 2000.

Markiewicz-Lagneau, Janina. "L'autobiographie en Pologne." *Revue française de Sociologie* 17, no. 4 (1976): 591–613.

Marrus, Michael R. *The Holocaust in History.* New York: Meridian Books, 1987.

Marrus, Michael R., and Robert O. Paxton. *Vichy France and the Jews.* New York: Basic Books, 1981.

Martin, Wallace. *Recent Theories of Narrative.* Ithaca: Cornell University Press, 1986.

Maza, Sarah. "Stories in History: Cultural Narratives in Recent Works in European History." *American Historical Review* 101, no. 5 (1996): 1493–1515.

Mendelsohn, Ezra. *The Jews of East Central Europe Between the World Wars.* Bloomington: Indiana University Press, 1983.

Michman, Dan, ed. *Belgium and the Holocaust: Jews, Belgians, Germans.* Jerusalem: Yad Vashem, 1998.

———. *Holocaust Historiography: A Jewish Perspective—Conceptualizations, Terminology, Approaches and Fundamental Issues.* London and Portland, Ore.: Vallentine Mitchell, 2003.

———. "Understanding the Jewish Dimension of the Holocaust." In *The Fate of the Euro-*

pean Jews, 1939–1945: Continuity or Contingency?, edited by Jonathan Frankel. Studies in Contemporary Jewry, vol. 13. New York: Oxford University Press, 1997.

Mintz, Alan. *"Banished from their father's table": Loss of Faith and Hebrew Autobiography.* Bloomington: Indiana University Press, 1989.

———. *Hurban: Responses to Catastrophe in Hebrew Literature.* Syracuse: Syracuse University Press, 1996.

Misch, Georg. *A History of Autobiography in Antiquity.* Vol.1. Translated by E. W. Dickes. Cambridge: Harvard University Press, 1951.

Moore, Bob. *Victims and Survivors: The Nazi Persecution of the Jews in the Netherlands, 1940–45.* New York: Arnold, 1997.

Moseley, Marcus. "Jewish Autobiography: The Elusive Subject." *Jewish Quarterly Review* 95, no. 1 (Winter 2005): 16–59.

———. "Life, Literature: Autobiographies of Jewish Youth in Interwar Poland." *Jewish Social Studies* 7, no. 3 (2001): 1–51.

Moyn, Samuel. "Judaism against Paganism: Emmanuel Levinas's Response to Heidegger and Nazism in the 1930s." *History and Memory* 10, no. 1 (Spring 1998): 25–58.

Myers, David N. *Re-Inventing the Jewish Past: European Jewish Intellectuals and the Zionist Return to History.* New York: Oxford University Press, 1995.

Nipperdey, Thomas. *Germany from Napoleon to Bismarck, 1800–1866.* Translated by Daniel Nolan. Princeton: Princeton University Press, 1996.

Nussbaum, Felicity A. "Toward Conceptualizing Diary." In *Studies in Autobiography,* edited by James Olney. New York: Oxford University Press, 1988.

Ofer, Dalia, and Lenore J. Weitzman, eds. *Women in the Holocaust.* New Haven: Yale University Press, 1998.

Parush, Iris. *Reading Jewish Women: Marginality and Modernization in Nineteenth-Century Eastern European Jewish Society.* Translated by Saadya Sternberg. Hanover, N.H.: University Press of New England for Brandeis University Press, 2004.

Patterson, David. *Along the Edge of Annihilation: The Collapse and Recovery of Life in the Holocaust Diary.* Seattle: University of Washington Press, 1999.

Paxton, Robert O. *Vichy France: Old Guard and New Order, 1940–1944.* New York: Columbia University Press, 1982.

Penslar, Derek. *Shylock's Children: Economics and Jewish Identity in Modern Europe.* Berkeley and Los Angeles: University of California Press, 2001.

Pinnock, Sarah K. *Beyond Theodicy: Jewish and Christian Continental Thinkers Respond to the Holocaust.* Albany: State University of New York Press, 2002.

Podnieks, Elizabeth. *Daily Modernism: The Literary Diaries of Virginia Woolf, Antonia White, Elizabeth Smart, and Anaïs Nin.* Montreal: McGill-Queens University Press, 2000.

Pohl, Dieter. *Nationalsozialistische Judenverfolgung in Ostgalizien 1941–1944: Organisation und Durchführung eines staatlichen Massenverbrechens.* Munich: R. Oldenbourg, 1997.

———. *Von der "Judenpolitik" zum Judenmord: der Distrikt Lublin des Generalgouvernements, 1934–1944.* Frankfurt am Main: Peter Lang, 1993.

Popkin, Jeremy D. "Historians on the Autobiographical Frontier." In *American Historical Review* 104, no. 3 (1999): 48 pars. <http://www.historycooperative.org/journals/ahr/104.3/ah000725.html> (1 Jul. 2005).

Powell, Lawrence N. *Troubled Memory: Anne Levy, the Holocaust, and David Duke's Louisiana.* Chapel Hill: University of North Carolina Press, 2000.

Poznanski, Renée. *Jews in France during World War II.* Translated by Nathan Bracher. Hanover: University Press of New England for Brandeis University in association with the United States Holocaust Memorial Museum, 2001.

———. "Le Sionisme en France pendant la Deuxième Guerre mondiale: Développements institutionnels et impact idéologique." In *Les Juifs de France: Le Sionisme et l'État d'Israel,* edited by Doris Bensimon and Benjamin Pinkus. Vol. 1. Paris: Actes du Colloques International organized by Ben Gurion University in Beersheva and the Institut National des Langues et Civilisations Orientales, 1987.

Presser, Jacob. *Ashes in the Wind: The Destruction of Dutch Jewry.* Translated by Arnold Pomerans. Detroit: Wayne State University Press, 1988.

Rabinbach, Anson. "The Reader, the Popular Novel and the Imperative to Participate: Reflections on Public and Private Experience in the Third Reich." In *History and Memory* 3, no. 2 (1991): 5–45.

Raphaël, Freddy, and Robert Weyl. "La double demeure: Les juifs d'Alsace et le sionisme." In *Regards nouveaux sur les juifs d'Alsace.* Éditions des dernières nouvelles d'Alsace. [n.p.]: Librairie Istra, 1980.

Rayski, Adam, ed. "La presse des organizations juives de résistance de la MOI face à l'extermination et au secret qui l'entourait." In *Qui savait quoi? L'extermination des Juifs 1941–1945,* edited by Stéphane Courtois and Adam Rayski. Paris: Éditions la Découverte, 1987.

Roseman, Mark. *A Past in Hiding: Memory and Survival in Nazi Germany.* New York: Henry Holt, 2000.

Rosenblatt, Paul C. *Bitter, Bitter Tears: Nineteenth-Century Diarists and Twentieth-Century Grief Theories.* Minneapolis: University of Minnesota Press, 1983.

Rosenwein, Barbara. "Worrying about Emotions in History." *American Historical Review* 107, no. 3 (2002): 821–45.

Roskies, David. *Against the Apocalypse: Responses to Catastrophe in Modern Jewish Culture.* Cambridge: Harvard University Press, 1984.

———. "Landkentenish: Yiddish Belles Lettres in the Warsaw Ghetto." In *Holocaust Chronicles: Individualizing the Holocaust through Diaries and Other Contemporaneous Personal Accounts,* edited by Robert Moses Shapiro. Hoboken, N.J.: Ktav, 1999.

Rubenstein, Richard L. *After Auschwitz: Radical Theology and Contemporary Judaism.* Indianapolis: Bobbs-Merrill Co., 1966.

Rubenstein, Richard L., and John K. Roth. *Approaches to Auschwitz: The Holocaust and Its Legacy.* Atlanta: John Knox Press, 1987.

Rudavsky, Joseph. *To Live with Hope, To Die with Dignity: Spiritual Resistance in the Ghettos and Camps.* Northvale, N.J.: Jason Aronson, 1997.

Sarkozy, Nicolas. *Georges Mandel: Le moine de la politique.* Paris: Bernard Grasset, 1994.

Scharf, Rafael F. "Literature in the Ghetto in the Polish Language: Z *otchlani*—From the abyss." In *Holocaust Chronicles: Individualizing the Holocaust through Diaries and Other Contemporaneous Personal Accounts*, edited by Robert Moses Shapiro. Hoboken, N.J.: Ktav, 1999.

Schorsch, Ismar. "The Emergence of Historical Consciousness in Modern Judaism." *Leo Baeck Institute Year Book* 28 (1983): 413–37.

Schulze, Winfried. "Ego-Dokumente: Annäherung an den Menschen in der Geschichte? Vorüberlegungen für die Tagung 'Ego-Dokumente.'" In *Ego-Dokumente: Annäherung an den Menschen in der Geschichte*, edited by Winfried Schulze. Berlin: Akademie Verlag, 1996.

Schwartz, Vanessa R. *Spectacular Realities: Early Mass Culture in Fin-de-Siècle Paris*. Berkeley and Los Angeles: University of California Press, 1998.

Scott, Joan W. "The Evidence of Experience." *Critical Inquiry* 17 (Summer 1991): 773–97.

Shandler, Jeffrey, ed. *Awakening Lives: Autobiographies of Jewish Youth before the Holocaust*. With an introduction by Barbara Kirshenblatt-Gimblett, Marcus Moseley, and Michael Stanislawski. New Haven: Yale University Press in cooperation with YIVO Institute for Jewish Research, 2002.

Shmeruk, Chone. "Hebrew-Yiddish-Polish: A Trilingual Jewish Culture." In *The Jews of Poland Between Two World Wars*, edited by Yisrael Gutman, Ezra Mendelssohn, Jehuda Reinharz, and Chone Shmeruk. Hanover, N.H.: University Press of New England, 1989.

Siekierski, Maciej. "The Jews in Soviet-Occupied Eastern Poland at the End of 1939: Numbers and Distribution." In *Jews in Eastern Poland and the USSR, 1939–1946*, edited by Norman Davies and Antony Polonsky. New York: St. Martin's Press, 1991.

Soucy, Robert. *French Fascism: The Second Wave, 1933–1939*. New Haven: Yale University Press, 1995.

Soyer, Daniel. "Documenting Immigrant Lives at an Immigrant Institution: Yivo's Autobiography Contest of 1942." *Jewish Social Studies* 5, no. 3 (1999): 218–43.

Starościak, Włodzimierz. *Żydzi w Dąbrowie Górniczej*. Dąbrowa Górnicza: Kawiarnia Literacka, 1995.

Sternhell, Zeev. *Neither Right nor Left: Fascist Ideology in France*. Translated by David Maisel. Princeton: Princeton University Press, 1996.

Steussy, Fredric S. *Eighteenth-Century German Autobiography: The Emergence of Individuality*. Vol. 69, Studies in Modern German Literature Series. York: Peter Lang, 1996.

Stola, Dariusz. "Early News of the Holocaust from Poland." *Holocaust and Genocide Studies* 11, no. 1 (1997): 1–27.

Stoltzfus, Nathan. *Resistance of the Heart: Intermarriage and the Rosenstrasse Protest in Nazi Germany*. New York: W. W. Norton, 1996.

Strauss, Herbert A. "Jewish Emigration from Germany—Nazi Policies and Jewish Responses (I)." *Leo Baeck Institute Year Book* 25 (1980).

Syrkin, Marie. "Holocaust Literature 1: Diaries." In *Encountering the Holocaust: An Interdisciplinary Survey*, edited by Byron L. Sherwin and Susan G. Ament. Chicago: Impact Press, 1979.

Todorov, Tzvetan. *Facing the Extreme: Moral Life in the Concentration Camps*. Translated by Arthur Denner and Abigail Pollak. New York: Henry Holt, 1996.

Toews, John E. "Intellectual History after the Linguistic Turn: The Autonomy of Meaning and the Irreducibility of Experience." *American Historical Review* 92, no. 4. (1987): 879–907.

Trunk, Isaiah. *Judenrat: The Jewish Councils of Eastern Europe Under Nazi Occupation.* Lincoln: University of Nebraska Press, 1972.

Turner, James Grantham. "Pepys and the Private Parts of Monarchy." In *Culture and Society in the Stuart Restoration: Literature, Drama, History,* edited by Gerald Maclean. Cambridge: Cambridge University Press, 1995.

Volkov, Shulamit. "The Dynamics of Dissimilation: *Ostjuden* and German Jews." In *Living with Antisemitism: Modern Jewish Responses,* edited by Jehuda Reinharz Hanover, N.H.: University Press of New England for Brandeis University Press, 1987.

von Greyerz, Kaspar. "Religion in the Life of German and Swiss Autobiographers (Sixteenth and Early Seventeenth Centuries)." In *Religion and Society in Early Modern Europe, 1500–1800,* edited by Kaspar von Greyerz. London: German Historical Institute and George Allen and Unwin, 1984.

von Ranke, Leopold. "On the Relations of History and Philosophy (A Manuscript of the 1830s)." In *The Theory and Practice of History: Leopold von Ranke,* edited by Georg G. Iggers and Konrad von Moltke. Indianapolis: Bobbs-Merrill, 1973.

Weber, Eugen. *France: Fin de Siècle.* Cambridge: Belknap of Harvard University Press, 1986.

———. *The Hollow Years: France in the 1930s.* New York: W. W. Norton, 1994.

Weintraub, Karl. "Autobiography and Historical Consciousness." *Critical Inquiry* 1, no. 4 (1975): 821–48.

White, Hayden. *The Content of the Form.* Baltimore: Johns Hopkins University Press, 1987.

Wiener, Wendy J., and George C. Rosenwald. "A Moment's Monument: The Psychology of Keeping a Diary." In *The Narrative Study of Lives,* vol.1, edited by Ruthellen Josselson and Amia Lieblich. Newbury Park and London: SAGE Publications, 1993.

Wisse, Ruth R. *The Modern Jewish Canon: A Journey through Language and Culture.* New York: Free Press, 2000.

Wright, Gordon. *France in Modern Times.* 5th ed. New York: W. W. Norton, 1981.

Wulf, Joseph. *Presse und Funk im Dritten Reich.* Gütersloh: Sigbert Mohn Verlag, 1964.

Wyschogrod, Edith. *An Ethics of Remembering: History, Heterology, and the Nameless Others.* Chicago: University of Chicago Press, 1998.

Yahil, Leni. *The Holocaust: The Fate of European Jewry.* Translated by Ina Friedman and Haya Galai. New York: Oxford University Press, 1987.

Yerushalmi, Yosef Hayim. *Zakhor: Jewish History and Jewish Memory.* Seattle: University of Washington Press, 1982.

Young, James E. "Between History and Memory: The Uncanny Voices of the Historian and Survivor." *History and Memory* 9, no. 1/2 (1997): 47–58.

———. "Memory and Monument." In *Bitburg in Moral and Political Perspective,* edited by Geoffrey Hartman. Bloomington: Indiana University Press, 1986.

———. "Toward a Received History of the Holocaust." *History and Theory* 36, no. 4, Theme Issue: Producing the Past: Making Histories Inside and Outside the Academy (1997): 21–43.

———. *Writing and Rewriting the Holocaust: Narrative and the Consequences of Interpretation.* Bloomington: Indiana University Press, 1988.

Zapruder, Alexandra. Introduction to *Salvaged Pages: Young Writers' Diaries of the Holocaust,* edited and collected by Alexandra Zapruder. New Haven: Yale University Press, 2002.

Zimmels, H. J. *The Echo of the Nazi Holocaust in Rabbinic Literature.* [Hoboken, N.J.]: Ktav, 1977.

zur Nieden, Susanne. *Alltag im Ausnahmezustand: Frauentagebücher im zerstörten Deutschland, 1943 bis 1945.* Berlin: Orlanda Frauenverlag, 1993.

———. "Aus dem vergessenen Alltag der Tyrannei: Die Aufzeichnungen Victor Klemperers im Vergleich zur zeitgenössischen Tagebuchliteratur." In *Im Herzen der Finsternis: Victor Klemperer als Chronist der NS-Zeit,* edited by Hannes Heer. Berlin: Aufbau-Verlag, 1997.

Acknowledgments

It is a privilege to acknowledge those individuals and organizations which have generously given me their time, caring, and support during these years of research and writing. They have made it possible for me to bring this book to fruition, although of course I bear full responsibility for its shortcomings.

In more ways than one, this book has benefited from the influence of Saul Friedländer. It began as a dissertation, which was shaped by the questions he posed about the historical representation of the Holocaust. His theoretical reflections encouraged me to immerse myself in the history of the Holocaust as history, to learn not only from historians but also from the people who had firsthand experience of this past. He has served as advisor and model through every stage of this project, and I am deeply grateful for his sustained involvement in my work.

I am fortunate to have had the opportunity to work with three other historians, each of whom has played a crucial role in my intellectual development. For fifteen years, Thomas A. Kohut has been a treasured mentor. He taught me to look for the human side of history, to try to empathize with people from the past and to understand their experiences on their terms. Indeed, it was his encouragement that set me on the path to become a historian. Thanks to his continued feedback on my work and unflagging support, I have never regretted embarking on that journey. David N. Myers has also been a dear teacher and intellectual guide. His rigorous engagement with each chapter of this book has left a deep imprint. He has managed to be simultaneously an incisive critic and warm supporter, and my work has been immeasurably enriched as a result. I have also been a grateful beneficiary of David Warren Sabean's passion for and dedication to teaching. He taught me that being a historian is most of all a way of thinking and asking questions, rather than an expertise of a narrowly defined place and time.

He has provided essential conceptual and line-by-line feedback on my writing, and I appreciate his inspiration and advice.

Over the course of my research and writing, a number of friends and colleagues have read drafts of my manuscript and offered helpful comments. I want to thank the members of the Williams College Department of History, especially the members of the History Department colloquium, to whom I presented my work in the spring of 2005 and whose comments were intellectually stimulating and enormously supportive. At different stages of the project, I have benefited from the insightful comments of the participants in UCLA's European History Colloquium, in Brandeis University's Colloquium in Modern Jewish Studies, and in the United States Holocaust Memorial Museum's Center for Advanced Holocaust Studies Summer Research Workshop on Jewish Holocaust Diaries and Early Memoirs. In particular, I would like to thank Rachel Feldhay Brenner, Manuela Consonni, Sylvia Fuks Fried, Amos Goldberg, Jack Kugelmass, Britta McEwen, Ofer Nur, Jared Poley, Antony Polonsky, Eugene Sheppard, Debora Silverman, Barry Tractenberg, and Teo Ruiz for their comments. I would also like to thank the anonymous readers of my manuscript, whose criticisms and suggestions were immensely valuable as I completed the final revisions of the book.

Everyone I have worked with at Yale University Press has made the process of preparing and producing the manuscript straightforward and even enjoyable. I am indebted to Larisa Heimert, who initially acquired the manuscript for Yale University Press, and to Christopher Rogers for conscientiously attending to the manuscript in the production phase in his capacity as executive editor. Lawrence Kenney skillfully copyedited my manuscript, and I am so grateful for his dedication to improving my prose. I also appreciate my agent, Jennifer Lyons, for agreeing to represent this book and for all of her work on my behalf.

Many institutions and organizations have financially supported the research and writing of this book. I am grateful for their generosity. Thanks to a Fulbright Fellowship and a Dorot Foundation Travel Grant, I was able to spend a year in Israel to conduct archival research. UCLA and Williams College supported two separate research stints in France, and Williams made possible a return trip to Israel. The generosity of the "1939" Club and of the United States Holocaust Memorial Museum's Center for Advanced Holocaust Studies furnished me with time to conduct research at archives in the United States. In addition, UCLA's Department of History and the UCLA Graduate Division provided support throughout my years in graduate school and while I was completing the writing of my dissertation.

I am indebted to the archivists and librarians in several institutions in Israel, France, and the United States who facilitated my research beyond my expectations. I would particularly like to thank the archivists, librarians, and staff of Yad Vashem, Jerusalem, especially Yaala Ariel-Joel, Nadia Kahan, and Sara Pechanac; the Wiener Library, Tel Aviv University; the Central Archives for the History of the Jewish People, Hebrew University of Jerusalem, Givat Ram; the Jewish National and University Library, Hebrew University of Jerusalem, Givat Ram; Massua Archives, Kibbutz Tel Yitzhak; Yossi Shavit at Beit Lohamei Haghetaot, Western Galilee; and Yehoshua Bichler at Moreshet Archives, Givat Haviva. In France, I am particularly appreciative of the help extended to me by Sylvie Sallé at the Centre de Documentation Juive Contemporaine, Paris; Françoise Aujogue at the Archives Nationales, Paris; and the archivists and staff of the Bibliothèque Nationale, Paris. In the United States, I extend my tremendous thanks to the archivists and staff at the Leo Baeck Institute, New York; and to the archivists, librarians, and curators at the United States Holocaust Memorial Museum, in particular Alexandra Borecka, Ferenc Katona, Aaron Kornblum, and Teresa Pollin. Suzy Snyder of the USHMM merits a special thank you for showing me diaries from the museum's collections and for generously letting me share her office with her while I read them. My thanks also extend to Sandy Garber for allowing me to read the original text of her grandmother's diary.

At Yad Vashem and the United States Holocaust Memorial Museum, I was able to attend the remarkable research seminars that each institute holds on a regular basis. I would like to extend my heartfelt thanks to Yehuda Bauer, who graciously served as my academic host in Israel. At the Center for Advanced Holocaust Studies at the United States Holocaust Memorial Museum, I am indebted to numerous individuals for the warm welcome I received and for giving me the valuable opportunity to present my research findings. My special thanks to Suzanne Brown-Fleming, Martin Dean, Robert Ehrenreich, Wendy Lower, Jürgen Matthäus, Ann Millin, Alexander Rossino, Paul Shapiro, and Madeline Vadkerty. I also am grateful to the editors at the USHMM's Center for Advanced Holocaust Studies for allowing me to use previously published material. Portions of chapter 2 originally appeared as "A Tale of Two Diarists: A Comparative Examination of Experiences in Eastern and Western Europe," in the occasional paper *Ghettos 1939–1945: New Research and Perspectives on Definition, Daily Life, and Survival,* published by the United States Holocaust Museum, Center for Advanced Holocaust Studies, copyright (c) 2005 by Alexandra Garbarini.

Throughout the years I have worked on this project, I have been fortunate to have wonderful friends and family who have contributed to this book with their ideas, advice, and support. I cannot furnish details here, but I tremendously appreciate the contributions of Shilpa Agarwal, Jill Bernheimer, James Brennan, Annelie Chapman, Leila Gerstein, Matt and Jessica Harris, Sara Hendren, Cathy

Johnson, Regina Kunzel, Jessica Lapenn, Gretchen Long, Christopher Nugent and Sarah Allen, Ilana Ruskay-Kidd, the extended Singer family, Stefanie Solum, Peter Starenko, Nancy Stockdale, K. Scott Wong, Jesse Zigelstein—and Emily Klein, who has been my constant phone companion over these many years. I especially want to thank my grandparents, Lillian and the late Charles Garbarini, for their love and support throughout my life. Five friends have amazed me with their generosity. I am indebted to Zvi Ben-Dor Benite and Amos Goldberg for the time they spent helping me with Hebrew translations; Alexandra Zapruder shared her passion for this subject with me and never tired of helping me sort out the intricacies of research, writing, and publishing; and to Daniel Hurewitz and Laura Kim Lee, who have patiently read multiple drafts of every chapter and conveyed an unflinching faith in my ability to pull this book together, I express my gratitude for immeasurably enriching my work and my life.

My parents, Ruth and Charles Garbarini, have been steadfast in their love and encouragement of my work. Their presence in my life is a daily blessing.

Finally, I want to thank my husband, Micah Singer. His humor, intelligence, and care have sustained me these many years. He has always given me the time and respect to follow my intellectual pursuits, and the love that helps to keep it all in perspective. Micah has my deepest gratitude and love.

INDEX